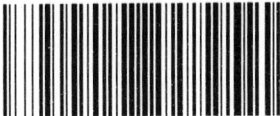

CW01475548

SCOTLAND'S
MEDIEVAL
QUEENS

For my son Lewis, my inspiration, with all my love

SCOTLAND'S MEDIEVAL QUEENS

FROM SAINT MARGARET TO MARGARET OF DENMARK

SHARON BENNETT CONNOLLY

PEN & SWORD
HISTORY

AN IMPRINT OF PEN & SWORD BOOKS LTD.
YORKSHIRE – PHILADELPHIA

First published in Great Britain in 2025 by
PEN AND SWORD HISTORY
An imprint of
Pen & Sword Books Ltd
Yorkshire – Philadelphia

ISBN 978 1 39909 812 0

Typeset in Times New Roman 10/12.5 by
SJmagic DESIGN SERVICES, India.
Printed and bound in the UK by CPI Group (UK) Ltd.

Pen & Sword Books Limited incorporates the imprints of Atlas, Archaeology,
Aviation, Discovery, Family History, Fiction, History, Maritime, Military,
After the Battle, Military Classics, Politics, Select, Transport, True Crime,
Air World, Frontline Publishing, Leo Cooper, Remember When,
Seaforth Publishing, The Praetorian Press, Wharncliffe Local History,
Wharncliffe Transport, Wharncliffe True Crime and White Owl.

For a complete list of Pen & Sword titles please contact
PEN & SWORD BOOKS LIMITED
George House, Units 12 & 13, Beevor Street, Off Pontefract Road,
Barnsley, South Yorkshire, S71 1HN, England
E-mail: enquiries@pen-and-sword.co.uk
Website: www.pen-and-sword.co.uk

or

PEN AND SWORD BOOKS
1950 Lawrence Rd, Havertown, PA 19083, USA
E-mail: uspen-and-sword@casematepublishers.com
Website: www.penandswordbooks.com

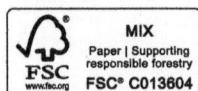

MIX
Paper | Supporting
responsible forestry
FSC
www.fsc.org   FSC® C013604

Scottish Queens: St Margaret to Margaret, the Maid of Norway

Ingebiorg (1) = Malcolm III = (2) St Margaret of Wessex

Ethelreda = Duncan II

Sybilla = Alexander I

David I = Matilda de Senlis

Malcolm IV   William I (the Lion) = Ermengarde de Beaumont

David = Matilda of Chester

Margaret → House of Balliol

Isabel → House of Bruce

Joan of England (1) = Alexander II = (2) Marie de Coucy

Margaret of England = Alexander III

Alexander

Eric II of Norway = Margaret

Margaret, the Maid of Norway

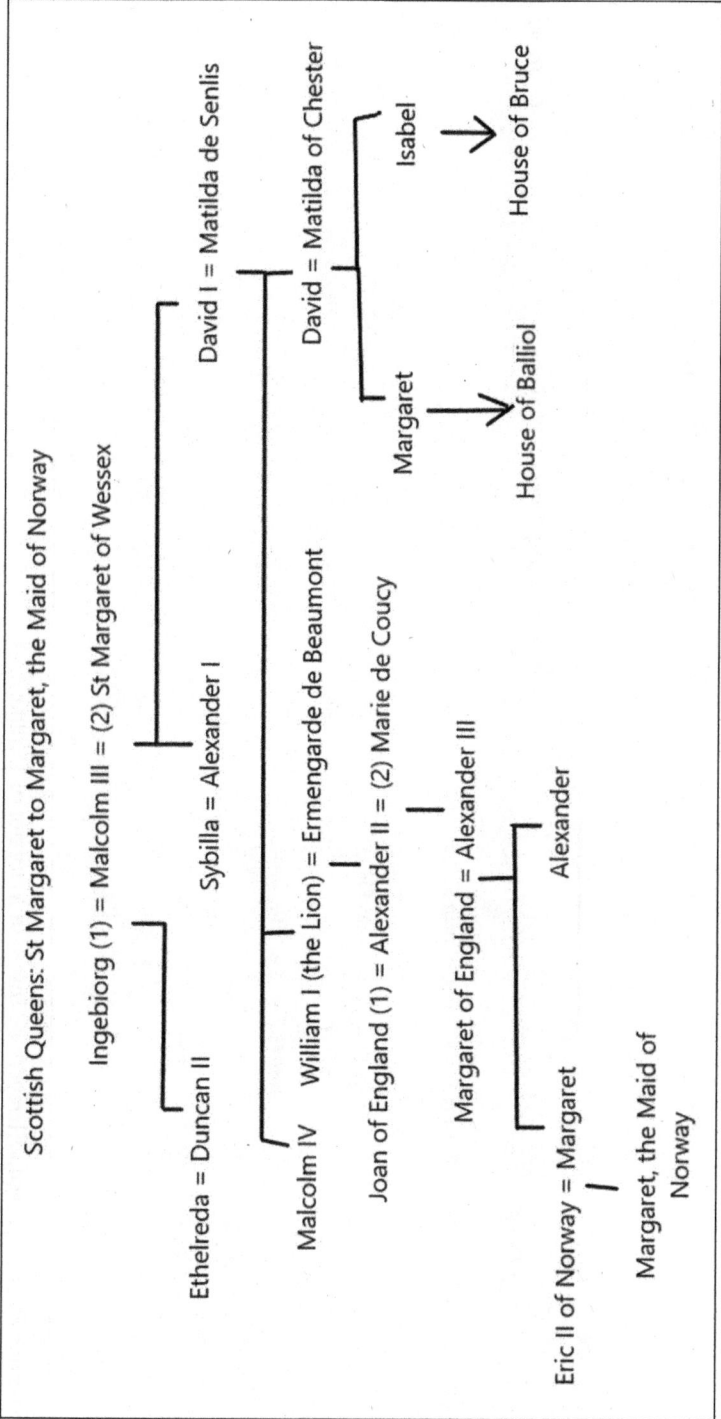

Scottish Queens 1: From St Margaret to Margaret, the Maid of Norway.

Scottish Queens: Elizabeth de Burgh to Margaret of Denmark

Isabella of Mar (1) = Robert I the Bruce = (2) Elizabeth de Burgh

Joan of the Tower (1) = David II = (2) Margaret Drummond

Walter Stewart = Marjorie Bruce

Elizabeth Mure (1) = Robert II = (2) Euphemia Ross

Robert III = Annabella Drummond

James I = Joan Beaufort

James II = Mary of Guelders

James III = Margaret of Denmark

Scottish Queens 2: From Elizabeth de Burgh to Margaret of Denmark.

Contents

Acknowledgements

Writing *Scotland's Medieval Queens* has been a truly memorable experience, and I would like to thank everyone who has helped and encouraged me throughout the process. I would like to thank the staff at Pen & Sword for their continued confidence in me, especially my editors, Sarah-Beth Watkins and Cecily Blench, and the rest of the team, including Laura Hirst, Lucy May and Rosie Crofts.

I would particularly like to thank Amy Licence, whose help, advice and friendship have been invaluable to me in my journey to become an author. I am also grateful to my fellow author, Kristie Dean, who has been a wonderful sounding-board, offering advice and encouragement throughout my writing career. And thank you to Elizabeth Chadwick for her constant support over the years. Thanks also go to some amazing historians and authors, especially Louise Wilkinson, Danna Messer, Carol McGrath, Toni Mount, Linda Porter, Janina Ramirez, James Wright and Sarah Bryson for the many little snippets of advice and encouragement.

Writing can be a lonely experience, you spend your time reading books for research, or sitting, staring at the computer screen, trying to think of something to write. But social media has changed all that, there are always friends just a 'click' away to give you a diversion or encouragement. I would therefore like to thank the readers of my blog, *History... the Interesting Bits*, for their wonderful support and feedback. I'd particularly like to thank Derek Birks, for getting me into podcasting; our podcast, *A Slice of Medieval*, has been great fun and, hopefully, entertaining. The online author community has proved invaluable to me. So, I would like to extend a special 'thank you' to Darren Baker, Matthew Lewis, Nathen Amin, S. J. A. Turney, Tony Riches, Matthew Harffy, Steven A. McKay, Giles Kristian, Justin Hill, Cathie Dunn, Paula Lofting, Samantha Wilcoxson, Lynn Dawson, Jacqueline Reiter, Virginia Crow, Stephanie Churchill and Prue Batten for all your support and encouragement with this book and the previous ones.

And thank you to the various historical sites I have visited over the years of research, York Minster, Lincoln Cathedral, the British Library, the National Archives, and all the wonderful staff who have been happy to talk about all things medieval. And to Jason Ubych at the Tain Museum, for clearing up my confusion between two different women named Euphemia Ross. I am particularly grateful to the staff at Queen Margaret's Chapel in Edinburgh, who offered early encouragement on this project; their enthusiasm spurred me on! And thanks especially to Dr Fiona Watson for answering a last-minute question about Robert the Bruce's inauguration when a reference threw a spanner in the works.

I would like to say an extra special 'thank you' to Sasha, Gill and Kai at Lindum Books in Lincoln for hosting my author talks and being a huge support to this local author. I am grateful to everyone at Gainsborough Old Hall and Conisbrough Castle, for being my places of refuge when I needed to get away from the computer. They are my havens from writer's block. A thank you must also go to my friends closer to home, particularly Sharon Gleave, Jill Gaskell, Di Richardson, Helen Walker, Jenny Smith and all my local friends, for their wonderful support and for dragging me out for a coffee every once in a while.

I reserve a special thanks to my family, especially to my mum and dad for all their love and encouragement, and for their own passion for history. And to my husband, James, thank you for putting up with all the history talks. I could not have done it without all of you. The biggest thank you has to go to my research assistant and son, Lewis Connolly, who has grown up travelling to various wonderful places with me in the process of making each of my books a reality. He has turned into a fabulous sounding-board for my ideas and arguments and provided much of the background research for *Scotland's Medieval Queens*, especially Lady Macbeth. A chip off the old block, if ever there was one, he is well on the way to becoming an excellent historian himself and I really value the many history-related conversations we have on a daily basis.

I will always owe a debt of gratitude to the great historians throughout history – to the present day – who have gallantly edited and translated the great chronicles of the medieval era, so that they are accessible and readable for all of us who have an interest in the period, but very little understanding of Latin. Every effort has been made to ensure the accuracy of this book. However, any errors that may occur are entirely my own.

Introduction

In the past, my idea for a book has been born out of the project I was working on in the moment. A prime example is *King John's Right Hand Lady: The Story of Nicholaa de la Haye*, which started as an article on my blog in 2015, became a few thousand words in the *Warrior Heroines* chapter in *Heroines of the Medieval World* and from there, Nicholaa was given a chapter of her own in *Ladies of Magna Carta: Women of Influence in Thirteenth Century England*. It was a short step, then, to dedicating a whole book to this incredible woman. All my previous books have developed in this way, from ideas inspired by *Heroines of the Medieval World*.

Until now.

The inspiration for *Scotland's Medieval Queens* came primarily from a conversation with my son after his GCSE English Literature class a few years ago. Lewis was studying *Macbeth* and was quite perturbed with the way Shakespeare had portrayed Lady Macbeth. In no uncertain terms, I was told, 'Mum, you need to set the record straight!'

So, I got to thinking…

In the bard's famous drama, also known as 'The Scottish Play', Lady Macbeth is not even given her name. Presented as a scheming, manipulative woman, Shakespeare did as good a hatchet job on Gruoch, a royal princess in her own right, as he had on Richard III. Unfortunately, there is no society established to repair Gruoch's reputation.

So, my son and Lady Macbeth gave me the kernel of an idea.

There is not enough information about Gruoch to write an entire book about her, but what if I start with her and develop the idea to include all of Scotland's medieval queens? If you have read my blog, or *Heroines of the Medieval World*, you will know of my interest in Scottish history and, in particular, St Margaret, the women of the Bruce family and Joan Beaufort, Queen of Scots as the wife of James I. I already had the beginnings of the book.

My second inspiration was Nigel Tranter. My introduction to Scottish history had been his wonderful *Bruce Trilogy*, which I devoured in my early twenties; and I have since read and enjoyed every one of Tranter's historical novels. Scottish history is fascinating! It is violent, politically charged and passionate. Being inconveniently situated on England's northern border was never easy for Scotland, but it has made for some great stories over the centuries. Scotland's story is often that of brother against brother, ambition and family rivalries causing feuds that threatened the stability of the crown itself. Such fissures, of course, grew and ruptured with the aid of English interference and encouragement. The King of England was always happy to play one side off against the other if it weakened Scotland's position.

And Scotland's medieval queens, be they Scottish, English, Danish or French, formed a big part of that story.

More often than not, these disputes north and south of the border were resolved in peace treaties, sealed by wedding bells. A number of English princesses and noblewomen found themselves married to Scotland's kings as a consequence. The longest period of peace between the two countries was in the thirteenth century, when Henry III's daughter, Margaret, married Alexander III, King of Scots. It is probably unsurprising, given the history between the two countries, that the long peace was shattered by the death of Alexander's granddaughter Margaret, the Maid of Norway, which gave Edward I of England the opportunity to direct Scotland's affairs. Little Margaret's death left the Scots throne vacant, with thirteen Competitors vying for the crown, staking their claims as Edward acted as adjudicator.

But I am getting ahead of myself, and we will come to Edward I and the Wars of Scottish Independence in due course. Suffice it to say, for the present, that Scotland's turbulent history is often linked with that of England.

If my son's pleas and my love for Scottish history were not enough to persuade me to write a book on Scotland's queens, *Outlaw King* would certainly have tipped the balance. The 2018 film that told the story of Robert the Bruce's fight to become King of Scots all but ignored the contribution of women to the Bruce's story. And yet the role of women, of the king's wife, daughter, sisters and the brave Isabella MacDuff, Countess of Buchan, was indeed significant. Their suffering at the hands of Edward I is legendary. *Outlaw King* ignores practically all of it – and all of them.

Scotland's Medieval Queens aims to put the women at the forefront of Scotland's story, to highlight their role and influence on Scottish history and on Scotland's kings, culture and landscape. These women, however, did not act wholly independently, so while this book brings their actions into the limelight, it will be always within the context of the wider story of Scotland, from the eleventh to the fifteenth century.

Sharon Bennett Connolly
Lincoln
October 2023

Prologue

Lady Macbeth

ollowing a prophecy, given by three witches, that he will be 'king hereafter', a brave Scottish general named Macbeth is consumed by ambition. Spurred to action by his wife, Macbeth murders King Duncan, laying the blame on the dead king's servants, and takes the Scottish throne for himself. He is then racked with guilt and paranoia. Forced to commit more and more murders to protect himself from enmity and suspicion, he soon becomes a tyrannical ruler. The bloodbath and consequent civil war swiftly take Macbeth and Lady Macbeth into the realms of madness and death. Whilst Macbeth is killed in battle, Lady Macbeth, tortured by what she has forced her husband to do, kills herself. This is the briefest summary of William Shakespeare's *The Tragedie of Macbeth*.

In *Macbeth*, also known as 'The Scottish Play', the eponymous character's wife is not even given her own name. She is 'Lady Macbeth', and she is imbued with evil and ambition. She is a character to be vilified and hated, driving her husband to yet greater crimes for the sake of a crown. She never professes love, nor sentimentality throughout the play. She is an intelligent, beautiful woman, but her passions are for power and supremacy. From the first time we meet her, in Act 1, Scene V, Lady Macbeth's character is firmly set as the woman who would push her husband to do anything to claim greater power:

> The Raven himself is hoarse,
> That croakes the fatall entrance of Duncan
> Under my battlements. Come you Spirits,
> That tend on mortall thoughts, unfex me here,
> And fill me from the Crowne to the Toe, top-full
> Of direst Crueltie: make thick my blood,
> Stop up th'accesse, and passage to remorse.
> That no compunctious vistings of Nature
> Shake my fell purpose, nor keepe peace between
> Th'effect and hit. Come to my Womans Brests,
> And take my Milke for Gall, you Murth'ring Ministers,
> Where-ever, in your sightless substances,
> You wait on Natures Mischiefe. Come thick Night,

And pall thee in the dunnest smoake of Hell,
That my keene Knife fee not the wound it makes,
Nor Heaven peepe through the Blanket of the darke,
To cry hold, hold.[1]

Where Macbeth can be swayed from his purpose by the strain of expectation and by superstition, Lady Macbeth is steadfast in her resolve. Her ambition is not for herself, but for her husband, as was expected in medieval times. A woman with ambitions for herself never fared well, just look at Empress Matilda, the rightful queen of England after the death of Henry I, vilified for her lack of deference to her brother, a mere earl, and kept from the throne by her cousin, King Stephen, simply because she was a woman. Stephen's wife, Matilda of Boulogne, on the other hand, is seen as a loyal supporter of her husband and praised as a dutiful wife, ambitious only for her husband and son. So, at least in one respect, Shakespeare's Lady Macbeth is acting as a wife should, a helpmate for her husband; but in this she divests herself of conscience and her femininity. She is strong in the areas her husband is weak, she is self-assured, single-minded and tenacious in her purpose. When Macbeth falters in his plans to murder King Duncan, it is Lady Macbeth who taunts him into proceeding, saying:

Was the hope drunke,
Wherein you drest your selfe? Hath it slept since?
And wakes it now to look so greene, and pale?
At what it did so freely? From this time,
Such I account thy love. Art thou affear'd
To be the same in thine own Act, and Valour,
As thou art in desire? Wouldst thou have that
Which thou esteem'st the Ornament of Life.
And live a Coward in thine owne esteeme?
Letting I dare not, wait upon I would,
Like the poor Cat i'th'Addage.[2]

For over 400 years, Shakespeare's version of Lady Macbeth has been the woman most people are familiar with. The scheming, ambitious woman who will stop at nothing to put her husband on the Scottish throne – and commit murder to keep him there. But is that the real Lady Macbeth? As many fans of Richard III will say, Shakespeare is fiction. He is telling a story to entertain, imbuing it with the moral judgements of his time, the early modern era. Unlike with Richard III, Lady Macbeth has no following with a desire to seek out the truth and right the wrongs done to her. Historians, however, have tried to address the bard's inaccuracies. But Shakespeare's shadow is long...

So, who was Lady Macbeth?

As you can imagine, with the passing of nearly a thousand years, the information on Lady Macbeth is scarce. Her name was Gruoch, and she was a royal princess, daughter of Boite mac Cinaeda and granddaughter, possibly, of King Kenneth II.[3] The inheritance of the Scots crown was very complex at the time. Known as tanistry, the crown did not necessarily pass to the eldest son of the king, but often to a different branch of the royal family, all of whom shared at least one great-great-grandfather and all of whom descended from Kenneth MacAlpin, the ninth-century King of Scots.[4] If nominated before the king's death, the successor was known as the tanaiste, or next heir.[5] Such a system ensured the succession of an adult king, but also fostered family rivalry, resulting in frequent murders and blood feuds. As the succession switched between various branches of the extended family, it is uncertain whether Boite was the son of Kenneth II or Kenneth III, though Kenneth II seems the most likely candidate as father. If so, Gruoch was, therefore, a niece of King Malcolm II of Scotland, who was the eldest son of Kenneth II and ruled from 1005 to 1034.[6] As a male member of the extended royal family, whether it was as the grandson of Kenneth II or Kenneth III, Gruoch's brother also had a claim to the Scottish throne. He is identified as Gille in a twelfth-century source and there is a suggestion that Gille's baby son, the last direct male heir of Kenneth II, was murdered as an infant by Malcolm II in 1033, as the *Annals of Ulster* record 'the grandson of Baete [Boite] son of Cinaed [Kenneth] was killed by Mael Coluim son of Cinaed [Kenneth].'[7] It is possible that Gille may also have been murdered on the orders of Malcolm II, who was intent on his grandson, Duncan, succeeding him and may have been clearing the field of possible rivals.

Gruoch's date of birth is unknown, but she appears to have been married at some point in the 1020s to a man named Gille Comgáin, which may mean she was born in the first decade of the eleventh century. The evidence for this first marriage is a tad sketchy; it is based on the parentage of her son, Lulach, but the sources contradict each other. The *Continuation of the Synchronisms of Flann Mainistreach* records Lulach as the son of Macbeth, while the *Annals of Ulster* record that 'Lulach son of Gille Comgáin, over-king of Scotland was killed in battle by Mael Coluim son of Donnchad' in 1058.[8] It seems possible, therefore, that Lulach was the son of Gille Comgáin and stepson of Macbeth. Although there is nothing specific that states that Gruoch was the mother of Lulach, it is likely that she was the wife of Macbeth, given the evidence of a charter, which states that '*Machbet filius Finlach... et Gruoch filia Bodhe, rex et regina Scottorum*' made grants to the church of St Serf, though the fact the charter also mentions King Malcom, son of Duncan, casts doubt on the authenticity of the document.[9] Lulach is further referenced in the twelfth-century *Cronica Regum Scottorum* as '*Lulac nepos filii Boide*' and identified as successor of King Macbeth.[10] If Lulach is the grandson of Boite and son or stepson of Macbeth, then it follows that Gruoch, Boite's daughter and Macbeth's wife, is Lulach's mother. And if Lulach was Macbeth's stepson, and Gille Comgáin's son, it would mean that Gruoch was the wife of Gille Comgáin before she married

Macbeth. Moreover, if Gruoch and Macbeth were from two different branches of the MacAlpin family, for instance if Macbeth was descended from Kenneth II while Gruoch was a granddaughter of Kenneth III, their union would strengthen Macbeth's position not only in Moray, but in the whole of Scotland.

If Gruoch was first married to Gille Comgáin, she was in the midst of a particularly nasty family feud. Gille Comgáin was a first cousin of Macbeth. Macbeth was the son of Findlaech mac Ruidrí, mormaer of Moray, a semi-independent region of north-eastern Scotland. Literally translated, mormaer means great steward and the holders of the title enjoyed semi-royal status, which may explain why they are sometimes referred to as kings. The mormaers of Moray, and other Scottish provinces, were often members of the extended royal family from which Scotland's kings were chosen.[11] Findlaech mac Ruidrí may, therefore, have been some relation to Malcolm II, King of Scots. The other possibility, though the evidence is later and uncertain, is that Findlaech was married to the unnamed youngest daughter of Malcolm II.[12] Although the family relationship is confusing, this may explain why Macbeth is identified as a nephew or grandson of Malcolm II in various sources.[13] Gille Comgáin was the son of Findlaech's older brother, Máel Brigte. In what appears to have been a family feud, or power struggle, the *Annals of Ulster* record the death in 1020 of 'Finnlaech son of Ruadrí king of Alba... killed by his own people.'[14] Findlaech was murdered by – or on the instigation of – his nephews, Máel Coluim and Gille Comgáin. Máel Coluim then succeeded his uncle as mormaer of Moray and was in turn succeeded by his younger brother Gille Comgáin, on his death in 1029.[15] Macbeth, younger than his murderous cousins, and probably only a teenager at the time, fled, perhaps to Ireland. According to *the Annals of Ulster*, 'Gilla Comgán son of Mael Brigte, earl of Moray was burned together with fifty people' in 1032.[16] Though Macbeth is not mentioned as the perpetrator, it is possible he exacted his revenge on Gille Comgáin, gathering supporters from among those disaffected by his rule. Many, certainly, lay the blame at his door. And it is not inconceivable that Macbeth had the support of Malcolm II, who saw in Gille Comgáin's demise the elimination of another possible threat to the succession of his grandson. Given the number of dead involved, it is likely that Gille Comgáin and his followers were trapped in his hall as it was burned down, perhaps during a feast, the doors barred from the outside to prevent escape. If Gruoch was Gille Comgáin's wife, it is possible that she and her small son were away at the time, otherwise they would have perished alongside the others. Another possibility is that Gruoch escaped – or was rescued – from the hall with Lulach before the fire took hold.

Macbeth succeeded as mormaer of Moray and it was only a short time after Gille Comgáin's death that Gruoch and Macbeth were married, putting an end to the murderous family feud. We may feel uneasy about Gruoch marrying her husband's murderer, if he was, but the union was political common sense. Gruoch, a mother with a young son and royal blood, was low on male protection; her brother had just been murdered, possibly by Malcolm II, and her infant nephew would be killed the following year. As the wife of Macbeth, Gruoch could feel secure in his protection as the new mormaer and may have extracted guarantees that Macbeth would look after Lulach's interests, given the way he raised the boy and even designated him as his heir. For Macbeth, Gruoch's royal blood and lands would strengthen his own claim to the Scots throne, if he was thinking that far ahead in 1032. One assumes that, because Macbeth did become King of Scots, it is something he always aspired to, but we cannot be sure. In 1032, we can be certain that his aim was to reclaim Moray, which he did.

In 1034, on 25 November, King Malcolm II died at Glamis. *The Annals of Tigernach* record the death of 'Mael-Coluímb son of Cinaed king of Scotland'.[17] It has been variously suggested that Malcolm II was assassinated, killed in battle or while fighting bandits. However, given that he had reigned for almost thirty years, and had come to the throne as an adult, it is just as likely that he was in his 50s or 60s and died a natural death. His grandson, Duncan, succeeded to the throne peacefully, helped no doubt by Malcolm's campaign of eliminating potential rivals. Duncan was the son of Bethoc, Malcolm II's daughter, and Crinan, earl (or mormaer) of Atholl and hereditary abbot of Dunkeld. He had been married before 1030 and had at least one son, Malcolm – the future Malcolm III Canmore – born in 1031, when he ascended the throne. His wife is named by fourteenth-century chronicler John of Fordun as Sybilla, a cousin of Earl Siward of Northumbria, while an early list of Scottish kings names her as Suthen; but no contemporary source gives her name or origins.[18] Duncan was probably in his mid-20s when he was invested as King of Scots at Scone just five days after his grandfather's death: he was certainly not the old man as depicted by Shakespeare. As he established himself on the throne, Duncan was aided by turmoil elsewhere. In England, following King Cnut's death in 1035, two of Cnut's sons, Harold Harefoot and Harthcnut, were embroiled in a power struggle for the throne. And in the north, Thorfinn, Earl of Orkney, was facing an internal power struggle.[19] Duncan was unable to expand on his grandfather's achievements and in 1038 faced an incursion by Eadulf of Bernicia, seeking revenge for Malcolm II's seizure of Durham twenty years before. Duncan needed the help of his brother, Maldred, regent of Strathclyde, to repel Eadulf.[20]

Duncan then went on the offensive and whilst he marched on Durham, his nephew, Moddan, was sent north to attack Caithness, part of the lands of Thorfinn of Orkney. Heavily outnumbered, Moddan was forced to retreat south, as Duncan's campaign into England in 1039 met with humiliating defeat. Returning north, Duncan decided to concentrate on one front at a time, taking his remaining army north to deal with Thorfinn. In the meantime, Thorfinn had allied with Macbeth to form a league to challenge Duncan. As Moddan was killed at Thurso, Duncan led an army against Moray, apparently unaware of Macbeth's alliance with Thorfinn.[21] The two armies met at Pitgaveny, near Elgin, on 15 August 1040.[22] Macbeth won the contest, with Duncan lying dead on the field of battle at the end of the day. With Duncan's sons still only children, Macbeth assumed the kingship unchallenged, with Gruoch by his side. According to W. F. Skene, Gruoch's own royal lineage may have boosted Macbeth's claim to the throne and certainly did not hinder it:

> In Kenneth, son of Dubh, and his son Grig, this line of kings came to an end; but the 'Irish Annals' record a Boede, son of Kenneth, whose grandson was slain in the year 1033; and it appears from the chartulary of St Andrews that Gruoch filia Boede was wife of Macbeth, son of Finnloech, and reigned along with him, while Lulach, his successor, is termed in one of the Latin lists, 'nepos filii Boede'; and thus the rights of that family may have passed to her husband and to Lulach, and given rise to their claims upon the throne.[23]

Gruoch is the first Scottish queen whose name is known to history; as we have seen, the name of Duncan's wife is unclear and open to conjecture. Duncan's young sons were taken into exile, and while they were at large and beyond his reach, Macbeth could never be wholly secure on his throne. His kingship, moreover, did not go unchallenged and in 1045 he faced an army led by Crinan, hereditary abbot of Dunkeld and father of Duncan I, at Dunkeld. Crinan probably sought to place his younger son, Maldred, on the throne as his grandson, Malcolm, was still only a teenager at the time. Macbeth's forces won the day. Crinan was killed in the fighting. A year later, Edward the Confessor gave permission to Siward, Earl of Northumbria, to mount an invasion of Scotland in the name of Malcolm, Duncan I's oldest son and heir.[24] Although the invasion initially succeeded in defeating Macbeth, he gathered reinforcements from his heartlands in the north and expelled Siward's forces.[25]

There were no further challenges to Macbeth's authority and the next eight years were peaceful. By 1050, Macbeth was in such a strong position that he was able to leave Scotland and go on pilgrimage to Rome, where he 'scattered money like seed to the poor'.[26] The pilgrimage would have been a combination of religious devotion and diplomatic networking; a chance for the King of Scots to be seen on the wider European stage. Their generosity towards the church during the pilgrimage had monastic writers recording that 'in his reign there were productive seasons'.[27] These appear to have been Macbeth's last few years of peace, however. Duncan's sons were now grown to manhood and Macbeth must have felt their threat. In 1052, when the Norman knights were expelled from England following the successful return from exile of Earl Godwin and his family, Macbeth welcomed many to Scotland. John of Worcester noted that 'Osbern, nicknamed Pentecost, and his comrade Hug surrendered their castles, and, approaching Scotland through Earl Leofric's territory, with his permission, were received by Macbeth, king of Scots.'[28] The Normans were expert cavalrymen, experienced in Edward the Confessor's wars against the Welsh. These knights fought alongside Macbeth's own forces when Earl Siward invaded Scotland in 1054, hoping to place Duncan's son Malcolm on the throne, as a client king of King Edward. Although the battle at Dunsinane was lost, the Normans sold their lives dearly; Siward's eldest son was killed, and the earl was unable to press any advantage.[29] Henry of Huntingdon gave a succinct summary of the campaign:

> Around this time Siward, the mighty earl of Northumbria, almost a giant in stature, very strong mentally and physically, sent his son to conquer Scotland. When they came back and reported to his father that he had been killed in battle, he asked, 'Did he receive his fatal wound in the front or the back of his body?' The messenger said, 'In the front.' Then he said, 'That makes me very happy for I consider no other death worthy for me or my son.' Then Siward set out for Scotland, and defeated the king in battle, destroyed the whole realm, and having destroyed it, subjected it to himself.[30]

Henry of Huntingdon's account may not be wholly accurate as John of Worcester states that Siward himself led the army. Worcester gives a fuller account of the battle:

> Siward, the vigorous earl of the Northumbrians, at the king's command, went to Scotland with a mounted force and a powerful fleet and joined battle with Macbeth, king of the Scots and when many thousands of Scots and all the Normans, whom we mentioned above, had been killed he put them to flight and, as the king commanded, he set up Malcolm, son of the king of the Cumbrians, as king. However, in that battle, his own son and many of the English and the Danes fell.[31]

Although Macbeth was forced to relinquish some lands and influence to Malcolm Canmore, the formerly exiled son of King Duncan, who established himself in Lothian and the southern kingdom of Strathclyde, Macbeth continued to control Scotland's heartlands north of the Forth.[32] The subsequent campaign was long and bloody as Malcolm extended his influence northwards. It was not until 1057 that Malcolm crossed the Mounth, ambushing Macbeth, cut off from his main army, at Lumphanan, west of Aberdeen, on 15 August.[33] Macbeth was killed in the battle, along with his personal bodyguard. The Scots king was buried on the island of Iona, where his rival King Duncan was also interred.[34]

Macbeth's forces may have been ultimately successful as it was not Malcolm who benefited from the outcome, but Lulach. On taking the throne, Macbeth had designated his stepson by Gruoch as his heir and it was Lulach who succeeded to the throne. The other possibility, of course, is that although Macbeth's forces were defeated, the Scots council elected Lulach to succeed his stepfather, ignoring the claims of the victorious Malcolm Canmore. Although he has been derisively nicknamed 'the Fatuous' or 'the Simpleton', Lulach clearly enjoyed much support, especially in Moray, and may have been seen as the better, for the Scots, alternative to Malcolm, who had been raised across the border in England.[35] His reign lasted less than a year and he was defeated and killed, 'by treachery', on 17 March 1058, at Essie in Strathbogie.[36] The chronicles are confusing and some suggest that Lulach was killed before Macbeth, who had earlier abdicated his throne in his stepson's favour, but had to take up the crown again following Lulach's death. Whichever order the battles happened, the outcome was the same, Macbeth and Lulach were both killed.[37] Lulach's wife does not appear in the records, so her name is unknown, as well as the year of her death; was she ever queen? Her existence is only evidenced by the fact she had two children. Lulach was not the last of his line and his son, Máel Snechta, was mormaer of Moray until 1078. A grant by *'Maelsnecte son of Luloeg'* to the church of Deer is recorded in a notice of grants between 565 and 1100.[38] He died in 1085, having spent his last years as a monk. He was succeeded as mormaer by his sister's son, Angus, who would be killed in battle at Strickathrow in 1130.[39]

Macbeth's reputation as a strong, wise, generous and pious king has been overshadowed by the Macbeth of Shakespeare. He is described as 'a tall man with a ruddy complexion and fair hair'.[40] Of his wife Gruoch, we have no description. We have very little record of Gruoch's movements, either as Macbeth's wife or before. We can assume that she spent the early years of her marriage to Macbeth in creating a household and raising her young son, Lulach. Once Macbeth attained the throne, Gruoch may well have assumed the traditional roles associated with queens, as an intercessor for those seeking the king's mercy or patronage, as a hostess in welcoming foreign envoys and powerful magnates to the Scottish court, and as a religious benefactor. Alongside her husband, Gruoch is recorded as a benefactor of the Céli Dé of Loch Leven, to whom they had granted estates in Fothriff (West Fife).[41] In the charter, the couple are identified as 'Macbeth son of Finlach... and Gruoch daughter of Bodhe, King and Queen of Scots'.[42] Part of the donated property was, in fact, named after Gruoch, Gruoch's Well on Benarty Hill.[43] This may actually suggest that the donated land belonged to Gruoch as part of her own inheritance. The fact that we have a grant given jointly by Macbeth and Gruoch suggests that the couple worked together during Macbeth's reign. Gruoch also accompanied her husband on his pilgrimage to Rome, a journey that must have been an exciting adventure for both of them. John of Worcester noted that 'Macbeth, King of Scotland, distributed alms lavishly at Rome.'[44] There is no record in the chronicles of any disharmony in the marriage. We know little else of Queen Gruoch. Despite already bearing a son, Lulach, she and Macbeth had no children that we know of; although it may be that she lost children by miscarriage or in early childhood before they came to the notice of chroniclers. This lack of a surviving heir of his own may have been what prompted Macbeth to adopt Gruoch's son as his successor. It does not appear to have affected Macbeth and Gruoch's relationship, from the scant evidence we have, that is.

We know nothing of Gruoch's death, no date is recorded nor even hinted at. She may have lived through the grief of losing her husband and son in battle and seeing Malcolm III Canmore ascend the throne and assert his authority over the whole of Scotland. Or she may have died years beforehand. William Shakespeare had her dying by her own hand, driven insane by her evil deeds:

> Of his dead butcher and his fiend-like queene,
> Who, as 't is thought, by selfe and violent hands
> Tooke off her life.[45]

However she died, Gruoch's final resting place, the one site that may give us a clue, is also lost to history. The story of Queen Gruoch, Lady Macbeth, is one shrouded in mystery, tantalisingly obscure. If only we could know more. The lack of information on Gruoch makes it easy for Shakespeare's interpretation to be accepted as fact, but it is more than likely an injustice to a woman who survived her first husband's gruesome death, protected her son and came to an agreement with Macbeth to become his wife, securing her son's future in the process, and later becoming queen as a consequence.

Chapter One

St Margaret, Queen of Scots

With the demise of Macbeth and, shortly afterwards, Lulach, the crown passed to the son of Duncan I. Máel Coluim mac Donnchada is better known in the anglicised form of his name as Malcolm III Canmore. Canmore (or Ceann Mór) is translated as 'Great Head' or 'Great Chief' and probably relates to his position as king, rather than the size of his cranium. When his father was killed by Macbeth, in battle, in 1040, Malcolm was only 8 or 9 years of age. He and his younger brother, Donald, were smuggled out of Scotland to be raised in England, where the English king gave him a small estate in Northamptonshire.[1] By 1058, Malcolm was now 26 or 27 and, with the support of England's king, Edward the Confessor, and Earl Siward of Northumbria, he was finally in a position to challenge Macbeth. The fact Siward supported Malcolm during his exile, and accompanied him with an army on his campaign to reclaim the throne in 1057 and 1058, lends credence to the suggestion that Malcolm's mother was a cousin of the Northumbrian earl, though at this time, we cannot know for certain. Malcolm was to reign for thirty-five years, establishing a firm hold on Scotland for himself and his descendants. The House of Canmore would rule Scotland until the death of Margaret, the little Maid of Norway, in 1290.

As he consolidated his position in Scotland, Malcolm married Ingibiorg. Ingibiorg was either the daughter or widow of Thorfinn, earl of Orkney, known as Thorfinn the Mighty, Macbeth's former ally. Thorfinn's death is usually given as 1064 or 1065, when he would have been well into his 50s. Thorfinn had married Ingibiorg Finnsdottir, the daughter of Finn Arnesson, a friend and ally of Harald Hardrada, King of Norway. Her mother, Bergljot, was Hardrada's niece and she was a cousin of Harald's second wife, Thora. Ingibiorg and Thorfinn had two sons, Paul and Erland Thorfinnson, who would rule Orkney together after their father's death. If this Ingibiorg did marry Malcolm III, then she was much younger than her first husband, as she gave Malcolm as many as three sons before her death, which must have occurred before 1069. The dates between Thorfinn's death and Malcolm's second marriage cast doubt on whether Ingibiorg was Thorfinn's widow. It may well be that she was the daughter of Thorfinn and Ingibiorg Finnsdottir, which would mean that she may have married Malcolm in the early 1060s rather than the mid-1060s. However, Rosalind K. Marshall argues that Ingibiorg was most likely Thorfinn's widow, as it is so stated in the *Orkneyinga Saga*, and there is no record of Thorfinn having a daughter with her mother's name.[2] Whether it was with his widow or his daughter, a marriage alliance between Malcolm and the earldom of Orkney would have extended Malcolm's influence over Caithness, Sutherland and other lands in the north, controlled by Orkney's earl.

We know very little of Ingibiorg. As the wife of Thorfinn, she would have probably resided at his main stronghold of Birsay in Orkney.[3] As Queen of Scots, she probably lived mainly at Dunfermline, which was Malcolm's preferred residence. She and Malcolm had at least two, possibly three sons, Duncan – the future Duncan II – Donald and Malcolm.[4] By 1069, however, Ingibiorg was no longer part of Malcolm's life. What had happened to Ingibiorg, we do not know. It is possible that she was repudiated due to an impediment to the marriage, such as consanguinity, but the most likely explanation is that Queen Ingibiorg had died, either from illness or as a result of complications in childbirth. Whatever the reason, Malcolm was now free to take another wife and he had settled his attentions on Margaret of Wessex.

The story of St Margaret, Queen of Scotland as the wife of King Malcolm III Canmore, started far away from the courts of Scotland and England, in eastern Europe. Margaret had an impeccable Saxon pedigree, she could trace her ancestry directly to Alfred the Great, King of Wessex, and his forebears. She was the daughter of Edward the Exile and his wife Agatha.

Edward the Exile was the son of Edmund II Ironside, King of England in 1016; Edmund was, in turn, the son of Æthelred II and his first wife, Ælfgifu of York. Edward's grandfather was, therefore, Æthelred II (the Unready) and his uncle was Edward the Confessor, England's king from 1042 until 1066. Edward the Exile's mother was Ealdgyth, the widow of Sigeferth, a thegn from East Anglia, who had been betrayed in 1015, along with another thegn, Morcar, by King Æthelred's son-in-law Eadric Streona, the treacherous ealdorman of Mercia. Streona had lured the two men into his chamber during a great assembly at Oxford and killed them. After the murders of the thegns, King Æthelred 'took possession of their property, and ordered Aldgyth [Ealdgyth], Sigeferth's widow, to be taken to the city of Malmesbury'.[5] Taking a stand against his father and Streona, however, 'while she was confined there the ætheling Edmund came thither, and, against his father's wish, took her to wife' sometime between the middle of August and the middle of September 1015.[6] Edmund then rode into the territories of Sigeferth and Morcar, in the Five Boroughs (Derby, Leicester, Lincoln, Nottingham and Stamford), 'invaded Sigeferth's and Morcar's territory, and subdued the people of those lands to himself'.[7]

Edmund and Ealdgyth, therefore, were probably married at the beginning of August. They would have two sons, Edward and Edmund, who may well have been twins or were born just one year apart. Edward was born in 1016, with Edmund being born no later than 1017. Their father spent the rest of 1015 and 1016 trying to encourage resistance to the constant Danish onslaught. As his father weakened and fell ill at Cosham, Edmund raised an army in the Midlands to confront Cnut. However, Eadric Streona then turned traitor and took forty English ships – and their men – with him as he submitted to Cnut. As a consequence, with the situation looking hopeless, the people of Wessex followed Streona's example and also submitted to Cnut, giving hostages as well as providing horses for the Danish king's army. One of the main aspects of England in this era was a distinct lack of unity; it was every man for himself, which meant mounting a concerted resistance to the Danish invasion was virtually impossible.

In early 1016, Edmund raised another army but was forced to disband it when his father and the London garrison failed to join him. The figurehead of the king was needed for the sake of unity and without him, few were willing to make a stand. A second army, this time with King Æthelred at its head, however, failed to make inroads against the Danes. After which, Edmund, along with Earl Uhtred of Northumbria, ravaged the Danish-held territories of Staffordshire, Shropshire and Cheshire. However, when Cnut attacked York, Uhtred was forced to withdraw north to protect his own lands; he was executed on the orders of Cnut, following his submission to the Dane.[8] King Æthelred died in London on St George's Day, 23 April 1016, 'after the great toils and many tribulations of his life'.[9] He was buried in Old St Paul's cathedral, London; his tomb was lost when the cathedral was destroyed in the Great Fire of London in 1666.

On Æthelred's death, according to John of Worcester, the leading men of the kingdom came together. Electing Cnut as their new king, they 'renounced and repudiated in his presence all the descendants of King Æthelred and made peace with him and swore fealty to him, and he swore to them that he would be a faithful lord to them, both in religious and in secular matters.'[10] England was split; the people of London and the south chose Edmund as king:

> He, raised to the height of royal dignity, undauntedly approached Wessex without delay and was received with great joy by the whole population, whom he very swiftly subjected to his rule. When they heard this many of the English hastily yielded to him voluntarily.[11]

Cnut then sailed to London with his whole fleet and laid siege to London. Edmund then spent the summer fighting a series of indecisive battles with the Danes. He managed to force Cnut's withdrawal from the capital, before defeating him at Brentford. However, when he was forced to withdraw to Wessex to raise more troops, the Danes once again besieged London, only to be defeated once more when Edmund returned. At Sherston in Wiltshire, ahead of a two-day battle in which neither side would claim victory, Edmund, 'addressing each man by name, exhorted and entreated them to remember that they strove for their country, children, wives and homes, and with those most inspiring words he fired the soldiers' spirits.'[12] As a testament to Edmund's personal courage, John of Worcester described the English king in the heat of battle:

> King Edmund Ironside made his presence felt in fierce hand-to-hand fighting in the front line. He took thought for everything; he himself fought hard, often smote the enemy; he performed at once the duty of a hardy soldier and of an able general.[13]

Unfortunately, Edmund was defeated by Cnut in battle at 'Assundun' (possibly Ashdon or Ashingdon in Essex) on 18 October of the same year; in the heat of the battle, the treacherous Eadric Streona once again turned and fled with his men. The English suffered heavy losses. Following a possible further battle in the Forest of Dean, Cnut and Edmund met at Alney in Gloucestershire and a compromise was reached, whereby Edmund would rule all lands to the south of the River Thames and Cnut would rule everything to the north. It was also agreed that Cnut and Edmund would be each other's heirs; whichever king survived longest would get everything. This understanding was cut short when Edmund died on 30 November, probably having succumbed to wounds received during the summer of vicious fighting, rather than the later story which circulated, telling of a grisly murder by a sword or arrow thrust into his bowels whilst visiting the latrines.[14]

With Edmund's death, and with his two sons being only toddlers, there was no further organised opposition to Cnut and the Danes were able to take possession of the entire country. As soon as he had established control, Cnut sent Edmund's infant sons to the court of the king of Sweden, Olof Stötkonung, apparently with instructions to have them killed. The Swedish king was understandably squeamish about murdering two toddlers and eventually sent them on to be raised in the relative safety of the court of the Grand Prince of Kyiv, Yaroslav the Wise, and his wife – Olof's daughter, Ingegerd. As young adults, Edward and Edmund later made their way to Hungary and helped in the restoration of the exiled Andrew of Hungary. Edmund is said to have married a Hungarian princess but died sometime before 1054. Around 1043 Edward married Agatha, whose origins are extremely obscure. She may have been a daughter of Yaroslav and Ingegerd of Kyiv. It is also possible that she was the daughter of Luidolf, Margrave of West Friesland and a relative of Holy Roman Emperor Henry III. According to John of Worcester, she was the daughter of Emperor Henry's brother.[15] Liudolf was the son of Gislea of Swabia by her first husband, Bruno of Brunswick; Emperor Henry was the same Gisela's son by her third husband, Emperor Conrad II.[16] We may never know. The couple had three children together. Margaret, the eldest, was born in either 1045 or 1046; her sister Christina was born around 1050 and her brother Edgar, the Ætheling, was born sometime between 1052 and 1056.

The family could have spent their whole lives in European exile, were it not for Edward the Confessor's failure to produce a legitimate heir with his wife, Edith of Wessex. In 1054 Edward, having realised that he needed to settle the question of the succession, sent an embassy to eastern Europe in search of his brother Edmund's children. Ealdred, Archbishop of York, spent several months at the court of Holy Roman Emperor Henry III, but was initially unsuccessful in arranging Edward the Exile's return to England, though the reasons for Edward's reluctance to return home are unknown. It may be that he was unwilling to uproot his young family from everything and everyone they knew; he would have known how that felt from his own early life. It was not until a second embassy arrived in 1056 that the prince was persuaded to return to his homeland. He arrived back on English soil in 1057, forty years after he was sent into exile. It is not known whether his family travelled with him or arrived later. In a tragic turn of events, just days after his return Edward the Exile was dead, before he had even seen his uncle the king. He was buried in St Paul's Cathedral, London. Whether his death was caused by nefarious means or simply a sad twist of fate is uncertain. The suspicion has been raised that another challenger for the throne, Harold Godwinson – the future Harold II – may have taken the opportunity to remove his rival; although it was likely that it was Harold who had escorted Edward back to England, as he was on the Continent at that time. So surely, had he intended murder, he would have done it sooner and far from English soil?

Whatever the circumstances, the death of Edward the Exile was a blow for Edward the Confessor's dynastic hopes. Little Edgar, now the Ætheling and accepted heir, was much too young to assume a political role. He and his sisters, along with their mother, were now under the protection of King Edward. They continued to live at court, where Edgar was adopted by Queen Edith, who raised him and saw to his education. Margaret and Christina were probably sent to the nunnery at Wilton, where the queen had been schooled, to continue their education. According to Turgot, Margaret's biographer,

> Whilst Margaret was yet in the flower of youth, she began to lead a very strict life, to love God above all things, to employ herself in the study of the Divine writings, and therein with joy to exercise her mind. Her understanding was keen to comprehend any matter, whatever it might be; to this was joined a great tenacity of memory, enabling her to store it up, along with a graceful flow of language to express it.[17]

By January 1066, when Edward the Confessor died, Margaret was approaching her 20th birthday, while Edgar could have been as young as 10 and was no older than 14. Due to his tender years, Edgar was passed over as a candidate for the throne, in preference for the older and more experienced Harold Godwinson, England's leading magnate as Earl of Wessex. He was crowned as King Harold II on 6 January, the day after the old king's death. Following Harold's own death at the Battle of Hastings on 14 October 1066, Edgar was proclaimed king by some of his supporters, including Archbishop Ealdred of York, the earls Edwin and Morcar and the city of London. As William continued to lay waste to the southern counties, Edgar's support melted away. In December, the leading clerics, including Archbishop Ealdred, the citizens of London and Edgar himself came to terms with the Norman invader at Berkhamsted and 'having given hostages, made him their submission, and swore fealty to him'.[18]

By 1068, Edgar the Ætheling had become involved in the opposition to Norman rule which had been festering in northern England. He was forced to flee north to Scotland when the rebellion was crushed by King William:

Edgar the Ætheling, with his mother Agatha, his sisters Margaret and Christina, and the last relics of the English nobility, resolved to sail for Wearmouth, and to seek a shelter at the court of Malcolm, King of Scotland. They could hardly have expected to find the man who was to have been their host, in the very act of ravaging their native country; but his savage occupation in no way lessened his friendly feelings towards them. He met them in person, he gave them the most hearty reception, and bade them dwell in his realm as long as it might please them.[19]

There seems to be some confusion as to whether Margaret and her mother and sister accompanied Edgar north in 1068, as he returned to England within a short time. It may be that the women's journey north was not until 1070. In that year, Symeon of Durham has Margaret and Malcolm meeting at Wearmouth when

it was announced to him [Malcolm] that Edgar Atheling and his sisters, fair maidens of royal birth, and many other very rich men fleeing from their estates, had come to shore in ships at that harbour. They therefore commended themselves to him; and when they came to him he spoke to them kindly, and granted them with his firmest peace to dwell in his realm so long as they would, with all their followers.[20]

Whichever year it was that the couple first met, Malcolm III Canmore remained in England as the exiles sailed to Scotland, continuing to ravage Northumberland in support of a northern rising against William the Conqueror. King Malcolm then marched north to greet his distinguished guests. And

Then began Malcolm to yearn after the child's [Edgar] sister, Margaret, to wife; but he and all his men long refused; and she also herself was averse, and said that she would neither have him nor anyone else, if the Supreme Power would grant, that she in her maidenhood might please the mighty Lord with a carnal heart, in this short life, in pure continence. The king, however, earnestly urged her brother, until he answered Yea. And indeed he durst not otherwise; for they were come into his kingdom … The prescient Creator wist long before what he of her would have done; for that she would increase the glory of God in this land, lead the king aright from the path of error, bend him and his people together by a better way, and suppress the bad customs which the nation formerly followed: all which she afterwards did. The king therefore received her, though it was against her will, and was pleased with her manners, and thanked God, who in his might had given him such a match.[21]

Although we do not know for certain what happened to Malcolm's first wife, Ingibiorg Finnsdottir, according to Nigel Tranter, in his *The Story of Scotland*, Ingibiorg and her sons were at Dunfermline when Margaret and her family arrived, receiving the exiles and looking after them until the king return. Although he doesn't cite his sources, Tranter says that Ingibiorg was then sent to the royal castle of Kincardine, with her children, where she soon died, 'not without suspicion of poisoning'.[22] It must be noted, however, that there is no contemporary mention of Ingibiorg still being alive when Margaret arrived in Scotland. She may have died or been put aside in favour of this new marriage to a descendant of Alfred the Great; her death seems most likely, perhaps in childbirth. Malcolm was therefore free to find another wife and marriage to Margaret was a prestigious one, though it would have been viewed by King William as a hostile act, as any children of the union would have a strong claim to the crown of England. Margaret was reluctant to agree to the marriage as she was more inclined to a religious life and had hoped to become a nun. Nonetheless, with pressure from Malcolm, her brother and, possibly, her own sense of obligation to the king who was sheltering her family, she eventually accepted his proposal. According to Turgot,

> While thus she was meditating upon the law of the Lord day and night, and, like another Mary sitting at His feet, and delighted to hear His word, rather in obedience to the will of her friends than to her own, yea by the appointment of God, she was married to Malcolm, son of King Duncan, the most powerful king of the Scots.[23]

Malcolm and Margaret were married at Dunfermline sometime in 1069 or 1070, in a small chapel beside the king's palace, by Fothad, the last Celtic Bishop of St Andrews.[24] By all accounts, it seems to have been a happy and successful marriage and partnership. Queen Margaret was a strong figure; she was pious but also worldly-wise. Having grown up on the Continent, she was familiar with many of the courts of Europe and had met some of its leading churchmen. Given that Malcolm had spent fifteen years in exile at the English court, he and Margaret may have had much in common. Said to be a modernising queen, Margaret brought luxury to the Scottish court and into the lives of the nobles of her new country. She was averse to the Celtic traditions of the court, associating the Gaelic language with the irregularities of the Scottish church. Margaret introduced a more rigorous attention to etiquette than had previously been seen in the rough-and-ready Scottish court, no longer encouraging the use of bards and druidic old men to recite the ancestry of Malcolm and Scotland's kings.[25] She introduced ceremony and luxury, not only to the court, but to the magnates throughout the kingdom. According to Turgot,

> By means of her temporal possessions [Margaret] earned for herself the rewards of heaven; for there, where her heart was, she had placed

her treasure also. And since before all things she sought the kingdom of God and His justice, the bountiful grace of the Almighty freely to her honours and riches in abundance. This prudent queen directed all things as it was fitting for her to regulate; the laws of the realm were administered by her counsel; by her care the influence of religion was extended, and the people rejoiced in the prosperity of their affairs. Nothing was firmer than her fidelity, steadier than her fervour, or juster than her decisions; nothing was more enduring than her patience, graver than her advice, or more pleasant than her conversation.[26]

A life of St Margaret was commissioned by her daughter, Matilda, when queen of England as wife of Henry I. It was written sometime between 1100 and 1107 by Turgot, Margaret's former chaplain and then prior of Durham. The biography emphasises the queen's compassion for children and the poor and stresses her piety, pointing to the severity of her self-denial and her frequent fasting. It also relates how

To these two excellent gifts of prayer and abstinence she joined the gift of mercy. For what could be more compassionate than her heart? Who could be more gentle than she towards the necessitous? Not only would she have given to the poor all that she possessed; but if she could have done so, she would have given her very self away.[27]

Turgot also reports how Queen Margaret employed spies to go throughout the kingdom in search of captive English of all ranks, who had been taken 'by violence of war and reduced to slavery, whom she restored to liberty by paying their ransom'.[28] According to her biographer, the queen had a love of etiquette and formality, she encouraged the wearing of bright colours and jewellery and insisted that the king 'should be accompanied in great state whenever he either walk or rode abroad'.[29] The queen

added to the state of the royal palace, so that not only was it brightened by the many-coloured apparel worn in it, but the whole dwelling blazed with gold and silver; since the vessels employed for serving the food and drink to the king and the nobles of the realm were of gold and silver, or at least were gilt and plated.[30]

Turgot warns us, however, that this display of splendour was not because it delighted Margaret, but rather 'because duty compelled her to discharge what the kingly dignity required'.[31]

Writing his biography for Margaret's daughter, Turgot was bound to be complimentary and to show the queen in the best light. It is clearly evident, however, that Margaret enjoyed a high reputation among the Anglo-Norman world, even in her own lifetime; Orderic Vitalis described her as 'eminent from her high birth, but even more renowned for her virtue and holy life'.[32] Theobald d'Étampes, a Caen-educated teacher and theologian, wrote to Margaret, asking for a position as one of her chaplains.[33] Margaret was a 'strong, complex and interesting character, as well as beautiful and notably religious'.[34] According to Nigel Tranter, Margaret carried with her, everywhere, a piece of the true cross, on which Christ was crucified. It is from this relic, which became known as the Black Rood of Scotland, that the Palace of Holyrood, in Edinburgh, takes its name.[35] Her life as Queen of Scotland did not prevent her pursuing an active religious life; indeed, Margaret's position gave her a unique opportunity to influence the practice of Christianity in Scotland. Margaret strived to bring the Church of Scotland into conformity with the practices of western Catholicism, and away from the tenets of the Celtic, or Columban, church, which held a lot of influence in the country and did not recognise the overlordship of the pope. The Columban Church celebrated Easter on a different day to the Catholic Church, as it included Sundays in its forty days of Lent, unlike the Roman Catholic Church. They also shared bread and wine among their congregation during communion, unlike the Roman church, which gave bread to the congregation, but reserved the wine for the celebrant and priests.

Having been raised on the Continent, amid the splendour of the churches in the Holy Roman Empire, Margaret believed that the wearing of beautiful vestments by the clergy was done for the glory of God; as far as she was concerned, the rough, homespun habits of the Columban clergy, did nothing to glorify God. She also believed in the strict hierarchy of the church, from the pope, through cardinals, archbishops, bishops, abbots and the clergy. The two churches even differed in the tonsures of their clergy; Roman priests shaved the crowns of their heads, whereas the Columban, or Celtic, priests, shaved their foreheads.[36] As Turgot put it, 'there were certain places in Scotland in which Masses were celebrated according to some sort of barbarous rite, contrary to the usage of the whole church'.[37] Queen Margaret encouraged the Scottish clergy, and its people, to receive communion more than once a year at Easter, to refrain from working on a Sunday and to observe the Lenten fast from Ash Wednesday, rather than the following Monday, and so bringing it in line with the practice of the Roman Catholic Church. Margaret also urged the clergy to celebrate mass with a common ritual and sought to forbid marriage between a man and his stepmother or sister-in-law, a practice forbidden in the Roman Catholic Church but permitted within the Celtic church.

Margaret was supported in all her reforms by her husband; indeed, if Malcolm III had not given his support, it is doubtful that Margaret's influence would have achieved much, if anything at all. His role in her attempts at religious reform is vague, although Malcolm did arrange a conference for the clergy to introduce a number of reforms. Margaret was present and embarrassed some of the clerics by knowing more than they did about the proper procedures of the church. She even had the papal manuals to quote from. It may well be that Malcolm was needed to facilitate the interactions between queen and clergy, as

Margaret's biographer claimed the queen's first language was English, whereas Malcolm was fluent in English and his native Gaelic and could have acted as translator for his wife.[38]

The queen founded a monastic community at Dunfermline, building the first major stone church in Scotland in the place where she had married:

> She had no sooner attained this eminent dignity, than she built an eternal memorial of her name and devotion in the place where her nuptials had been held. The noble church which she erected there in honour of the Holy Trinity was to serve a threefold purpose; it was intended for the redemption of the king's soul, for the good of her own, and for securing to her children prosperity in this life and in that which is to come.[39]

Queen Margaret sought the aid of Lanfranc, Archbishop of Canterbury, with whom she corresponded often, in the foundation of Dunfermline. She asked that he send monks from the cathedral monastery at Canterbury, to become its first community. The revered archbishop responded reverentially to Margaret's appeal, and to her request for him to become her own spiritual adviser:

> Lanfranc, unworthy archbishop of the holy church of Canterbury, sends greetings and his blessing to Margaret, the glorious queen of the Scots.
>
> In the brief span of a letter I cannot hope to unfold the joy with which you flooded my heart when I studied the letter that you sent me, o Queen beloved of God. With what holy cheer the words flow on which are uttered by the inspiration of the Holy Spirit! I am convinced that what you had written was said not by you but through you: by your mouth of a truth he spoke, who says to his disciples, 'Learn of me, for I am meek and lowly in heart.' It is as a result of Christ's teaching here that you, who are born of a royal line, brought up as befits a queen and nobly wedded to a noble king, are choosing me as your father – a foreigner of neither birth nor worth, who is ensnared in sin: and you ask me to accept you as my spiritual daughter, I am not what you think me to be; but may I be so because you think it. Do not continue under that misapprehension: pray for me that I may be a father fit to pray to God for you and have my prayers granted. Let there be a mutual exchange between us of prayers and good works. Those that I render are small indeed; but I am confident that I shall receive far greater benefits in return. From now on then may I be your father and be you my daughter.
>
> I am sending your glorious husband and yourself our very dear brother Dom Goldwin as you asked me to, and two other brothers

with him; for he could not accomplish single-handed what is required in God's service and your own. I do most urgently entreat you to strive to complete the work that you have begun for God and your souls' welfare as quickly and effectively as you can. Should you be able to achieve it with the help of others, or wish to do so, we most fervently desire that our own monks should return to us, for in the positions they held they were really indispensable to our church. But let it be your decision: in all respects we entirely desire to render you obedience.

May the Lord almighty bless you and mercifully free you from all your sins.[40]

Although it started as a priory, Dunfermline was elevated to an independent abbey in 1128, at the instigation of Margaret's son, David I.[41] The Queen's Ferry crossing on the Firth of Forth, for which Margaret had persuaded her husband to remit the charges for genuine pilgrims going further north to St Andrews, was named for Queen Margaret. According to Turgot, the church was

beautified with rich gifts of various kinds, amongst which, as is well known, were many vessels of pure and solid gold for the sacred service of the altar, about which I can speak with the greater certainty since, by the queen's orders, I myself, for a long time, had all of them under my charge.[42]

The queen 'also placed there a cross of priceless value, bearing the figure of our saviour, which she had caused to be covered with the purest gold and silver studded with gems, a token, even to the present day, of the earnestness of her faith'.[43] As well as her foundation at Dunfermline Abbey, which became the burial place, or necropolis, for many of Scotland's kings and queens, Margaret also rebuilt in stone the abbey on Iona, which had been burned down. And at Edinburgh Castle, the small chapel which still bears her name was built in her honour during the reign of David I, the queen's youngest son.[44]

Queen Margaret, therefore, was instrumental in pushing through the reforms of the Scottish church. However, not everything went in her favour, and she suffered one reverse when King Malcolm appointed their fourth son, Æthelred, to the position of lay abbot of Dunkeld, and therefore the primacy of the Columban Church. The position was hereditary and had been held by the boy's great-grandfather, Crinan, from a similar early age. Æthelred fully embraced his new post and became a priest of the church, marrying without his parents' permission; although permitted in the Celtic church, a priest was not allowed to marry in the Roman Catholic Church. Æthelred's wife is said to have been the daughter of the late King Lulach (d. 1058). It may well be that these actions were the cause of Æthelred later being barred from the succession. He was not entirely disowned by his family, as it seems that he was with his mother when she died in 1093. Margaret and Malcolm would have a large family, with six sons and two daughters growing to adulthood. According to Turgot, Margaret was no 'less careful about her children than she was about herself. She took all heed that they should be well brought up, and especially that they should be trained in virtue.'[45] Margaret took great care in educating her children, ensuring they were given the essentials for their future royal careers. She was quite the disciplinarian and 'charged the governor who had care of the nursery to curb the children, to scold them, and to whip them whenever they were naughty, as frolicksome childhood will often be.'[46] Turgot went on to say that it was 'thanks to their mother's religious care, her children surpassed in good behaviour many who were their elders; they were always affectionate and peaceable among themselves, and everywhere the younger paid due respect to the elder.'[47]

The eldest son of Malcolm and Margaret, Edward, died in 1093 in his early 20s, within days of his father. As we have seen, another son, Æthelred, who may have been styled Earl of Fife, became Lay Abbot at Dunkeld and died around 1097. Following their father's death and the succession dispute between Malcolm III's brother Donald III, and his oldest son by Ingibiorg, Duncan II, Margaret's youngest son, David, had fled to England with his brothers, Edgar and Alexander. Donald had initially usurped the throne on Malcolm's death but was himself deposed by Duncan in May 1094. When Duncan was killed at the Battle of Monthechin in November of the same year, Donald again seized the throne. Margaret and Malcolm's second son, Edmund, moreover, had sided with his uncle in order to become co-ruler. Edmund ruled south of the Forth/Clyde boundary, while Donald ruled the north, although there is no indication that he was ever crowned. Donald and Edmund were both deposed in 1097, in favour of Edmund's brother, King Edgar, who had the support of not only his uncle, Edgar the Ætheling, but also of King William II Rufus of England. Edgar the Ætheling drove Donald from the throne; the deposed king was mutilated and imprisoned before dying in 1099. Edmund fared better. He became a monk, joining the Cluniacs at Montacute Abbey, Somerset, where he died at an unknown date, having never married. King Edgar himself, fourth son of Margaret and Malcolm, died on 8 January 1107. Unmarried and childless, he was succeeded by his brother, Alexander I, who had been married to Sybilla, an illegitimate daughter of King Henry I of England, but we will look at this relationship more closely in the next chapter, as we will Alexander's successor, David I, the sixth and youngest son of the royal brood.

Malcolm and Margaret also had two daughters: the oldest, Edith, changed her name to Matilda on marrying King Henry I of England, and was the mother of Empress Matilda, whose attempts to claim the crown on her father's death were thwarted by her cousin, King Stephen. Margaret's second daughter, Mary, married Eustace III, Count of Boulogne, and was the mother of Matilda of Boulogne, wife of Stephen, King of England.[48] Matilda and Mary were educated at Wilton Abbey, in the charge of Margaret's sister, Christina. Edith/Matilda was unhappy in her aunt's care and later said: 'I ... went in fear of the rod of my aunt Christina ... and she would often make me smart with a good slapping and the most horrible scolding, as well as treating me as being in disgrace.'[49] Christina's treatment of Matilda included forcing the girl to wear a veil, supposedly to hide her beauty from visiting men. However, this caused controversy when she married King Henry I, as it raised the question of whether she had ever taken her vows – or been veiled – as a nun. At the inquiry into this question in 1100, Matilda insisted she had not, saying: 'that hood I did indeed wear in her presence, chafing and fearful ... but as soon as I was able to escape out of her sight I tore it off and threw it in the dirt and trampled on it. This was my only way of venting my rage and hatred of it that boiled up in me.'[50]

Living on England's northern border as they did, Malcolm and Margaret continued to support Margaret's brother, Edgar the Ætheling; in 1075, he was welcomed 'with great honour' at the Scottish court on his return from Flanders and 'the king Malcolm and his sister gave him and all his men countless treasures, and very honourably sent him out of their domain again.'[51] As King of Scots, Malcolm also had claims to Cumbria and Northumbria and in 1069/70, he made raids into Northumberland. King William I responded by sending an army north and the eventual peace treaty saw Malcolm's oldest son by Ingibiorg, Duncan, being sent south to England as a hostage and guarantee of his good faith. Duncan would eventually reign, briefly, as Duncan II but was killed in battle in 1094. The most notable of Malcolm's raids into Northumberland were in 1079 and 1091, with the aim of gaining control over the county. When a diplomatic mission, aided by his brother-in-law, Edgar the Ætheling, in 1092 failed, he invaded northern England again in 1093, taking his eldest son by Margaret, Edward, with him. The resulting siege of Alnwick saw King Malcolm killed and Edward so seriously injured that he succumbed to his wounds just a few days later, at Jedburgh.

Many of the chroniclers of the time record Margaret's reaction to the news of the deaths of her husband and oldest son. John of Worcester told of Margaret's grief:

> Margaret, queen of the Scots, was so deeply affected by the news of their death, that she fell dangerously ill. Calling the priests to attend her without delay, she went into the church, and confessing her sins to them, caused herself to be anointed with oil and strengthened with the heavenly viaticum; beseeching God with earnest and diligent prayers that he would not suffer her to live longer in this troublesome world. Nor was it very long before her prayers were heard, for three days after the king's death she was released from the bonds of the flesh, and translated, as we doubt not, to the joys of eternal salvation.[52]

The *Anglo-Saxon Chronicles* recorded:

> when the good Queen Margaret heard this – her most beloved lord and son thus betrayed – she became anguished in mind to the point

of death and went to church with her priests, and received her rites and prayed to God that she might give up her spirit.[53]

According to Margaret's biographer, Turgot, the queen's health had been failing for some time; for six months, she had been unable to ride a horse and had rarely risen from her bed. Thoughts of her children were at the forefront of her mind, and she had entreated Turgot:

> There are two things which I beg of you. One is, that as long as you survive you will remember me in your prayers; the other is, that you will take some care about my sons and daughters. Lavish your affection upon them; teach them before all things to love and fear God; never cease instructing them. When you see any one of them exalted to the height of an earthly dignity, then, as at once his father and his master in the truest sense, go to him, warn him lest through means of a passing honour he become puffed up with pride, or offend God by avarice, or through prosperity in this world neglect the blessedness of the life which is eternal. These are the things, said she, which I ask you – as in the sight of God, who now is present along with us two – to promise me that you will carefully perform.[54]

Margaret died just days after the battle at Alnwick, on 16 November, possibly on receiving the news of the deaths of her husband and eldest son, although the fact her body was weakened, by her frequent fasting and self-denial, may have hastened her death. One of the priests attendant upon the queen related her last moments to Turgot and reported that the queen's son, Edgar,

> who, now, after his father, holds in this realm the reins of government, having returned from the army, entered the queen's bedroom. Conceive his distress at this moment! Imagine to yourself how his heart was racked! He stood there in a strait; everything was against him, and whither to turn himself he knew not. He had come to announce to his mother that his father and brother were slain, and he found his mother, whom he loved most dearly, at the point of death. He knew not whom first to lament.[55]

Queen Margaret was buried in the abbey she had founded at Dunfermline, 'opposite the altar and the venerable sign of the Holy Cross which she had erected'.[56] King Malcolm was initially buried at Tynemouth, but later moved to join his wife at Dunfermline.

The queen's personal piety was renowned for the severity of her fasting and self-denial. The story of her life, written by Turgot, emphasises her compassion for children and the poor. Her religious zeal may well have arisen from her childhood in eastern Europe, a region which had only just recently – and not entirely – converted to Christianity. In the *Vita Sanctae Margaretae*, Turgot said of Margaret: 'Her understanding was keen to comprehend any matter, whatever it might be; to this was joined a great tenacity of memory, enabling her to store it up, along with a graceful flow of language to express it.'[57] The *Anglo-Saxon Chronicles* said of Margaret: 'This aforesaid queen afterwards performed many useful works in that land to the glory of God, and also throve well in the royal estate, just as was natural to her.'[58] John of Worcester also recorded Margaret's piety:

> For while she lived, she devoted herself to the exercise of piety, justice, peace, and charity; she was frequent in prayer, and chastened her body by watchings and fastings; she endowed churches and monasteries; loved and reverenced the servants and handmaids of God; broke bread to the hungry, clothed the naked, gave shelter, food, and raiment to all the pilgrims who came to her door; and loved God with all her heart.[59]

Margaret's sons honoured their mother's memory, encouraging the popular cult of St Margaret, that developed soon after the queen's death, in order to foster the idea that she should be made a saint. Such an honour would serve to enhance the political and religious status of their family. One of the miracles attributed to her was that in 1199 Scotland's king, William the Lion, was persuaded against launching an invasion of England after experiencing a vision while holding a vigil at Margaret's tomb at Dunfermline. Her canonisation took some time, however, and finally took place in 1250, when her remains were translated to a new shrine within Dunfermline Abbey. In 1673, Pope Clement X named her patroness of Scotland. The shrine housing St Margaret and Malcolm III, and many of the tombs of Scotland's kings, was despoiled in 1560, at the height of the Reformation. The saintly relics, however, had already been removed to a safe place. Saint Margaret's head was enclosed in a separate reliquary. When Mary, Queen of Scots, was awaiting the birth of her son, the future King James VI, the head was brought to her at Edinburgh Castle and thereafter remained at Craigluscar for some time. In 1597, Saint Margaret's head was entrusted to John Robie, who was on his way to study with the Jesuits at Douai. It remained at the Jesuit College at Douai for the next two hundred years and was supposedly hidden away during the French Revolution, but has since disappeared. Following the Reformation, the remainder of the relics of both Margaret and Malcolm were removed to Flanders, from where they were taken to Spain by Philip II and reinterred in a chapel in the Royal Monastery of the Escorial in Madrid.[60]

Margaret was a direct descendant of King Alfred the Great of Wessex; her Saxon royal blood, alone, ensured that she would not be allowed to follow her inclination for a religious life, she was too valuable on the marriage market. However, through her efforts to reform the Scottish church, it could be said that she found a better way to worship God. Her legacy was cemented through the work of her son, David I, who continued in her policy of church reform; while her Saxon blood found its way back into the English royal family through her daughter, Matilda, and her marriage to Henry I, continuing into the Plantagenet dynasty through her granddaughter, Empress Matilda. Her two granddaughters, Matilda of Boulogne and Empress Matilda, would find themselves on opposing sides in the contest for the throne between the empress and King Stephen.

> Quaint legends to our hearts endear
> Ours sainted Scottish Queen:
> Alone, unseen, oft strayed she here
> In thoughtful mood, serene;
> Thus oft from yonder ancient towers
> She sought from pomp to dwell,
> And pondered o'er life's fleeting hours
> Beside her cherished well.[61]

Chapter Two

The Daughters-in-Law of St Margaret

I f King Malcolm and Queen Margaret had been married in 1070, and given that their eldest son Edward died shortly after his father, the couple's surviving sons would have still been in their teens when their parents died. This may explain why, when Malcolm III Canmore was killed at the siege of Alnwick on 13 November 1093, he was succeeded as king, not by one of his many sons, but by his brother Donald III, also known as Donald Bane (the Fair or the White, perhaps referring to the colour of his hair). As we have seen, it had long been the tradition in the Scottish monarchy that the crown did not pass from father to son but from king to the senior adult male in the family. In this case, Malcolm's brother. Born in the 1030s, Donald would have been in or approaching his 60s when he seized the throne. Tradition has it that he spent most of his brother's reign in exile in the kingdom of the Isles. His acceptance as king is seen as a backlash against the Anglo-Saxon influences of Malcolm's reign and a desire to return to Celtic traditions. Donald had a daughter, named Bethoc, but we know nothing of his wife; given Donald's age at his accession, his wife may have been long dead. It is from Bethoc that John Comyn would make his claim to the throne in 1291, following the death of Margaret, Maid of Norway, when there was no clear successor to the crown. Bethoc was married to Uhtred of Tynedale, son of Earl Waltheof of Northumbria and it is from this marriage that Hextilda of Tynedale was born; Hextilda married Richard Comyn, and the couple were the ancestors of John Comyn, giving him descent, through Donald III, from Duncan I and Malcolm II.[1]

Donald III may have thought Malcolm's sons by Queen Margaret too young to challenge his rule, but he had not reckoned on Malcolm's older son, Duncan, by his first marriage to Ingibiorg. Duncan had been given to William the Conqueror as a hostage to his father's good behaviour in 1072 and was held in Normandy, alongside Ulf, the son of the late king, Harold II. Both were freed and knighted by Robert Curthose on the Conqueror's death in 1087, after which Duncan travelled to England, where he remained at the court of William II Rufus, serving in Rufus's army. It was William Rufus who gave his support to Duncan when he made a bid for the throne in May 1094, defeating Donald and driving him into the Celtic hinterland. According to Florence of Worcester:

the Scots elected for their king Donald, brother of King Malcolm, and expelled from Scotland all the English who belonged to the kings' court. Duncan, king Malcolm's son, hearing of these events, besought king William, in whose army he then served, to grant him his father's kingdom, and obtaining his request swore fealty to him. He then hastened to Scotland, with a host of English and Normans, and expelling his uncle Donald reigned in his stead. Thereupon some of the Scots banded together and slew nearly all his men, a few only escaping with him. But afterwards they restored him to the throne, on condition that he should no longer harbour either Englishmen or Normans in Scotland, and permit them to serve in his army.[2]

Duncan had spent most of his life abroad, living in Normandy and then at the English court. He was seen as an outsider supported by a foreign occupying army. When the Scots rose against these Norman allies, Duncan was forced to negotiate and agreed to send the majority of his foreign supporters back to William II Rufus. This proved to be a fatal mistake, as Donald, who had fled into the Highlands, now saw the opportunity to challenge his nephew. Duncan was ambushed on 12 November 1094, and killed at the battle of Monthechin, though the chronicles differ as to the identity of his killer and the manner of his death. Florence of Worcester states: 'Meanwhile, the Scots perfidiously murdered their king, Duncan, and some others, at the instigation of Donald, who was again raised to the throne.'[3] The *Annals of Inisfallen* record that 'Donald son of Duncan' killed 'Duncan son of Malcolm King of Scots' in 1094 and 'took the kingship of Alba.'[4] While the *Chronicle of John of Fordun* claims that 'Duncan, King Malcolm's illegitimate son' was 'slain at Monthechin by the Earl of Mernys... Malpetri, in Scottish, Malpedir, through the wiles of his uncle Donald' and was buried 'in the island of Iona'.[5] And the *Annals of Ulster* confusingly records that 'Duncan son of Malcolm, king of Scotland, was treacherously killed by his own brothers Donald and Edmund' in 1094.[6] While Edmund was, indeed, Duncan's half-brother, Donald was his uncle, though Duncan did also have a full brother named Donald, which may explain the confusion.

The *Annals of Ulster* may have assigned the blame for Duncan's death on Donald and Edmund as they were the main beneficiaries of Duncan's demise, though they may not have administered the fatal blow themselves. In his chronicle, John of Fordun corroborates the *Annals'* claims:

> [Malmesbury,] writing about the aforesaid Edmund, says: – Of the sons of the king and Margaret, Edmund was the only one who fell away from goodness. Partaking of his uncle Donald's wickedness, he was privy to his brother Duncan's death, having, forsooth, bargained with his uncle for half the kingdom.[7]

Whether he was killed in battle or murdered by his uncle and brother, or by Malpedir, the outcome was the same. Duncan II was dead and the crown was back in the hands of Donald III. Duncan left a widow and child to mourn him. He was married, though we do not know when, to Ethelreda of Northumbria, daughter of Gospatric, Earl of Northumbria. As an exile from England since his earldom was given to Waltheof, the surviving son of Earl Siward, in 1072, Gospatric had been given the castle of Dunbar and its surrounding area by Malcolm III. Through his mother, Gospatric was the grandson of Uhtred the Bold, Earl of Northumbria, while his successor, Waltheof, was Uhtred's great-grandson. Duncan and Ethelreda had one son, William fitz Duncan, who would have fled into exile with his mother following Duncan's death. It seems likely that Ethelreda sought shelter with her brother, also called Waltheof, lord of Allerdale in Cumbria, and married again. The *Chronicon Cumbriæ* records that Waltheof granted Broughton, Ribton and Little Broughton jointly to his sister Ethelreda and Waltheof, son of Gillemin, who must have been Ethelreda's second husband.[8] According to the *Chronicon Cumbriæ*, William fitz Duncan eventually succeeded his cousin, Alan, son of Waltheof, as lord of Allerdale.[9] Eighty years later, in the reign of William the Lion, William fitz Duncan's descendant, Donald Macwilliam, rebelled:

> in the year 1179, William, king of Scotland, with his brother Earl David, and a large army, advanced into Ross against Macwilliam, whose real name was Donald Bane, and fortified two castles there – namely, Dunschath and Ederdone; and when he had fortified these, he hied him back to the southern tracts of his kingdom. But after seven years were overpast, seeing that this man went on in his wonted wickedness, the king, with a numerous army, and in very strong force, set out for Moray against this same enemy of his, Donald Bane, who said he was sprung of royal seed, and was the son of William, son of Duncan the Bastard, who was the son of the great Malcolm, king of Scotland, called Canmore. This man, relying upon the treachery of some disloyal men, had first, indeed, wrested from his king the whole of Ross, by his tyrannous insolence; and then, having for no little time held the whole of Moray, he had seized upon the greater part of the kingdom, with fire and slaughter, and aimed at the whole thereof. Now, while the king was making some stay, with his army, at the town of Inverness, and had been harassing Donald Bane and his adherents by daily plundering and spoiling, it fell out, one day, that some of his men, whom he had as usual sent out, to the number of two thousand, throughout the woods and country to plunder and to reconnoitre, lo! all of a sudden, stumbled unawares upon Macwilliam and his troops lurking in a moor which is called Macgarvy, near Moray. Macwilliam, seeing that those of the king's army were few in comparison with his own men, engaged them at

once, and charged them. But they manfully and fearlessly withstood him with all their might, and, by God's help, slew him, with five hundred of his men, and routed the rest, on Friday the 31st of July – thus giving him the meet reward he had earned. They then brought away his head to the king, as a gazing-stock for the whole army.[10]

With Duncan dead, and his descendant's challenge to the throne long into the future, Donald III was back on the throne. He would share power with Edmund, now the eldest surviving son of Malcolm III. With only a daughter, and no sons, Duncan may have recognised Edmund, his eldest nephew, as his heir; they agreed a power-sharing arrangement in which Edmund was made co-King of Scotland, ruling the lands south of the Forth/Clyde, with Donald ruling the lands to the north.[11] Although Edmund may have seen this move as practical and the best way to guarantee that he succeed to the throne on Duncan's death, it alienated him from his brothers, Edgar, Alexander and David, who fled into exile in England 'for fear of him [Donald]'.[12] What happened to another brother, Æthelred, the lay abbot of Dunkeld, at this time, seems uncertain. He may already have died, but as John of Fordun states, nothing is really known: 'About Ethelred I find nothing certain, in any writings, as to where he died or was buried; except that, as some assert, he lies buried in Saint Andrew's Church at Kilremont.'[13] What is certain is that Æthelred, who appears as Malcolm and Margaret's third son in most genealogies, does not feature in William II Rufus's plans for Scotland when he determines to replace Donald and Edmund with Edmund's younger brother, Edgar.

The dual monarchy of Donald III and King Edmund lasted until 1097, though there appears to be little information regarding the nature of their rule. According to John of Fordun, Edgar Ætheling, Queen Margaret's brother,

> saw that Donald had wickedly usurped the throne of Scotland, which, by right, belonged to his nephews, and that he would not restore it, though more than once besought thereto by ambassadors, by a friendly intervention, he was stirred to wrath.[14]

When negotiation failed, Edgar Ætheling turned to William II Rufus for help:

> So he gathered together from all sides a vast number of his friends, and being strengthened by the aforesaid King William's help, set out against Donald in order to drive him out, and appoint, as king of Scotland, his nephew, Edgar, a younger son of King Malcolm and his sister Margaret.[15]

When the two armies met, the matter appears to have been decided by the champions of both sides, whereby a certain knight of English birth, named Robert, the son of the aforesaid Godwin, and the heir and rival of his father's prowess, being accompanied by only two knights, charged the enemy, and slew their mightiest, who stood out, like champions, in front of the line of battle. So, before the armies had neared one another, Donald and his men were put to flight; and thus, by the favour of God and the merits of Saint Cuthbert, Edgar happily achieved a bloodless victory.[16]

Donald was blinded and imprisoned at Rescobie in Forfarshire, where he died in 1099, 'dispatched by the contrivance of David, the youngest brother and the power of [King] William [II]'.[17] Another source reports that 'He was blinded and slain by Edgar, son of Malcolm, and was interred at Dunkeld, and afterwards translated to the isle of Iona.'[18] Other sources claim he lived until 1107, when he was killed on the orders of Alexander I.[19] He was eventually buried on Iona. Edmund, on the other hand, was tonsured and 'doomed to perpetual imprisonment' at the Cluniac monastery at Montacute in Somerset and 'on his near approach of death, ordered himself to be buried in his chains'.[20] Edmund died sometime after 1097 and was buried at Montacute.

The new king, Edgar, had been invested as King of Scots by William II Rufus in 1095, after he had campaigned with the English king against the rebel earl of Northumbria, Robert de Mowbray. However, it was not until 1097 that he was able to mount an effective challenge to his uncle and brother, with the support of his maternal uncle, Edgar Ætheling. King Edgar's reign, from 1097 to 1107, appears to have been, on the whole, peaceful. He neutralised a potential threat from Magnus Barelegs, King of Norway, by agreeing a treaty in which he recognised Norwegian sovereignty of the Hebrides.[21] This willingness to relinquish any claim to the Hebrides demonstrates Edgar's south-facing policies, and thus the neglect of the political core of his ancestral kingdom. Edgar was continuing the Anglo-Saxon focus of his parents' realm. This is also seen in the marriage of his sister, Edith (also known as Matilda) to England's new king, Henry I, in 1100. His religious policies followed a similar tone, repopulating Dunfermline with monks from Canterbury when he began a programme of rebuilding at the abbey. Edgar also remembered his family. In a charter dated to 1095, 'Edgar ... King of Scots' made grants for the souls of 'Malcolm our father and Margaret our mother ... and Edward and Duncan our brothers' by charter dated 1095.[22] Edgar died, still only in his 30s, either at Dundee or Edinburgh Castle, on 6 or 8 January 1107. He was buried alongside his parents, in the church at Dunfermline Abbey, in front of the high altar.[23]

There is no record that Edgar ever married, and therefore he had no son to succeed him. The crown passed to his younger brother, Alexander I, who, like his brother before him, succeeded to the throne as a vassal of the English crown. Alexander was born around 1177 or 1178 and was, therefore, 30 or so when he ascended the throne in 1107, 'as the King Henry granted him'.[24] He had probably spent the years between his father's death and Edgar's accession in exile in England, with Edgar and their younger brother, David. John of Fordun provides a largely flattering assessment of Alexander I as king:

> Now the king was a lettered and godly man; very humble and amiable towards the clerics and regulars, but terrible beyond measure to the rest of his subjects; a man of large heart, exerting himself in all things beyond his strength. He was most zealous in building churches, in searching for relics of saints, in providing and arranging priestly vestments and sacred books; most open-handed, even beyond his means, to all newcomers; and so devoted to the poor, that he seemed to delight in nothing so much as in supporting them, washing, nourishing, and clothing them.[25]

Early in the reign, however, tensions arose between Alexander and his youngest brother, David, who had been bequeathed a significant portion of southern Scotland, incorporating Cumbria and Lothian, by his brother Edgar.[26] Alexander was reluctant to relinquish control of such a significant portion of his kingdom but was forced to yield when faced with the threat of military intervention from Henry I of England, who sided with David.[27] Although this early confrontation strained the relationship between the kings, Alexander was still Henry's vassal and in 1114 he led an armed force into Wales as part of Henry's campaign in the principality.[28] It was also with the help of England that Alexander continued with the reforms of the Scottish church which had been initiated by his mother. A devotee of St Cuthbert, like his brother Edgar, who had credited the saint with his victory over Donald III, Alexander was present at the translation of the saint's remains to its new shrine in Durham cathedral:

> The body of St. Cuthbert, the bishop, was exposed to view while Ranulph was bishop, and was clearly found to be uncorrupted, as well as the head of St. Oswald, king and martyr, and the relics of St. Bede and other saints, by Ralph, abbot of Séez, afterwards bishop of Rochester, and the monks of Durham, in the presence of earl Alexander, the brother of Edgar, king of Scots, and afterwards king himself. Having been permitted to assist on so sacred an occasion, he caused a shrine to be made at the cost of many gold and silver marks, in which the sacred body was deposited, wrapped in new vestments.[29]

And it was from Durham that Alexander sought to fill the vacant bishopric of St Andrews; Turgot, prior of Durham, who had been his mother's close spiritual adviser and biographer. However, Alexander was determined that the Scottish church would not be subordinate to the English church and refused to allow either Turgot or his successor, Eadmer, to profess obedience to the archbishops of Canterbury and York. In 1072, in the reign of Malcolm III, a compact had been agreed between the Archbishops of York and Canterbury, by which all of Britain north of the Humber would be under the jurisdiction of the Archbishop of York, including Scotland's churches. And so, when the Archbishop of York claimed the right of consecrating the Bishop of St Andrews as his suffragan, this was resisted by Alexander, who maintained that the Bishop of St Andrews, as the *Episcapus Albania*, was the head of the Scottish church, and that the Scottish church was independent. As a consequence, having been approved by Henry I, Turgot was eventually consecrated at York on 1 August 1109, but without the profession of obedience. Turgot struggled to establish his authority and to deal with the various factions, including the king. The pope, Paschal II, wrote to him twice with advice but when Turgot sought permission to go to Rome to speak with the pope in person, Alexander would not permit it. After falling ill in June 1115, Turgot retired to Durham, where he died on 31 August that year.[30]

Turgot was succeeded as Bishop of St Andrews by Eadmer, a monk from Canterbury, whose selection by Alexander I was approved by Henry I. Eadmer was initially given the ring of office, by the king, but not the pastoral staff. This was likely in response to the investiture controversy between lay and ecclesiastical powers, where kings and pope were in conflict over who had the right to appoint and invest clergy. Alexander relented the following month, when he was about to go to war, and allowed Eadmer to take the pastoral staff from the altar of St Andrews. His full consecration, however, was further delayed by the sees of Canterbury and York claiming the right to install him as bishop. Eadmer supported Canterbury but York had the backing of the pope. Alexander, on the other hand, would allow neither as each required a profession of obedience. After consulting with the Bishop of Glasgow and two Canterbury monks, Eadmer restored the staff and ring to St Andrews and returned to Canterbury in about 1121. Eadmer was eventually replaced by Robert, prior of Scone Abbey, in 1124 but he was still not consecrated at the time of Alexander's death later in the year.[31] Robert's consecration as Bishop of St Andrews was eventually performed by Thurstan, Archbishop of York, in 1138, in the reign of King David, Alexander I's successor.

Not all of Alexander's dealings with the church were a confrontation over the jurisdiction of the English archbishoprics. Alexander intended to establish the Augustinians at the cathedral at Dunkeld, but was thwarted by the established clergy and so instead founded the monastery of canons of the island of Emonia (Inchcolm), by Inverkeithing.[32] King Alexander and his men were caught in a violent storm whilst crossing at Queensferry. They managed to reach land on the island of Inchcolm and were sustained by a hermit who was dedicated to the service of St Columba. The hermit

> earnestly devoted himself to it at a certain little chapel on the island,
> content with a meagre diet consisting of the milk of one cow, shells

and little fish that he gathered from the sea. The king with his very large number of fellow soldiers gratefully lived on this food of his for three days on end under compulsion from the wind. But on the previous day when he was giving up hope of surviving, as he was being buffeted by the very great danger of the sea and the madness of the storm, he made a vow to the saint that if he brought him safely to the island along with his men, he would leave on the island such a memorial to his glory as would serve for asylum and solace to sailors and victims of shipwreck. This is how it came about that he founded a monastery of canons in that same place, just as it can be seen at the present day.[33]

And according to John of Fordun, it was Alexander who brought the remains of his father, Malcolm III, from his original resting place at Tynemouth home to Scotland, to be laid to rest in Dunfermline Abbey.[34] The king often looked to the south when filling clerical and monastic vacancies. Around 1114, he colonised his new foundation of Scone Abbey with Augustinian canons from Nostell Priory in Yorkshire, appointing Robert, the future Bishop of St Andrews, as its first prior:

He [Alexander] it was who bestowed the Boar's Chase upon the blessed Andrew. He it was, likewise, who gave so many privileges to the aforesaid church of the Holy Trinity, at Scone. He had founded and built it on the spot where both the Scottish and Pictish kings had whilom established the chief seat of government; and, when constructed with a framework of stone, according to the custom of that time, he had had it dedicated – to which dedication, by strict order of the king, nearly the whole kingdom flocked. That church, indeed, with all its pertinents, he freely made over, God so ordering it, to the governance of canons-regular called from the church of Saint Oswald at Nostle (Nastlay, near Pontefract), and of the others after them who should serve God, until the end of the world.[35]

Although Alexander's focus appears to have been on the church, he did initiate some changes to royal administration. Charters to Durham and Scone Priory indicate that King Alexander had a chancellor, the first known in Scotland.[36] Alexander's reforms also included the introduction of sheriffs into Scotland, in order to maintain the king's peace.[37] His constable, Edward, commanded his household knights, who were predominantly from an Anglo-French background. According to Orderic Vitalis, this Edward was the son of Earl Siward, Earl of Mercia, which must be a mistake as Siward was earl of Northumbria; however, it does suggest that Edward was also from England rather than a native Scot.[38] Alexander's seal was very similar to that of William II Rufus but the king in majesty was uncrowned.[39] The king also began a programme of castle-building, including the palace of

Stirling. Alexander also fulfilled his martial duties as king, as Walter Bower attests in his *Scotichronicon*:

> [Edgar] was succeeded by his brother Alexander nicknamed 'the Fierce'. He is called 'the Fierce' because his uncle the earl of Gowrie gave him as a baptismal gift the lands of Liff and Invergowrie. When he became king, he began to build a royal palace at Liff, when behold certain ruffians of the Mearns and Moray made an attempt to capture the king by night within the precincts of the palace, and when they were trying to break down the doorposts, one of the king's chamberlains called Alexander Carron cunningly led the king out through a latrine. He went aboard a galley at Invergowrie, and made for the southern regions of Scotland, gathered together a large army, and hurried against the rebels. Because God had supported him in time of danger, he wished to show his gratitude to Him. So he founded a monastic church at Scone, and after he had given them the lands of Liff and Invergowrie as endowment and glebe, he quickly resumed his expedition along with his men. When they arrived at the Water of Spey, his enemies were massed together in a great army on the opposite bank; and as the water was rising excessively high, the king was advised not to ford the Water until it subsided. He was blazing with anger at the sight of his enemies threatening conspiracy, and not being able to contain himself, he handed over his banner to his chamberlain (the aforesaid Alexander) to carry; and these two were the first to attempt the ford; the army followed, and the enemy was turned to flight.[40]

One of the primary duties of a king is to marry and produce heirs; at least one son, preferably two – the heir and the spare. This guarantees the succession and offers stability to a country. Even daughters were useful to a king, their marriages cementing alliances with friends and enemies alike. Alexander I was married shortly after his accession to the throne. His bride was offered to him by Henry I of England. She was Sybilla, also known as Sybilla of Normandy, one of the King of England's many illegitimate offspring. King Henry had more than twenty illegitimate children and as many as five were by the same mother, his mistress, or concubine, Sybilla Corbet. Orderic Vitalis refers to Sybilla of Normandy as 'the daughter of King Henry by a concubine'.[41] It is highly likely that Sybilla Corbet was Sybilla's mother. She was the daughter of a Shropshire landowner named Robert Corbet. Her children with the king included Reginald, Earl of Cornwall, and a young man named William, who was described as the queen's brother when he accompanied the younger Sybilla to Scotland.[42] Sybilla Corbet is also reputed to have been the mother of Robert, Earl of Gloucester, Henry I's oldest son and the stalwart supporter of his legitimate sister, Empress Matilda, during the Anarchy.[43]

After the end of her relationship with the king, Sybilla Corbet would go on to marry Herbert FitzHerbert, who held lands in Yorkshire and Gloucestershire, and have a further five children.[44]

The date of Alexander's marriage to Sybilla is unknown, though it is thought to have been shortly after his accession to the throne, possibly in 1107 or 1108, and before his involvement in the English campaign in Wales in 1114.[45] It was in a charter dated to 1114 or 1115 that Alexander and Sybilla jointly refounded Scone Abbey, whereby they are referred to as 'Alexander ... King of Scots, son of King Malcolm and Queen Margaret and ... Sybilla, Queen of Scots, daughter of King Henry of England.'[46] Another unknown is Sybilla's age at the time of her marriage as her birth was unrecorded. Alexander was in his 30s, while most historians agree that it is likely that Sybilla was born in the mid-to-late 1090s and probably in her mid-teens. Although born out of wedlock, as the acknowledged daughter of King Henry I of England, Sybilla was considered a suitable wife for King Alexander. Henry I's illegitimate daughters played an important role in his foreign and domestic policies; no fewer than ten of them were married into the upper classes of the Norman-French nobility to cement political alliances.[47] Sybilla's illegitimate status was of less significance than the fact her father was the King of England. The marriage was intended to bind Alexander even closer to England and to King Henry personally, who was already his brother-in-law, having married Alexander's sister, Matilda of Scotland, shortly after becoming king. The union was also aimed at securing peace along the Anglo-Scottish border. In his chronicle, William of Malmesbury recorded the marriage, though did not name Sybilla and added 'there was ... some defect about the lady either in correctness of manners or elegance of person.'[48] Malmesbury stated that Alexander 'did not sigh much when she died before him, for the woman lacked, as is said, what was desired, either in modest manners, or in elegant body'.[49] Unfortunately William of Malmesbury does not elaborate further on this defect, nor on the reasons behind such an unflattering description of the Scottish queen. No other chronicler mentions any defect. It is possible that Malmesbury was playing down the queen's attributes, and the impact of her death on the king, in order to find favour with her brother-in-law David, Alexander I's younger brother and heir.

Although some historians have interpreted the childless marriage as also being loveless, perhaps drawing on Malmesbury's depiction of Sybilla, most actually agree that, although there were no children, it was a happy and loving marriage.[50] With this distance of time, it would be difficult to be certain either way. However, despite the lack of an heir, Alexander did not repudiate his wife, although that could always be as a result of who her father was. Rosalind Marshal suggests that Alexander loved Sybilla, and mourned her deeply when she died, founding a church in her memory.[51] Alexander and Sybilla's court is said to have been one of splendour, with reference to Arab stallions and Turkish men-at-arms.[52] They issued a number of charters together, including the one founding Scone Abbey, mentioned above. Scone was the ancient site for the installation and crowning of Scotland's kings, it was the centre of royal power in Scotland. Sybilla's inclusion in the foundation of the Augustinian priory there demonstrates how she had become an integral part of the Scottish ruling dynasty.[53] She and Alexander also made a joint offering to the cathedral church of St Andrews. Sybilla also made grants, as an ecclesiastical patron, in her own right. She granted the manor of Beath in Fife to Dunfermline Abbey, the monastery founded by her husband's parents, Malcolm III and Queen Margaret, their final resting place. Sybilla attested one of the four surviving charters from Alexander I's reign, demonstrating her presence at court and involvement in the affairs of state. Significantly, it may have been Sybilla who acted as peacemaker between the king and Eadmer, when he became Bishop of St Andrews. As we have seen, due to the investiture controversy that was causing issues throughout Europe, with kings and bishops in disagreement over the validity of lay investiture, Eadmer accepted the ring of office from King Alexander, but not the staff. The staff had been placed on the altar at the cathedral of St Andrews and it seems likely that Sybilla was the one who broached the compromise whereby Eadmer would take the episcopal ring from the king, but the pastoral staff from the altar. When Eadmer arrived at the cathedral church of St Andrews to take up the pastoral staff, Queen Sybilla was there to greet him.[54]

Queen Sybilla died suddenly on the Island of the Women at 'Loch Tay, the cell of the canons of Scone' on 12 or 13 July 1122 and was buried at Dunfermline.[55] Afterwards, the king granted the island on Loch Tay, and its surrounding lands, to the canons at Scone, to pray for the soul of Queen Sybilla, and himself.[56] Alexander did not remarry after Sybilla's death, leaving the crown to his brother, David, on his own death in 1124. Although he and Sybilla had no children, Alexander did have one illegitimate son, Malcolm, who appears to have challenged David for the throne after his father's death. Orderic Vitalis stated that 'Malcolm, illegitimate son of Alexander' claimed the crown after Alexander's death but was defeated by David. He again invaded Scotland with an army in 1130 but this time was defeated by 'Edward the son of Siward ... cousin of King David'.[57] Robert de Torigny states that Malcolm invaded Scotland in 1130, but does not say what happened to him afterwards.[58] Malcolm made two failed attempts on the throne, in 1124 and 1130. His eventual fate is unknown. As for Alexander I:

> Now King Alexander, than whom no man was more devoted to the clergy, more bountiful to strangers, or more unbending towards his own people, paid the debt of nature at Strivelin [Stirling], in full health of body and faculties, on the 24th of April 1124, and, being taken away from this life, gave up the ghost to heaven, and his body to the ground. He was buried in state at Dunfermline on the day of Saint Mark the Evangelist, near his father, in front of the great altar, after having completed seventeen years and twenty-one days on the throne.[59]

Queen Sybilla has left little imprint on history, beyond her name as a witness on a surviving charter and the founding of Scone Abbey. That she did not bear children, and therefore an heir for Alexander I, means that she did not have living descendants to keep her memory alive and memorialise her life and deeds, as Queen Margaret had. Her significance is, perhaps, not in her impact on Scotland but rather the physical link that she represented between the kingdoms and dynasties of England and Scotland, and thus demonstrating Scottish acceptance of Norman rule in England.[60]

When he came to the throne on Alexander's death, King David was already married. As the sixth and youngest son of Malcolm III Canmore and Margaret of Wessex, David would never have expected to succeed to the throne. At least, not until it became obvious that Alexander and Sybilla would have no children. David was born in or before 1085 and spent much of his early life at the English court.[61] After he and his brothers fled to England following Malcolm III's death in November 1093, David was placed in the household of the future King Henry I. He was also granted a small estate in Normandy, close to Henry's own Norman lands.[62] David may have briefly returned to Scotland in 1097, accompanying his brother Edgar's army in the defeat of their uncle, Donald III. Tradition has it that it was David who schemed to have his defeated uncle blinded after his capture.[63] However, David soon returned to England, where Henry was crowned king in August 1100. A few months later, on 11 November, King Henry married David's sister, Edith, who would be known as Queen Matilda in her new kingdom. As a consequence of his position as the queen's brother, David was to receive considerable patronage from his new brother-in-law, rising fast and high in Henry's service, both in the form of offices and lands.[64]

On his death in 1107, David's brother, King Edgar, had bequeathed him the rule of Scottish Cumbria and eastern Scotland south of Lammermuir, lands stretching from the northern edge of Loch Lomond to the Solway in the south, and into Tweeddale in the east.[65] Understandably, the new King of Scots, Alexander I, was reluctant to relinquish such a vast amount of territory and only acquiesced after the threat of military action from Henry I. The affair caused a permanent rift between the two brothers. Had it not been for the lack of an heir from Alexander's marriage to Sybilla, David may well have envisioned that his future lay in England. Especially after 1113, when his marriage was arranged by Henry I. As John of Fordun put it, 'Before this King David was raised to the throne, the king of the English, his sister the good Queen Matilda's husband, gave him to wife Matilda, the daughter and heiress of Waldeof, Earl of Huntingdon, and Judith, who was the niece of the first King William.'[66] David's bride was the rich, high-born heiress, Matilda de Senlis. Matilda was the widowed Countess of Northampton and Huntingdon, having been married to Simon de Senlis (or St Lis) sometime around 1090. She was already the mother to at least three, perhaps four, children. *Ingulphs' Chronicle of the Abbey of Croyalnd* tells a rather juicy story of how Matilda came to be the wife of Simon de Senlis. Ingulph suggests that Matilda's mother was initially the intended bride:

William was desirous to give his said niece in marriage to a certain Norman, of noble birth, by name Simon of Senlis. She declined his hand, because the said Simon halted in one leg. The king, being excessively enraged at this, gave the earldom of Huntingdon, with all the lands pertaining thereto; to the said Simon; on which, dreading the wrath of the king, accompanied by her daughters she took to flight, and being utterly despised, and held in extreme hatred by all through the just judgment of God, concealed herself a long time in various spots and hiding-places.

At length, however, this wretched woman confessed her wickedness, and shewed extreme penitence for the nefarious destruction of her husband; and so remained unmarried to the end, being from that time an object of suspicion to all and deservedly despised. Earl Simon, however, before-named after much deliberation, took her eldest daughter, Matilda by name, to wife, by whom he had offspring, Simon, Waldev [Waltheof], and Matilda, who are still young and in their infancy.[67]

Matilda was the daughter of Waltheof, earl of Northumberland, and granddaughter of Siward, the pre-Conquest Earl of Northumbria who had defeated Macbeth in 1054 and helped to establish Malcolm III on his throne. Earl Waltheof had the unfortunate distinction of being the only English lord to be executed during the reign of William I. Married to the king's niece, Judith of Lens, he was executed in 1076 for his part in the Revolt of the Earls against William the Conqueror, though historians are still debating the extent of Waltheof's involvement; it is possible he simply knew of the plans of the earls of Hereford and East Anglia. In his chronicle, Ingulph suggests that there was some collusion on the part of Judith in accusing and convicting her husband of treason.[68] Matilda was the eldest of the three daughters the couple had together. As she had no brothers, she would inherit at least one of her father's earldoms. The earldom of Northumbria, which Waltheof was given in 1072 following the expulsion of his cousin, Gospatric, was forfeited on his death, though Matilda would still hold a claim to the title. However, before becoming earl of Northumbria, Waltheof had been created earl of Huntingdon and Northampton and it was these two earldoms that Simon de Senlis claimed as Matilda's husband.

Simon was probably granted the earldom and the town of Northampton by William Rufus in 1089, which would have been around the time he and Matilda were married, and the Senlis family retained the earldom for the next 100 years.[69] Simon de Senlis had taken part in the First Crusade in 1096, was captured while campaigning in the Vexin in 1098 and subsequently ransomed and built Northampton Castle. He probably died in 1111, when Northampton Castle reverted to the crown for a short time, but certainly no later than 1113. Simon died whilst in France and was buried at the Cluniac priory of La Charité-sur-Loire.[70] Of their children, Simon was the oldest and though he would eventually inherit the earldom of Huntingdon and Northampton, it did not pass to him immediately and was held for some time by David, as Matilda's second husband. However, he was restored as earl of Northampton and Huntingdon at some point between 1138 and 1141, by King Stephen, for whom he fought at the First Battle of Lincoln on 6 February 1141. Waltheof joined the church and eventually became abbot of Melrose Abbey, in Scotland. Matilda married firstly Robert fitzRichard, Lord of Dunmow, and later Saher de Quincy. Matilda and Saher's grandson, also named Saher de Quincy, was first earl of Winchester and a rebel baron during the reign of King John.[71]

The combination of royal blood, extensive landed estates, and two earldoms, as well as a claim to a third, would have made Matilda de Senlis an attractive marriage prospect and a suitable bride for a Scottish prince. It gave David footholds on both sides of the border and placed him in the topmost echelons of the English nobility. However, the marriage would have considerable repercussions for future Scottish monarchs. As well as a claim to the earldom of Northumbria, that would be revived by David's heirs, the marriage gave Scotland's kings a substantial amount of land in England, for which they would owe allegiance to the King of England. In 1127, for instance, by which time he was King of Scots, David was the first lord to swear the oath to uphold the rights of Empress Matilda to succeed to the English throne on her father's death. David was probably about 30 when he married, with Matilda perhaps as much as ten years older. Given that her father was executed in 1076 and she was the eldest of three children, Matilda was probably born around 1072. After their marriage, David held the earldoms of Huntingdon and Northampton in right of his wife and their children were given precedence over the children of Matilda's first marriage. As is so often the case with medieval couples, we have no record of whether the marriage was loving, or loveless. As David had been at the English court since his childhood, it is possible that he and Matilda knew each other before they married. Matilda was coming to an age when women no longer bore children, and yet managed to give birth another four times. As she was only in her early 40s, Matilda would still have been fertile, but the risks to her life and that of any child was greater because of her age. To face the dangers of childbirth even once, in order to give her second husband a family and the all-important heir, certainly suggests a commitment to the marriage on Matilda's part. David and Matilda had four children together, two sons and two daughters. One son, Malcolm, was tragically killed when a toddler; he was reportedly murdered by a Scandinavian monk in his father's service, who is said to have savagely attacked the child with his artificial iron hand. Needless to say, the murderous monk was executed: David ordered that he be torn apart by wild horses.[72] A second son, Henry of Scotland, was born in 1114 or 1115. He married Ada de Warenne, by whom he had several children, but we shall look further into Henry and Ada in the next chapter. David and Matilda's two daughters, Claricia and Hodierna, died young and unmarried. On his marriage, David acquired the honour of Huntingdon, English lands stretching from Yorkshire to Middlesex, but mainly concentrated in the shires of Northampton, Huntingdon,

Cambridge and Bedford.[73] The chronicler, Andrew of Wyntoun, recorded David's marriage to Matilda, and the birth of Henry:

> The quhilk to name than had Dame Maud,
> (As wes the Qwene hys systyr cald)
> The Erlys dochtyr off Hwntyntowne [Huntingdon] Willame,
> than haldyne off gret renowne,
> And hys ayre. On hyr body
> He gat a sown, wes cald Henry,
> Fadyre-lik in all his dedys,
> Quha that hys tyme seis, or redis:
> He wes Erle off North wmbyrland;
> All Hwntyntown wes in his hand.[74]

David's marriage appears to have been a turning point in his life. It is from this time that he developed an interest in religious patronage, founding the abbey at Selkirk for the housing of Tironensians, a rather austere order of monks based at Tiron near Chartres.[75] Their convent relocated to Kelso, eventually becoming the richest abbey in Scotland.[76] David even undertook a pilgrimage, to visit St Bernard of Tiron in person, but the abbot died before his arrival.[77] Matilda and their son, Henry, were both witnesses to the foundation charter for Selkirk Abbey in 1120.[78] And to that of Kelso Abbey dated to 1119/1124.[79]

David came from a pious family. His mother would later become a saint, his aunt, Christina, was abbess of Romsey abbey and his sister, Queen Matilda, was renowned for her acts of piety, which were witnessed by David, as John of Fordun tells us of an event David himself related to Abbot Baldred:

> I will, however, relate one thing she did, which I heard from the mouth of David, a king renowned and never to be forgotten, and whereby, in my opinion, how she behaved to Christ's poor will be clearly enough brought out. When, says he, I was still a youth serving at the king's court, one night while I was in my lodging with my fellows, doing I know not what, I was called by the queen herself to her chamber, and went there accordingly; and lo! a house full of lepers, and, standing in the midst, the queen, who, having laid aside her cloak, and girded herself with a linen cloth, put water into a basin, and began to wash and dry their feet, pressing them, when dry, between her hands, and kissing them most devoutly. 'What doest thou, madam?' said I to her. 'Surely, if the king knew of such a thing, he would never deign to touch, with his lips, thy mouth defiled by such rottenness.' She then, smiling, said: – 'Who knows not that the feet of the everlasting King are to be preferred to the lips of a king who must die? Of a truth, therefor called I thee, that thou might, by

31

my example, learn to do such works.' Then, taking up the basin, 'Do,' said she, 'what thou didst behold me doing.' At these words, I was sore afraid, and answered that I could on no account undergo that. For as yet I knew not the Lord, and His Spirit had not been revealed unto me. She, however, went on persisting; so I laughed out, 'Have mercy on me!' and hied me back to my fellows.[80]

David instituted a policy of religious reform throughout his lands. He appointed his chaplain John, as Bishop of Glasgow, the senior episcopal office in the territories that constituted Cumbria.[81] At David's request, Bishop John was consecrated by Pope Paschal II himself.[82] An inquest into the see's landed endowments, in the 1120s, highlighted that many had been sequestrated and so new endowments were provided and the foundations laid for a new cathedral, which would be consecrated in 1136.[83] Again, David's wife, Matilda, was on the witness list, appearing as *Matildis comitissa*.[84] David was to continue his church reforms after he became king, founding monasteries for the Tironensian, Cistercian and Augustinian orders, and establishing a Cluniac priory on the Isle of May. By enlarging the Benedictine priory at Dunfermline, he turned it into the second richest abbey in Scotland.[85]

When Alexander died in 1124, David was not the only candidate for the Scottish throne. Alexander had been survived by a son, Malcolm, though of questionable legitimacy, and there was also William fitzDuncan, legitimate son of David and Alexander's half-brother, Duncan II. Neither Malcolm nor William, however, had the support of Henry I to press their claim to the throne. As a consequence, it was David who succeeded to the crown, with Matilda as his queen. He was around 40 years of age, middle aged by medieval standards, and Matilda may have already celebrated her 50th birthday. The couple had one surviving son, Henry, who would have been approaching 10 years of age. Matilda's younger son by her first marriage, Waltheof, also made his home in Scotland. In 1128, Waltheof, named as '*Waldef filio Reginæ*' (Waltheof the queen's son) witnessed a charter dated to 1128, by which King David made grants to the church of St John in the castle of Roxburgh.[86] And in 1148, 'Richard, the first abbot of Melrose, died, and Walteve [Waltheof] the brother of Henry earl of Northumberland and of Simon earl of Northampton, was made abbot of Melrose.'[87] A life of the abbot 'containing many marvellous stories' was written, about fifty years after his death, 'in a continued strain of eulogy, by Josceline, a monk of Furness'.[88] Waltheof was said to be 'beloved' by his stepfather, David, who brought him with him to Scotland when he succeeded to the throne in 1124:

> there he completed his education along with his friend Ailred, afterwards Abbot of Rievalle. ... He resolved to embrace the monastic life ... retired to the convent of St. Oswald's at Nostell where he was admitted into the order of Canons Regular of St. Augustine. While he held the office of sacristan in that monastery he was called by

the unanimous voice of the canons in Kirkham to be their Prior ...
The excellent order and discipline maintained at Kirkham ... brought
the virtues of Waltheof's character so much into notice that when the
see of York was vacant the clergy would have elected him Archbishop
if they had not been prevented by King Stephen ... (Waltheof)
resigned the Priorship and retired into the Cistercian convent at
Warden in Bedfordshire, where he began his novitiate in that order
greatly to the displeasure of his brother Simon, Earl of Northampton,
who ... endeavoured ... to deter him from it. ... Waltheof removed
to the monastery at Rievalle. He continued at Rievalle till the year
1148 when he was elected Abbot of Melros. ... Upon the death of
Robert, Bishop of St. Andrews, in 1159, Waltheof was unanimously
fixed upon to succeed him; but he declined. He died in August, 1159,
and was buried in the Chapter House at Melrose.[89]

The religiously devout new king, who was familiar with the English ecclesiastical
tradition of coronation, had some reservations about the inauguration ritual of a
Scottish king. In Scotland, the king was enthroned on the Stone of Destiny at Scone
Abbey and acclaimed by his nobles. There was no official church involvement
in the ceremony and David had to be persuaded to undergo the pagan ritual by
his spiritual advisers.[90] Unfortunately, there is no record that Matilda, as David's
queen, was ever given a coronation. Scotland must have been quite a culture shock
for both Matilda and David, who had spent most of the past thirty years in England.
The Gaelic culture of much of the kingdom would have appeared barbaric to him.
Conversely, David was an unknown character to most Scots, and many would not
have wanted this anglicised king on the throne.[91]

Although he had not settled any English knights on his Scottish lands before
he became king, David did so from 1124, granting land to men on whom he would
rely for support and advice. One such knight was Robert de Brus, who was granted
Annandale. Others followed, including Hugh de Morville and Robert Avenel, but
none were given lands north of the River Forth. These Norman knights integrated
themselves into Scottish society by marrying Gaelic heiresses, 'gaining large lands
and putting down those roots'.[92] In those northern lands, the heartland of the kingdom,
David trusted to the loyalty of the Gaelic Earls of Fife and Strathearn.[93] It must have
been a delicate balancing act and a dangerous time for David, trying to establish his
rule over a kingdom in which he had been born, but which was fundamentally alien
to him. As a consequence, he faced a rebellion from Alexander I's illegitimate son,
Malcolm, in 1124. Married to the daughter of Somerled, lord of Argyll, Malcolm
enjoyed widespread support among the Gaelic regions of Scotland. In 1130,
Malcolm allied with Angus, Earl of Moray, a descendant of Macbeth's stepson,
King Lulach, and marched against David. The opposing forces met at Strathcaro,
where the rebels were crushed, and Earl Angus killed. Malcolm managed to escape
and spent the next four years causing trouble for David, until he was captured

and imprisoned at Roxburgh Castle.[94] The rebellion gave David the opportunity to impose his authority on Moray, building royal castles, introducing colonists and forming alliances with native families such as the earls of Atholl and Caithness.[95]

Although unremarked by the chroniclers observing David's reign, it was in 1130 or 1131 that Queen Matilda breathed her last. She died on either 22 or 23 April and was buried at Scone Abbey.[96] It must have been a difficult time for the king, who had acceded to the throne on 23 April, to lose his wife on the anniversary. David granted the church of Tottenham, part of Matilda's estates, to Holy Trinity in London 'for the weal of his own soul and for the souls of his sister, Matilda the Queen, and of his wife, Matilda the Queen, and of all his ancestors'.[97] The queen is mentioned in a charter to Dunfermline Abbey, dated to sometime after 1147, probably 1150, in which

> King David, exercising the royal authority and power, with the assent of Henry his son and of Matilda the Queen, his wife, and with the assent of the bishops, earls and barons of his kingdom, the clergy and the people acquiescing, confirms to the church of Dunfermline the gifts of his predecessors.[98]

Rather than being a confusion of the date of Matilda's death, it seems most likely that this charter was a copy and reissue of the charter given to Dunfermline in 1128.

Although we have no idea of the extent of his grief at the death of his wife of sixteen years, we do know that David never remarried, even though he had only one surviving son and heir. Young Henry was now a teenager of 14 or 15 summers, and may have felt the loss of his mother keenly. David would eventually confer Matilda's earldom of Huntingdon on Henry, in order to avoid performing homage to King Stephen for his English lands, when Stephen seized the crown in 1135. Henry and his older half-brother, Simon de Senlis, would be in dispute over who had the greater right to their mother's earldoms until Stephen restored it to Simon some time between 1138 and 1141. Matilda and David's marriage provided the foundation for the continuing line of Scots kings, establishing primogeniture as the rule for royal inheritance. Though he gets Matilda's ancestry a little wrong, the *Chronicle of Huntingdon* records:

> But David the King of Matilda the Countess ... the daughter of Ivette [Judith], the granddaughter [sic] of William the Conqueror, gave birth to Count Henry, the father of William the King [who begat] Alexander King, the father of Alexander the last.[99]

Queen of Scots for just six years, Matilda de Senlis left little mark on Scotland beyond securing the dynasty. A handful of charters demonstrate her patronage to religious houses, usually in consort with her husband. The fact that her son from her first marriage, Waltheof, accompanied the family to Scotland when David succeeded to the throne offers a suggestion that Matilda was close with her children. There is evidence of deep affection, in the fact that Matilda, despite being in her forties and the increased danger faced in childbirth, gave her husband four children, though only one, Henry, survived to adulthood. The marriage had not only fulfilled Matilda's duties as wife to continue David's dynasty, but Matilda's lands had also given David a secure financial base from which he could extend his influence, not only on the earldoms of Huntingdon and Northampton, but also on David's own lands in southern Scotland. In addition, this wealth gave David considerable independence to pursue his own reforms within church and state once he became king. He would also continue to press a claim to the earldom of Northumberland on his wife and son's behalf; a claim that would continue to be pursued through several generations of Scottish kings.

King David would survive his wife by over twenty years, instituting political and religious reform and extending Scottish territory further south than any Scots king had done before him. His wife's lands afforded him a platform from which to support his niece, Empress Matilda, in her struggle against King Stephen, the man who usurped the throne. We shall look more into that shortly. David, King of Scots, youngest and last surviving son of Malcolm III Canmore and Margaret of Wessex, died while at prayer in Carlisle on 24 May 1153 and was succeeded by his grandson, Malcolm IV the Maiden. Walter Bower recorded his eulogy:

> He reigned for twenty-nine years, two months and three days. He was pious and Godly, lavish in alms, energetic among his own people, wise and careful in the just extension of his kingdom, and, in a nutshell, he blossomed brilliantly in all the virtues; thus he always produced abundance of the ripe fruit of good deeds. How powerful he was as a king, what great conquests he made justly, or what great abbeys and houses of God he founded, Ailred, as will appear below, will truthfully declare to readers, as he laments his death. He revealed no haughtiness in his character, no cruelty in his words, nothing that was dishonourable in what he said or did. There was not a king like him among the kings of the earth in his own time, since he was pious, wise, humble, modest, sober, chaste and tranquil, while this present life animated his bodily frame.[100]

Chapter Three

Peace with a Marriage

A nd now we turn to a woman who would never become Queen of Scots herself but, as the mother of two Scottish kings, is often referred to as the Queen Mother of Scotland.[1] Related to some of the most powerful barons of the age, and a second cousin to the King of France, Ada de Warenne would become a useful bargaining tool in negotiations with the King of Scots. Ada was probably born in the early-to-mid-1120s. She was the youngest daughter of William de Warenne, second Earl of Warenne and Surrey, and Isabel de Vermandois. Through her mother, she was a great-granddaughter of King Henry I of France.

Ada had two brothers, William and Reginald, who were the third Earl of Warenne and Surrey and Baron of Wormegay, respectively. A third brother, Ralph de Warenne, does not appear to have married and disappears from the records after 1147. Ada's one sister, Gundreda, would marry Roger de Beaumont and become Countess of Warwick. Through her mother's first marriage to Robert de Beaumont, Earl of Leicester, Ada had nine further half-siblings, including Waleran de Beaumont, Count of Meulan and – later – earl of Worcester, Robert de Beaumont, second Earl of Leicester, and Hugh de Beaumont, who, in 1138, was made Earl of Bedford. He was also known as Hugh le Poer, because he was the younger brother, rather than because of his financial situation, though his father had not actually left him any land or titles, just a substantial rent charge on his father's properties in Paris.[2] Ada also had six half-sisters, one of whom became a nun, while another, Isabel, was the mistress of King Henry I before marrying Gilbert de Clare, first earl of Pembroke. They all, except the nun, of course, made good marriages. Ada's niece, Isabel de Warenne, heiress to the earldom of Warenne and Surrey, would marry William of Blois, the younger son of King Stephen and, following his death, Hamelin, illegitimate half-brother of Henry II of England.

When her father died, in 1138, it was Waleran de Beaumont, twenty years Ada's senior, who became the head of the large Beaumont/Warenne family. As is almost always the case with medieval women, we know nothing about Ada's childhood. We can, however, assume that she was taught the skills needed by a woman of rank, such as needlework, dancing, music and the management of a noble household. Her mother, who had raised two separate broods of children, would have ensured that Ada had all the skills needed to take on the responsibilities of a noblewoman. As distant kin to the Norman kings of England and the Capetian kings of France, Ada's family connections were of the highest quality, which made her a valuable commodity on the marriage market. The first mention of her in the chronicles, therefore, is on the arrangements for her marriage. Ada's proposed bridegroom was Prince Henry of Scotland. Born in or around 1115, Henry was probably about eight to ten years older than Ada.

Henry was the only surviving son of King David I of Scotland and his queen, Matilda (or Maud) of Huntingdon, widow of Simon (I) de Senlis, who had died before 1113. As we have seen, Matilda was the daughter of Waltheof, Earl of Northumbria, and Judith, a niece of William the Conqueror.[3] King David was the youngest of the six sons of Malcom III Canmore and his second wife, Margaret of Wessex, great-granddaughter of Æthelred II (the Unready) and a descendant of King Alfred the Great of Wessex. King David's sister, Matilda (known as Edith before her marriage), was the first wife of King Henry I of England and had, ironically, been sought as a bride by Ada's father William, Earl Warenne, in the 1090s. As a younger son with little chance of gaining the throne, David had spent much of his youth at the court of King Henry I in England, learning his trade as a knight and courtier. He had been preceded on the Scottish throne by one half-brother, Duncan II, and three of his older brothers, Edmund, Edgar and Alexander. David had succeeded his older brother, Alexander I, as King of Scots on 23 April 1124, when Henry was about 9 years old. Prince Henry was described by the chronicler, John of Fordun as 'a meek and godly man, and of a gracious spirit, in all things worthy to have been born of such a father'.[4]

On his marriage to Matilda, arranged by his brother-in-law King Henry, David acquired lands in Northampton, Bedford, Cambridge and Huntingdon, as well as lands stretching from South Yorkshire to Middlesbrough, which would become known as the 'honour of Huntingdon'.[5] By the first Treaty of Durham, agreed in February 1136, King David had refused to do homage to Stephen, intending to abide by his oath of 1127 to support Matilda's claim to the throne. In his place, he allowed his son to do so. Henry was given Doncaster and the lordship of Carlisle. He also received his mother's inheritance, the honour and earldom of Huntingdon, paying homage for these lands to King Stephen at York.[6] At Stephen's Easter court that same year, Henry sat at the king's right hand, his royal birth giving him precedence ahead of the English earls. This infuriated Earl Ranulf of Chester, who had wanted Carlisle for himself, and Simon (II) de Senlis, Henry's own older half-brother, who maintained a rival claim to the Huntingdon lands. The two barons withdrew from the court in disgust.[7] As the grandson of Earl Waltheof, Henry also asserted his claim to the earldom of Northumberland. David surrendered Newcastle as a conciliatory gesture, in return for a promise that Henry's rights to Northumberland be addressed in the future.[8] When Stephen refused to relinquish Northumberland, Scottish raids into the county were renewed. David was ostensibly arguing that he was supporting his niece, Empress Matilda, in her struggle with Stephen over the English crown, though his actual motives were far from selfless. He had been quick to seek peace with Stephen, who was married to another of his nieces, Matilda of Boulogne, in 1136 and to back the empress now was accompanied by a strong dose of self-interest. The *Gesta Stephani* was generous in assessing the Scots king's dilemma:

> In Scotland, which borders on England, with a river fixing the boundary between the two kingdoms, there was a king of a gentle heart, born of religious parents and equal to them in his just way of living. Since he had in the presence of King Henry, together with the other magnates of the kingdom, or rather first of all of them, bound himself with an oath that on King Henry's death he would recognise no-one as his successor except his daughter or her heir, he was greatly vexed that Stephen had come to take the tiller of the kingdom of the English. But because it had been planned and carried out by the barons themselves without consulting him he wisely pondered the ultimate result and waited quietly for some time to see what end the enterprise would come.[9]

In the early months of 1138, David had taken advantage of Stephen's preoccupation with the siege of Bedford castle, to lead a foray into Northumberland. The Scots king was apparently spurred on by a letter from his niece, according to the *Gesta Stephani*. Empress Matilda, at last,

> sent him a letter, stating that she had been disinherited and deprived of the kingdom promised to her on oath, that the laws had been made of no account, justice trampled under foot, the fealty of the barons of England and the compact to which they had sworn broken and utterly disregarded, and therefore she humbly and mournfully besought him to aid her as a relation, since she was abandoned, and assist her as one bound to her by oath, since she was in distress.[10]

Whether acting in response to his niece's pleas, or in his own interests, David 'sent out a decree through Scotland and summoned all to arms, and giving them free licence he commanded them to commit against the English, without pity, the most savage and cruel deeds they could invent.'[11] According to the *Gesta Stephani*, Scotland,

> which is also called Albany, is a land hemmed in by marshy places, well supplied with productive forests, milk and herds, encircled by safe harbours and rich islands, but it has inhabitants that are barbarous and filthy, neither overcome by excess of cold nor enfeebled by severe hunger, putting their trust in swiftness of foot and light equipment; in their own country they care nothing for the awful moment of the bitterness of death, among foreigners they surpass all in cruelty. From this people then and from the nearer parts of Scotland the king collected a mass of rebels into an incredible army and led it towards England.[12]

David moved his army into England in January 1138. He besieged Wark Castle and led a chevauchée further south. However, he retreated into the Scottish borders when Stephen brought a substantial force against him. The king,

> receiving intelligence by a messenger that his enemies had made an irruption, and were devastating the lands, burning the vills, and besieging castles and towns, he marched with a strong force into Northumbria. He did not long remain there, having, with some difficulty, accomplished the object he had in view. Those who are well acquainted with the facts, relate that, for nearly six months, a terrible irruption was made by numerous enemies of different races into Northumbria and the adjacent country, both far and near. Multitudes were taken, plundered, imprisoned, and tortured; ecclesiastics were put to death for the sake of the property of their churches; and scarcely any one can compute the number of the slain on the enemy's side or our own.[13]

From Roxburgh, David awaited the departure of the English army before renewing his campaign. The Scots ventured across the border, once again, on 8 April, this time targeting the coastal regions of Northumberland and County Durham in a campaign of plunder and waste.[14] Stephen was now heavily occupied in the south, in campaigns against various rebel barons, including William Fitz Alan, who was married to a niece of Robert, Earl of Gloucester, and Arnulf of Hesdin, who held Shrewsbury Castle against the king.[15] Having offered his support to Stephen on his accession in 1135, Robert of Gloucester had finally made a move in favour of his half-sister, the empress, issuing a *diffidatio*, a chivalric device which was a formal statement of renunciation of allegiance and homage to Stephen.[16] According to William of Malmesbury, Robert

> sent representatives and abandoned friendship and faith with the king in the traditional way, also renouncing homage, giving as the reason that his action was just, because the king had both unlawfully claimed the throne and disregarded, not to say betrayed, all the faith he had sworn to him.[17]

David took advantage of these distractions and again crossed the river Tees with a Scottish army in July. He sent two Scottish barons to lay siege to Wark Castle, while he headed further south. Eustace fitz John, deprived of Bamburgh Castle by King Stephen, but still in control of Alnwick, chose to add his own forces to those of King David. The army opted to march past Bamburgh, until the garrison, believing themselves impregnable, taunted the Scots from the safety of the castle's formidable walls. The Scots promptly attacked, broke down the barricades and killed everyone in the castle. Bernard de Baliol, who had sworn homage to King

David for his northern lands, was sent north by King Stephen and he and Robert de Brus (Bruce) were tasked with discussing terms with the Scots; if the Scots went home, Prince Henry would be given the earldom of Northumberland. David rejected the offer.[18]

King Stephen was beset on all sides, with invasion from the Scots, rebellion in England, and Geoffrey of Anjou, Empress Matilda's husband, causing trouble in Normandy. The king employed all his senior commanders in putting out the fires, including his highly capable wife, Queen Matilda. In the late summer of 1138, following the capitulation of Shrewsbury, after which Stephen had hanged the entire garrison, the queen

> besieged Dover with a strong force on the landward side, and sent word to her friends and kinsmen and dependants in Boulogne to blockade the fortress by sea. The people of Boulogne proved obedient, gladly carried out their lady's commands and, with a great fleet of ships, closed the narrow strait to prevent the garrison receiving any supplies.[19]

This military pressure, combined with the persuasive power of Robert de Ferrers, father-in-law of the rebel garrison's commander, Walchelin Maminot, caused Walchelin to surrender to the queen, probably in late August or early September. The retribution meted out to the Shrewsbury garrison provided a final persuasive argument to those holding Dover.

David's nephew, William fitz Duncan, son of David's older half-brother, Duncan II, inflicted a defeat on an English army at Clitheroe in Lancashire. David now overplayed his hand by allowing his troops from Galloway to plunder the English countryside, the Gaelic levies enslaving their female captives.[20] The ferocity of the Scottish assaults united the northern barons in their determination to put an end to these all-too-frequent forays into England. With Stephen, his loyal generals and his wife occupied with rebels in the south of England, the defence of the north fell to Thurstan, Archbishop of York since 1115; he was approaching his 70th year. Placing the archbishop in command was a move which would prevent baronial squabbling over seniority. Thurstan called for a crusade against the Scots and mustered his army at York. The Scots refused all offers of negotiations, so the archbishop marched the forces of the north to Northallerton, in Yorkshire, just 30 miles north-west of York. The army was preceded by the banners of St Peter, St John of Beverly and St Wilfrid of Ripon, flying on a mast which itself was mounted on a carriage.

On 22 August 1138, with the carriage supporting the standards placed on the summit of the southernmost of two hillocks, to the side of the Darlington Road, the troops were arrayed to the front of the standards. Above the emblems of the saints a banner read 'Body of the Lord, to be their standard-bearer and the leader of their battle'.[21] It was from this pious display that the ensuing battle, the Battle of the Standard, would get its name. The English forces were formed in three groups, with dismounted men-at-arms in the front rank, a body of knights around the standards and the shire levies deployed at the rear and on both flanks. The Scots were drawn up on the northern hillock, with men-at-arms and archers in the front and the poorly equipped men from Galloway and the Highlanders in the rear. The unarmoured men from Galloway complained bitterly about being placed in the rear and demanded the rightful place of honour in the front of the battleline, so much so that King David, against his better judgement, allowed them to spearhead the attack. Prince Henry took command of the right flank, constituting the troops from Strathclyde and the eastern Lowlands and a body of mounted knights. The left was formed of west Highlanders. The king led the small reserve, made up of the men from Moray and the East Highlands.[22]

The presence of the standards of the apostle and two Yorkshire saints, and a contingent of Picts among the Scottish army, led to the sense, among the English, that they were on a noble crusade. According to Henry of Huntingdon, the Bishop of Durham then gave a rousing speech, before the bishops and priests retreated from the field:

> Rouse yourselves, then, gallant soldiers, and bear down on an accursed enemy with the courage of your race and in the presence of God. Let not their impetuosity shake you, since the many tokens of our valour do not deter them. They do not cover themselves with armour in war; you are in the constant practice of arms in time of peace, that you may be at no loss in the chances at the day of battle. Your head is covered with the helmet, your breast with a coat of mail, your legs with greaves and your whole body with shield. Where can the enemy strike you when he finds you sheathed in steel … It is not so much the multitude of a host, as the valour of a few which is decisive. Numbers, without discipline, are an hindrance to success in the attack and to retreat in defeat. Your ancestors were often victorious when they were but a few against many.[23]

As the English soldiers shouted out 'Amen! Amen!' in response to the bishop's speech, the Scottish army advanced with their own battle cry of 'Albani! Albani!' on their lips.[24] The men of Galloway launched the initial attack and 'bore down on the English mailed knights with a cloud of darts and their long spears'.[25] The lightly armoured Scots had no protection against the hail of arrows and English swords, though through their sheer ferocity, they temporarily broke the English front rank. They could get no further: 'The whole army of English and Normans stood fast around the Standard in one solid body.'[26] It was a stalemate that Prince Henry attempted to break by leading a mounted charge against the English forces. Although he sustained heavy losses, the prince broke through the English ranks and continued on towards the enemy's rear, reaching the horse lines. The English closed ranks before the Scots foot soldiers could take advantage of the gap created by the prince's charge. The chronicler, Henry of Huntingdon, reserves praise for his namesake, Prince Henry: King David's

> brave son, heedless of what his countrymen were doing, and inspired only by his ardour for the fight and for glory, made a fierce attack, with the remnant of the fugitives on the enemy's ranks … But this body of cavalry could by no means make any impression against men sheathed in armour, and fighting on foot in a close column; so that they were compelled to retire with wounded horses and shattered lances, after a brilliant but unsuccessful attack.[27]

Finding himself marooned behind enemy lines, the prince ordered his men to discard any identifying badges and mingle with the English forces until they could make their escape.[28] The ruse worked and the prince was able to make his way back to Carlisle.

According to Huntingdon, the men of Galloway were put to flight when their chief fell, pierced by an arrow. Fighting along the line, and having seen what befell the Gallwegians, the remainder of the Scots army began to falter. Seeing that the battle was lost, men began to flee, in small numbers at first, but soon the greater part of the army was in retreat. King David had chosen the greatest of the Scottish knights as his personal guard, who remained steadfast almost to the last. Once they saw the battle was lost, they persuaded the king to call for his horse and retreat, rather than risk death or capture. Henry of Huntingdon reports 11,000 Scottish dead, while the English had few casualties, with Gilbert de Lacy's brother the only English knight to fall on the field of battle.[29] The English, however, failed to pursue or harry the fleeing Scots and David was able to march his surviving army north, to join the forces which had been besieging Wark since June. Satisfied that they had seen off the Scottish threat, the English withdrew, leaving only a small contingent in the field to reduce Eustace fitz John's castle at Malton. The Scots retreated over the border and negotiations for peace began:

> After the war between the two kings had lasted for a long time, created terrible disorder, and brought widespread calamity, a peace mission was sent out by God's will; travelling to and fro between the two kings, who were exhausted by the slaughter, destruction, ceaseless anxieties, and hardships, the envoys succeeded in restoring harmony between them.[30]

A truce was arranged at Carlisle at the end of September 1138 and negotiations for a lasting peace began in earnest shortly afterwards. On 9 April 1139, the Treaty of Durham was concluded between King Stephen and King David of Scotland. Alberic of Ostia, the papal legate, was deeply involved in the negotiations between the two sides, as was Stephen's queen, Matilda of Boulogne, King David's own niece. Richard of Hexham gave details of Alberic's involvement, and that of the queen:

> He also besought, with much entreaty, the king of England, respecting the renewal of a peace with the king of Scotland. Matilda, queen of the English, lent her aid to his wishes by her private entreaties, being by no means indifferent to the preservation of peace between her husband and the king of Scotland, her uncle; for King David had two sisters, Mary and Matilda; the latter married King Henry; Mary, the earl of Boulogne had taken in marriage, and of her begat this Matilda, his heiress. But King Stephen took her for his wife with the earldom of Boulogne.[31]

The queen's diplomatic skills are in evidence throughout the treaty process. Richard of Hexham's detailed account demonstrates how diligently Queen Matilda worked towards peace with the Scots, aided by Alberic, although the final agreement was not reached until shortly after Alberic had returned to the Continent:

> During the course of these proceedings, [Alberic] was engaged most discreetly and earnestly in treating with several persons, and especially with the queen of England, respecting the renewal of peace between the two kings. Finding that the queen's mind was much set upon the accomplishment of this object, with her mediation, and backed by her feminine shrewdness and address, he frequently appealed to the king himself regarding this matter. They found him at first stern, and apparently opposed to a reconciliation; for many of his barons who had suffered severe losses from their variance, eagerly urged him on no account to make peace with the king of Scotland, but to avenge himself upon him; but notwithstanding all this, the zeal of a woman's heart, ignoring defeat, persisted night and day in every species of importunity, till it succeeded in bending the king's mind to its purpose. For she was warmly attached to her uncle David, the king of Scotland, and his son Henry, her cousin, and on that account took the greatest pains to reconcile them. The legate, seeing the affair progressing in this way, derived fresh confidence in his intercourse with the king, from the better hope which had sprung up, and gave his attention to his other concerns.[32]

The contents of the agreement were kept secret for almost a year, an indication that Stephen knew they would be hard for his barons to swallow. The terms were, indeed, extremely favourable to the defeated Scots. All the lands that Prince Henry had held in 1138 were returned to him, save for the castles at Bamburgh and

Newcastle, for which he was recompensed with two towns of equal value in the south. Furthermore, Henry was confirmed as earl of Huntingdon and created earl of Northumbria, a title which encompassed Northumberland, Durham, Cumberland, Westmoreland and parts of Lancashire north of the Ribble.[33] It was agreed that English law would remain in force in these regions, but that the barons within the earldom were permitted to do homage to Prince Henry, saving only their allegiance to King Stephen. In return, King David and his son promised a permanent peace and provided four hostages. Richard of Hexham reported that the 'agreement was signed at Durham on [April 9, 1139], by Henry son of the king of Scotland, and their barons, in the presence of Matilda, queen of England, and many earls and barons of the south of England'.[34] He goes on to say that, after the conclusion of the treaty, Matilda then accompanied her cousin, Prince Henry, to Nottingham, where Stephen was holding court. Henry did homage for his new earldom and spent the summer in southern England.

Although the text of the treaty is now lost, it seems likely that the prince's marriage to Ada de Warenne, sister of the third Earl of Warenne and Surrey and half-sister of the Beaumont twins, was included in the terms of the Treaty of Durham. According to the *Chronicle of Melrose*, the marriage was arranged on the insistence of Queen Matilda:

> At the instance of the queen peace was made between the two kings, and Northumberland was given to Henry, the son of king David. Earl Henry married the countess Ada, the daughter of William, earl of Warren, [and the sister of William the younger,] and of Robert, earl of Leicester, and of Waleran, count of Mellent [Meulan], whose mother was sister of Ralph, earl of Perona, the kinswoman of the king of France.[35]

Orderic Vitalis gave a more romantic slant to the story, claiming

> Henry, the son of King David of Scotland, favoured the agreement; he loved Adelina [Ada], the daughter of William earl of Surrey, and asked for her hand in marriage. Bound by such a close tie, he was whole-heartedly in favour of the pact with the Normans and English, for he saw the force of his counsellors' argument that it would be a valuable source of strength for himself and his people.[36]

Shortly after the treaty was signed, Prince Henry joined King Stephen's court for a time, accompanying Stephen on campaign, which came with not a little risk. Whilst Stephen's forces besieged Ludlow, 'this Henry was dragged from his horse by an iron hook, and nearly taken prisoner, but was gallantly rescued from the enemy by King Stephen'.[37] It was probably during his stay with Stephen's court that Henry married his bride; the marriage perhaps intended to draw Henry into Stephen's corner by allying him in marriage to the family of his staunchest supporters, the Beaumont twins. Ada's father, William de Warenne, 2nd Earl of Surrey, had died in May 1138, so the head of the family was now Ada's oldest half-brother, Waleran de Beaumont, Count of Meulan. It would have been Waleran who gave approval of the marriage on his family's behalf. On her wedding day, which took place sometime between the conclusion of the Treaty of Durham and Henry's return to Scotland, Ada became Countess of Huntingdon and Northumberland and Lady of Haddington and Crail. Ada would have been in her mid-teens, with Henry, at the age of 24, about ten years older. Although she would never become queen, before her death, she would be thought of as Queen Mother of Scotland as the mother of Malcolm IV and William I, both kings of Scotland.

It was not until after Michaelmas (19 September) 1140 that Ada and Prince Henry returned to Scotland. A disgruntled Ranulf, Earl of Chester, angry that the Scottish prince had been given Carlisle and Cumberland – both lands to which he nursed his own claims – apparently planned to ambush the prince on his journey north. Queen Matilda became aware of Chester's intentions and, in order to thwart the recalcitrant earl, she persuaded her husband, the king, to accompany the Scottish heir and his party to the border.[38] This event caused the frustrated earl to pursue his own aims, which would lead to the Battle of Lincoln in 1141 and Stephen's capture by Empress Matilda's forces.

The marriage having formed part of the peace treaty, it failed in its primary function, to seal a lasting accord between the two kingdoms, and relations with England remained fractious. This probably came as no surprise to anyone at the time, given the unrest engendered by Stephen's seizure of the English crown and Empress Matilda's determination to win it back. It would have been remiss of the Scots to not take advantage of England's woes to advance their own aims. That is not to say, however, that the marriage in itself was not a success. Ada appears to have taken to her new role as the wife of Scotland's future king, settling into a life of duty as a wife, mother, feudal lady and religious benefactor. She is most frequently styled '*Ada comitissa regis Scottorum*'.[39]

From the moment she arrived in Scotland, as David I's wife Queen Matilda had died in 1131, Ada was the first lady of the Scottish court. Although her public role was severely limited by her frequent pregnancies throughout the first decade of her marriage. She appeared as a witness on three of her husband's charters between 1139 and 1142, at Jedburgh, Selkirk and Huntingdon; this last demonstrating that she travelled throughout her husband's lands in England and Scotland.[40] She also witnessed a charter by King David, to Dryburgh Abbey, sometime in 1152 or 1153, appearing second on the witness list behind Prince Henry.[41] Relations with King Stephen broke down permanently in 1141, when the English king gave the earldom of Huntingdon to Prince Henry's older, half-brother, Simon de Senlis, along with the lands in the Midlands that comprised the honour of Huntingdon.[42] Henry had been involved in the government of Scotland, alongside his father, since 1144, taking some of the burden from the now-ageing king. The prince was recognised as '*rex designatus*' or 'king-designate'. Henry shared his father's policies of modernisation in Scotland, helping to transform it into a European-style kingdom. Henry's lands in Northumberland, north of the Ribble and the Tees, were ruled by him as part of an extended Scottish-Northumbrian realm.[43] Prince Henry issued coins in his own name at Bamburgh, Carlisle and Corbridge and endowed numerous religious houses within the region, demonstrating a sensitivity to local interests. When the time came, he stood sponsor for Henry Plantagenet, 18-year-old son and heir of Empress Matilda, when, at Carlisle on 22 May 1149, 'Henry, the son of the empress ... the daughter of king Henry the first, and the son of the earl of Anjou, was honourably received by David the king of the Scots at Carlisle, and there received arms of knighthood from him.'[44]

According to the *Gesta Stephani*, David, ever one to see to his own interests, used the occasion to launch a further, ultimately abortive, incursion into northern England:

> While the kingdom of England was in this wretched and frightful state of disorder and disturbance Henry, the lawful heir to England, received advice from his adherents to get the emblems of a knight's rank from his father, or else from the King of Scots, his intimate and special friend, and then with renewed vigour rise up against the king and gain with resolution and spirit what was rightfully his. So taking with him Roger Earl of Hereford, and the sons of some men of birth, that they might receive the honour of a knight's arms at the same time as himself, he sent messengers ahead and hastened to make his way to the King of Scotland. The king, having already had word that he would arrive, met him gladly and cheerfully, and welcoming him in fitting fashion, with the respect due to a king, ungrudgingly bestowed on him the splendid emblems of a knight's dignity and promised him very ready aid in vanquishing his enemies; and gathering together a vast number of Scots, with the Earl of Chester and some adherents of his party joining him to make his army a very large one, he approached the city of York as though he intended to storm it. When, behold, King Stephen, having had a warning beforehand from the citizens to come to their aid, suddenly arrived with a highly-equipped body of knights, and arraying his army in military fashion with resolution and skill made an immediate advance on the enemy; and had not they, hearing of the king's approach and knowing already his pre-eminent prowess, become discouraged from fear of him and withdrawn to safer positions, he would have triumphantly overwhelmed them all together. So when the King of Scotland and his allies observed that King Stephen's forces were stronger and were continually being reinforced, as the most vigorous warriors were streaming in to him from the different parts of England, whereas they on the other hand

had already collected all they could and been far from matching his strength, inferior as they were in valour and numbers they lost heart, gave up hope of a fight and, dispersing in different directions, went back to their homes individually.[45]

Prince Henry took the opportunity to hold out an olive branch to the Earl of Chester, offering to marry one of his daughters to the earl's son as a resolution to their differences. Although the wedding never materialised, the thought was there. In 1150, Henry and his father co-founded a Cistercian house at Holmcultran, Cumberland, for monks from Melrose Abbey. It was to be one of the prince's last major acts. The prince had fallen seriously ill in 1140 but was supposedly cured at the intervention of a visitor to the Scottish court, the Irish reformer, St Malachy. However, his health may have been gradually failing ever since, or it may be that he suffered a sudden illness. He died on 12 June 1152, probably at Peebles, at the relatively young age of 37. He left his wife, Ada, still only in her late 20s, a widow with five young children. The year of 1152 was a year of tragedy for Ada, as the *Chronicle of Melrose* reports that 'Henry, earl of Northumberland, the son of David, king of Scots, died, as did also his daughter Matilda.'[46] Henry and Ada's sixth child, Matilda, not yet 7 years old and possibly only a baby, died shortly after her father.[47] The couple had

> three sons; namely, Malcolm, the future king of Scotland; David, who was afterwards Earl of Huntingdon and Garviach; and William, who was also to be afterwards king – and as many daughters. One, Ada, was given in marriage to Florence [Florent], Count of Holland. The second, Margaret, wedded Conan, Duke of Brittany and Earl of Richmond, and bore him a daughter, named Constance, who was given in marriage to Geoffrey, brother of Richard, king of England. Of her this Geoffrey begat a son, named Arthur, who was afterwards drowned at sea, a daughter named Alice, who conceived of Peter Mauclerk, and bore a son, named John, afterwards Duke of Brittany, and another daughter, named Eleanor, who perished at sea, with her brother Arthur. Earl Henry's third daughter, Matilda, moreover, departed this life in the same year as her father.[48]

In this comprehensive list of Ada and Henry's descendants, it has to be noted that the Arthur and Eleanor who were 'drowned at sea' are, in fact, Arthur of Brittany, who was murdered by or on the orders of his uncle, King John, and Eleanor of Brittany, who was kept in perpetual imprisonment in England by her uncle, King John and, subsequently, her cousin, Henry III.

By all accounts, it appears that Henry would have made an impressive Scottish king; he was brave in battle, exhibited strong leadership qualities and would have continued his father's work in advancing Scotland's interests. Chroniclers boasted of his kingly qualities and he was greatly mourned on both sides of the Anglo-Scottish border. John of Fordun gives a fitting tribute:

> Now this Henry, the king's only son. Earl of Northumberland and Huntingdon, a youth of comely mien, with his father's virtues budding within him, was taken away from this life on the 12th of June 1152, before he had completed the years of the first bloom of youth. He was a most handsome lad, amiable to all men, the expected successor to the throne, a prince of most unassuming spirit, a well-disciplined and pious man, devout towards God, and a most compassionate guardian of the poor; in short – to recount all his good qualities – he was in all things like his father, save that he was a little more fair-spoken. Leaving the three sons above mentioned, and two daughters surviving him, he was, amid very deep mourning and wailing on the part of both Scots and English, buried near Roxburgh, at the Monastery of Calkhow (Kelso), which his father had reared from its very foundations, and endowed with ample possessions and great honours.[49]

Henry and Ada's eldest son, 11-year-old Malcolm, became David I's heir and their second son, William, inherited his father's earldom of Northumberland. Shortly after Henry's death, King David took 10-year-old William to Northumberland to receive the homage of the barons. Ada was to spend twenty-six years as a widow and it is in this period that her dedication to her estates and people, and to Scotland, shines through. Through her own cosmopolitan outlook, Ada is credited with encouraging European values and norms within the society of the Scottish nobility.

Ada did not forget her Warenne roots and encouraged knights from the great Warenne honours in England and Normandy, as well as from Northumberland, to settle in Scotland. It seems likely that Ela, who married Duncan (II), Earl of Fife, was a daughter of Reginald de Warenne, Baron of Wormegay, and therefore one of Ada's nieces. Ada's great-nephew, Roger, the grandson of Ada's half-brother, Robert de Beaumont, Earl of Leicester, had joined the church and found great favour in Scotland; he became chancellor of Scotland and was elected as Bishop of St Andrews in 1189. Ada must also have kept one eye on English affairs, following the exploits of her brothers and half-brothers in the contest for the English throne. Her family losses included her mother's death in 1147, the same year that her brothers William, Earl of Warenne and Surrey, and Waleran, Count of Meulan and Earl of Worcester, left England to take part in the Second Crusade. Waleran would survive the expedition and return home; his younger half-brother, William, was not so fortunate and was killed at the Battle of Mount Cadmus.

Ada's chief dower estates were the burghs and shires of Haddington and Crail, with lands also in Tynedale at Whitfield, near Hexham, and in the honour of Huntingdon, at Harringworth and Kempston. It seems likely that Ada's main residence was in Haddington, where she is still well thought of to this day, and where Ada founded a priory for Cistercian nuns sometime before 1159.[50] She refers to it as 'my burgh of Haddington'.[51] It was in her widowhood, as the dowager Countess of Northumberland and Queen Mother of Scotland, that Ada's own patronage and interests come to the fore. Although they do not give the full picture of Ada and her holdings, her numerous surviving charters shed light on her lands and responsibilities. Her charters included grants of land, varying in size from half a carucate to a full toft, to various religious houses, including Dunfermline Abbey, Kelso Abbey, Dryburgh Abbey and Newbattle Abbey, Bearford. St Andrews Cathedral Priory benefited greatly from Ada's largesse, receiving land in Crail, a full toft from her burgh at Haddington and 'one silver merk annually in Pitmilly for the soul of Earl Henry, for building the new church and for lighting, to be paid by Malise'.[52] Further common pastureland held by Malise in Pitmilly was to be granted to St Andrews Cathedral Priory and their hospital.[53] Grants to Hexham Priory in Northumberland included

> all Whitfield except the lands of Robert son of William (of Dilston) and Joel of Corbridge, by the same boundaries of which she held it of Earl Henry and King William afterwards, and wasteland which she and Robert the chaplain through her cultivated and populated; for a rent of 6 pounds of pepper yearly at Michaelmas.[54]

Although the majority of her endowments were to Scottish religious houses, Ada also confirmed gifts to convents in England, including Wardon Abbey and Nuneaton Priory, founded by Ada's half-brother Robert, Earl of Leicester, which was to receive 20 *solidi* rent annually; this latter was confirmed by Pope Alexander III, who referred to Ada as 'Ade comitisse Scotie' (Countess of Scots).[55] The Cathedral at Durham received a sum of money for prayers for Ada's health, following a bout of illness.[56] It is notable that these gifts were not to religious institutions that were traditionally in the Warenne sphere of influence, but rather associated with her life as a princess in Scotland. Ada supported fourteen religious houses, in total, ten of which were in Scotland. These houses covered almost the full spectrum of religious groups, with donations to the Benedictines, the Tironensian monks, the Augustinian and Arrouaisian canons, the Cistercian monks and nuns, the Premonstratensian canons, Fontevriste nuns and a hospital.[57]

Several grants were made to individuals, including Ada's chaplain, Robert, who received grants of land in Whitfield, including land 'to be held of Hexham priory in fee'. In another, a man named William Carpenter received a grant of one toft and common pasture in Crail. While Alexander de St Martin, Ada's chief baron and the sheriff of Haddington, was granted the land of Athelstaneford 'by the same boundaries by which King David gave the same land to him'.[58] Alexander de St Martin's brother, Adulf, killed a fellow knight, Malcolm de Moreville, in a hunting accident. Land at Langlaw was given to the abbey at Dryburgh in reconciliation.[59] As an example of Ada's continued patronage, one grant is a confirmation to Matthew, the son of her chaplain, Robert, of the land at Whitfield, 'to be held as it was before the war'.[60] The war referred to is most likely that of 1173–74, in which King William was captured by the English. Two of Ada's charters were witnessed by her youngest son, referred to as 'David, my son'; he was the only one of Ada's children to witness her charters. And while Alexander de St Martin witnessed no less than twelve charters, other witnesses included Ela, Countess of Fife and Thorald, archdeacon of Lothian. Other vassals who appeared as witnesses in Ada's charters were from such prominent families as the Giffards and Balliols.[61]

The charters demonstrate not only the size of Ada's landholdings, but also the breadth of her patronage, both to individuals and to the church. The number of charters in her own name also suggests that Ada had a hands-on approach to the management of her estates and the distribution of her largesse. We can be certain that, as the Queen Mother of Scotland, Ada had her own household, which included her chaplain, Robert, and a clerk named William, although we know little else of its composition. Her grants to religious foundations were a demonstration of her piety, but also an expected social obligation. She had clearly embraced her life and family in Scotland, choosing to patronise institutions associated with her new home, rather than the Cluniac foundations of her Warenne birth family.

Ada and Henry had three sons, two of whom became kings of Scots; Malcolm IV, William I and David, who was the fifth Scottish earl of Huntingdon. Although Ada's youngest son, David, never became King of Scots, he was to have great influence on the Scottish succession in later generations. During his brother Malcolm's reign, in 1163 David was sent to England as a hostage, but returned to Scotland in 1165, following Malcolm's death and the accession of his remaining brother, William. Until William married and produced a son and heir of his own, David was now the heir to the Scots throne. He married Matilda of Chester, the granddaughter of Ranulf de Gernons, Earl of Chester; the same Ranulf who had been denied Carlisle and Cumberland in favour of Prince Henry, and who had attempted to ambush Prince Henry and Ada on their return to Scotland in 1140. It is through the daughters of David and Matilda that Robert de Brus (grandfather of Robert the Bruce, King of Scots) and John Balliol (later John, King of Scots) both based their claims as Competitors to the Scots throne in the 1290s. They were two of the thirteen Competitors who vied for the crown following the extinction of the senior royal line with the death of 8-year-old Margaret, known as the Maid of Norway, granddaughter and heir of Ada's great-grandson, Alexander III.

Ada and Henry also had three daughters.

The eldest, Ada, was born around 1142. In August 1162, she was married to Florent III (or Floris), Count of Holland, and was given the county of Ross in Scotland as her marriage gift. This younger Ada died sometime after 1206; she and Florent had between eight and ten children, including two sons, Dirk and William, who each became Count of Holland in turn. It was through his descent from Ada that Florent (or Floris) V, Count of Holland, also claimed his place as one of the Competitors to the Scottish throne in 1292. The Count asserted that his descent from Ada, older sister of David, should give him precedence over David's daughters and their descendants. He also stated that David had relinquished his rights to the Scottish crown in return for lands in Garrioch in north-east Scotland, and that William I had then settled the succession on Ada. Unfortunately, Count Florent was unable to produce any written evidence to support his claims.[62]

A second daughter, Margaret, was born around 1145. In 1160 she married Conan IV, Duke of Brittany, and was the mother of the duke's sole surviving heir, Constance, Duchess of Brittany. Constance was to marry, as her first husband, Geoffrey Plantagenet, third surviving son of Henry II and Eleanor of Aquitaine. He was also a grandson of Empress Matilda. Constance's son – and Margaret's grandson – Arthur, Duke of Brittany, was cruelly murdered by, or on the orders of, his uncle, King John. His sister, Eleanor, was to be a perpetual prisoner of the English crown from her capture in 1203 to her death in 1241, aged 57. Duke Conan died in 1171, leaving Margaret a widow at the age of 26. Sometime between the duke's death, in February 1171, and Easter 1175, Margaret was married to Humphrey III de Bohun of Trowbridge, Hereditary Constable of England in the service of King Henry II. Humphrey died in 1181, leaving a daughter, Matilda, and son, Henry, who was to become the first Bohun Earl of Hereford.

King David died less than twelve months after his son, Henry, on 24 May 1153. He did not live to see his nephew, Henry of Anjou, Empress Matilda's son, succeed King Stephen in 1154, as Henry II; reinstating the line of Henry I that the empress and David had fought so hard for. David was succeeded by his grandson, Malcolm, who became King of Scots at the age of 12 – possibly even on his 12th birthday – as Malcolm IV. The accession of Malcolm surpassed all the ambitions of his Warenne grandfather; William de Warenne, the second earl, who had sought a royal bride for himself. He had not lived to see his daughter marry the heir to the Scottish throne, but he would have approved of it; Malcolm's accession to the throne would have been the culmination of his aspirations for the family.

Henry and Ada's eldest son, Malcolm, was born between 23 April and 24 May 1141. He was later known as Malcolm the Maiden, due to his youth, religious devotion and the fact he remained chaste and unmarried.[63] He had become his grandfather's heir following his father's death, at which time he had been placed into the custody of Duncan, Earl of Fife, and taken on a progress around Scotland north of the Forth, following the old Celtic tradition of showing the heir to the people of the kingdom. In this way, David hoped to guarantee a peaceful succession when the time came. When King David died less than twelve months after his son, Malcolm succeeded him. The chronicles make no mention of Ada playing a part in the politics of Scotland during her eldest son's kingship. She did appear at court often and was present for many of the important occasions; she was also a witness to no less than sixteen of Malcolm's charters. Ada did, moreover, take great interest in the futures of her children, arranging the marriages of her three surviving daughters and working hard to persuade her son to marry.

The chronicler, William of Newburgh, relates a story of the lengths Ada had to go to in order to encourage her reluctant son to choose a bride. Ada went so far as to present her son with a young woman of noble birth, in his bed. Not wishing to cause an argument with his mother, Malcolm did not send her away and allowed the lady to spend the night in his royal bed; while he slept on the floor, wrapped in his cloak. Ada, it seems, was relentless in her attempts to persuade Malcolm to marry, until the young king tired of her constant nagging and begged her to hold her peace.[64] While William of Newburgh makes it sound as if Ada was pushing for grandchildren, or tempting her son to lose his innocence, Ada's constant attempts to discuss marriage with Malcolm had a political motive as much as a personal one. She was well aware of the importance of royal marriage, not just for the continuation of a dynasty and political alliance, but also for the strength and stability of the monarchy itself. An heir made the kingdom less vulnerable to internal unrest and external interference. Ada, moreover, was not the only one eager to see the young king settle down with a wife. The Scottish *curia regis* (royal council) continued to pressure Malcolm to find a bride, even after his mother had given up. Arnold, Bishop of St Andrews encouraged Malcolm to follow the example of his recently married sisters. The king, however, was no more swayed by the bishop and his royal council than he was by his mother. It seems that he was eager to hold onto the highest ideals of Christian knighthood and remain chaste, as plans for him to marry Constance of Brittany came to nothing.[65] Malcolm's relative youth may also have led him to believe that he had many years ahead of him and plenty of time before he needed to settle down and raise a family.

Malcolm's kingship faced several challenges. In November 1154, the young king was faced with a revolt from Somerled, Earl of Argyll. The unrest was to continue for several years, with Somerled only suing for peace in 1159, having been deprived of his chief supporters, the MacHeths, father and sons, who had been reconciled with the king in 1157.[66] Malcolm's greatest challenge, however, was his larger neighbour, England. While David I had taken advantage of the civil war in England during Stephen's turbulent reign, the accession of Henry II in 1154 changed the political landscape entirely. In 1157, 'Malcolm, king of the Scots, went to Henry, king of England, at Chester, and there became his vassal, upon the same terms as his grandfather had been the vassal of the old king Henry, preserving in every respect his dignities.'[67] This homage suggests that Malcolm was accepting that he was a vassal of Henry II, as his grandfather had been a vassal of Henry I. He was also forced to resign his lordship of Northumberland, Cumberland and Westmorland, although the honour of Huntingdon was returned to the Scots king and his brother and heir, William, was given the lordship of Tynedale. In 1158, there was a further, less agreeable, meeting 'between Henry, king of England, and Malcolm, king of the Scots; but they parted from each other not upon the best of terms, and therefore the king of Scots was not made a knight at that time.'[68]

In 1159, Malcolm, his brother and others joined Henry II and the English army on an expedition to Toulouse and 'On his return from this army, Malcolm, the king of the Scots, was made a knight, at Tours, by Henry, king of England.'[69] Although the *Chronicle of Melrose* states the knighting ceremony took place at Tours, most sources agree that it was at Périgueux.[70] The expedition met with initial success and the army overran the county of Toulouse before laying siege to the city itself. However, the siege had to be abandoned when King Louis VII of France intervened in support of the Count of Toulouse. By the end of the year, Henry and Malcolm were back in Limoges, crossing to England shortly afterwards. In the same year, Malcolm sent representatives to the papal court, during which the Bishop of Moray was made papal legate to Scotland:

> William, bishop of Moray, and Nicolas, at that time the chamberlain of the king of the Scots, paying a visit to the Roman court, on the service of king Malcolm, of their own free will went to see pope Alexander, at Agnania, which is beyond Rome. They were received by him with due honour. William returned in the year following, having been appointed the legate for the kingdom of Scotland.[71]

Malcolm returned to Scotland in 1160 and to a revolt of six earls led by Feterth, Earl of Strathearn, angry at the king's expedition with the English army. As the *Chronicle of Melrose* recounted, the

> king of Scotland, returned from the expedition to Tolouse [sic]; and having reached the town called Perth, he was besieged therein by earl Fereteatht and five other earls, who were incensed against him because he had gone to Toulouse, and who wished, therefore, to take him prisoner. This presumptuous design of theirs was unsuccessful. Upon three several occasions, king Malcolm went with a large army into Galloway, and at length he subdued them.[72]

Mediation by the clergy led to an uneasy peace and their abandoning of besieging Malcolm at Perth. Unrest then arose in Galloway and Malcolm made several forays into the region before the end of the year, when Fergus, lord of Galloway, submitted to the king.[73] It was the last major unrest by any Scottish earls for not only Malcolm's reign, but also for that of his brother, William I.

Like his grandfather before him, Malcolm continued the royal patronage of the Scottish church. In 1160, the king presided at the consecration of the new Bishop of St Andrews:

> Ernald, abbot of Kelso, was elected to the episcopal see of St. Andrew's, in Scotland, upon the day of St. Brice, the bishop [13 Nov.], (which this year fell upon a Sunday); and on the Sunday

following, that is to say, on the day of St. Edmund [20 Nov.], he was consecrated at St. Andrew's, in Scotland, by William, bishop of Moray, the legate of the apostolic see, in the presence of king Malcolm, and the bishops and abbots and earls of the realm.[74]

And in 1163, 'Richard, the chaplain of king Malcolm, was elected to the bishopric of St. Andrew's.'[75] The following year, Malcolm founded the abbey of Cupre.[76]

Malcolm was again summoned to meet Henry II in 1163. Despite falling ill at Doncaster, he was still expected to complete the journey to Henry's court and arrived at Woodstock at the end of June. It seems that Henry wanted to assert his supremacy over Britain, as a group of Welsh rulers had also been called to attend the English king. On 1 July, Malcolm renewed his oath to Henry and handed over hostages, the most senior of whom was his own youngest brother, David, soon to be made earl of Huntingdon, and 'a firm peace was established between him and Henry, king of England'.[77] Homage given, Malcolm returned to Scotland, where he faced a revolt led by Somerled, Lord of the Isles, 'who had been in a state of wicked rebellion for twelve years against his natural lord, Malcolm, king of Scotland, landed at Renfriu, with a large army which he had collected together in Ireland and various other places; but at length God's vengeance overtook him, and he and his son', and a countless number of his followers, were there slain by a few of the people of that district.[78] Malcolm appears to have never fully recovered from the illness he suffered on his journey south and frequently complained of pains in his head and feet. He planned a pilgrimage to Santiago de Compostela, to pray for healing, but was unable to undertake it. He died at Jedburgh on Thursday 9 December 1165, aged 24:

> Malcolm, the king of Scotland, of pious memory, died at Jedburgh, on the fifth of the ides of December [9th Dec.], which fell upon the fifth day of the week; he was in the twenty-fifth year of his age, and in the twelfth of his reign. His corpse was carried to Dunfermline by all the people, with much honour, and there it was buried.[79]

We do not have Ada's response to the death of her first-born son, but it cannot have been easy for her, only in her 40s herself and already a widow of thirteen years. Malcolm was succeeded by his brother William, later known as William the Lion. William had succeeded his father as earl of Northumbria in June 1152, when he was about 10 years old. Ada appears to have been less influential at court during the reign of her second son. He had ascended the throne as a grown man, who had already seen war, rather than a boy, as Malcolm had been. She witnessed only five of William's charters in the thirteen years between his accession and her death, and none after 1173. Her advancing years and occasional illnesses may have been the reason, rather than any loss of regard on her son's part.

Ada de Warenne, Countess of Huntingdon, died in 1178, although where and of what she died has gone unrecorded. She had spent forty of her 55 years in Scotland, first as the wife of Scotland's heir and then as mother to two of her kings. Although there is no surviving eulogy for Ada, she is remembered in charters of donations to religious houses by her children, her household and her vassals. Several of her household officials, including Alexander de St Martin and Hugo de Moreville, named their daughters after Ada.[80] It is hard to assess Ada's contribution to Scottish history beyond her securing the Scottish succession for generations, and her own patronage of religious houses, particularly the nunnery at Haddington. Bower's *Scotichronicon* records 'The Countess Ada also, the wife of Waltheof's brother Henry, after the death of her husband, and at the instigation (it is said) of the same Abbot Waltheof, founded the monastery at Haddington for nuns of the Cistercian Order.'[81] She is believed to be buried in the Haddington area, most likely at the convent she founded, although the exact location of her grave is lost to history. It is interesting to note that in 1198 her grandson, the future Alexander II, would be born in her old palace at Haddington, after her dower lands were passed on to Queen Ermengarde; these estates would henceforth form the core of the dower lands for all subsequent Scottish queens.

If Orderic Vitalis is to be believed, although the marriage was a dynastic one, sealing peace between England and Scotland, it was also a love match. And although Ada's marriage was a success on a personal level, and for Scotland as a whole, it failed to secure the lasting peace with England that had been the intention of the 1139 Treaty of Durham. It is, with hindsight, hard to believe that anyone seriously expected it would. And maybe they didn't. Peace between England and Scotland was ever transitory and the kings on both sides of the border would keep it only as long as it suited them. As the surviving information from her charters show, Ada de Warenne, Countess of Huntingdon and Northumberland, spent her entire adult life, forty years, in service to her family, her adopted country and her friends. The dignity by which she bore herself, both as a wife and a widow, is clearly indicated by the foundations she patronised and the contributions made by all three of her sons, to Scotland and its history. Though she was never Queen of Scotland, Countess Ada fully deserved the title and accolade of Queen Mother of Scotland.

Chapter Four

Queen Ermengarde

As the second son of Countess Ada and Prince Henry, William had succeeded his father as earl of Northumbria in June 1152, when he was about 10 years old. His grandfather, King David, personally took William to Newcastle to receive the homage of the men of Northumberland.[1] With Malcolm touring Scotland as king-designate and William receiving the homage of his earldom of Northumbria, David hoped to ensure a smooth succession at his death. William lost the earldom, however, when his brother, Malcolm IV surrendered the northern counties of England to Henry II in 1157; he was given lands in Tynedale, worth £10 per annum, in compensation. This loss of Northumberland was never forgotten and was to colour William's future dealings with the English crown throughout his reign, resulting in humiliation for William and Scotland. As John of Fordun explained it, 'William ... had always been on bad terms with the English, and their lasting foe, forasmuch as they had taken away his patrimony, the earldom of Northumberland.'[2] Despite the bitterness over the loss of his earldom, William still accompanied his brother on the English expedition to Toulouse, and he was, apparently, knighted by Malcolm, at Périgueux, following the king's own elevation to the knighthood by Henry II.[3]

On their return to Scotland, Malcolm and William were faced with rebellion by disaffected barons who were incensed at their king's readiness to join the English on campaign. William helped his brother to break the siege they were subjected to at Perth and accompanied him on the campaigns into Galloway. In 1163, William was in attendance on Malcolm in a meeting with King Henry II at Woodstock, where the Scots king did homage to the English king, as was their younger brother, David, who was to remain in Henry II's custody as a hostage. In appearance and demeanour, William was more like his Warenne ancestors than Malcolm had ever been. He had even used the Warenne surname when earl of Northumberland.[4] This perhaps suggests that he identified more closely with his mother's Anglo-Norman kin than with his father's Scottish ancestry. One chronicler observed that Scottish kings considered themselves 'as Frenchmen in race, manners, language and culture; they keep only Frenchmen in their household and following and have reduced the Scots to utter servitude'.[5] Such a remark must surely be an exaggeration, but may be an indication of how William's own separation from his Gaelic roots were perceived.

When Malcolm IV died, 'William, his brother, succeeded him; and on the vigil of the Lord's Nativity [24 Dec.] he was elevated to the throne, according to the kingly manner.'[6] As Fordun puts it, following Malcolm's death

> the prelates and all the lords of Scotland met at Scone, at the command of his brother William, then warden of the kingdom, and there, with one accord, set up the latter as king. So, on Christmas Eve, that is, the fifteenth day after the king's death, this William, the friend of God, the lion of justice, the prince of peace, was consecrated king by Richard, bishop of Saint Andrews, with other bishops to help him, and raised to the king's throne.[7]

On his inauguration at Scone Abbey, on Christmas Eve 1165, William was 22 years old. He came to the throne as a grown man, who had already seen war, rather than a boy, as Malcolm had been, and was ready to assert his authority and pursue his own interests. With that in mind, when he met with King Henry II in Normandy in 1166, William requested the restoration of the earldom of Northumberland, but was refused. It was reported that the two kings parted on bad terms.[8] Anglo-Scottish relations were damaged further two years later, when William approached Louis VII of France for his aid in the matter. The news sent Henry into such a rage that he tore the cover from the bed on which he was seated and stuffed the bedding straw into his mouth.[9] Nevertheless, William and his brother David were again at the English court in 1170, where David was knighted. They attended Henry II's council at Windsor on 5 April of that year. Having taken the opportunity to visit his Huntingdon estates, William was back in London by 14 June, for the coronation of Henry's eldest son, also Henry, at Westminster Abbey. He would be known as Henry the Young King, rather than Henry III, and died in 1183, six years before his father. Both William and his brother David performed homage to the Young King after the controversial ceremony.[10] Thomas Becket, the exiled Archbishop of Canterbury, had forbidden the coronation, which was performed by Archbishop Roger of York, in the presence of most of the senior clergy in England.

In 1173, when the Young King and his brothers, Richard and Geoffrey, rebelled against their father, the younger Henry promised that he would return the northern counties of England to the Scots king, and the earldom of Huntingdon with Cambridgeshire to the king's brother, David, in return for Scottish support in the rebellion. William considered the offer. Consulting his barons in the summer of 1173, his counsellors advised against getting involved, while his young household knights pressed for war. It was decided to ask Henry II to return Northumbria, and to renounce homage if he refused. It should have come as no surprise when King Henry refused: 'Hereupon William, king of the Scots, hoping that he would find a remedy for old injuries in this new strife, waged a fierce war against his kinsman and lord, Henry, king of England, following herein evil counsels.'[11] William joined the Young King's rebellion, forming an alliance with Louis VII of France and Count

Philippe of Flanders, who both promised mercenaries would be sent to England in support. This was the start of Scotland's long tradition of alliances with France, against England, which would become known as the *Auld Alliance*. On 20 August 1173, the Scottish forces moved south, to Alnwick, Warkworth and Newcastle. Although they were unable to take the castles, 'the Scots cruelly destroyed the greater part of Northumberland with fire, and with great ferocity put the inhabitants to the sword.'[12] They moved on to Carlisle, in the west, but having again failed to take the castle, they pulled back to Roxburgh after receiving news that a new English force was advancing. This force, under Ranulf de Glanville, the justiciar, burned Berwick.

A truce was agreed until 13 January 1174, before the English returned south to deal with an invasion from Flanders. The truce was later extended to 24 March 1174, after a payment of 300 marks by the Bishop of Durham to King William.[13] At the end of the truce, the Scots, accompanied by Flemish mercenaries, again advanced into England. While William's brother, David, joined the rebels at Leicester, the king ravaged the Northumberland coast and besieged both Wark-on-Tweed (on the Northumberland–Scotland border) and Carlisle castles, but, ill-prepared for siege warfare, failed to take either. The castles at Appleby and Brough surrendered to the Scots, but they were resisted at Prudhoe Castle, near Newcastle, from where they moved north to Alnwick after hearing of an approaching English army. On 13 July, while much of the Scottish army was spread out in raiding parties, the Scots were caught unprepared by an English force. A large proportion of the Scots nobility were captured. King William's horse was killed, the king trapped beneath. William surrendered to Ranulf de Glanville and was taken south, with his feet bound by a rope passed under his horse's belly, as an added humiliation:

> On the morrow, William, king of the Scots, was taken prisoner at Alnwick, and conducted (sorrowing as he went) to Richmond, where he was kept in custody for a time, but with all due respect. As soon as the intelligence reached the king of England, by his orders he was sent across into Normandy, and this welcome treasure was laid up in safety in the tower of Falaise.[14]

King William was taken first to Newcastle and then to Northampton, where he appeared before Henry II on 24 July.[15] He was sentenced to imprisonment and transported to Falaise in Normandy. Moreover, William's sister Margaret, dowager Duchess of Brittany and Countess of Richmond, after her brother's capture, was imprisoned at Rochester castle and then moved to Rouen. However, on hearing of the king's capture, his younger brother David 'hastily abandoned Leicester, which he was besieging, and he and his followers took themselves back to Scotland as they best might.'[16]

The price of his freedom would be high. In the Treaty of Falaise, sealed on 8 December 1174, King William was to publicly submit himself and his kingdom to King Henry in order to obtain his release. In addition, the Scots king had to promise hostages and surrender the key castles of Berwick, Roxburgh, and Edinburgh to King Henry II.[17] The treaty also stipulated that 'the church of Scotland shall henceforward owe such subjection to the church of England as it should do'.[18] King William arrived back in Scotland in February 1175, having spent two months in England until the handover of the Scottish castles had been completed. David returned with his brother. Their sister, Margaret, had also been released from captivity and was married to Humphrey de Bohun; their son was born the next year. During the king's absence, Galloway had erupted in revolt after Uhtred, Lord of Galloway, had been murdered by his brother Gilbert, in September 1174. William was unable to quash the rising immediately as Gilbert had appealed to King Henry to become his vassal, making it difficult for William to act against him without the express permission of the English king as William's overlord.[19]

William met King Henry at York, on 10 August 1175, where he confirmed the treaty and publicly performed homage and fealty to King Henry for his kingdom of Scotland as well as his English estates. William also promised to enforce the subjection of the Scottish church to English jurisdiction and instructed his nobles and clergy to make their own submissions to the English king:

> The earls and barons, and all the greater and more powerful personages through the realm of Scotland, did their allegiance to Henry, king of England, in the presence of William, their king, and gave him hostages; and the bishops of the same kingdom swore fealty to him upon the Word of Truth. This was done at York.[20]

The humiliation of the Scots was complete; the country was now a vassal of England, with English garrisons in the major Scottish castles south of the Forth. And the matter of William's claims to Northumberland and Cumberland was put to rest: as far as Henry was concerned the counties belonged to England. The earldom of Huntingdon was also confiscated. It was restored to William in 1184, after which he promptly resigned it and 'immediately on which, in presence of the king, he conferred the earldom on his brother David'.[21] Furthermore, the harbouring of felons, fleeing justice from one country into the other, was forbidden.[22] As the Scottish chronicles recorded, their people paid a high price for their king's freedom:

> The Scots purchased his liberty by surrendering the independency of the nation; and with the consent of the Scottish barons and clergy, William became the liegeman of Henry for Scotland and all his other territories, and in 1176 the Church of Scotland was required to yield obedience to the English Church.[23]

As Gerald of Wales put it in his tract *De instructione principum*, completed about 1214,

> Having taken William prisoner, he (Henry ii.) subjected Scotia, and thus adding nobly to the Anglican crown an unexpected increase, greatly extended the bounds of his kingdom from the Southern Ocean to the northern Isles of Orkney, comprehending the whole island, as it is enclosed by the ocean, with a powerful hand in one monarchy. Because, from the time when the Picts and Scots first occupied the northern parts of the island, it is not recorded in any authentic writing that this was done by any one after the time of Claudius Caesar, who not only added Scotia to the Britannic kingdom, but also the Orkney Isles to the Roman empire.[24]

The required twenty Scottish noble hostages included the king's only surviving brother and – until he had children of his own – heir, David, and his kinsman Duncan (II), Earl of Fife. Several retainers of William's ageing mother, Countess Ada, were also among the hostages, including Hugh Gifford, William de la Hay and William de Mortemer.[25] William had returned from his captivity to the revolt in Galloway, which he managed to quash, but in 1179 the King of Scots was forced to go north, to answer the threat of Donald Ban Macwilliam, grandson of Duncan II, Malcolm III's son by his first wife, Ingibiorg, who was gaining support for a challenge to the throne and a return to the royal line of Duncan. Understandably, Macwilliam thought the crown was rightfully his. William built two new castles at Redcastle and Dunskeath and confirmed to his brother David the earldom of Lennox and lordship of Garrioch, thus controlling the roads to Moray and Ross. Things quietened down for a time, but in April 1181, when the king and David were in Normandy, Donald Ban Macwilliam led an uprising in Moray and Ross, apparently gaining full control of the two earldoms. One royal retainer, Gillecolm the Marischal, surrendered the castle of Auldearn and then joined the rebels.[26]

As the rebellion rumbled on, William was also – again – facing unrest in Galloway, where Gilbert of Galloway had failed to pay the money he had owed to Henry II since his earlier uprising. Gilbert died on 1 January 1185 and shortly after King William invaded Galloway, alongside Gilbert's nephew Roland, son of Uhtred of Galloway, who had been murdered by Gilbert, his own brother, in 1174. On 4 July 1185, William and his allies defeated the main force of Gilbert's followers and in July 1186, King William presented Roland to King Henry at Carlisle. By 1190, Roland had been granted the lordship of Galloway by King William while Gilbert's son, Duncan, was made lord of Carrick.[27] As a result, Galloway remained at peace well into the thirteenth century, until the death of Roland's son, Alan, in 1234. With Galloway subdued, in 1187 King William was finally able to quash the rebellion in the north, leading his considerable army as far as Inverness. On

31 July, at the now-lost site of 'Mam Garvia', in Ross, Roland of Galloway faced the rebels in battle where over 500 of them were killed, including Donald Ban Macwilliam, whose head was sent to the king. [28]

As a consequence of the uprising in the north, William was forced to look to overhauling royal government in the region, reorganising the systems set in place by his brother and grandfather. He strengthened and extended the network of castles and restructured the system of sheriffdoms.[29] The overlordship of Henry II caused additional problems for King William in the Scottish church; the archbishops of York and Canterbury both claimed the homage of the Scottish clergy. William also had a long-running dispute with the papacy, with five successive popes, in fact, over the appointment of a Bishop of St Andrews, with neither approving of the other's candidate. It started in 1177, when 'Master John called Scot was elected to the see of St Andrews. King William was totally opposed, and confident in the royal power had Hugh his chaplain consecrated as bishop in the church of St Andrew in accordance with his wishes.'[30] Ignoring William's candidate and 'in the presence also of sir John de Monte Celio, the cardinal who had been appointed a legate from the lord pope's side in Scotland in particular, the grace of the Holy Spirit was invoked, and all and sundry cast their votes for the archdeacon, and jointly elected him as bishop with no dissent.'[31]

King William was incensed:

> At that time William king of Scotland, on hearing that the archdeacon had been elected bishop without him being consulted or giving any consent or approval, took it badly; and unable to hide the anger aroused in his mind, he burst out with these words: 'By the arm of St James' (for this was his usual oath) 'as long as I live he will never enjoy the bishopric of St Andrews, nor will he exercise episcopal authority in that see.' Soon therefore the property and revenues of the bishop were seized, and the king ordered that both John and all the others connected in any way with his family or household be condemned to exile.[32]

The expelled bishop, John Scotus, travelled to Rome to plead his case and Pope Alexander promised his support. The pope wrote to King William, asking that he welcome Scotus back with 'proper filial affection' or face the consequences of an interdict. It was John Scotus himself who persuaded the pope against issuing the interdict.[33] The pope then sent Scotus back to Scotland with the papal nuncio, Alexius, and King William reluctantly allowed the party to enter the country. Agreement was reached in 1180, by which John Scotus, 'in conformity with the dignity of the church of St Andrews and the king's honour he was to be consecrated to the episcopal see by whatever bishops he wanted'.[34] The English king sided with the popes on the matter and in 1181 King William was excommunicated by the Archbishop of York; the Scottish people, as a whole, were subsequently excommunicated by the bishop of Durham. The sentence of excommunication was lifted in 1182,

> at the urgent request of the envoys of the king of Scotland namely, Jocelyn, bishop of Glasgow, Arnold, abbat of Melrose, Osbert, abbat of Kelso, and Walter, prior of Saint Columba of the Isle, pope Lucius the Third absolved William king of Scotland from the sentence of excommunication, and his kingdom from the interdict, at the palace of the Lateran, at Rome, in presence of his cardinals.[35]

In a letter to King William, Pope Lucius ordered

> that the sentence of excommunication pronounced by the said archbishop upon the king, and that of interdict upon his kingdom, and the sentence of excommunication pronounced by the said bishop upon certain persons of his kingdom, ought reasonably and upon numerous grounds to be set aside. Wherefore, paying due deference to the before-named king as our most dearly beloved son in Christ, we have, by the common consent of our brethren and with the Apostolic authority, remitted all the sentence which was pronounced by the before-named bishop for the cause before-mentioned, against him or his people, or his kingdom, and have enacted that he and his people shall not be held to be excommunicated, nor his kingdom to be under interdict, in consequence of our sentence above-written. Wherefore, we do by our precept, by these Apostolic writings, command the whole of you that you will in no way hesitate to treat with him as a Catholic king and as holding communion with the Apostolic See, but will rather in all things pay him the honour that is his due. For the more assured we feel of the sincerity of his duteousness to the churches and ecclesiastical persons of his realm, the more abundantly do we wish him to be honoured in all things in which, with due respect to God, we can be honoured. Given at Velletari, this sixteenth day before the calends of April.[36]

The dispute over the bishopric of St Andrews rumbled on, but in 1183, both John Scotus and William's candidate, Hugh the Chaplain, resigned their rights. A compromise was reached whereby Hugh was confirmed as Bishop of St Andrews and Scotus was compensated with the bishopric of Dunkeld. King William was still dissatisfied and in 1186 both bishops were summoned to Rome. Hugh refused to go and was excommunicated. John Scotus returned to Scotland in 1188 with a letter of confirmation from Pope Clement III. The pope also wrote to Henry II,

> enjoining, your exalted royal highness with all the affection we possibly can, that, in consideration of your veneration for Saint

Peter and ourselves, as also in consideration of the persecutions which there is no doubt he has endured, you will earnestly advise William, the illustrious king of the Scots, our most dearly-beloved son in Christ, and induce him, and if necessary compel him with that royal authority in which you are his superior, and which has been conceded by him to your royal highness, to cease, by setting aside every pretext for the same, all the rancour of his indignation which, through the malice of certain whisperers, he has entertained against the said bishop.[37]

William finally conceded to the pressure. And, in 1189, following Bishop Hugh's death,

Roger, a son of the nobleman who was earl of Leicester, and a kinsman and chancellor of the lord king William, was elected to the bishopric of St Andrews on 13 April (a Friday); and in 1198 he was consecrated to his episcopal see by Richard bishop of Moray on the first Sunday in Lent, in the presence of the king, etc. And he served as bishop-elect for ten years, and as a consecrated bishop for three years and a half.[38]

Even as the dispute continued, the papacy and the Scots king were on such good terms that 'Pope Lucius, however, hearing of the fame of King William – that he was zealous for God, and took great pains in maintaining the laws of his kingdom – sent over, by them, to his best beloved son, with his fatherly blessing, a golden rose, set upon a wand, also of gold.'[39] The Golden Rose was a tribute to 'a king of exceptional religious zeal'.[40] On 13 March 1192, Pope Celestine III issued the papal bull, *Cum universi*, recognising the Scottish church as a 'special daughter' of the apostolic see and subject to Rome without an intermediary. Thereby denying the claims to superiority of both York and Canterbury.[41]

Unusually for a king in this period, by 1180 William had been on the throne for fifteen years and was still unmarried, a fact which must have irked his mother until the day she died. Given the lengths she had gone to in order to get Malcolm to marry, one cannot imagine that she had been any less persuasive with William. Unlike Malcolm's chaste lifestyle, however, William had several illegitimate children, including a daughter, Isabella, and in 'A.D. 1183. William, king of the Scots, gave, in honourable manner, his daughter Isabella in marriage to Robert de Brus. She was his issue by the daughter of Robert Avenel'.[42] Isabella was widowed some time before 1191, when, 'the king of Scots gave his daughter Isabella (the widow of Robert de Brus), in marriage to Robert de Ross, at Haddington'.[43] Another daughter, Ada, was married to Patrick, Earl of Dunbar in 1184 and in 1193 King William married a third daughter, 'Margaret to Eustace de Vesci, at Rokesburch [Roxburgh]; she was his issue by the daughter of Adam de Hythusum.'[44] There is a suggestion by Walter Bower that William had married Margaret's mother, referring to her as William's first wife, 'a daughter of Adam de Whitsome, by whom he fathered a daughter Margaret'.[45] It may be that Bower was confusing two of William's daughters who shared the name Margaret, this Margaret who was illegitimate and his legitimate daughter by Queen Ermengarde. When William was desperately ill in 1195, his barons swore fealty to 'his daughter Margaret as his true heir, unless he should have a son by his queen Ermengarde. He had fathered this daughter Margaret by a daughter of Adam de Whitsome.'[46] However, by this time, William had a daughter, also named Margaret, by his queen and it is most likely that it was this Margaret to whom the barons swore fealty, especially given that part of the negotiations included discussing possible husbands for Margaret: the elder Margaret was already married. The elder Margaret must have been illegitimate, otherwise she would have been proposed as William's heir. Following this logic, William had never been married to the elder Margaret's mother. William also had an illegitimate son, Robert of London, who was endowed with royal lands and donated lands to Lindores Abbey.[47] Another son was Henry Galightly, whose own son, Patrick Galithly, was one of the Competitors for the crown in 1291.

In spite of these children, however, until he married, William's heir was his younger brother, David. With this in mind, William was looking for a bride. Henry II, always happy to remind William that he was the Scots king's overlord, exercised his right to choose William's bride. In 1184, William was at King Henry's court to discuss a possible marriage with Henry's granddaughter, Matilda of Saxony. As the daughter of Henry the Lion, Duke of Saxony and granddaughter of Henry II, Matilda's royal status and close relationship to the English king would serve to reflect William's own royal status. The match was forbidden by the pope on the grounds of consanguinity; both Matilda and William were descendants of Malcolm III and St Margaret. Moreover, Henry may not have wanted to waste his politically useful granddaughter on a king he had already subjected to his will.

In May 1186, during a council at Woodstock, King Henry suggested Ermengarde de Beaumont as a bride for King William. Ermengarde was the daughter of Richard, Vicomte de Beaumont-sur-Sarthe, who was himself the son of Constance, one of the many illegitimate daughters of King Henry I of England. With such diluted royal blood, she was hardly a prestigious match for the King of Scots. William felt slighted but he reluctantly accepted the marriage after consulting his advisers, the offer sweetened by a generous payment for the wedding celebrations and the return of two of the forfeited Scottish castles, as a wedding present.[48] We have, of course, no record of Ermengarde's thoughts on the marriage, nor of whether she was aware of the fact it was seen as an insult to the Scots king. The wedding took place 'with great magnificence, on the nones of September [5 Sept.] (being the sixth day of the week [Friday], the moon being in her eighteenth day), in the royal chapel in the park at Woodstock, in the presence of the king himself'.[49] The wedding mass was celebrated by Baldwin, Archbishop of Canterbury.[48] Following the ceremony, King Henry hosted four days of festivities; Edinburgh Castle was one of the castles returned to the Scots as part of Ermengarde's dowry.[50] Although we do not know Ermengarde's birth date, at the time of the marriage, she was referred to as 'a girl', suggesting that she may have only just reached the age of 12, the legal age to marry for girls.[51] It has been suggested that Ermengarde's tender age may also have been the reason for his reluctance to marry her.[52] We do not know the year of birth of Ermengarde's first daughter, Margaret. It is usually given as between 1187 and 1195. If Ermengarde gave birth to Margaret the year after her marriage, it seems highly likely that she was at least 14 or 15 years old at the time of her wedding. However, a later birthdate in the 1190s would suggest that Ermengarde was younger at the time of her marriage and was given time to mature before bearing children. The king's growing need for an heir would, perhaps, indicate that Ermengarde was old enough to bear children at the time of their marriage, and that describing the bride as 'a girl' was alluding to her youth, but not her actual age. Unfortunately, the vagaries of chroniclers means that we cannot say for certain.

King William agreed to provide Ermengarde with £100 of rents and forty knights' fees in Scotland, for the financial maintenance of her household; she also had dwellings and lands at Crail and Haddington, lands which had previously been held by William's mother, Ada de Warenne.[53] After the wedding, King William accompanied King Henry to Marlborough whilst the Scottish queen was escorted to her new home by Jocelyn, Bishop of Glasgow, and other Scottish nobles. Between 1187 and 1195, Queen Ermengarde gave birth to two daughters, Margaret and Isabella. Finally, in 1198, 'Alexander, the son of William, king of the Scots, was born on the day of St. Bartholomew the apostle [24 Aug.], and at his birth many rejoiced.'[54] The future Alexander II was born at Haddington; he was the first legitimate son born to a reigning Scottish king in seventy years. A third daughter, Marjory, was born sometime later. Although she does not appear as a witness on any of King William's extant charters, Queen Ermengarde appears to have played an active role in Scotland, with William allowing her an increasingly influential part in public affairs.[55] One disgruntled canon, in 1207, complained that Walter, a royal chaplain, had obtained the bishopric of Glasgow by not only bribing the king's chamberlain, but also Queen Ermengarde.[56] The queen may also have offered patronage to relatives, including one Richard de Beaumont, perhaps a brother or cousin, who received substantial lands in Crail.[57] As the king's health declined as he aged – he was already 46 when he married Ermengarde – the queen took on more responsibilities, especially where her children were concerned.

In 1189, King William experienced a stroke of luck with the death of his overlord, Henry II, in England. The Scots king travelled south and met Henry's successor, King Richard, at Canterbury, where he did homage for his English lands. Desperate for money for his crusade, on 5 December 1189, Richard abandoned his lordship of Scotland in the quitclaim of Canterbury; King William was released from the homage and submission given to Henry II, the castles of Roxburgh and Berwick were returned and the relationship between the kingdoms reverted to that in the time of Malcolm IV:

> Richard, by the grace of God, king of England, duke of Normandy
> and Aquitaine, earl of Anjou and Poitou; to the archbishops, bishops,
> abbots, priors, earls, barons, justiciaries, sheriffs, and all his ministers
> and lieges of the whole of England – Greeting: Know ye that we
> have given back to our cousin William, by the grace of God, king of
> Scots, his castles of Berwick and Roxburgh, with all their pertinents,
> as his by right of inheritance, and to be held for ever by him and his
> heirs in the said kingdom. Furthermore, we have remitted unto him
> all customs and bargains which our father Henry, king of England,
> of happy memory, extorted by fresh escheats, through his capture.
> Provided, of course, that the said king do wholly and fully unto us,
> for his lands in England, what his brother Malcolm, king of Scots,
> did unto Our ancestors, as he was bound by law to do. And we
> shall do unto him and his successors, whatever Our ancestors were
> bound by law to do: to wit, in safe-conduct in coming to court, and
> returning from court, and, while tarrying at court, in procurations,
> and dignities, and honours, and all the privileges of the same, due,
> by law, from old time (according as it shall be ascertained by four
> of our lords, elected by the said King William, and four lords of the
> kingdom of Scotland, elected by us), after William the Bastard, the
> conqueror of the said kingdom of England, and his heirs, obtained
> the said kingdom of England.[58]

The cost to the Scots was to be 10,000 marks, but Scotland was independent once again.[59] Richard, however, refused to sell Northumberland back to William; instead, he sold a life-interest in the earldom to the Bishop of Durham. The Scots king remained on good relations with King Richard, paying 2,000 marks towards his ransom in 1193 and meeting him at Nottingham in April 1194, where William asked for two favours. The first favour was a request to be granted an honourable escort and daily subsistence allowances during his visits to the English court: this was granted but not put into effect until the reign of King John. For the second favour, William asked to be granted the earldom of Northumberland, the lordships of Cumberland and Westmorland and the earldom of Lancaster, last held by the Scots in the 1140s. This second favour was, unsurprisingly, refused by Richard.[60] The Scots king carried one of the three swords of state at Richard's solemn crown-wearing at Winchester on 17 April 1194. Two days later, the Bishop of Durham surrendered the earldom of Northumberland; William offered 15,000 marks for it and Richard made a counteroffer saying that William could have the earldom but not its castles, which William refused. The matter remained unresolved.

In the spring of 1195, King William fell gravely ill at Clackmannan, causing a succession crisis, the sum of his legitimate children being one, possibly two, daughters at this time – and no son. The Scottish barons appear to have been divided, between recognising William's oldest legitimate daughter, Margaret, as his heir, or marrying Margaret to Otto, Duke of Saxony, grandson of Henry II, and allowing Otto to succeed to the throne. The earl of Dunbar led a faction who claimed that both solutions were contrary to the custom of the land, so long as the king had a brother who could succeed him.[61] This must have been a worrying time for Ermengarde, not only for the health of her husband, but for her own status in Scotland, should her daughter be disinherited. Not to mention the concern that Margaret, then aged only 8, might be married at such a young age to secure the succession. In the event, the discussion was moot as the king recovered from his illness and three years later the queen gave birth to Alexander, the much-desired son and heir. Chronicler John of Fordun described the relief and celebration felt throughout the country at the birth of the heir to the Scots throne:

> Now this most fortunate king of Scotland, William, had, nearly twelve years ago, with great splendour and rejoicings, taken to wife Ermyngarde, daughter of the Viscount of Beaumont, who was the son of the daughter of William the Bastard's eldest son, Robert Curthose. By her he had a son, named Alexander, – to the great gladness of his people, and the refreshment of the whole kingdom of the Scots, as the after course of these annals will show forth. He was born at Haddington, on Saint Bartholomew's Day, in the year 1198. In every place in the whole country, the common folk used to forsake their menial work on this day, wherein they first heard tidings of his birth, and spend it in joy; while priests and churchmen donned the alb, and walked in procession, with loud voice glorifying God in hymns and canticles, and humbly praising Him.[62]

For the last years of the century, William was again occupied with unrest in the north. Before going on campaign in October 1201, he had the Scottish barons swear fealty to his son, Alexander, now 3 years old, a sensible precaution, given he was approaching his 60th birthday. And in 1205, the king's brother 'Earl David performed his homage to his nephew Alexander, the son of king William'.[63]

Relations with England had changed again in 1199, with the accession of King John, the youngest son of Henry II. During the reign of King Richard, William had agreed with the justiciar, William Longchamp, and backed Arthur of Brittany as the king's heir. John may well have remembered this and felt less inclined to be amenable to William. Soon after John's accession, King William asked for the return of Northumberland. The two kings met at Lincoln in 1200, with William doing homage for his English lands and John asking for the discussion over Northumberland to be deferred until Whitsun 1201. John kept putting the matter off until the two kings finally met for formal talks at York from 9 to 12 February 1206 and again from 26 to 28 May 1207, although we have little record of what was discussed. William was confirmed in his lands in Tynedale and John granted Arbroath Abbey trading privileges in England.[64] However, John appears to have been prevaricating, suggesting another meeting in October 1207, which the Scots rejected. The dispute over Northumberland remained unresolved. In the meantime, the death of the Bishop of Durham meant John took over the vacant see and set about building a castle at Tweedmouth. The Scots, seeing this as a direct threat to Berwick, destroyed the building works and matters reached a crisis point in 1209.

After many threats, and with both sides building up their armies, the two kings met at Norham, Northumberland, in the last week of July and first week of August 1209. The Scots were in a desperate position, with an ailing and ageing king, and a 10-year-old boy as heir, whilst the English, with their Welsh allies and foreign mercenaries, had an army big enough to force a Scottish submission. Queen Ermengarde appears to have acted as a mediator between the two kings, although the subsequent treaty, agreed at Norham on 7 August, was humiliating for the Scots.[65] They agreed to pay 15,000 marks for peace and to surrender hostages, including the king's two oldest legitimate daughters, Margaret and Isabella. As a sweetener, John promised to marry the oldest princess to one of his sons; although Henry was only 2 years old at the time and Richard was just 8 months, whilst the girls were probably in their mid-to-late teens. Isabella would be married to an English noble of suitable rank, an earl at least. John would have the castle at Tweedmouth dismantled, but the Scots would pay an extra £4,000 compensation for the damage they had caused to it. The king's daughters and the other Scottish hostages were handed into the custody of England's justiciar at Carlisle on 16 August.[66]

How the girls, or their parents, thought about this turn of events, we know not. Given John's proven record of prevarication and perfidy, King William may have hoped that the promised marriages would occur in good time but may also have expected that John would find a way out of the pledges he had made. According to Bower, a further meeting between the two countries, at Alnwick in 1210, agreed that William should resign his English lands to his son, Alexander, who would then pay homage to King John for these lands. It was agreed that henceforth, no matter who the Scots king was, it would be the heir to the Scottish throne who would perform homage and fealty to the English king 'for the grant of the said lands and honours'.[67] William and John met again at Durham in February 1212, a meeting in which 'The queen of Scotland was present and acted as mediator, an extraordinary woman, gifted with a charming and witty eloquence.'[68] The queen's efforts bore fruit and peace between the two countries was renewed, as 'There in the presence of the nobles of both kingdoms and the revered lady the queen of the Scots a formula for achieving peace and love, to be observed between the kingdoms and their kings for ever, was worked out anew and confirmed by charters given by both parties.'[69] It was also agreed that the Scottish prince, Alexander, should be given an English wife. With at least one of the prince's older sisters already intended for a son of King John, marrying Alexander to one of John's daughters would further bind the Scots to the Plantagenet cause. It was also agreed that Prince Alexander, now aged 14, should be knighted. The ceremony took place at Clerkenwell on 4 March 1212:

And to join them with a stronger bond of love, Alexander the king of Scotland's son was sent by his father with the utmost pomp and splendour and invested with the sword of knighthood by the king of England at London, on the middle Sunday of Lent, Letare Jerusalem, on 8 March in his fourteenth year, along with twenty noble and wellborn boys of the kingdom. The king of England sent him back with generous gifts, and he returned to his father about Easter.[70]

Ermengarde may have taken a more prominent role in the negotiations of 1212 as King William's health began to fail. Their son, Alexander, was still only a teenager and so it would have fallen to the queen to take part in the talks. William had been a physically active king almost to the very last moment. In the spring of 1211, having recently recovered from illness, he led an army into the field against Guthred Macwilliam, who had been expelled from Ireland by King John, only to invade Ross. The king refortified the mottes at Dunskeath and Redcastle and was active in Moray from about the end of June until the autumn of 1211. Although the rebels were scattered, and many killed, Guthred Macwilliam remained at large. In October, the king moved on to Forfar, leaving Malcolm, Earl of Fife, in command in Moray. He could not prevent Guthred from attacking and firing one of the castles in Ross and the king could do nothing in retaliation as the winter weather set in, making campaigning impossible.[71] After he was knighted in London, Prince Alexander returned to Scotland with mercenaries provided by John, intending to suppress Guthred's rebellion. He was not needed, however, as Guthred was betrayed and captured. He was taken to Moray in chains, and then on to Kincardine, where he was beheaded.[72]

In January and February 1213, when both the Scots and English kings were close to the border, a meeting was proposed, but William resisted and could not be persuaded to meet with John. He was probably already very ill and was in his 70th year as, according to Fordun,

> The king of England, also, came as far as Norham, to have an interview with the king of Scotland; but as this king was at that time lying sick at Haddington, the interview did not come off. Nor was the Lord Alexander, the king's son – although the king of England had asked this very urgently – allowed to go to him; for they feared his wiles.[73]

According to Bower, the Scots feared 'the evil intentions of King John. If he had control over the person of the son and heir of the king of Scotland, and consequently of the king – for as the laws bear witness a king's son should be called – they suspected that it would not be easy for Alexander to return.'[74]

As William's health failed, Queen Ermengarde appears to have taken on more responsibilities and exerted her influence on the court. The king rallied in 1214, so that he was well enough to travel to Elgin in the summer, where he came to an accord with John, the new earl of Caithness, and received the earl's unnamed daughter as a hostage.[75] The journey took its toll on the king, and he suffered some sort of collapse. He was taken, in easy stages, to the royal castle at Stirling, where he saw his lords for the last time. With the queen in attendance, William urged his barons and bishops to accept Alexander, now 16 years old, as king. King William I, later known as William the Lion, died on 4 December 1214, aged about 71, having reigned for a total of forty-nine years, almost to the day:

> William, king of Scotland, of holy memory, going the way of all flesh, departed to the Lord by a happy death, in the forty-ninth year of his reign, in the seventy-second year of his age, on the second of the nones of December [4 Dec.], leaving his kingdom in a state of profound peace. His son Alexander, (being now in the seventeenth year of his age,) attended by a vast concourse of the nobility, proceeded to Scone, and there, according to the royal custom, and with the usual solemnities, he assumed the government of the realm of Scotland upon the eighth of the ides of December [6 Dec.], in equal honour and peace.[76]

The chronicler John of Fordun was generous in his praise of King William and even attributed a miracle to him:

> He there lingered for some time, failing in strength from day to day; and after his son had been accepted as the future king, by the bishops earls, and barons, William departed this life, full of goodly days, and at a good old age, charging his familiar friends and officers about paying back all debts and services in full, as became a good prince. And fully armed with thorough devoutness, a clear shrift, true charity, the viaticum of Christ's body, and the rest of the sacraments, while his kingdom abode in the deepest peace, breathed he out his last breath, in a blissful end, and flitted to Christ's presence, we trust, about the third hour of the night, on Thursday, the 4th of December, in the aforesaid year – the forty-ninth of his reign, and the seventy-fourth of his age. How great was that distinguished king's worthiness in God's sight, may be gathered from a certain miracle, which was on the following wise. Upon one occasion – namely, in 1206 – between Candlemas and the 1st of March, this king went, under the safe-conduct of some English nobles, to John, king of England, at York; and after a stay of four days there, when his business was over, he sped safely back. At that time, at York, in the presence of many nobles of England and Scotland, a boy was, by his touch and blessing, healed of a grievous sickness, which was upon him; while

all wondered and stood aghast. But that he was beloved by worthy
men, even as he was by God, is shown in this case, for instance.[77]

On the morning after her husband's death, Queen Ermengarde was 'in a state of
extreme mourning and worn out with grief'.[78] The prelates and nobles attempted
to rouse Ermengarde from her melancholy by asking that she arrange the late
king's funeral, but the queen would not be moved. They left Ermengarde with
her grief and took the young king, Alexander, to Scone, where he was crowned as
King Alexander II on 6 December. King William was then buried at Arbroath on
10 December. The new king and his mother then presided over the royal Christmas
feast at Forfar but returned to Stirling in January 1215. They then visited Arbroath,
to see the tomb of King William.[79] Queen Ermengarde had been much younger than
her husband, the king, possibly by as much as thirty years. She would, therefore,
continue to live for many years into her son's reign.

King Alexander II sided with the English barons in their struggle against the
tyranny of King John, making an alliance with the northern barons, who agreed
to press for a decision on the future of Alexander's sisters, and a resolution of
the lordship of the northern counties. He raided the northern English earldoms,
exploiting the unrest in England to renew Scottish claims to these counties,
besieging Norham in October 1215 and receiving the homage of the leading men
of Northumberland on 22 October 1215.[80] In the summer of 1216, Alexander took
the castle and town of Carlisle and in September the Scots king marched his army
the length of England, from Scotland to Dover, to pay homage to the dauphin,
Louis, for his English lands. The papal legate to England, Cardinal Bicchieri Guala,
denounced Louis and his supporters and

> pronounced the sentence of excommunication against the said Louis
> and all his supporters, and declared that it proceeded from the pope
> himself; moreover he included in this same sentence our lord the
> king of the Scots and all his nobility, and did not hesitate to place the
> lands of all of them under interdict.[81]

The sentence of excommunication even extended to Queen Ermengarde.
Following John's death in October 1216 and the defeat of the French rebel army
at Lincoln in May 1217, Alexander's position in England became precarious.
England's status as a papal fief saw Alexander and Scotland put under interdict.
The Scots king surrendered Carlisle Castle at Berwick on 1 December 1217 and
submitted to Henry III at Northampton later in the same month.[82] The sentences of
excommunication were lifted:

> Our lord Alexander, the king of-Scotland, was absolved from the
> bond of excommunication by the lord archbishop of York, and by the
> lord bishop of Durham, at Berwick, upon the kalends of December

[1 Dec.], by authority of the legate, who was resident in England, and the third day afterwards the mother of the said king was absolved by the lord bishop of Durham.[83]

With King Alexander's submission, there followed an unprecedented almost eighty years of unbroken peace between England and Scotland. The peace was sealed with a marriage in June 1221:

> On the Saturday next before the feast of St. John the Baptist [19 June], our lord Alexander, the king of Scotland, married at York the daughter of John, and the sister of Henry, king of England; and after the nuptials had been celebrated with the exceeding splendour which was fitting such an occasion, he conducted her into Scotland, to the great joy of all the inhabitants of both kingdoms.[84]

Another marriage soon followed, when, in London on 30 October,

> In the same year, by the consent of the kings of England and Scotland, and by the advice of the nobility of both realms, the lady Margaret, the daughter of William, king of Scotland, of holy memory, and the sister of our lord king Alexander, was given in marriage to Herbert de Bure, the justiciary of England and Scotland.[85]

Queen Ermengarde must have felt relief that her son had found a bride, and hoped that an heir would soon follow. She may also have been satisfied that her eldest daughter, Margaret, once thought of as the heir to the Scots throne, was also finally settled in matrimony. Though there was complaint from some sides that Margaret had been pressed into a disparaging marriage when she had been promised a prince as a bridegroom. Hubert de Burgh, her new husband, was King Henry III's justiciar, as he had been for King John, but was of minor nobility and did not receive his earldom of Kent until after his marriage to Margaret. Princess Margaret was no young bride, however; if she had been born in 1187, then she was already in her mid-30s and even if she was born as late as 1195, she would have been in her mid-20s, rather old for a medieval princess to marry her first husband. As for Margaret's sisters, 'Isabella, the daughter of William, that king of good memory, and the sister of Alexander, the king of Scotland, returned from the wardship of the king of England, being still unmarried.'[86] Isabella was eventually married in May 1225, to Roger Bigod, the young Earl of Norfolk. The wedding took place at Alnwick, in Northumberland, which may have meant that Queen Ermengarde was able to attend. Over ten years younger than his bride, and still underage, Roger became a ward of his brother-in-law, King Alexander.

Queen Ermengarde devoted her later years to founding an abbey at Balmerino, a parish in the district of Cupar in the county of Fife. The parish consisted of the villages of Kirkton and Galdry, 993 inhabitants, of whom sixty-two were in the village of Balmerino:

> This place, of which the name, of Celtic origin, signifies 'the town of the sea,' or 'Sailors' town,' most probably derived that appellation from its position on the estuary of the river Tay. It appears to have been distinguished, at a very early period, for the mild temperature of its climate, and the salubrity of its atmosphere; and early in the 13th century, it was selected by Queen Ermengard, widow of William the Lion, and mother of Alexander II, as a place of occasional resort, for the benefit of her health.[87]

The dowager queen raised the money to found the Cistercian abbey, paying 1,000 merks to purchase the land and acting as overseer to the building project. The abbey was built of red stone, quarried locally. Dedicated to Saint Edward the Confessor, the abbey was populated by monks from Melrose Abbey. Queen Ermengarde appears to have had a particular veneration for the sainted English king, as the only other religious gift we can attribute to her was to the hospital of St Edward at Berwick.[88] Queen Ermengarde and her son, Alexander II, are credited with founding the abbey at Balmerino together:

> He, also, together with his mother Ermengarde, founded and endowed the abbey of Saint Edward of Balmurinath (Balmerino), whither was sent the brotherhood of Melrose, with the Lord Alan, the abbot thereof, on the day of Saint Lucy the Virgin, in the year 1229; and there, four years afterwards, was buried that same noble queen Ermengarde, his mother – to wit, in the year 1233, the forty-seventh after her betrothal.[89]

The queen had lived long enough to see three of her four children settled in marriage, and may have met her first grandchild, a daughter born to Princess Margaret in 1227. In the same year, Henry III's brother Richard, Earl of Cornwall, arrived in Scotland to speak with Queen Ermengarde. The object of the discussions was the queen's youngest daughter, Marjory.[90] The earl's proposals were attractive to neither the Scots nor his brother and negotiations came to nought, but the fact that it was Ermengarde that Richard approached, rather than the king, clearly demonstrates the queen's continuing influence on her family. Her youngest daughter was not married until August 1235, when

> The lady Marjory, the sister of our lord Alexander, the king of the Scots, was married at Berwick, upon the day of St. Peter ad Vincula [1 Aug.], to the earl of Pembroke. There were present at the marriage the king himself and the chief of the nobility of his realm; and on

the other side were G., the marshal of England, and the bridegroom, together with a large number of the English nobles.[91]

The bridegroom, Gilbert Marshal, Earl of Pembroke, died in 1241.
The queen did not live to see the wedding as in 1233,

> Ermergerdis of good memory, the mother of king Alexander, and the queen of William, king of Scotland, died on the third of the ides of February [11 Feb.], after having been married forty-seven years; and she was buried in the abbey of St. Edward, of Balmorinac, which she herself had founded.[92]

The queen was buried before the high altar of the abbey to which she had dedicated her years of widowhood. Although the surviving records hint at the queen enjoying substantial authority in Scotland, especially where her family are concerned, we have few specifics. That she was entrusted with negotiating with the English emissaries, in 1209 and again in 1212, suggests that she possessed impressive diplomatic skills, and that King William had considerable confidence in his wife's abilities. Their partnership defined Scottish history for a generation. Furthermore, the queen's evident grief at her husband's death attests to a deep affection within the union, an affection that not only defined the marriage, but also the whole family, with the queen continuing to exert her influence on the relationships of her children in the years after her husband's death.

Having served as queen for twenty-eight years and as its dowager queen for a further nineteen years, Ermengarde de Beaumont defined the role of Queen of Scots for subsequent consorts. Her memory cast a long shadow.

Chapter Five

The Foundations of Peace

King Alexander II of Scots ascended the throne at the tender age of 16 years. Born on 24 August 1198, he was the only legitimate son of King William I, known as the Lion, and was 'baptized by Jocelyn, the venerable bishop of Glasgow'.[1] He was recognised as his father's heir at Musselburgh on 12 October 1201, when 'the nobility of the land swore fealty to Alexander, the king's son, on the fourth of the ides of October'.[2] And in 1205, Alexander's uncle 'Earl David performed his homage to his nephew Alexander, the son of king William'.[3] Even as a young prince, Alexander was an integral part of his father's policies. In negotiations with King John of England, it had been agreed that each king 'should support the other so far as he was able in any just disputes, and that whoever of the two outlived the other should protect the other's heir as if he were his own son, should Support him and make every effort to put him into possession of his kingdom'.[4] In the discussions in 1212, it 'was also agreed there that within six years the king of England should give as wife to Alexander the king of Scotland's son a lady of such quality and position as would satisfy him and bring honour to the kingdom of Scotland'.[5] King John also claimed the right to be the one to knight the 14-year-old prince:

> And, for the knitting of a stronger bond of love, Alexander, the son of the king of Scotland, was sent with the greatest pomp and state, by his father, to the king of England, by whom he, together with some noble and highborn boys of the kingdom, was girded with the sword of knighthood, in London, on the middle Sunday of Lent – that is, 'The Lætare, Jerusalem' – the 8th of March, in the fourteenth year of his age. Then the king of England sent him away with gifts, and he went back to his father about Easter.[6]

On his return to Scotland, Alexander proceeded north into Moray and Ross, to help deal with the rebellion by Guthred Macwilliam. By the time he arrived in the region, Guthred had been 'seized and fettered through his own men's treachery, was brought before the king's son, the lord Alexander, at the king's manor and castle of Kincardine, and was there beheaded, and hung up by the feet'.[7] With King William frequently ill, and approaching his 70th year, it appears that, in spite of his tender years, Alexander was not being shielded from the duties and responsibilities

75

that would be expected of him as a king. He was a king in training. His father died on 4 December 1214 and the next day,

> the Earls of Fife, Stratherne, Atholl, Angus, Menteith, Buchan, and Lothian, together with William, bishop of St. Andrews, took the king's son, Alexander, a lad of sixteen years and a half; and, bringing him as far as Scone, they raised him to the throne, in honour and peace, with the approval of God and man, and with more grandeur and glory than any one until then; while all wished him joy, and none gainsaid him. So King Alexander, as was meet, held his feast in state, at Scone, on that day (that is to say, Friday), and the Saturday following (namely, the Feast of St. Nicholas), as well as the next Sunday.[8]

On the Monday after his inauguration, the young king, along with his uncle, rode to the bridge at Perth where

> he met his father's body, which was being taken down, in great state, to Abirbroth (Arbroath), to be buried, as the king himself, before his death, had directed. And thus, followed by all the nobility of the whole kingdom, save a few of the nobles who guarded the uttermost parts of the kingdom, William, the kindly king of Scots, and to be had in kindly remembrance for everlasting, was buried on Wednesday, the 10th of December, in front of the high altar, in the church of the monastery of Abirbrothoc (Arbroath), which he had himself caused to be built up from the very foundations, to the honour of God and Saint Thomas the Martyr, Archbishop of Canterbury; and which he had, after endowing it with many estates and possessions, committed to the monks of Kalkhow (Kelso). May God be gracious unto his soul! Amen.[9]

Earl David, King William's younger brother, acted as pall bearer, alongside other earls, and 'afterwards, at the king's burial, he stood by as chief mourner, as became a brother'.[10]

Despite his youth, there was no suggestion of a regency and Alexander assumed the full responsibilities of the King of Scots. After spending Christmas at Forfar, with his mother, and epiphany at Stirling, Alexander then moved on to Edinburgh, where he held his first parliament and reappointed many of his father's choices as officers of state. Alexander II succeeded at a critical time for Scotland. Scottish royal authority was still weak in the strongly Gaelic-Norse extremities of the realm. To the south, King John, was behaving as if he was Scotland's overlord, having won so many concessions in recent years.[11] There was also the threat of alternative claimants to the throne. Male primogeniture was not an established rule of succession in Scotland

and until the accession of Malcolm IV the crown had frequently passed to the oldest male royal, rather than the oldest son of the king (or grandson, in Malcolm's case). Alexander's uncle David could have pursued a claim to the throne, but the challenge materialised from the senior Macwilliam claimant, Donald Bân, just weeks after Alexander's inauguration.[12] The rebellion was swiftly suppressed, however, and by mid-June 1215, Donald was dead.[13] Meanwhile, things were hotting up south of the border. At about the same time Donald Bân Macwilliam's head was being delivered to Alexander, King John was fixing his seal to Magna Carta. Alexander had his own axe to grind with John and his constable Alan, Lord of Galloway, had ensured his king's interests were included in the negotiations. One of the clauses of the Great Charter specifically addressed the grievances of the Scots:

> Clause 59: We will treat Alexander, king of Scots, concerning the return of his sisters and hostages and his liberties and rights in the same manner in which we will act towards our other barons of England, unless it ought to be otherwise because of the charters which we have from William his father, formerly king of Scots; and this shall be determined by the judgement of his peers in our court.[14]

King Alexander was brother-in-law to two of the rebel barons opposing King John. Robert de Ros and Eustace de Vescy were married to the king's illegitimate half-sisters, Isabella and Margaret respectively. They must have kept him informed of events south of the border and the progress towards civil war, as Alexander prepared to capitalise on King John's woes. On 19 October, he moved south and with 'his entire army, began to lay siege to the castle of Norham'. After having 'continued the siege for forty days, and finding that he made no progress, he withdrew. On the eleventh of the kalends of November [22 Oct.], our lord Alexander, the king of the Scots, received the homage of the barons of Northumberland at Felton.'[15] By the end of 1215, however, only one castle, Carlisle, had fallen to Alexander. The rest of the northern fortresses held out against him and in January 1216, John launched an offensive north:

> In the month of January, there occurred an unprecedented destruction of vills and towns in Northumberland, and in the southern parts of Scotland. For king John having heard that Alexander, the king of Scots, had laid claim to Northumberland, and had received the homage of the barons of that district, took with him his mercenary soldiers and marched towards Scotland with great energy.[16]

The barons of Yorkshire fled ahead of John's advance;

> they were so terrified that they fled for protection to the king of Scotland; and when they reached his presence they did homage to

him, and one and all of them swore fealty to him, and gave him security upon the reliques of the saints, upon the third of the ides of January [11 Jan.], in the chapter-house of the monks of Melrose.[17]

Before fleeing, the Yorkshire barons had burned their own crops so that John's troops would have no sustenance, but John, in turn 'and in his revenge devastated their vills and towns, and estates and farms, with fire and sword ... so that, between the two, a large portion of the district was destroyed by fire'.[18] Wark, Alnwick, Mitford, Morpeth and Roxburgh were all destroyed within one week.[19] Nothing was achieved by John's offensive as, in February, Alexander launched a counter-offensive into Cumberland, raiding as far as Carlisle. And with the landing in Kent of Louis, the heir to the French throne who had been invited to take the English crown by the rebels, John's position in the north proved untenable. As Louis made inroads in the south, Alexander established his control of the north, leading his army against Carlisle and taking the town's surrender on 8 August.[20] Although the castle held out against him, Alexander established the Scottish administration for the whole of Cumberland and Westmorland in the town.[21] Towards the end of August, Alexander left Carlisle and travelled to the south coast of England, meeting Louis at Dover, where 'He was welcomed, with honour, by Louis; and, having made a stay there of fifteen days or upwards, after treating of, and secretly winding up, sundry matters with him, he at length made ready to cross over to his own country.'[22] John, however, seized the opportunity afforded by Alexander's absence, to break the Scots' lines of communications and once again threaten the north, forcing Alexander to retrace his steps. The king was back in Scotland by the time of John's death, on the night of 18/19 October 1216, at Newark.

The death of the despised king changed the course of the war. Many barons, disillusioned with Louis's preference for his own men at the expense of rewarding his English allies, could now unite around the new king, Henry III; a child just turned 9 years of age who could not be blamed for the shortcomings of his father. A reissued edition of Magna Carta made no mention of the Scots' grievances; that was something that could be dealt with when the child-king came of age. To make matters worse, Alexander, his barons and even his mother were excommunicated by the papal legate to Henry's court, Bicchieri Guala. The whole of Scotland was placed under special interdict.[23] Alexander had proven himself a quick-witted, resilient military leader, despite his tender years, and now proved to be a pragmatist. Accepting the deteriorating situation in which he found himself, he travelled south, meeting the king at Northampton to pay homage to Henry for his English possessions and relinquishing his hold on Carlisle. Negotiations for a lasting peace would drag on for over two years and the question of the northern counties remained unresolved in the final agreement, concluded at York in June 1220:

The king of Scotland bound himself to wed the eldest sister of the king of England, while the latter bound himself to see that the Scottish king's sisters – whom his own father had formerly taken, as already said, to get them married – were worthily mated; and they both took an oath on the Body to that effect, before a certain Pandulph, the English legate, and a good many other lords of either kingdom. Thus a peace was established, which was to last time without end; and they returned home in peace.[24]

While Alexander was to have one of Henry III's sisters as a bride, the promise to marry the Scots king's own sisters had been diluted; they were no longer to marry Henry III and his brother, Richard, but 'suitable' non-royal English husbands.[25]

With peace established with England, Alexander II could now turn his attentions to Scotland and consolidating his own power. One bone of contention for the young king was that the king-making ceremony in Scotland, the inauguration, was a secular one, rather than an ecclesiastical coronation and anointing with holy oil. Alexander was determined to rectify this, seeing the Scottish ceremony as a stigma which could be perceived as Scottish kings being inferior to English kings, who were crowned and anointed in an ecclesiastical ritual. Alexander asked the papal legate in Scotland to crown and anoint him, but the issue was referred to the pope, who rejected Alexander's request after pressure from England. He would try again and again, but always be rebuffed; even in peacetime, the English king would be opposed to such a move, and the papacy was ever appreciative of the influence of the most powerful nation in the British Isles.[26]

Meanwhile, in June 1221, Alexander II was married to Henry III's sister, Joan of England. Joan was the oldest daughter of King John and his second wife, Isabelle d'Angoulême. Born 22 July 1210, she was the third of five children; she had two older brothers, and two younger sisters would have joined the family by 1215. Even before her birth, Joan was mooted as a possible bride for Alexander. The humiliating treaty of Norham in 1209 forced on an ill King William, who was threatened with invasion by John, not only obliged William to pay £10,000 and hand over thirteen hostages, but also gave John the authority to arrange the marriages of William's two daughters.[27] As we have seen, the intention was that one of the daughters would marry one of John's sons, while Alexander would marry one of John's as yet unborn daughters. A further treaty in 1212 agreed to the marriage of 14-year-old Alexander II to 2-year-old Joan. However, the agreement seems to have been made as a way of preventing Alexander from looking to the Continent – in particular, France – for a potential bride, and, by extension, allies. As early as 1200, when Alexander was only 2 years old, Philip II, King of France, promised his daughter, Marie, who was a similar age, 'in marriage to Alexander, the son of William, king of Scotland'.[28]

Nevertheless, this did not stop John from looking further afield for a more favourable marriage alliance for Joan. Nor did it stop Alexander II from siding with the barons against King John; Alexander was, in fact, one of the signatories of Magna Carta. As mentioned earlier, Clause 59 of the charter specifically refers to the return of the King of Scots' sisters and their fellow Scottish hostages and guarantees him the same privileges and rights as the other barons of England.[29] John later refused a proposal from his old ally, King Philip II of France, for Joan to marry Philip's son John, and settled instead, in 1214, for a marriage with his old enemies the de Lusignans. Joan was betrothed to Hugh X de Lusignan: Hugh was the son of John's rival for the hand of his wife Isabelle in 1200. Isabelle's engagement to Hugh IX was broken off in order for her to marry John.

Following the betrothal to Joan, Hugh, Lord of Lusignan and Count of La Marche, was given custody of the towns of Saintes, Saintonge and the Isle of Oleron as pledges for Joan's dowry. Left in the custody of her future husband's family when John returned to England, Joan was kept well away from the intrigues and crisis caused by her father's increasing tyranny in 1215. Her father's death in October 1216, however, did not dissolve the agreement with the Lusignans. In 1218, the widowed Isabelle d'Angoulême, having been given no role in the upbringing or governance of her young son, King Henry III, left England to go home to Angoulême, where she was countess in her own right. She may also have thought that she would be closer to Joan, now 8 years of age, and could supervise the arrangements for Joan's marriage to Hugh de Lusignan. Her four other children remained in England, supervised by guardians. Given her tender years, little Joan was still four years from the minimum age that it was permitted for girls to marry. In 1220, in a scandalous *volte-face*, Hugh repudiated Joan and married her mother, his father's former betrothed – so poor 9-year-old Joan's erstwhile future husband was now her stepfather.

Isabelle d'Angoulême wrote to her 12-year-old son, King Henry III, excusing her actions and saying Sir Hugh de Lusignan could not yet marry Joan, on account of her tender years, but was in desperate need of an heir. Isabelle claimed she married Hugh herself to prevent him looking to France for a suitable bride, and to safeguard the Plantagenet lands of Poitou and Gascony. The letter read:

> To her dearest son Henry, by the grace of God king of England, lord of Ireland, duke of Normandy and Aquitaine, count of Anjou, Isabella by that same grace queen of England, lady of Ireland, duchess of Normandy and Aquitaine, countess of Anjou and of Angoulême, sends health and her maternal benediction.
>
> We hereby signify to you that when the Counts of La Marche and Eu departed this life, the lord Hugh de Lusignan remained alone and without heirs in Poitou, and his friends would not permit that our daughter should be united to him in marriage, because her age is so tender, but counselled him to take a wife from whom he might speedily hope for an heir; and it was proposed that he should take a wife in France, which if he had done, all your land in Poitou and Gascony would be lost. We therefore, seeing the great peril that might accrue if that marriage should take place, when our counsellors

could give us no advice, ourselves married the said Hugh, count of March; and God knows that we did this rather for your benefit than our own. Wherefore we entreat you as our dear son, that this thing may be pleasing to you, seeing it conduces greatly to the profit of you and yours; we earnestly pray that you will restore to him his lawful right, that is, Niort, the castles of Exeter and Rockingham, and 3500 marks, which your father, our former husband, bequeathed to us; and so, if it please you, deal with him, who is so powerful, that he may not remain against you, since he can serve you well – for he is well-disposed to serve you faithfully with all his power; we are certain and undertake that he shall serve you well if you restore him to his rights, and, therefore, we advise that you take opportune counsel on these matters; and when it shall please you, you may send for our daughter, your sister, by a trusty messenger and your letters patent, and we will send her to you.[30]

However, instead of sending Joan back to England, as you might expect, the now 10-year-old princess went from being Hugh's betrothed to his prisoner. She was held hostage to ensure not only Hugh's continued control of her dower lands, but also the transfer of his new wife's dower as queen. At the same time, England was withholding Queen Isabelle's dower against the return of Joan and her dower lands. Negotiations to resolve the situation went on for several months. In the meantime, despite her captivity, Joan's older brother, Henry III, and his advisers were already looking to arrange a new marriage for her. On 15 June 1220, the conference in York, between Alexander II and Henry III, saw the Scots king agree to marry Joan, with a provision that he would marry Joan's younger sister, Isabella, if Joan was not returned to England in time. It was also agreed that Alexander's oldest sister Margaret would marry, not Henry III as had been agreed in the 1209 Treaty of Norham, but Hubert de Burgh, Henry's justiciar and chief adviser. On 3 October 1221, 'Hubert de Burgh justiciar of England married Margaret the sister of King Alexander in London on the Sunday after Michaelmas in the presence of Henry king of England, who gave her away at a gathering of the nobility of England.'[31]

In the end, when Joan was not returned in time for the original date set for the wedding, Alexander offered to wait for his bride, rather than risk the fledgling peace that had been established between the neighbouring countries.[32] Negotiations for Joan's return were long and difficult and not helped by the fact Hugh was threatening war in Poitou. Eventually, after papal intervention, agreement was reached in October 1220 and Joan was surrendered to the English. Joan and Alexander II were married on 19 June 1221, at York Minster. Joan was just weeks from her 11th birthday, while Alexander was 22. The Archbishop of York performed the ceremony, which was witnessed by Henry III and the great magnates of both realms. Henry III's Pipe Rolls suggest the wedding was followed by three days of celebrations, costing £100.[33] Talking of her wedding day, John of Fordun's *Chronicle of the Scottish Nation* recounted:

> the following year, after Whitsunday, Alexander, king of Scotland, in great state, and with a great bevy of knights, proceeded, again under a safe-conduct, to York, as had been agreed between those kings the year before; and, on the Friday before the Nativity of Saint John the Baptist, he was, to the great joy of both sides, betrothed to the English king's eldest sister, named Joan, as yet a girl of very tender age. And so our lord the king went safely home again with his betrothed, who, when she grew up, turned out very handsome, and comely, and beautiful.[34]

And the *Chronicle of Melrose* recorded:

> On the Saturday next before the feast of St. John the Baptist [19th June], our lord Alexander, the king of Scotland, married at York the daughter of John, and the sister of Henry, king of England; and after the nuptials had been celebrated with the exceeding splendour which was fitting such an occasion, he conducted her into Scotland, to the great joy of all the inhabitants of both kingdoms.[35]

The day before the wedding, Alexander had assigned dower estates to Joan, worth an annual income of £1,000, including Jedburgh, Crail and Kinghorn.[36] However, part of the dower was still held by Alexander's mother, the dowager queen Ermengarde, and Joan was not entitled to the income until after her mother-in-law's death in 1233. This left Joan financially dependent on Alexander from the beginning, a situation which mirrored that of her mother's marriage to King John and severely curbed Joan's independence, as it had her mother's. There is a suggestion that Joan was not enamoured with Scotland and its society, and that she found it difficult to settle into the Scottish court. We cannot know this for certain. However, we do know that she faced several challenges, not least of which was her age. Despite being married, Joan still had some growing up to do but her youth also meant that she did not have the maturity or experience to hold her own against her domineering mother-in-law. And, although she was given considerable leeway in the early years of her marriage, she was, eventually, hampered by the fact she failed to produce the desired heir. Joan's position was further hindered from time to time by tensions between her husband and brother.

In this, though, she seems to have found her purpose. Joan regularly acted as intermediary between the two kings. Alexander often used Joan's personal letters to her brother as a way of communicating with Henry on an unofficial level, bypassing the formality of official correspondence between kings. One such letter is a warning, possibly on behalf of Alexander's constable, Alan of Galloway, of intelligence that Haakon IV of Norway was intending to aid Hugh de Lacy in Ireland. In the same letter, Joan assured Henry that no one from Scotland would be going to Ireland to fight against Henry's interests.[37] Another letter, this time from Henry, was of a more personal nature; written in February 1235, it informed Joan of the marriage of their 'beloved sister' Isabella to the Holy Roman Emperor Frederick II, news at which he knew Joan 'would greatly rejoice'.[38] In December 1235, Alexander and Joan were summoned to London, possibly for the coronation of Henry's new queen, Eleanor of Provence. This would have been a long and arduous journey for the Scottish monarchs, especially in the deepest part of winter.

Although she was never given a place in her husband's councils, as Ermengarde had been accorded by King William, Henry's use of his sister as an intermediary suggests she did have some influence over Alexander; this theory is supported by the fact that Joan accompanied Alexander to negotiations with the English king at Newcastle in September 1236 and again at York in September 1237. Henry was keen to establish a permanent peace on his northern border, though on England's terms. In 1234, Henry had granted Joan the manor of Fenstanton in Huntingdonshire, and during the 1236 negotiations she was granted that of Driffield in Yorkshire, thus giving Joan an income independent of Scotland.[39] Many have seen this as an indication that Joan was intending to spend more time in England and the thirteenth-century chronicler Matthew Paris hints at an estrangement between Joan and Alexander, although we cannot be certain.[40] The 1236 and 1237 councils were attempts at resolving the ongoing claims by Alexander that King John had agreed to gift Northumberland to him as part of the marriage contract between Alexander and Joan. Henry, of course, denied this. With the mediation of a papal legate, agreement was eventually reached in York at the 1237 council, with both queens, Joan and Eleanor of Provence, present. Alexander gave up the claim to Northumberland in return for lands in the northern counties with an annual income of £200.[41]

Following the summit, as her husband returned to his Scottish kingdom, Joan travelled south:

> In 1237 the kings Henry and Alexander met at York on St Maurice's Day with their queens and magnates of both kingdoms. They negotiated there on difficult business of the kingdoms for fifteen days in the presence of Otto the legate of the lord pope. Once the negotiations were complete, the king of Scotland returned home safely; but the queen of Scotland went to Canterbury with the queen of England on a pious exercise, and died near London in the following year on 4 March in the arms of Henry king of England and Richard [earl] of Cornwall the said queen's brothers. They arranged for her body to be honourably buried in the church of the nuns of Tarrant.[42]

Travelling with her sister-in-law, Eleanor of Provence, Joan's pilgrimage to the shrine of Saint Thomas Becket at Canterbury could have been for a number of reasons. Given that Joan was now 27 and Eleanor already married for two years, and neither had yet borne a child, it is possible that both women were praying for an heir to their respective husbands' thrones. Joan may also have been already in the early stages of her final illness. She stayed in England for the rest of the year, spending time with her brothers, Henry and Richard, Earl of Cornwall. Much of the stay seems to have been informal and pleasurable. Joan spent Christmas at Henry's court and was given new robes for herself, her clerks and servants, in addition to gifts of deer and wine. Her sister Eleanor, Countess of Pembroke, widow of William II Marshal and future wife of Simon de Montfort, was present, with their niece the Countess of Chester and their cousin, the captive Eleanor of Brittany. In late January, arrangements were made for Joan's return to Scotland, but she fell ill before she could travel north. Only 27 years of age, Joan died on 4 March 1238 at Havering-atte-Bower in Essex. Her brothers were at her side. Before her death, she had had time to get her affairs in order, as testified by the rolls of Henry III:

> 1238. 18 March. Sandleford. The king has granted to J. queen of Scots while she lives that if she happens to die, her executors may hold in their hands the manors of Driffield and Fenstanton for two years from Michaelmas in the twenty-second year, in order to make execution of [the testament] of the aforesaid queen as would seem best for the king, so that they would hold those manors in their hand, as has been agreed between the king and the aforesaid executors, by a certain price. Order to Robert of Crepping to take the manor of Driffield into the king's hand and keep it safely until the king orders otherwise, saving to the aforesaid executors the corn in the land, rent of assise and all stock found in the same manor up to Michaelmas in the twenty-second year.[43]

According to Matthew Paris, 'her death was grievous, however she merited less mourning, because she refused to return [to Scotland] although often summoned back by her husband'.[44] Paris's observation does not take note of the fact Joan was planning her return to Scotland when she fell ill, nor that she would have had a difficult journey, had she returned north over the winter months. And just because the King and Queen of Scots were in two different countries when Joan died, we cannot infer that the couple had officially, or unofficially, separated. There is no record to say, either way. The *Chronicle of Melrose* recorded their queen's death:

> The lady Johanna, queen of Scotland, was attacked by a severe illness when in the neighbourhood of London,-where she died, on the 4th of the nones of March [4 March], in the arms of her brothers Henry, king of England, and Richard, duke of Cornwall, after having received the sacraments of the church. She died childless. Her brothers buried her

body, with great grief and with equal magnificence, in the church of the nuns of Tarent.[45]

Joan's will requested that she be buried at the Cistercian nunnery of Tarrant in Dorset. The convent benefited greatly from Henry III's almsgiving for the soul of his sister; in 1252, more than thirteen years after her death, the king ordered a marble effigy to be made for her tomb. The memorial did not survive the upheaval of the Reformation of the sixteenth century.

The debacle of Joan's betrothal and imprisonment by Hugh de Lusignan, and her apparently unhappy marriage to Alexander II, are prime examples of the lot of a Plantagenet princess. She was too young to have any influence when Magna Carta was issued, but her husband had been a part of its creation, although it seems to have had little relevance to her as an English princess and Scottish queen. However, Joan rose above her marriages and found a purpose in her pursuit of peace between England and Scotland. She was a conduit to maintaining communications, even when relations were tense. Joan was also lucky to enjoy a happy, close relationship with her siblings, especially her brothers, Henry III and Richard, Earl of Cornwall, although once she married, she seems to have had little contact with her mother, Isabelle d'Angoulême, hundreds of miles away in France and with her new Lusignan family to concentrate on.

We do not know the depths of Alexander's grief for his wife, or if he grieved for her at all. They had been married for sixteen years, but there is no record that Joan had ever fallen pregnant. The King of Scots was approaching his 40th birthday and had one child, a daughter named Marjory who would marry Alan Durward, one of the leading members of his administration after 1244.[46] But Marjory was a girl, and illegitimate, and Alexander needed a son and heir. Worse, the king had no surviving close male relative who could succeed. His uncle, Earl David, his father's youngest brother, had died in 1219 and David's son, John the Scot, had died in 1237. John had inherited the earldom of Chester through his mother and was married to Elen, daughter of Llywellyn the Great by King John's illegitimate daughter, Joanna, Lady of Wales. Although they had been married for fifteen years, the couple was childless at John's death, aged only 30. Alexander recognised his cousin, Robert de Brus, lord of Annandale, as heir presumptive, while at the same time beginning the search for a new wife.

As yet, King Henry III had no daughters and his surviving sisters were both married, Isabella to the Holy Roman Emperor and Eleanor had secretly married Simon de Montfort at the beginning of the year. As a result, Alexander would have to look elsewhere for a bride, and he did not seek Henry III's approval of his final choice; the King of England was no longer the overlord of the Scots king. That he looked to France, England's old enemy, would bring Scotland and England to the brink of war, the situation exacerbated by a feud that had erupted among the nobility of Scotland.[47] Alexander II married again just over a year after Joan's death. His bride was Marie de Coucy, the elder daughter of Enguerrand (III) de

Coucy and his third wife, Marie de Montmirail. Known as 'the Great', Enguerrand was lord of Coucy, in Picardy, and a great-grandson of King Louis VI of France.[48] Matthew Paris admired Marie for her beauty.[49] Aged about 20, with a high social standing and considerable wealth, Marie was a suitable match for Alexander. The union harked back to the Franco–Scottish alliance of 1216–1217, when a teenage Alexander had supported the invasion of England by Louis, the eldest son of Philip II of France. It may even be that Alexander had met his future father-in-law, Enguerrand de Coucy, when he visited Louis in Dover. The Chronicle of Melrose recorded the event: 'Alexander, the most noble king of Scotland, took to wife the lady Mary, the daughter of the illustrious Ingeran [sic] de Cuchi, on the ides of May [15 May], being Whitsunday, at Roxburgh.'[50] As did John of Fordun in his *Chronicle of the Scottish Nation*:

> As, therefore, the king had begotten of her [Joan] neither son nor daughter, he, on Whitsunday, the 15th of May 1239, by the advice of his lords, took to wife, at Roxburgh, the daughter of a nobleman, Ingram [sic] of Coucy. This lady was named Mary; and of her the king begat a son on whom the father's name was bestowed. So Alexander, the first-born of the king of Scotland, was born at Roxburgh, on the day of St. Cuthbert's translation, Wednesday, the 4th of September, when his father was beginning the forty-fourth year of his age, and was well-nigh at the end of the twenty-seventh of his reign.[51]

The wedding had taken place just fourteen months after the death of Queen Joan and the wait for a royal heir ended two years later, when Queen Marie was safely delivered of a son, also named Alexander:

> 1241: In this same year, the eldest child of our lord Alexander, king of Scotland, was born at Roxburgh, on the day of the translation of St. Cuthbert, the day before the nones of September [Wednesday, 4 Sept.], being the fourth day of the week, and the child was named Alexander. He was born in the commencement of the forty-fourth year of the age of his father; the twenty-seventh year of his reign then drawing towards its conclusion.[52]

In providing King Alexander II with a son and heir, Marie had achieved her primary purpose as the king's wife. She had secured the succession. There is thought to have also been a short-lived daughter, named Ermengarde, after Alexander's mother.[53] To have only one surviving child was a precarious situation, but it would not matter if the prince survived the perils of childhood. It is difficult to assess the extent of Marie's influence on Scottish culture and politics, beyond her position as the king's wife and mother of the heir. She arrived in Scotland with 'an impressive train of followers', though most would have returned to France after the wedding.[54] Her chancellor, Master Richard Vermand, may have accompanied her from home, his possible origin being from Vermand, near Coucy.[55] Marie's nephew, Enguerrand de Guines, became an influential Scottish magnate, marrying Christiana de Lindsay in about 1280. He would succeed as lord of Coucy in 1311.[56]

Relations with England remained tense, but in 1242, in advance of his expedition to Poitou, Henry III had finally relinquished to Alexander the northern manors agreed on in the treaty of 1237. The two kings had also made a provisional agreement on the marriage of the infant prince, Alexander, with Henry's 2-year-old daughter, Margaret.[57] Good relations between the two kings were restored, but only for a short time. It all started with an internal feud in Scotland,

> while King Alexander was visiting Moray with the queen, news came of the arrival home of the king of England from overseas, and they hurried in the direction of that king. On meeting King Alexander that noble officer [Walter] Bisset put extreme pressure on him to spend two nights with him at his castle of Aboyne. The king stayed with him for only one night; but the same [Walter] with the lord king's permission remained in the company of the lady queen for four nights.[58]

Alexander moved on to Haddington, where the 'nobles, magnates and knights' had gathered for a tournament at the end of which Patrick, the claimant to the earldom of Athol, died in suspicious circumstances.[59] The house in which Patrick was lodging was burnt to the ground, with him in it. Patrick, Earl of Dunbar, along with the Comyns, accused Walter Bisset, lord of Aboyne, and his nephew, John, of the murder. According to Bower, Bisset had an alibi. He was with the queen:

> Many blamed [Walter] Bisset for this crime. But how could he be involved in that crime on that night when he had to look after the queen at his castle of Aboyne? Since many people say many things, some say that he was not there in his own person, but his equipment and knights and all his armed strength were there with his knowledge. But the queen was ready to take an oath that the said Sir [Walter] was never inclined to attempt such a horrific act. 'Rare therefore is the trust which should be invoked' etc. The same [Walter] Bisset had all those who took part in and were responsible for this conflagration excommunicated in his own chapel and in all the churches of Scotland with the lighting and extinguishing of candles. In addition he asked the lord bishop of Aberdeen to publish the said sentence in [all] the churches located in his diocese, and that on the same day the bishop would confirm it. And this was done.[60]

Wyntoun suggests that the queen had already left Bisset's residence by the time of the murder, 'The Qwene syne to Forfare rade.'[61] Despite the support of the king and queen, Bisset's protestations of innocence were not enough. He and his nephew were outlawed from Scotland and took a vow to depart for the Holy Land and remain there for the rest of their lives. However, the Bissets did not travel so far and only fled to the court of Henry III, who also appears to have been unconvinced of their guilt. John became one of the king's household knights. As the *Chronicle of Melrose* put it, 'the accursed traitor Walter Biset and his accomplices ceased not to pour into the ears of Henry, king of England, the poison of discord'.[62] Apparently, they complained vociferously to Henry III of their treatment and accused Alexander of harbouring King Henry's enemies, fortifying castles along the Anglo-Scottish border, including Hermitage Castle in Liddesdale. They also claimed Alexander was making an alliance with King Louis IX of France, and planning with Earl Patrick of Dunbar to invade England.[63] In the midst of all this, the queen suffered a personal tragedy. Her father was killed in a rather bizarre riding accident. As Enguerrand de Coucy was crossing

> a certain ford, his horse's foot struck upon some obstacle; and he fell backwards into the depths, [into which however he was dragged by his own stirrup with violence and disastrous result.] And as he fell headlong his sword slipped from the sheath and transfixed his body. And so submerged and pierced and torn by the sword he departed from this temporal light to gather the fruit of his ways.[64]

The business of state must go on, however, and Enguerrand's successor 'John, his son and sole heir, for love of the queen of Scotland his sister afforded aid, as was said above, and counsel to the king of Scotland.'[65]

The King of England decided he must act:

> Having got together a numerous army, Henry, king of England, came to Newcastle-upon-Tyne, to wage war against Alexander, king of Scotland, forasmuch as a certain castle, which is called Hermitage (at Castleton), had been reared by the Scots, in the marches between Scotland and England, in Liddesdale. So King Alexander, with his army well equipped, went to meet him, as far as Caldwell, where all the chiefs renewed their fealty to our lord the king; and thus, all of one mind, they marched on as far as Pentland, ready to come to blows with the king of England, if he should enter Lothian. But, at the instance of the Archbishop of York, and other great men, peace was restored between the kings; and the king of Scotland sped safely home again.[66]

The King of England mustered a considerable army, consisting of up to 1,200 knights, while Alexander had only 500 knights but a substantial force of foot soldiers. In the event, war was averted thanks to the diplomatic skills of Richard, Earl of Cornwall, and the Archbishop of York. In the subsequent peace settlement, Alexander recognised Henry as his liege lord, but only for the lands he held personally in England, not for Scotland. He did, however, promise that neither he nor his heirs would make war on England, nor damage it by making a treaty with England's enemies. Henry, on his part, agreed that the King of Scots could contract marriages where he pleased, without the endorsement of England's king. Moreover, Henry promised not to make war on Scotland. The treaty acknowledged and confirmed Scotland's independence. It also confirmed the future marriage of Alexander's son and heir with Henry's daughter.[67] The Bissets did not recover their Scottish lands and would remain dependent on Henry's patronage.

With peace with England restored, King Alexander returned to Scotland. In 1249, he decided to mount a naval expedition to the Hebrides. Alexander had offered to buy the islands, which were in the hands of Haakon IV, King of Norway, in 1244, but was refused. The Scots king's mounting suspicion of the MacDougalls, who were vassals of both Scotland and Norway, was countered with the naval expedition cruising the waters of the Inner Hebrides. In July 1249, the ships were moored in Oban Bay, off the island of Kerrera, when

> the illustrious king of the Scots, was seized with a severe illness while he was on his journey to the parts of Argyll, and was carried to the island of Cerverei, where (after he had received the sacraments of the church) his happy spirit was removed from this world, and associated with all the saints in heaven, as we trust. But as for his body, it was removed to the church of Melrose (as he had himself given directions in his lifetime), and was there committed to the bosom of the earth as befitted a-king. At the time of his death he was in his fifty-first year, and in the thirty-fifth year of his reign; he died on the fifth day of the week, on the eighth of the ides of July, [Thursday, 8 July], leaving his kingdom to his son Alexander, a boy nearly eight years old, who, according to the custom of the kingdom, was appointed king, and placed upon his father's throne by the nobility on the third of the ides of July [13 July], and was honoured by all as the lawful heir.[68]

The chronicler John of Fordun further provided an assessment of Alexander in his recording of the king's death:

> That renowned king of Scots, Alexander ii., while he was on his way to restore peace to the land of Argyll, was overtaken by grievous sickness, and carried across to an island which is called Kerneray (Kerrera); and there, in the year 1249, after he had partaken of the sacraments of eternal salvation, his blissful soul was snatched

away from this life, and joined – as we believe – all the saints in the heavens. But his body was brought down to the church of Melrose, as he himself had willed in his lifetime; and after the obsequies due had been solemnly celebrated, after the manner of kings, it was there committed to the bosom of the earth, on Thursday, the 8th of July, about the ninth hour, in the fifty-first year of his age, and the thirty-fifth of his reign – for he was sixteen years and a half old when he was made king. While he lived, he was a most gentle prince towards his people, a father to the monks, the comforter of the needy, the helper of the fatherless, the pitiful hearer and most righteous judge of the widow and all who had a grievance, and, towards the church of Christ, a second Peter.[69]

Where Queen Marie was at the time of her husband's death is unknown. It is unlikely that she was with her husband while he was on a military campaign, so she was probably in one of the royal residences further south, in the company of her 7-year-old son, when the news reached her. The queen ensured that the young prince was taken to Scone immediately for his inauguration as King Alexander III. As the child arrived at Scone, arguments erupted among the magnates about the order of ceremonies, whereby many thought that the king had to be knighted before his inauguration, 'because the lord Alan Dorwart [Durward], then justiciary of the whole of Scotland, wished to gird Alexander with the sword of knighthood on that day'.[70] Others argued against any delay in consecrating the new king, and feared that 'a country without a king was, beyond a doubt, like a ship amid the waves of the sea, without rower or steersman'.[71] It was decided, therefore, to proceed with the coronation and confer the knighthood on the king at a later date and so the barons and prelates

led Alexander, soon to be their king, up to the cross which stands in the graveyard, at the east end of the church. There they set him on the royal throne, which was decked with silken cloths inwoven with gold; and the bishop of Saint Andrews, assisted by the rest, consecrated him king, as was meet. So the king sat down upon the royal throne – that is, the stone – while the earls and other nobles, on bended knee, strewed their garments under his feet, before the stone. Now, this stone is reverently kept in that same monastery, for the consecration of the kings of Albania; and no king was ever wont to reign in Scotland, unless he had first, on receiving the name of king, sat upon this stone at Scone, which, by the kings of old, had been appointed the capital of Albania.[72]

The ceremony over, 'a highland Scot suddenly fell on his knees before the throne, and, bowing his head, hailed the king in his mother tongue' and proceeded to recite the young king's genealogy back through all the generations.[73]

Queen Marie was given no significant role during the minority of her son. As queen mother, she was assigned a third of Scottish royal revenues, according to Matthew Paris, who estimated her share as between 4,000 and 7,000 marks a year.[74] On 19 June 1250, she was at Dunfermline Abbey with her son to mark the canonisation of St Margaret, the eleventh-century Queen of Scots, and witness the translation of her remains to a new shrine, joining in the celebrations that accompanied the event:

> Again, in the second year of King Alexander iii., on the 19th of June 1250, this king, and the queen his mother, with bishops and abbots, earls and barons, and other good men, both clerics and laymen, in great numbers, met at Dunfermline, and took up, in great state, the bones of the blessed Margaret, sometime queen of Scots, out of the stone monument where they had lain through a long course of years; and these they laid, with the deepest devoutness, in a shrine of deal, set with gold and precious stones.[75]

King Alexander and a group of

> companions chosen for this purpose, lifted up the casket containing the bones of the king along with that, now raised, which held the remains of the queen, without expending any effort or encountering any obstacle. They solemnly placed both coffins in tombs which had been decked out elegantly for that purpose, as the congregation sang and a choir of prelates followed in solemn procession, on 19 June.[76]

The kings of Scotland and England met at York for the Christmas period, where

> all things were happily settled, even as they had before been arranged; while the kings and the lords of both kingdoms swore, with their hands upon the most holy Gospels, that they should thenceforth be faithfully kept. Never did any of the English or British kings, in any past time, keep his pledges towards the Scots more faithfully or more steadfastly than this Henry; for, nearly the whole time of his reign, he was looked upon by the kings of Scotland, father and son, as their most faithful neighbour and adviser; – a thing which never, or seldom, had happened, save in the days – alas! so few – of Richard Coeur de Lion.'[77]

In October 1250, Queen Marie had crossed to France, where she had inherited property from her father, 'for the sake of visiting her country and her relatives'.[78] Before her departure, she

> came to the lord king to salute him, he enriched her with many honours and gifts, even as it is the king's custom to afford to all

91

foreigners gifts and honour; and requested her to return without interval of delay when she should be called to the wedding of her son Alexander the second [sic] whom the nobles of Scotland had raised to the throne.[79]

She was back in England the following year, with a large retinue accompanying her, to attend the wedding of her son to Margaret of England, at York on 26 December 1251. She was present, therefore, when

> Alexander, king of Scotland, therefore, a boy of nine, there received the honour of knighthood at the hands of Henry, king of England, on Christmas Day, amid the greatest joy and good wishes of the lords of either kingdom; and, on the morrow – that is, on Saint Stephen's Day – the king of England gave his first-born daughter, named Margaret, in marriage to the king of Scotland.[80]

Twenty new knights were made alongside the young king on Christmas Day, they 'were all decorated with choice and costly robes, as was fitting in a so renowned noviciate'.[81] Attending the King of Scots was

> the queen, his mother, called for this from foreign parts; and many nobles accompanied her, not of Scotland only, but also many from France, whence she took her origin. For she had obtained, as is the custom for widows, the third part of the revenues of the kingdom of Scotland, amounting to four thousand marks and more, besides other possessions which she had received from the gift of her father Engelram [sic]; and she proceeded exceedingly loftily with a magnificent and numerous retinue.[82]

The wedding ceremony was conducted on St Stephen's Day, the day after Christmas and 'because the people hurrying in troops and masses crushed one another inordinately that they might be present and see the celebration of such nuptials, the celebration of marriage was performed in the earliest morning, secretly and before the expected time'.[83] The whole event must have been spectacularly extravagant and colourful:

> For a thousand knights and more appeared there on behalf of the English king at the wedding clothed in silk and, to speak in the vulgar tongue, in *cointisse*. And on the morrow they threw all those aside, and presented themselves at court in new robes. And on behalf of the king of Scotland sixty knights and more, and many the equivalent of knights, adorned with sufficient appropriateness, presented themselves there to the gaze of all.[84]

With her young son now married, and no role in the governance of Scotland, Marie would divide her time between Scotland and France. In 1250, her brother Ralph died on crusade, leaving the lordship of Coucy in the hands of his younger brother, Enguerrand. The succession of her second brother, whilst still a boy, and his subsequent imprisonment by King Louis IX, in 1256, occupied Marie's attention for some time. It was perhaps in order to appease Louis that Marie agreed to marry Jean de Brienne, the Grand Butler of France. Jean's father had been crowned king of Jerusalem in 1210 and emperor of Constantinople in 1231.[85] Raised at the French court, with King Louis and his brothers, Jean was a widower, his first wife having died in 1252, and bore the lofty but empty title of King of Acre.[86] News of the marriage annoyed Henry III, who did not want to see even more French influence over Scotland. When Marie and Jean sought a safe conduct from the English king, to travel through England into Scotland, Henry insisted that they swear an oath not to harm him or the kingdom. They returned to Scotland in 1257 and both were appointed to the ruling council in 1258, though with limited influence. During this stay, the queen received a regrant of all her jointure lands, guaranteeing that her Scottish revenues were secure. There is a suggestion that Marie and Jean had a daughter, Blanche, by some sources, but this is far from certain.[87]

Marie separated from Jean in 1268 and returned to Scotland:

> Mary the mother of King Alexander, wife of John d'Acre, fled from her husband and came to Scotland from overseas. At length John bishop of Glasgow made peace between them at the insistence of the king of Scotland, who had written to the husband saying that he would himself receive 500 marks from her dower in Scotland every year, while she might remain in Scotland.[88]

Her son, who was now 27 and with children of his own, secured an agreement for her to remain in Scotland at her pleasure, assigning Jean de Brienne an annual pension of 500 merks from her dower.[89] In 1276, she was again granted a safe conduct from England, this time to visit the shrine of St Thomas Becket, just as her predecessor, Queen Joan, had done in 1237. Queen Marie may have known of her son's plans for his second marriage, and even helped with the initial negotiations, to Yolande de Dreux, in October 1285. But she did not live to witness the nuptials, dying that summer. She was buried at Newbattle Abbey, in a tomb she had already had prepared for her remains. The dowager queen was in her 60s.

It is hard to assess the extent of Queen Marie's influence on Scotland, beyond the fact she gave the country its much-needed son and heir. Although she had only been Scotland's queen for a decade, she enjoyed considerable prestige, primarily because of her French connections but in part as a result of her own personality. She was present at the big moments in her son's life, such as his wedding day, and in the life of Scotland, especially the translation of the relics of St Margaret and her husband, Malcolm III, into their new tomb at Dunfermline Abbey. Marie's marriage, however, had caused tensions with England. The fact these tensions had been overcome without bloodshed was a testament to the strong relationship Alexander II and Henry III had built up during the lifetime of Queen Joan, and the inclinations of both kings towards peace between the nations. These familial links were strengthened further by the marriage of Marie's son, Alexander III, to Henry's daughter Margaret. The two unions with England resulted in over seventy years of peaceful relations between the two countries, even if they were sometimes tense.

Chapter Six

An Enduring Peace

lexander III was only two months shy of his 8th birthday when he became King of Scots in 1249. He was inaugurated as king on 13 July 1249, five days after his father's death. As his father had repeatedly failed to get the pope to agree to Scottish kings being anointed with holy oil, the young king was inaugurated in the same ceremony as his predecessors, enthroned on the ancient 'Stone of Destiny', consecrated, and invested with a mantle, with his genealogy proclaimed by a Gaelic bard. Afterwards, the magnates of the kingdom made their obeisances to their new king.[1] The arrangements for the ceremony were not without dispute, with Alan Durward insisting on the right to knight the young king before he was crowned, while others argued that the priority was to crown the child and the knighthood could come later; a kingdom without a king was like a ship without a rudder. Durward was defeated and the young king was installed without first being knighted. The ceremony ended with the recitation of King Alexander's illustrious heritage:

> There suddenly appeared a venerable, grey-haired figure, an elderly Scot. Though a wild highlander he was honourably attired after his own fashion, clad in a scarlet robe. Bending his knee in a scrupulously correct manner and inclining his head, he greeted the king in his mother tongue, saying courteously: 'God bless the king of Albany, Alexander mac Alexander, mac William, mac Henry, mac David.' And so reciting the genealogy of the kings of Scots he kept on to the end. ... 'Hail Alexander, king of Scots, son of Alexander, son of William, son of Henry, son of David, son of Malcolm, son of Duncan, son of Bethoc, daughter of Malcolm, son of Kenneth, son of [Malcolm, son of Donald, son of Constantine, son of Kenneth, son of] Alpin, son of Eochaid [or Achay], son of Aed Find, son of Eochaid, son of Domnall Brecc, son of Eochaid Buide, son of Aedan, son of Gabran, son of Domangart, son of Fergus Mor, son of Erc, son of Eochaid Munremor, son of Engusafith, son of Fethelmech Aslingith, son of Enegussa Buchin, son of Fethelmech Romaich, son of Sencormach, son of Cruithlinch, son of Findachar, son of Akirkirre, son of Ecthach

Andoch, son of Fiachrach Catmail, son of Ecddach Ried, son of Coner, son of Mogolama, son of Lugchag Etholach, son of Corbre Crangring, son of Daradiomore, son of Corbre Findmor, son of Coneremor, son of Ederskeol, son of Ewen, son of Eliela, son of Iair, son of Dethach, son of Sin, son of Rosin, son of Ther, son of Rether, son of Rowem, son of Arindil, son of Mane, son of Fergus the first king of the Scots in Albany.'[2]

The problem facing Scotland in 1249 was that Alexander II had, apparently, made no provision for what would happen if he were to die before his son came of age. Malcolm IV had come to the throne at the age of 12 while Alexander II had been 16; neither had needed a regency, assuming full powers as king the moment they succeeded. Alexander III was still only 7 years old and in no way could be thought mature enough to rule without a regent or regency council. Scotland had never had a child-king. The laws of succession prior to the establishment of primogeniture, which was still in its infancy, had guaranteed that the crown would go to the senior adult male within the royal family. Now the crown passed from father to son, an adult succession could not be assured. And was not in this case. Although she must have been aware of Blanche of Castile assuming the regency for her young son, Louis IX, in France in 1226, there is no evidence that Marie de Coucy sought, or was offered, the regency in Scotland.[3] Initially, it appears that most of the officers appointed by Alexander II continued their duties into the reign of Alexander III; there was no clean sweep of officials in the new administration. The leading magnates distributed the responsibilities of regency amongst themselves. The Scots appear to have more closely followed the recent example of England following King John's sudden death in 1216 and the subsequent long minority of Henry III, who was only 9 at his father's death.

This first regency government continued for two and a half years. Royal acts were issued under a new great seal and a special seal for the king's minority.[4] Though not the most senior in rank, Alan Durward's position as justiciar, and husband of Alexander's half-sister, may have put him in a position to lead the regency council, even if he was not sole regent. It is possible that Durward pushed for the right to knight the young king in order to set himself above the other magnates with whom he shared power.[5] After all, William Marshal had knighted 9-year-old Henry III before his coronation, and then taken up the regency of the kingdom. Durward was opposed by Walter Comyn, Earl of Menteith, who led the rising Comyn faction, excluded from the government between 1249 and 1251, though they did appear as witnesses on thirteen of the acts done in the king's name in that time. Alexander II may have left an effective administration in place for his son, but it was not without its challenges and excluding the Comyns – the faction who had brought down the Bissets – meant that he did not leave a united country. Among the magnates, there were two clearly defined camps, the Dunbars and the Comyns. Alan Durward and his fellow justiciar, David de Lindsay, were not allied to either faction. Durward had been strong enough to orchestrate the return of the Bissets to Scotland in late 1249 and, as justiciar, was able to keep the Comyns in order, at least for a time. Henry III did not interfere with the regency arrangements across the border, perhaps suggesting that he was content, for now, with the establishment and composition of the regency council.

Young King Alexander's marriage had been arranged when he was still in the cradle. In 1242,

> And while these things took place ... and good-will was restored both on the part of the king of England and on the part of the king of Scotland, betrothal was celebrated between Alexander, first-born son of the king of Scotland, and Margaret, daughter of the king of the English, by intermediation of the lord [bishop] of Durham, that in the king's absence the kingdom might be more firmly established.[6]

By 1251, the regency government was having trouble containing the excesses of the Comyn family and their adherents. They failed to prevent their attacks on churches and other lands. Henry was already unhappy with the Durward administration, which had revived the appeal to the papacy to allow for an anointing ceremony to be included in the coronation and was also asking for Scottish church taxes to go to Scottish crusaders, rather than Henry III's military enterprises. King Henry wanted not only a more effective government in Scotland, but one that was sympathetic to English interests. According to John of Fordun, 'the magnates of Scotland saw the danger in the country being under the governance of a boy king, and that his councillors, who were perhaps the greatest men of the whole kingdom, were swayed by the advantages each one had to gain.'[7] In order to avoid the dangers of the self-interested magnates, and on the advice of the clergy, an embassy was despatched

> to Henry, king of England, to the end that the treaty of peace formerly made between him and the late king Alexander might be renewed, and most firmly secured by an alliance through a marriage to be contracted between the young king Alexander and this same King Henry's daughter. So, when this embassy came to London, the king of England granted all their demands to their hearts' content.[8]

In return, Henry despatched his own embassy to Scotland, with an invitation, and safe conduct, for the young king, along with his advisers and magnates, to meet with him at York over Christmas 'in order to settle the aforesaid business'.[9] With the royal families of both Scotland and England staying at York Castle over the

Christmas period, the meeting between the two kings and their advisers resulted in everything being happily settled, at least to Henry's satisfaction. The kings and the lords of both kingdoms swore upon the most holy Gospels, to uphold the terms agreed upon. Negotiations were followed by the ceremonial:

> Alexander, king of Scotland, therefore, a boy of nine, there received the honour of knighthood at the hands of Henry, king of England, on Christmas Day, amid the greatest joy and good wishes of the lords of either kingdom; and, on the morrow – that is, on Saint Stephen's Day – the king of England gave his first-born daughter, named Margaret, in marriage to the king of Scotland.[10]

The wedding was conducted in York Minster early in the morning of 26 December, so as to minimise the danger caused by the vast crowds gathering to view the great magnates of the two kingdoms in all their finery. Matthew Paris records the splendour and extravagance of the wedding banquets:

> for the celebration of the nuptials as was fitting between so great personages. Now there had come together there an exceedingly numerous host both of the clergy and of the knighthood of either realm, that the serenity of so important nuptials might shine with greater lustre and extent.[11]

The accompanying feasts were bountiful and extravagant, as Paris reports:

> And if I should expound more fully the abounding diversity of the banquets, the variety of changed robes, the pleasure of the applauders of jesters, the great numbers of those at table together, the extravagant narrative would arouse derision in the ears and minds of those who were not there.[12]

Before returning home to Scotland, Henry agreed to pay Alexander 5,000 silver merks as Margaret's dowry.[13] For his part, King Alexander performed homage to Henry III for the lands he held from the English king, but when asked to perform homage for Scotland itself,

> the king of Scotland replied that he had come thither in peace and for the honour of the king of England, and by his command, to wit to be allied to him by mediation of a matrimonial alliance, and not to reply to him about so difficult a question. For he had not held full deliberation or suitable counsel concerning this with his chief men, as so difficult a matter demanded.[14]

Henry III apparently accepted the rejection with equanimity, for he

> refused to becloud with any commotion so placid a festival, or
> to distress a king so young and his younger spouse, especially as
> he had come when summoned as with the greatest joy to wed his
> daughter; but dissembled everything, passing it over for the time
> in silence.[15]

The celebrations ended in controversy when

> At this time Alan, the Doreward, and certain others were there
> accused to the king of Scotland, of an intention to betray him;
> whereupon many persons were compelled to resign their offices;
> and others, in the selfishness of their fear, consulted only their own
> safety, by basely returning homewards.[16]

According to the *Chronicle of Melrose*, the accusations arose out of a scheme
by Alan Durward to get the pope to legitimise the daughter he had by his wife,
Marjory, the young king's illegitimate half-sister. He 'and his accomplices, had
despatched messengers and presents to the pope'.[17] Had he succeeded, then it
would have meant 'that if any accident should happen to the king of Scotland,
they should succeed him in the kingdom as its lawful heirs. Had he succeeded
in this, he would without doubt have been a traitor towards the king and the
queen.'[18] According to John of Fordun, it was Robert, abbot of Dunfermline,
the king's chancellor, who 'was accused of intending to legitimate, by the great
seal, the king's illegitimate sister (namely, the wife of Alan, the Hostiary), so
that she might become the king's heiress in the succession to the throne'.[19]
Whatever the facts of the story, it was enough to cause the downfall of the
Durward administration. Now the father-in-law of the young Scottish king
Henry III intervened to reorganise the Scottish government, ousting Durward
and his friends and installing justiciars, a chamberlain and a chancellor who were
all Comyn adherents. The government had swung from one faction to the other
and one wonders if Henry should have taken a little time to investigate further
before choosing a side. The changes were done with the pretence that Alexander
had made the decision himself as the Scottish magnates acquiesced to Henry's
dispositions. Suggesting Alexander was perhaps more mature than you would
expect of a 10-year-old, John of Fordun reported that

> The king of Scotland, having, by the advice of the king and magnates
> of England, arranged and regulated everything with moderation,
> went home again with his consort, and, disguising his intentions,
> awaited better times for correcting excesses of this kind.[20]

The newly married children departed York for Scotland at the end of January, with little Queen Margaret, only a couple of months younger than her husband, bidding a no doubt tearful farewell to her parents.[21] They travelled by Berwick-on-Tweed to Roxburgh and onto Linlithgow, where they arrived in April 1252. From there, they moved on to Edinburgh Castle, which was to be the young couple's principal residence. The queen was also allotted two representatives, Robert de Noreis and Stephen Bauzan, to travel with her and look after her interests.[22] A doting father, Henry III had made provision for everything and on the return of the young king and his new queen to Scotland, their household was established along Henry's guidelines, the Scottish royal household becoming an extension of the English royal household.[23] There was frequent communication between the two households, with Henry appointing Robert de Ros, an Anglo-Scottish baron, as guardian to his daughter and son-in-law, with John de Balliol, another Anglo-Scottish baron, being appointed sometime later; de Noreis and Bauzan were recalled to England.[24] Such appointments mirrored Henry's only childhood under the tutelage of two baronial guardians. Queen Margaret's household was under the supervision of Mathilda de Cantiloupe, who was a widow of one of the stewards from King Henry's household.

Margaret was an unhappy little queen, suffering from homesickness for her family. It is hardly surprising. She was 10 years old, miles away from her family, friends and the life she had known. Everything was unfamiliar. She detested the grim fortress that was Edinburgh Castle and did not like the Scottish weather. She had grown fond of King Alexander but was kept apart from him most of the time, Robert de Ros having strict instructions that the couple were not to sleep together at such tender ages, it being considered detrimental to the health of both bride and groom. The child wrote miserable letters home to England, telling her mother and father of her unhappiness. Her parents petitioned for Margaret to be allowed to travel south to visit her mother, but the Scots refused to allow her to leave, presumably afraid that she would not be seen again if she were allowed to travel to England. In 1255, Margaret's mother, Eleanor of Provence, sent one of her own physicians to Scotland to visit her daughter. Reginald of Bath found the Scots queen to be pale and depressed, and

> when master Reginald had learned the troubles of her mind and
> body he severely reproved her guardians and magistrates. And after
> disputes and words of bitter altercation and even of threatening, he
> accused all the nobles of the king and queen and the guardians of the
> kingdom as being guilty of treason, convicted and menaced them.[25]

The unfortunate physician himself fell ill whilst in Scotland and barely had time to write to the queen of England before succumbing to his illness, saying

> that he had come thither under an inauspicious star; for he had
> seen that their daughter was unfaithfully and inhumanly treated

among those unworthy Scots, and because he had blamed them the Northerns had prepared for him snares of death.[26]

In the meantime, Alan Durward had recovered Henry III's favour as the political situation in Scotland was also deteriorating. Durward had answered the English king's call for aid in his military campaign in Aquitaine in 1254, also accompanying the future Edward I to Burgos in Castile, for his marriage to Eleanor of Castile. Actively speaking against the Scottish administration,

> not only did he recover the friendship of the king of England, but he became in turn the accuser of his accusers and their accomplices, before the king of England, in many points. Hereupon there arose a great dissension among the nobility of the kingdom of Scotland.[27]

The earl of Menteith and his allies had managed to alienate much of their support in Scotland. King Henry wrote to the earls of Dunbar, Strathearn and Carrick, demanding that the situation be resolved.

According to Matthew Paris, in his *Chronica majora*, an enraged King Henry sent more representatives north to ascertain what was going on in Scotland. This time it was Richard, earl of Gloucester, and John Mansel who arrived at Edinburgh Castle without any forewarning and apparently disguised as members of the household of Robert de Ros. Once inside, they were joined by their own retainers, a handful at a time, until their entire force was within the castle, and they no longer had to fear being overpowered. Queen Margaret met with the earl and Mansel

> with confidence, and complained grievously that she was unfitly guarded or rather imprisoned in that castle, a dreary and solitary place, wholly lacking wholesome air or verdure, as being near the sea. Nor was she permitted, so she said, to go about in her realm, or to keep a special household, or even the girls whom she desired to have, as attendants and chambermaids. Nor was the king her husband permitted to have conjugal access to her, or to rejoice in mutual embraces. And whether anything secret was added to her complaints is unknown.[28]

As Richard of Gloucester and John Mansel had been listening to the complaints of the Scots queen, Durward and the earl of Dunbar had staged a coup, seizing Edinburgh Castle, and therefore, taking custody of the king.[29]

> At the same time, while the king [of England] was daily more and more moved by complaints and importuned by communications from the queen of Scotland and her friends, he called together an

army and turned his reins and standards toward Scotland, intending to bring a serious charge against Robert de Ross and John Balliol, knights and men of great power and authority. For he was assured, so he asserted, by frequent secret communications from his vassals, that they had treated both the king and queen and the kingdom of Scotland otherwise than as was fitting and expedient.[30]

The continuing unrest among the factions in Scotland, added to the young queen's unhappiness, spurred Henry III into action. In August 1255, negotiations between all factions and the two kings resolved nothing, with the Comyns rejecting all proposals. Henry himself travelled north with his queen, staying at Wark on the Scottish border in September 1255. The new arrangements for the Scottish government were settled on or around 4 September, Alexander III's 14th birthday.[31] Durward and his supporters,

> taking the king and queen with them, went to meet the king of England at Wark, and after they had held a short and amicable preliminary conversation, the king of Scotland returned home the same day, but his queen remained there with her mother.[32]

The two royal couples were frequently in each other's company for the next two weeks, with only 9 miles separating the respective residences of the kings at Roxburgh and Wark. Margaret's younger sister, Beatrice, had also accompanied her parents and Queen Margaret spent some time at Morpeth with her mother and sister.[33] Henry was then invited to Roxburgh, where

> he was met by the king of Scotland, who received him with the greatest joy, and brought him into the church of Kelso with a great procession. Here, after having held a conference, he entrusted the king and the realm to the earl of Dunbar and his adherents, and so returned to his own country after a kingly banquet had been served.[34]

The Comyn faction had also sent representatives to the discussions at Kelso, but they refused to agree to a document prepared by the Dunbar faction. An assembly of seventeen lay and eight ecclesiastical magnates was formed to approve the appointment of a new council of fifteen established to rule Scotland for the remainder of the minority of the young king; until he was 21, in fact.[35] At the same time, King Alexander issued a declaration promising to treat Margaret 'with matrimonial affection and every consideration befitting our Queen and the daughter of so great a prince'.[36] Matthew Paris sums it up nicely:

> So everything being pacified and arranged to his wish, when the lord king of the English and the queen had had sufficient mutual

conference with the king of Scots and the queen their daughter the king hastened his return to the southern parts of England.[37]

It should come, perhaps, as no surprise that the new administration lasted barely two years. By 1257, we read that 'Walter Comyn earl of Menteith and his accomplices were frequently cited before King Alexander and his counsellors to answer many serious complaints, but did not appear.'[38] In early 1257, Queen Margaret received a visit from her brother, Edward, which must have been a pleasant interlude, considering the gathering storms. She and Alexander spent August in England, attending the festivities of the Feast of the Assumption at Woodstock before continuing on to London, where they were entertained by John Mansel.[39] That same October, Walter Comyn and his supporters 'seized the king at night as he lay asleep in bed at Kinross, and shamefully took him with them before dawn to Stirling on the morning after the feast of St Simon and St Jude in 1257. They also seized by force the king's great seal.'[40] Queen Margaret was also taken into custody, she was 'removed and guarded carefully, lest she should take after her father'.[41] According to Matthew Paris, they 'upbraided the queen moreover in that she had incited and summoned her father to come upon them as an enemy with his army, and do lamentable destruction'.[42] The growing political unrest in England, which was inexorably moving towards civil war in the contest between Henry III and Simon de Montfort, meant Henry was only able to aid his son-in-law in a limited capacity. However, Alexander III, now 16, was becoming increasingly independent and self-confident and himself summoned a parliament to meet at Stirling in mid-April 1258. It took months to hammer out a settlement, but by September a unified council was established, with four each from the Comyns and Durward, alongside the queen mother, Marie de Coucy, and her husband, Jean de Brienne, that survived until Alexander fully established his personal rule in 1260.[43] As the young king was becoming more confident, and growing into his authority, Alexander travelled to England. Alexander was able to press a beleaguered Henry III for payments of Queen Margaret's dowry amounting to some 4,000 marks – the payments being, by then, over nine years in arrears. Queen Margaret arrived a few days after her husband,

> very near to her confinement, coming for the sake of visiting the king and the queen and England, and, God willing, to be delivered there near to them. And she was conducted by the venerable man bishop [Henry] of Whithorn. And her younger brother Edmund met her; and she was received in formal procession at St. Albans in the hour of vespers, and honourably entertained. In the morning she set out for London. – And when she was received, there were there at the same time three kings and as many queens: and who could without admiration think of their splendour and nobility? – And when the queen had been presented to her parents the bishop, loaded with

precious and diverse gifts, returned to Scotland as quickly as he could.[44]

Queen Margaret was five months pregnant when she left Scotland, and had not informed the Scots council of her condition before leaving for England, lest they insist that she stay in Scotland until after the birth.

Alexander III was not at Windsor for the birth of the baby. He had returned home from England in late 1260 to deal with the inheritance of the earldom of Menteith, in dispute following Earl Walter's death in 1258. As he hurried north, he left his wife in the capable hands of her mother at Windsor, but not before exacting a promise from King Henry that he would not try to keep the Scottish queen in England after the birth. Henry agreed that Margaret and the child would be returning home forty days after her safe delivery, or by Easter at the latest. The king also promised that should his daughter die in childbirth and the baby survive, he would send the babe to Scotland.[45] Queen Margaret was to remain at Windsor, where she spent Christmas with her parents and there awaited the birth of her first child, the heir to the Scottish throne, in February 1261.[46] The baby was a girl: 'That same year – on the last day of February, to wit – was born the king's first-born daughter, named Margaret, who was afterwards betrothed to the king of Norway.'[47] The little princess was christened on Easter Sunday, 24 April 1261, and she and her mother set off on their return journey to Scotland in late May.[48] Perhaps learning from the lessons of the very recent past, arrangements were made for a regency council of thirteen named bishops, earls and barons, should King Alexander die before the baby was brought to Scotland.

Alexander III's reign, once he reached his majority, saw a steady progress in growth, both, politically and economically, which rendered Scotland robust, stable, and flourishing as the century advanced. This was aided by Alexander's consolidation of the western boundaries of the country. The Western Isles had long owed their allegiance to Norway, rather than Scotland, though Alexander II had died during a campaign to bring them into the Scottish kingdom. In 1263, King Haakon IV of Norway arrived in the region 'with eight score war-ships, having on board 20,000 fighting men' and 'took the castles of Bothe (Bute) and Man, and sacked the churches along the sea-board'.[49] The Norwegian king raided into Lennox and Loch Lomond. Alexander III mustered his army and marched against the Norwegians, confronting them just as their fleet was driven ashore by storms. After the ensuing Battle of Largs, both sides claimed victory, but the Norwegians had lost heart and Haakon sailed north to Orkney, where he died in December. The failure of the campaign, combined with the submission to Alexander III of the King of Man, and the lack of enthusiasm for Norwegian rule demonstrated by the Western Isles, who had no wish to antagonise the Scottish crown, persuaded Magnus VI to negotiate for peace, it being agreed in 1266 in the form of the Treaty of Perth, 'which ceded the Western Isles to the Scottish crown in return for a down payment of 4000 merks, and an annual rent of 100 merks in perpetuity'.[50]

Whilst Alexander III was fulfilling his military duties as a king, Margaret was performing her primary duty as a queen. On 21 January 1264, she gave birth to a son, named after his father:

> In this year, upon the day of St. Agnes [21 Jan.], the queen of Scotland (being then at Jedburgh), gave birth to a son, who, at his father's desire, was named Alexander, when he was baptized by Gamelin, bishop of St. Andrew's. And it happened that on the same day upon which the king of Scotland was informed that God had given him a son, intelligence also arrived that the king of Norway was dead. Rejoiced by these twofold tidings of joy, the king gave thanks to God, who exalts the humble and humbles the proud.[51]

As the Scots rejoiced at the arrival of their prince, England was descending into civil war. King Henry and his son and heir, Lord Edward, were captured by the forces of Simon de Montfort, following their defeat in the battle of Lewes on 14 May 1264. De Montfort effectively became the ruler of England, for a time at least, until he was defeated and killed at the battle of Evesham on 4 August 1265. It must have been a worrying and stressful time for the Scots queen, her father and brother held captive while her mother travelled to France to elicit European aid for the struggle against de Montfort. As Edward was held in captivity, 'Oliver, the venerable abbot of Driburgh, was despatched to Edward, on the part of his sister, the queen of Scotland; and when his arrival was told to Simon, he conducted him into the presence of Edward.'[52] Unfortunately, we have no record of what was discussed in the meeting, though we can surmise that it was nothing dangerous as Simon de Montfort remained in the room all the time that Edward conversed with the abbot. Queen Margaret probably wanted to express her familial love and support to her brother. King Alexander sent practical support in the form of a contingent of Scottish knights, prior to Evesham. The King of Scotland

> from motives of sheer goodwill assigned three men from each hide to form an expedition to go to the aid of the king of England and his own kinsman [Prince] Edward. But when the downfall of Simon and his accomplices had become known, the Scots were generously sent away by the English prince and returned home.[53]

Lord Edward spent the next couple of years campaigning against the remnants of Simon de Montfort's forces and in 1267 was in Northumberland, where he captured John de Vescy at Alnwick Castle. Being so close to Scotland, it would have been remiss not to visit with his sister and brother-in-law. The family reunion appears to have been a happy one, as Edward 'turned aside to confer with the king of Scotland at Roxburgh. The king of Scotland and Queen Margaret, the sister of the said Edward, and almost the whole nobility of Scotland met him. After many expressions of joy and congratulation on both sides, they returned home happy.'[54] According to Bower, Edward was accompanied by Edmund and so the queen was reunited with both her brothers. It was a year for family reunions as 'Afterwards the king of Scotland, accompanied by the queen, went to York with a small select band of knights to console his father-in-law the king of England over his aforementioned tribulations and difficulties.'[55] The family gatherings continued as Christmas was spent at Berwick 'with almost all the magnates of his realm. Present also was Edmund, the younger son of the king of England, in order to have some talk with his sister the queen of Scots, and to provide companionship for the king of Scotland.'[56] The reunions continued into 1268, when Alexander's mother, Marie de Coucy, left her husband and returned to Scotland. The king arranged for her to remain in the country at her own pleasure, assigning her estranged husband an allowance from the dowager queen's revenues.[57] Two years later, in October 1269, Margaret and Alexander were visiting her parents in London. They accompanied Margaret's father and brothers, Edward and Edmund, to Westminster Abbey when the relics of St Edward the Confessor were translated to his new shrine at the heart of the remodelled abbey. Margaret was deeply affected by her father's death in 1272, her grief probably exacerbated by the fact she could not travel south to console her mother as she was pregnant. To add to her misery and stress, her brother Edward was taking part in the latest crusade, his wife Eleanor of Castile with him: 'Queen Margaret of Scotland, deeply distressed by her various trials, chiefly by the death of her father and by anxiety about the return of her brother.'[58] No more children were born to the couple in the 1260s, though it is possible that Margaret suffered one or more miscarriages in that time. Her next child was born nine years after the birth of Prince Alexander, on 20 March 1273. Margaret was now in her early 30s and the birth was a difficult one, from which she was slow to recover. The child, a boy named David, was said to be delicate.[59]

It was against this background of grief for her father, worry for her brothers – Edmund had accompanied Edward on crusade – and the trials of childbirth that a sad incident happened while Margaret was staying at Kinclaven Castle that summer. The *Chronicle of Lanercost* recites the lamentable tale. The queen

> went forth one beautiful evening after supper from Kinclavin to take the air on the banks of the Tay, accompanied by esquires and maidens, but in particular by her confessor, who related to me what took place. There was present among others a certain pompous esquire with his page, who had been recommended to him by his brother in the presence of his superiors. And as they were sitting under the brow of the bank, he [the esquire] went down to wash his hands, which he had soiled with clay in playing. As he stood thus bending over, one of the maids, prompted by the Queen, went up secretly and pushed him into the river-bed.
>
> 'What care I ?' cried he, enjoying the joke and taking it kindly, 'even were I further in, I know how to swim.'

Wading about thus in the channel, while the others applauded, he felt his body unexpectedly sucked into an eddy, and, though he shouted for help, there was none who would go to him except his little page-boy who was playing near at hand, and, hearing the clamour of the bystanders, rushed into the deep, and both were swallowed up in a moment before the eyes of all. Thus did the enemy of Simon and satellite of Satan, who declared that he had been the cause of that gallant knight's destruction, perish in sight of all; and the matron, led away unduly by affection for her parents, received rebuke for her selfish love, and showed herself before all men wounded to the heart by overpowering anguish.[60]

The unfortunate squire is said to have been given to Margaret as a gift from her brother, Edward, during his visit in 1267.[61] He claimed to be the one who had killed Simon de Montfort, with his own sword, during the battle of Evesham, renamed by many of the time as the Murder of Evesham. Maybe it was these claims that prompted the chronicler to call the young man 'pompous', seeing a certain justice in the squire's drowning. The same cannot be said for the poor, almost forgotten, young page who jumped in the river to try to save the young man. Queen Margaret was greatly distressed by the two deaths, probably compounding the grief over her father's loss. By referring to the queen's 'selfish love', the chronicler is making a veiled accusation that there was something more going on between Margaret and the unfortunate squire, but there is no suggestion anywhere else that Margaret was anything but loyal and devoted to her husband. Having just endured a difficult childbirth, one cannot imagine, either, that Margaret had the time or inclination to conduct a love affair with a lowly squire. Perhaps the Lanercost chronicler's imagination was running away with him somewhat?

Margaret's concerns for her brother, at least, proved to be unfounded. On hearing of his father's death, Edward, now King Edward I, left the Holy Land to return home. He took a rather leisurely and circuitous route, stopping on the Continent to visit his possessions there and depositing his toddler daughter, Joan of Acre, with her grandmother, Jeanne de Dammartin, Countess of Ponthieu, where the little princess was to be raised for the next few years. It had been intended that Edward's coronation would be held the Sunday after Easter, when 'Alexander king of Scots along with his wife and children was specially invited by Edward to be present at his coronation in London.'[62] The ceremony was delayed, however, by Edward holding a great council at Lyons. The English king finally landed at Dover on 2 August 1274 and on 19 August, Edward

was solemnly anointed and crowned on the 14th of the kalends of September by the Archbishop of Canterbury, Brother Robert of Kilwardby. The nobles of the land attended the ceremony with a countless multitude, redoubling the display of their magnificence in honour of the new king. But my lord Alexander King of Scotland, who attended with his consort and a train of his nobility, exceeded all others in lavish hospitality and gifts.[63]

Attending her brother's coronation was to be one of Margaret's last duties as queen and just six months later she fell seriously ill during a visit to Fife. At the age of just 34, 'on the 26th of February, the said queen of Scotland, Margaret, King Henry's daughter, and this King Edward's sister, died at the castle of Cupar, and was entombed beside King David, at Dunfermline.'[64] The chronicler of Lanercost wrote a moving tribute to the English princess who had been Queen of Scotland since the age of 10:

> She was a woman of great beauty, chastity, and humility – three [qualities] seldom united in one individual. When her strength was failing many abbots as well as bishops collected to visit her, to all of whom she refused entrance to her chamber; nor from the time that she had received all the sacraments from her confessor, a Minorite Friar, until her soul passed away, did she admit any other to discourse, unless perhaps her husband happened to be present. She left behind her three children – Alexander and David and a daughter Margaret, all of whom followed their mother in a short time, owing, it is believed, to the sin of their father.[65]

Queen Margaret did not live to see her daughter, Margaret, married to King Eric II of Norway, nor did she see her oldest son, Alexander, marry Margaret of Flanders on 14 November 1282 at Roxburgh. The wedding of the heir to the throne had been a magnificent affair:

> in this year Alexander the son of King Alexander III married the noble young daughter of the lord count of Flanders at Roxburgh on the Sunday next after the feast of St Martin in the Winter with the full approval of Flemish knights and ladies. Very many bishops of Scotland, abbots, earls and barons met here for the ceremony, and joyfully went on with the festivities for fifteen days after the marriage had been royally celebrated, after which they eventually returned home.[66]

It is, perhaps, a blessing that Queen Margaret did not live to see the deaths of all three of her children in a few short years. Prince David had always been a delicate child and died, at the tender age of 8 years, at Lindores in June 1281.[67] Wyntoun's chronicle recorded the event as 1280:

> A thowsand and twa hundyr yhere
> Foure scor oure tha to rekyn clere,

Lady Macbeth by Daniel Nikolaus Chodowiecki, 1778. (Rijksmuseum)

Genealogical Chronicle of the English Kings: Edmund II Ironside and his descendants, Edward the Exile, Edgar, Margaret (Queen of Scots) and Christine. (Courtesy of the British Library Catalogue of Illuminated Manuscripts)

Malcolm III and Margaret of Wessex, depicted in the Seton Armorial. (Public domain)

KING MALCVM CAMNOIR MARIIT SANCT
MERGRET OF DVNFERMLIN QVHA BVRE TO HIM
ANE SONE CALLIT EDVERD QVHILK SVCCEDIT TO
THE CROVN AND DEIT V OVT SVCCESSIOVN
GOTTIN OF HIS BODY AND EFTER SVCCEDIT
TO HIM KING ROBERT BRVCE NERREST TO
YE SAID EDVERD OF BLVDE

Malcolm III and Margaret of Wessex, depicted in the Forman Armorial. (Public domain)

Edinburgh Castle. (Daniel Gleave)

Above and left: Memorial to the 1138 Battle of the Standard, Northallerton; Ada de Warenne's marriage to Prince Henry of Scotland was one of the clauses of the subsequent Treaty of Durham. (Author's collection)

Queen Margaret, daughter of Henry III and first wife of Alexander III. (Courtesy of the British Library Catalogue of Illuminated Manuscripts)

Seal of Yolande de Dreux, Queen of Scots, Duchess of Brittany, 1263–1330. (Wikipedia)

Jedburgh Abbey, where Yolande married Alexander III. (Author's collection)

Melrose Abbey, burial place of Alexander II and Robert the Bruce's heart. (Author's collection)

Off Dawy, this thryd Alysawndrys sone,
Off this lyff all his dayis war done.
Dede he wes in to Stryvelyn,
And enteryd in Dunfermlyn.[68]

The young prince was buried among his ancestors in Dunfermline Abbey. His passing was lamented by John of Fordun as the beginning of Scotland's grief:

> David, moreover, had departed this life before him, at Strivelyn [Stirling] Castle, at the end of the month of June 1281, amid the deep wailing of all the Scots, and the still deeper wailing of the king; and he lies buried in the monastery of Dunfermline. His death was the beginning of Scotland's sorrows to come. Alas! woe worth the day, O Scotland! for, even though thou had known that so many days of mourning and tears were in store for thee, evils so great are hastening upon thee without fail. 'That, if thou knew, thou ne'er could think to bear them.'[69]

Margaret, the Scots king's oldest child, now queen of Norway, died in childbirth on 9 April 1283. Her surviving daughter, Margaret, was to be Alexander III's only grandchild and he had her recognised as his heir following the death of Prince Alexander on 28 January 1284, at Lindores Abbey, just one week after his 20th birthday, after 'a lingering illness, with which he suffered a degree of mental aberration'.[70] It had been such a short time since the young prince's wedding:

> But alas! this great joy [the prince's wedding] was, within a short time, followed by deep mourning. For this Alexander, this gallant youth, who, it was hoped, would have been the heir to the Scots throne, died, the next year, at Lindores, in the twentieth year of his age, and was buried at Dunfermline, amid the boundless grief of the whole people, the tears and groans of all the clergy, and the endless sobs of the king and the magnates.[71]

By April 1284, it was apparent that Prince Alexander's wife, Margaret, was not with child and provision was made for her as the Scottish prince's widow:

> Confirmation, addressed to Margaret, daughter of Guy, count of Flanders, widow of Alexander, eldest son of the king of Scotland, of the grant to her of a dower of 1300 marks, to be paid yearly on the first of August, from the revenues of Berwick, and 200 marks from his manor of Linlitheu, in the diocese of St. Andrews, which latter sum, if the manor could not produce it, was to be made up from Berwick.[72]

A delegation from Flanders arrived at the Scottish court to take Margaret home:

> Now after the death of Alexander the first-born son of the said [1284] King Alexander, four knights sent by the count of Flanders came to the lord king of Scotland so as to take the daughter of the said count, the widow of his recently deceased son Alexander, to her father. The king and his counsellors deliberated long on this and finally agreed that the said lady could return to her father without taking an oath of allegiance to the lord king for her dower. And so it was done, and returning home they were sent away with gifts.[73]

When Queen Margaret died, Alexander III showed no inclination to remarry, despite being only 34. He had three surviving children, two sons and a daughter, so the dynasty was secure. All that came crashing down with the successive deaths of all three of those children in such a short space of time. It must have been devastating for Alexander III, to see his entire family disappear like that, one after the other. However, he was king and had his country to think about, not just his own despair. In February 1284, Alexander had persuaded the magnates of Scotland to recognise his little granddaughter as his heir, but a son would always be preferable, and the Scottish king began the search for a new wife:

> Also in this year, that is ten years after the death of the queen, King Alexander, on the advice of his prelates and lords, sent a solemn embassy consisting of Thomas Charteris the chancellor, Patrick de Graham, William de Sinclair and John de Soules, knights, to seek out for him a spouse born of noble stock. After the feast of the Purification of Blessed Virgin they went off to France, whence they successfully brought home to Scotland Joleta or Yolanda, the most beautiful of ladies, a daughter of that noble man the count of Droco (or Dreux as it is commonly called), with great pomp and with an impressive escort of Frenchmen.[74]

It was his mother, Marie de Coucy, who found her son's bride, Yolande de Dreux, Countess of Montfort, though the dowager queen died before the wedding took place.[75] Yolande was Scotland's Queen Consort for only four months and fourteen days. In that short time, she carried the hope of a nation – and its king – to secure the Scottish succession.

Born into a cadet branch of the French royal family, probably sometime in the mid-1260s, Yolande's father was Robert IV, Count of Dreux, who died in 1282 and her mother was Beatrice de Montfort, who died in 1311. Beatrice was the daughter of Count Jean I de Montfort l'Amoury and his wife Jeanne de Chateaudun. Beatrice was therefore a great-great-niece of Simon de Montfort, Earl of Leicester, and heiress to the impressive de Montfort estates. She was also the stepdaughter of

Queen Marie's second husband, Jean de Brienne.[76] One of six children, Yolande had two brothers and three sisters. Little is known of Yolande's childhood but we can imagine that as a junior member of the Capetian dynasty, she grew up amidst some privilege and splendour. And whilst Yolande had been growing into adulthood, Scotland had been experiencing a 'golden age', a period of relative peace and prosperity. That peace and prosperity was now under threat with the uncertainty over the succession. The embassy sent in search of a bride for their king had the hopes of the entire nation on their shoulders. Their successful mission saw Yolande arrive in Scotland that same summer, accompanied by her brother John. The king and Yolande were married at Jedburgh, also known as Jedworth:

> *The Castle of Jedburgh* was of great antiquity, though the precise time of its erection, and the name of its original founder, are unknown; it was a place of much strength, and the favourite seat of Malcolm IV., who died here in 1165. It was the frequent residence, also, of many others of the kings, among whom were, William the Lion, Alexander II., and Alexander III., whose son, Alexander, was born here in 1263, and who, after the death of his children, celebrated in this castle, with unusual pomp, his subsequent marriage with Jolande, daughter of the Count de Dreux.[77]

Walter Bower, in his *Scotichronicon*, reflects the mood of celebration and hope that accompanied the lavish wedding and feasting:

> In 1285 Lord Alexander king of Scotland married Yolanda the daughter of the count of Dreux on the feast of St Callixtus pope and martyr. Very many nobles of France and Scotland along with an innumerable multitude of both sexes met for the ceremonial celebration of their wedding in royal fashion. After the wedding was over the French, gladdened by all sorts of gifts, returned home in good spirits, although a few remained behind with the queen.
>
> I cannot recall having read of such a famous feast ever before in Scotland. But alas! an unusual feast of this kind a short time later brought forth for the Scots a fast, or that herald of sickness, an insatiable hunger. In order that the place might grace the feast and the feast might harmonise with the place, they deliberately chose to celebrate the royal wedding at Jedwood. The said place is called after the river, which is the Jed, and the forest, which is 'wood' in our native language.[78]

Alexander and Yolande were married at Jedburgh Abbey, Roxburghshire, on 14 October 1285, the feast of St Calixtus, in front of a large congregation made up of Scottish and French nobles. Yolande was probably no more than 22 years of age, while Alexander was in his 44th year. The celebrations must have been magnificent, as Walter Bower, writing in hindsight, describes them as foreshadowing the grief to come:

> While everything was going on at the royal wedding according to due custom, a kind of show was put on in the form of a procession amongst the company who were reclining at table. At the head of this procession were skilled musicians with many sorts of pipe music including the wailing music of bagpipes, and behind them others splendidly performing a war-dance with intricate weaving in and out. Bringing up the rear was a figure regarding whom it was difficult to decide whether it was a man or an apparition. It seemed to glide like a ghost rather than walk on feet. When it looked as if he was disappearing from everyone's sight, the whole frenzied procession halted, the song died away, the music faded, and the dancing contingent froze suddenly and unexpectedly. Laughter is [always] mixed with grief, and mourning takes over from extremes of joy: after such splendour the kingdom lamented ingloriously, when a short time afterwards it lost itself and as a consequence its king.[79]

The marriage was one of the shortest in British royal history – and the shortest of any English or Scottish king, lasting less than five months. Tragedy struck on 19 March 1286, after Alexander had spent the day attending a council meeting in Edinburgh. When the meeting broke up, he set off on horseback to join his wife at Kinghorn Castle in Fife. It was said he wanted to be there to celebrate her birthday and he may also have recently discovered that she was pregnant with the much-desired heir. For whatever the reason, he was eager to get to her and took only a small escort of three men and two local guides but

> the king was delayed by the ferry at [South] Queensferry until dusk on a dark night. When advised by his companions not to go beyond Inverkeithing that night, he spurned their counsel, and with an escort of knights hurried by a precipitous track towards Kinghorn Regis.[80]

It seems that, with bad weather closing in and daylight fading, several people counselled against continuing the journey, including the ferryman at the River Forth and the bailie at Inverkeithing, who argued that Alexander should stay the night and continue his journey in the morning as a heavy storm was brewing. Only eight miles from his destination, Alexander would hear none of it and insisted on continuing his journey. He somehow lost his escort in the dark and worsening weather but continued alone and 'To the west of that place beside the shore his horse stumbled in the sand, and alas! the noble king, too negligently attended by his followers, broke his neck and expired.'[81] It was not until the next morning that the king's body was found on the foreshore of Pettycur, just a mile from his destination. The most likely explanation was that his horse had stumbled, throwing the king, whose neck was broken in the fall, although at least one historical fiction writer has suggested foul play while others have suggested the king was drunk.

One thing is certain: Alexander III was seen as one of the greatest of Scotland's medieval kings. The chroniclers were vociferous in their praise of him. The *Chronicle of Lanercost* described Alexander as 'the best king that the Scots ever had'.[82] John of Fordun was particularly effusive in his praise:

> How worthy of tears, and how hurtful, his death was to the kingdom of Scotland, is plainly shown forth by the evils of after times. This king reigned thirty-six years. All the days of the life of this king, the Church of Christ flourished, her priests were honoured with due worship, vice was withered, craft there was none, wrong came to an end, truth was strong, and righteousness reigned. Moreover, rightly, and by reason of the merits of his uprightness, was he called king: seeing that he ruled himself and his people aright, allowing unto each his rights; and if, at any time, any of his people rebelled, he curbed their madness with discipline so unbending, that they would put a rope round their necks, ready for hanging, were that his will and pleasure, and bow themselves under his rule. By reason whereof he was looked upon with equal fear and love, both far and near, not only by his friends, but also by his adversaries, – and especially by the English. And all the time he lived upon earth security reigned in steadfastness of peace and quiet, and gleeful freedom. O Scotland, truly unhappy, when bereft of so great a leader and pilot; while – greater unhappiness still! – he left no lawful offspring to succeed him. Thou hast an everlasting spring of mourning and sorrow in the death of one whose praiseworthy life bestowed, on thee especially, such increase of welfare.[83]

The dead king, the last in the direct male line stretching back to Malcolm III and Margaret of Wessex, the last king of the royal house of Dunkeld, was buried at Dunfermline, among his illustrious ancestors. There followed months of uncertainty in Scotland. She had lost one of her most successful kings and the succession was in turmoil. Little Margaret, the Maid of Norway, had been recognised by the council as Alexander's heir, but Alexander's queen was pregnant; and if she gave birth to a boy, he would be king from his first breath. A regency council was established to rule until the queen gave birth. In the event, Yolande either suffered a miscarriage, or the child was stillborn. Some sources, the *Lanercost Chronicle* in particular, have questioned whether Yolande was pregnant at all, suggesting that she was intending to pass off another woman's baby as her own and being particularly harsh towards the young queen:

113

They [the regency council] governed the country for six years, transacting the affairs of the people, and, before all, of the Lady Queen, widow of Alexander, assigning a portion as her terce. But she, resorting to feminine craft, was pretending to be pregnant, in order to cause patriots to postpone their decision, and that she might more readily attract popularity to herself. But just as a woman's cunning always turns out wretchedly in the end, so she disquieted the land with her pretences from the day of the King's death till the feast of the Purification, nor would she admit respectable matrons to examine her condition; [and], in order that she might return ignominy upon those from whom she had received reverence and honour, she determined to deceive the nation for ever by foisting on herself the child of another. She caused a new font to be made of white marble, and she contrived to have the son of a play-actor to be brought [to her] so that it might pass for hers; and when as many as collected to dance by license [in honour of] so important an accouchement had come to Stirling (the place where the aforesaid lady was staying) at the time for her to be brought to bed (which she herself had arranged beforehand), her fraud was detected and revealed by the sagacity of William of Buchan, to the confusion of all present, and to all those willing to trust her who heard of it afterwards. Thus did she, who was first attracted from over the sea only by the prospect of wealth and was united to the King in marriage, depart from the country with shame.[84]

However, there are major discrepancies in the chronicle's apparently malicious account and tradition has the baby buried at Cambuskenneth. The throne passed to little Margaret and arrangements began to have her brought to Scotland, but we will look into her in the next chapter. Queen Yolande continued to reside in Scotland for some time, possibly at Stirling Castle, and was confirmed in her dower properties, which included an annual income of £200 from Berwick; she also had estates in the sheriffdom of Stirling and a horse stud at Jedburgh. The royal exchequer was still paying Yolande the revenues from her jointure lands in 1288, suggesting the dowager queen was still living in Scotland at that time.[85]

It was not until May 1294 that Yolande married for a second time; Arthur of Brittany was a similar age to Yolande and was the son and heir of Jean II, Duke of Brittany and earl of Richmond and Beatrice of England, the sister of Alexander III's first wife, Queen Margaret. Yolande was the second wife of Arthur, who already had three sons, Jean, Guy and Peter, by his first wife, Marie, Vicomtesse de Limoges. It is possible that Arthur chose Yolande as a bride due to the impressive de Montfort territories that she stood to inherit from her mother, although there were legal wranglings between Yolande and her younger sister, Jeanne, who also claimed the lands. Yolande and Arthur had six children together. Their eldest daughter, Joan, was born a year after their marriage and married Robert, Lord of Cassel; she died in 1363. Beatrice was born around 1295 and married Guy, Lord of Laval; she lived until 1384. Their only son, John, was probably born 1295/6 and married Joan of Flanders. Of the three youngest daughters: Alice was born in the late 1290s and married Bouchard VI, Count of Vendôme and died in 1377; Blanche was born in 1300 and died young; and Mary was born in 1302 and became a nun, dying in 1377.

Arthur succeeded his father as Duke of Brittany in 1305 and ruled until his death in 1312. He was succeeded by John III, his eldest son by his first marriage. However, John's death in 1341 sparked the War of the Breton Succession when Yolande's son, John de Montfort, claimed the duchy in place of Joan of Penthièvre, daughter of Guy (Arthur's second son by his first wife), who was married to Charles of Blois, nephew of King Philip VI of France. Joan and Charles were therefore backed by the French crown, while Edward III of England supported the claims of John de Montfort; the war eventually became part of the greater conflict, now known as the Hundred Years' War. When John fell ill and died in 1345, the war continued in the name of his 6-year-old son – Yolande's grandson – another John (John IV, Duke of Brittany) and finally ended in John's favour with the treaty of Guérande in April 1365. After being widowed for a second time, Yolande did not remarry. During her time in Brittany, Yolande continued to administer to her Scottish estates; in October 1323, a safe conduct to Scotland was granted to a French knight 'for the dower of the Duchess of Brittany while she was Queen of Scotland'.[86] It seems uncertain when Yolande died. Sources vary between 1324 and 1330, although she was still alive on 1 February 1324 when she made provision for the support of her daughter, Marie, who had become a nun.

These arrangements for her daughter are the last mention of Yolande in the historical record, the date of her death as uncertain as that of her birth. Her brief time as Queen of Scots was long in her past, though the consequences of her all-too-short marriage, and the lack of a legitimate male heir, were still reverberating throughout the Scottish kingdom.

Chapter Seven

Scotland's First Queen Regnant

I need to start this chapter with a disclaimer. I was originally going to include little Queen Margaret's story in the previous chapter but decided that Scotland's first queen regnant deserved a chapter of her own. Indeed, Margaret was not only Scotland's first queen regnant, but she was also the first queen regnant in the whole of the British Isles. The story of Margaret, the Maid of Norway, is short and sad. The little girl died before her 8th birthday, and before she ever set foot in the country of which she was queen. Her death set into motion a chain of events that would see Scotland torn apart by war for years to come.

Margaret's claim to the Scottish throne came from her grandfather, Alexander III. Alexander had come to the throne at the age of 8 and had proved to be a very capable and strong monarch. He had married, on 26 December 1251, Margaret, the daughter of Henry III of England and Eleanor of Provence. With three children born to the couple, they must have felt content that the succession was secure. Their eldest daughter, Margaret, was born in February 1261 at Windsor Castle and was recognised as the heir to the Scots throne until the arrival of her oldest brother. Of their two sons, Alexander was born in 1264 at Jedburgh and David was born in March 1273. However, there followed a succession of tragedies, starting with the death of Queen Margaret in February 1275 at Cupar Castle, aged only 34. Just six years later, the couple's youngest son, 8-year-old David, died in June 1281 at Stirling Castle; he had always been a delicate child, but the grief of losing his youngest child, on top of the grief of losing his queen and lifelong companion, must have been hard for Alexander III to take.

One happy event in the midst of the tragedy was the marriage of 20-year-old Margaret of Scotland to 13-year-old Erik Magnusson around the 31 August 1281. The marriage was intended to foster better relations between Scotland and Norway after several years of prickly relations in the aftermath of the 1266 Treaty of Perth, when the Scots finally secured control of the Western Isles and Man. The marriage, for which Alexander III promised 14,000 marks and a resumption of the payment of the annual 'due' for the Isles, ended any lingering tensions between the two countries.[1] Margaret's dowry included the estates of Rothiemay in Banffshire, Belhelvie in Aberdeenshire, Bathgate in West Lothian and Ratho in Midlothian. The treaty also specified that Margaret and her children would be in the Scottish line of succession after Alexander III's sons and the sons of Alexander's sons.

The Kyngys dowchtyr off Scotland
This Alysandrys the thryd, that fayre May
Wyth the Kyng wes weddyt off Norway:
Margret scho wes callyd be name,
Comendyt fayre, and off gud fame.
Off August that yhere the twelfft day
Hyr wayage scho tuk on till Norway.
In the Assumptyowne off oure Lady
Scho thare ressawyd wes honorably.
Suppos, off caws as hyr behowyd,
Swa fra hyr kyn scho wes removyd,
Hyr hart stad in gret hewynes;
Wyth honowre yheit scho ressawyd wes.
Off the mast Byschape off that land
Scho Qwene was made, the crown berand.[2]

Erik II Magnusson had become King Erik II of Norway the year before, in 1280, with a royal council ruling for the underage king. Erik was the son of Magnus the Lawmender, King of Norway, and his wife, Ingeborg, daughter of Eric IV, King of Denmark. King Magnus had hoped to have young Erik crowned as his co-ruler, but passed away before the coronation ceremony could be performed. The marriage promised a closer, friendlier, relationship between Scotland and Norway. Margaret was seven years older than her groom and, indeed, rather old for an unmarried princess; her mother had been married at the age of 10 and most princesses would expect to be married before their 16th birthday. This may denote a lack of suitable bridegrooms among the ruling houses at the time. Edward I had been married for over twenty-five years by 1281 and had fathered a brood of children, but his only surviving son at this time was 7-year-old Alphonso, Earl of Chester, who would, sadly, succumb to illness in August 1284. Alexander III may also have delayed looking for a husband for Margaret following the death of Queen Margaret, when the princess was 14. But now, the 20-year-old princess was getting married at the cathedral in Bergen:

> Now a little before this, that is in 1281, Margaret daughter of King Alexander III was married to the king of Norway called Hanigow or Eric. Leaving Scotland on 12 August she crossed the sea in state, along with Walter Bailloch earl of Menteith and his countess, the abbot of Balmerino and Bernard de Mowat, as well as many other knights and nobles, and on the eve of the Assumption of Our Lady she arrived in Norway and was honourably received by the king. She was crowned by the archbishop of that kingdom, although it was against the wishes of the said king's mother.[3]

The Lanercost chronicler appears to have his facts slightly skewed, but does go into greater detail. He names the Norwegian king as Magnus, and ages him by five years. He does suggest that Erik was the one who pressed for the marriage, sending embassies to Scotland to negotiate on his behalf:

> At this time the King of Norway died, leaving as successor his son called Magnus [sic]; who hearing that the King of Scotland had an amiable, beautiful and attractive daughter, a virgin, of suitable age for himself (being a handsome youth of about eighteen years), could not rest until a formal mission, divines as well as nobles, had been sent twice to obtain her as his spouse in marriage and consort on the throne.[4]

The chronicler goes on to say

> the union was very distasteful to the maiden, as also to her relations and friends (seeing that she might wed elsewhere much more easily and honourably), yet it was at the sole instance of her father, the king, that the bargain was made that he should give her a dowry 17,000 merks, primarily for the contract of marriage, but secondarily for the redemption of the right to the Isles.[5]

The chronicler was perhaps being a little unfair to Margaret; marrying a reigning monarch was certainly not dishonourable and the union was advantageous to Scotland's continuing possession of the Western Isles. It was a match of great significance to Scotland, ending decades of tension with Norway. If Margaret had any reservations, it was probably due to Erik's age; she was marrying a teenager, a boy, not a man, who was seven years her junior.

The chronicle goes on to say that Margaret's crossing to Norway was not without its dangers and praises Margaret's grace and culture as Norway's new queen:

> On the morrow of S. Laurence she embarked at … with much pomp and many servants, and after imminent peril to life which they ran on the night of the Assumption of the Holy Virgin, at daybreak on the said festival they lowered their sails at Bergen. Shortly afterwards she was solemnly crowned and proclaimed before all men by a distinguished company of kinsmen. She comported herself so graciously towards the king and his people that she altered their manners for the better, taught them the French and English languages, and set the fashion of more seemly dress and food.[6]

Unfortunately, we have very little information on Margaret's life in Norway, nor of her relationship with Erik. It cannot have been easy for her, with such a young husband and, it is said, with a mother-in-law, Ingeborg of Denmark, who, according to Bower, was against the marriage and undermined her position as queen and dominated the Norwegian court. The following year, at the age of 14, the young king came of age. At about the same time, Margaret would have discovered she was pregnant. The future must have looked bright for the young couple, becoming king and queen in reality, rather than just in name, and with a baby – possibly a son – on the way. After just eighteen months of marriage, tragedy struck as the queen delivered her first child.

> But this same Lady Margaret queen of the Norwegians, when she had lived with the king her husband for a year and a half, went the way of all flesh on 9 April at the beginning of the same year in which her brother Alexander died. By her the Norwegian king had only one daughter, also called Margaret. She likewise passed away when she reached maturity.[7]

Barely more than a child himself, King Erik was now a widower with a baby daughter to raise. Queen Margaret died at Tonsberg, either during or shortly after, giving birth to her namesake daughter, and was buried in the cathedral of Christ Church at Bergen, where she had been so recently crowned.

> A thowsand twa hundyr four scor and thre
> Yheris efftyr the Natyvyte,
> Dame Margret Qwene off Norway Endyd,
> and cloysd hyr lattyre day.'[8]

Despite his grief, King Erik still looked to the interests of his baby daughter and the promises made by Alexander III and within a year of his wife's death,

> The king of Norway, after the death of his wife Margaret, daughter of the said King Alexander, also sent a solemn embassy to the lord king of Scotland to seek and receive for the use of his abovementioned daughter – Alexander's granddaughter, that is – rents of 700 marks on certain lands, according to agreements entered upon by those kings and confirmed in writing. The king certainly welcomed this embassy kindly, and on the advice of his magnates he dispatched them honourably to the Norwegian king with great gifts of different kinds.[9]

The notes of the *Scotichronicon* clarify Erik's claims for the revenues, and explains further that Erik pursued the payment of his wife's dowry beyond the death even of his daughter, having it confirmed by Edward I in 1292:

> it appears from a claim made by King Eric in June 1292 to Edward I as lord superior of Scotland (Stevenson, *Documents*, 1, 312-17,

no.252) that Margaret's dowry had consisted of 7000 marks in cash and 700 marks by way of revenues from Specified lands in Scotland to be paid Margaret had been recognized as heir presumptive to the Scottish throne on 5 Feb. 1284 (APS, 1, 424), and Alexander had continued to pay over to Eric the revenues as agreed; it was only during the interregnum after 1286 that payments stopped; King Eric was successful in 1292 in obtaining an order from King Edward that payments should be resumed for his lifetime.[10]

For Alexander III, even more tragedy was to follow in January 1284 when his son and heir, Alexander, died aged just 20. Alexander's death sparked a succession crisis for Scotland's king. He had no brothers or uncles to succeed him; his only heir was his 8-month-old granddaughter, Margaret, in Norway. That same year Alexander obtained, from his nobles, a recognition of 'the illustrious girl Margaret … as our lady and right heir of our said lord king of Scotland'.[11] However, as we have seen, the death of his last surviving child also prompted Alexander III to look for a new wife. And on 1 November 1285, at Jedburgh Abbey, Alexander married Yolande de Dreux, in the hope of producing a legitimate male heir. A little over four months later, while riding through the night – and a violent storm – to be with his bride, Alexander's horse appears to have lost its footing and thrown its rider. The king's body, with his neck broken, was found on the beach the next day, just a mile from where his wife was staying, at Kinghorn in Fife. With the new queen pregnant, six Guardians were appointed to rule the kingdom until the arrival of Alexander's posthumous heir. However, Yolande either miscarried, or the baby was stillborn and by the end of the year it was clear that Scotland had to look elsewhere for a ruler. Alexander's only surviving heir was now 3-year-old Margaret of Norway:

> When indeed the great prince Alexander III was dead, and likewise all the children fathered by him and also all his lawful heirs and relatives descended in any way (either lineally or collaterally) from King William his grandfather, except for one very little girl called Margaret, the daughter of Margaret queen of Norway the late daughter of the said King Alexander, the kingdom of Scotland was Vacant without a king as ruler for six years and nine months, just as someone had prophesied long before: 'The land will be desolate, bereft of its glorious prince for six years and nine months.'[12]

Scotland was left in the hands of six guardians, in the name of the 'community of the realm', namely, Sir William Fraser, Bishop of St Andrews, Duncan, Earl of Fife, Alexander Comyn, Earl of Buchan, Robert, Bishop of Glasgow, Sir John Comyn and James the Steward of Scotland from the region to the south of the Forth.[13] Unfortunately, Duncan of Fife died just a short time later. Within weeks of Alexander's death, Robert de Brus and John Balliol had both made attempts on the crown and the south-west was raised in rebellion. However, the majority of Scots, represented by the six guardians, gave their backing to Margaret, the Maid of Norway. Brus and Balliol were forcibly held in check.

At her birth, Margaret's future had looked bright. She was a Norwegian princess who would be destined to play an important role in her country's foreign policy by making a prestigious marriage with one of the royal families of Europe. Her education, supervised by Bishop Narve of Bergen, where she resided, would have been tailored to provide her with the tools she needed for this future. Her grandfather's death, and her own position as his heir, promoted Margaret to being one of the most desirable heiresses in Europe. The Norwegians saw the advantage in securing Margaret's succession to the Scottish throne, as an opportunity to recover the Western Isles and various sums of money that had remained unpaid. However, as it was believed at the time that a woman could not rule alone, it was the choice of Margaret's husband that was of prime importance to all. As early as 1284, Alexander III had, following the death of his last son, floated the idea that England and Scotland might unite through marriage. In response to a letter of condolence from his brother-in-law, Edward I, Alexander had suggested that, through his tiny granddaughter, 'much may yet come to pass'.[14] When Alexander still had the prospect of producing an heir of his own, Edward saw little advantage in the idea of marrying Margaret to his only son and heir, Edward of Caernarfon, born in 1284. With Alexander III's death, Scotland was now Margaret's dowry, and Edward I was presented with the prospect of his son inheriting England after him, whilst also being King of Scotland as Margaret's husband.

> During the above-mentioned period of years Edward Longshanks king of England, knowing that the aforesaid girl called Margaret (daughter of the king of Norway and also the grand-daughter of his own sister) was the true and lawful heir of the king of Scotland, and striving with all zeal and effort to join and unite that kingdom of Scotland to his kingdom, appointed and established in 1289 six special proctors and eminent envoys, namely the bishops of Durham and Carlisle, the earls of Lincoln and Warenne, William de Vesci Knight, and Henry dean of York, to agree, arrange and negotiate between himself and the aforesaid guardians and the other estates of the kingdom about the contracting of a marriage between his son and heir Edward of Caernarfon and the aforesaid Margaret then heir to Scotland.[15]

With the guardians maintaining an uneasy peace between the competing claims of Margaret, Robert de Brus and John de Balliol, Erik II of Norway sought the help of Edward I of England. Messengers were sent between the English and Norwegian courts and in spring 1289 serious negotiations began. On 6 November

1289, an international summit was held at Salisbury, in England. The Norwegian ambassadors met with Edward and his advisers. It's possible the Scottish guardians had also sent representatives, but some sources say the Scots were excluded from these initial talks. Many Scots barons, including the Bruces, Comyns and Balliols, may have also been hoping to wed Margaret to their own sons, but they could hardly compete against a marriage with the son of the King of England. It was decided that Margaret would be brought to Scotland only when the country was 'at peace'.[16] The summit proved successful, and it was agreed that Margaret would marry Edward of Caernarfon, Edward I's son and heir, within the next twelve months. For the Scottish, the marriage alliance promised an end to the years of uncertainty and to the latent threats they had been facing since 1286. For Margaret, a marriage alliance with England gave the Maid a powerful protector and Edward I was so keen that he applied for papal approval for the match even before the terms had been finalised with the Scots.[17]

In March 1290, the community of Scotland, comprising over 100 Scotsmen of substance, met to ratify the marriage agreement. They wrote to Edward expressing their will to proceed with the wedding. The Guardians of Scotland, however, had sworn an oath to preserve Alexander III's kingdom intact and undiminished for his eventual heirs, and their overriding concern now was to safeguard Scotland's future independence. It was agreed at Brigham that, although Edward and Margaret were not yet of marriageable age, they would be regarded as married on Margaret's arrival from Norway – and Edward of Caernarfon would be King of Scotland from that moment. The business of Scottish government and law was to remain in Scotland and be run by a resident viceroy or lieutenant.[18] There was no common ground, however, on the issue of royal fortresses: Edward I wanted to appoint all custodians as a guarantee of security, but the Scots saw this as a demand for the surrender of sovereignty. In the final agreement, ratified at Northampton, the point is glossed over with an agreement that keepers would be appointed by the 'common advice of the Scots and the English king'.[19] The reason Edward acquiesced on – or, rather, failed to push – the castles issue was the news that Margaret had already left Norway. Edward wanted the deal signed and sealed before the Scots' hand was strengthened by the physical possession of their queen. In the final agreement, the Scots got a clear statement safeguarding their independence. Edward promised

> that the kingdom of Scotland would be as free and quit of all
> subjection of service as had satisfactorily and freely been the case
> with regard to customs and rights, both ecclesiastical and secular, in
> the time of the aforesaid King Alexander, according to what appears
> in a certain instrument contained in the Pleading of Baldred Bisset.
> So also that if the marriage did not last, or one of the parties to the
> contract died without issue while the other survived, the kingdom
> was to be freely and absolutely restored and returned to the nearest

heirs, without any subjection, saving to the king of England his right as far as it was competent from ancient times.[20]

The details now settled, the Scots Guardians sent envoys to Norway, to fetch their queen;

> So, in order that the said matter might be carried through to the end wished for, the nobles of Scotland solemnly despatched to the king of Norway, two knights, distinguished for their knowledge and character – Michael of Wemyss and Michael Scot – to perform the marriage, and bring the girl to the kingdom.[21]

Margaret had set sail in August 1290 in a Norwegian vessel; accompanied by Bishop Narve of Bergen, she was bound for Orkney, which was still Norwegian soil. There, she was to be transferred into the custody of an embassy of Scottish knights, sent by William Fraser, Bishop of St Andrews, who were to escort the little queen, at that time styled 'lady of Scotland', to Scone for her inauguration.[22] In preparation for the Maid's arrival, Edward I sent the bishop of Durham north to supervise her reception. He also sent gifts of jewels for his future daughter-in-law; and the magnates of Scotland began to assemble at Scone Abbey, Perth, in anticipation of the enthronement of their new queen. However, storms drove the Maid's ship off course, and she landed at the place now known as St Margaret's Hope, South Ronaldsay, on Orkney. Representatives from both England and Scotland now made the journey north to greet the young queen, receiving the news en route that Margaret had sickened and died. Margaret died at Orkney, in the arms of Bishop Narve, either from the effects of a severe bout of seasickness, or possibly from eating rotten food during the voyage. She was 7 years old.

As the Scottish and English messengers returned south with news of the Maid's death, Margaret's body was returned to Norway. She never set foot in her kingdom of Scotland. She was buried beside her mother, in the north aisle of the cathedral of Christ Church, in Bergen.[23] The cathedral has since been destroyed. Margaret's father confirmed the identity of the body before her burial, an act that proved significant in 1300, a year after Erik's death, when a woman appeared in Bergen, claiming to be Margaret. Reports say the woman appeared to be 40 years old, when Margaret would have only been 17. She gained popular support, despite the king's identification of Margaret's body, before finally being convicted as 'the False Margareth'; she was burned at the stake in 1301. Erik had died in 1299, so did not live to see the pretender.[24]

As for Scotland, Walter Bower, in his *Scotichronicon*, lamented the deaths of Alexander III's heirs, and what it meant for Scotland:

> The death of the brothers Alexander and David and of their sister Margaret and of her daughter Margaret was the beginning of the

future woes of Scotland. Alas, Scotland! for even if you had known
so many days of mourning and tears were in store for you, such
great and such manifold evils were inexorably hastening upon you:
Even if you had known how great they were, you could never have
imagined that you would bear them.[25]

The tragedy of Margaret's death brought an end to the rule of the House of Dunkeld,
begun with Malcolm III Canmore in 1058, and plunged Scotland into crisis:

Upon her death, a dispute straightway arose between John of Balliol
and Robert of Bruce the elder (for there were three then alive, called
by the same name: to wit, Robert, this elder noble – his son – and his
grandson, who, afterwards, was king of the kingdom of Scotland, by
right and inheritance).[26]

Edward I's intervention with his judgement of the Thirteen Competitors for the
crown, and his backing of John Balliol as the next king, saw the beginning of
Scotland's Wars of Independence. Marred not only by English invasion, but also
the in-fighting among the Scottish nobles, it was not until Robert the Bruce emerged
victorious that Scotland found her feet again.

The story of Margaret, Maid of Norway, is truly tragic. She never had the
chance to grow up, marry, be a queen. Her significance lies in the fact that the
magnates of Scotland were prepared to accept her as their monarch. Had she lived,
she would have been the first female to be crowned as queen regnant in the British
Isles. She would have achieved what Empress Matilda failed to do in England in
the mid-twelfth century. And it would have happened peacefully.

Chapter Eight

The House of Balliol

T he death of Margaret, Maid of Norway, plunged Scotland into crisis. There was no clear successor to the little queen. The magnates of the realm discussed among themselves who should succeed to the throne, but they came to an impasse and felt unable to decide who should rule,

> partly because it was a difficult and troublesome case, partly because different people felt differently about that right and vacillated repeatedly, partly because they were justifiably afraid of the power of the parties which was great and much to be feared, and partly because they had no superior who by the strength of his power could demand the execution of their decision or compel the parties to observe it.[1]

In the end, the barons decided to seek outside help. They sent

> a formal embassy to Edward king of England, so that he might become the supreme judge in this case and declare the rights of each party, and by his power might duly restrain the party against whom he pronounced his verdict in accordance with the requirements of the law.[2]

There were thirteen Competitors to the Scots crown, who each agreed to submit their claim to the judgement of Edward I of England. Although it seems strange, with the benefit of hindsight and Edward I's subsequent interference in Scottish affairs, to imagine the Scots submitting to the English king's arbitration, in 1290, Edward had a reputation as a legalist and the power to not only make a decision, but to enforce it.[3] Most of the claimants could trace their descent from Prince Henry, son of David I, and his wife, Ada de Warenne. It was through the daughters of David and his wife, Matilda of Chester, that Robert de Brus (grandfather of Robert the Bruce, King of Scots) and John Balliol (later John, King of Scots) both based their claims as Competitors to the Scots throne in the 1290s, as did John de Hastings, Lord of Abergavenny.[4]

Ada and Henry also had three daughters, and their descendants threw their names in the ring. The eldest daughter, Ada, who was born around 1142, was married to Florent III (or Floris), Count of Holland and was given the county of Ross in Scotland as her marriage gift. Ada died sometime after 1206; she and Florent had between eight and ten children, including two sons, Dirk and William, who each became Count of Holland, in turn. It was through his descent from Ada that Florent (or Floris) V, Count of Holland, claimed his place as one of the Competitors to the Scottish throne in 1292. The count claimed that his descent from Ada, older sister of David, should give him precedence over David's daughters and their descendants. He also claimed that David had relinquished his rights to the Scottish crown in return for lands in Garrioch in north-east Scotland, and that William I had then settled the succession on Ada. Unfortunately, Count Florent was unable to produce any written evidence to support his claims and failed to secure the nomination of King Edward to become King of Scots.[5] Others included John Comyn, Lord of Badenoch, Patrick, Earl of Dunbar, William de Vesci, Nicholas de Soules and William de Ross.[6] Even Erik II put a claim in, as his daughter's heir, though his argument was a weak one.[7]

By November 1292, Scotland had been without a monarch for two years. Edward I travelled to Berwick-on-Tweed, where he

> ordained that fifty distinguished Scotsmen who were experts in the law should be appointed as arbiters. These men were appointed, and the king added to their number thirty Englishmen whom he had chosen. He made them swear to consider the claims of all the candidates and to bring the business of the Scottish succession to a satisfactory conclusion.[8]

It took some time to narrow down the field, with Edward showing his influence in every part of the proceedings:

> Accordingly, when this had been arranged, the often-mentioned king chose twenty-four men distinguished by their knowledge, age, character and loyalty and sensible men whatever their status or rank, of whom twelve were from England and twelve from Scotland. When they had taken a solemn oath to speak the truth, he ordered them to exclude all the others who claimed a right to the throne (for there were very many), and bearing in mind their sworn oath and the danger to their souls to decide after careful enquiry between the said John (namely de Balliol) and Robert de Brus senior, and by their decision to show plainly which of them had the nearer or clearer right to the realm of Scotland so that he might succeed the aforesaid King Alexander by right of proximity according to the approved customs of the kingdom.[9]

John de Balliol and Robert de Brus, senior, emerged as the leading contenders. Balliol made his claim as the grandson of Margaret, the eldest daughter of David and Matilda, while Brus's claim was as the son of Isabel, Earl David's second daughter. Brus claimed that, as he was the grandson of Earl David, while Balliol was the earl's great-grandson, he was, therefore, a generation closer to the royal line, even though he descended from the second daughter, rather than the oldest. As an additional argument, Brus could also point out that he had been designated as heir apparent by Alexander II.[10] As you can imagine, there were arguments to be made for both candidates, which included lengthy pleadings, consultations with lawyers, the Scottish barons and churchmen from England and Scotland. After much deliberation, a decision was made:

> At the time appointed, the persons above named, to whose consideration the affair was committed, having met the three pretenders to the throne of Scotland also before named, it was clearly decided by the former that the claims of the lords R. de Bruce and J. de Hastings ought to be treated as null and void; and they declared that the right to the throne was vested in John de Baliol as the nearest in blood. Whereupon, having first done fealty to our lord the king of England for the whole Scottish territories, on the feast of St. Edmund, king and martyr, the said lord John was, with all due ceremonies, according to the usages anciently established, solemnly placed on the royal throne of Scotland on St. Andrew's day [30 November], at Scone, in the presence of the lords J. de Warrenne and H. de Lincoln, the earls who attended on the part of the king of England; the homage due to the king of England, as the supreme lord, for the whole kingdom with its dependencies, having still to be done.[11]

Both John of Fordun and Walter Bower suggest that Edward settled on John Balliol because Balliol would agree to swear fealty to Edward as his overlord. According to both chroniclers, when asked if he would hold Scotland as a vassal of King Edward, Robert de Brus replied

> If I can get the aforesaid kingdom by means of my right and a faithful assize, well and good; but if not, I shall never, in gaining that kingdom for myself, reduce it to thraldom – a kingdom which all the kings thereof have hitherto, with great toil and trouble, kept free from thraldom, in security of peace.[12]

When Balliol was called forward and asked the same question, he,

> after having quickly deliberated with his council, which had been quite bought over, fell in with the aforesaid king's wishes, that he

should hold the kingdom of Scotland of him, and do him homage for the same. Thereupon, the parties were, soon after, called up; and, in presence of the nobles of Scotland and England, Edward pronounced John Balliol to be the lawful heir in the succession to the throne, and by his award decided that he had the stronger right.[13]

After the decision was announced, John was taken to Scone Abbey where, on 30 November 1292,

the feast of St Andrew, John Balliol was made king of Scotland in the usual manner. At the monastery of Scone there was a huge stone set in the church near the high altar, hollow and shaped in the form of a round seat: it was the custom for future kings to be placed on it, as it were, in the manner of a coronation. The task of enthroning the new king of Scotland in this manner belonged by hereditary right to the earl of Fife. The king had to swear that he would rule justly, defend the holy mother church and his subjects, and would make good laws and maintain those already in force until his death. When the new king was thus placed on the stone of Scone, a solemn Mass was celebrated, and the king remained seated on the stone except during the elevation of the Host.[14]

So, who was John de Balliol, King John of Scotland? For most of his life, Balliol was no royal. He was not born to be king, merely one of the many Anglo-Scottish magnates. He was born in 1249, either on his family's English estates or in Picardy.[15] He was the fourth son of John Balliol of Barnard Castle, County Durham. His father was the founder of Balliol College, Oxford and died in 1269. King John's mother was Dervorguilla, second daughter of Alan, Lord of Galloway, and his wife, Margaret. Margaret was the eldest daughter of David, Earl of Huntingdon, younger brother of Malcolm IV and William the Lion, and his wife, Matilda of Chester. The king's three elder brothers, Hugh, Alan and Alexander, had all died by 1278, and John succeeded as lord of Bywell and inherited the patrimony which centred on Barnard Castle, although he was not confirmed in his lands until a year after Alexander's death.[16] Various other Balliol lands had been distributed as dowers to his mother and two of his sisters-in-law, Agnes de Valence and Aliénor de Genouve, the widows of Hugh and Alexander, respectively.[17] When his mother died in 1290, he also inherited the ancient lordship of Galloway, centred on Buittle Castle.

Before 7 February 1281, John was married to Isabella de Warenne, daughter of John de Warenne, sixth Earl of Warenne and Surrey.[18] A charter dated 27 Mar 1281 records a grant of property by 'Dervergulla de Balliol' to 'her son John de Balliol and the king's cousin Isabella daughter of Earl Warrenne his wife'.[19] John de Warenne was the son of William de Warenne, the fifth earl, and his second wife, Matilda Marshal, herself the eldest daughter of renowned knight William Marshal,

Earl of Pembroke, regent for Henry III. Isabella brought her husband some impressive family connections. Her mother was Alice de Lusignan. Alice was the daughter of King John of England's widow, Isabelle d'Angoulême, and Hugh X de Lusignan and half-sister to Henry III of England. Isabella was, therefore, Henry's niece and a first cousin of King Edward I. Born in around 1224, at the time of their marriage, Alice was seven years older than her 16-year-old husband. The marriage was part of Henry III's much-despised policy of patronising his Lusignan siblings and thus was condemned by Matthew Paris, who claimed that the marriage was 'beyond the bride's station'.[20] After the wedding, John received two extra robes at Christmas, and in 1248, although he had yet to reach his majority, received some of his father's lands, probably in order for John to support himself and his new wife.[21] John's mother, Matilda, had died in 1248, in her mid-50s. Choosing to be laid to rest with her Marshal family, rather than either of her husbands, Matilda was buried at Tintern Abbey, Monmouthshire. Her three Bigod sons and their Warenne half-brother carried their mother's bier into the church, where she was laid to rest close to her mother, Isabel, two of her brothers, Walter and Ancel, and her sister, Sybil.

Through her parents, Isabella was related to the royal families of England and France, as well as some of the most prominent families in England, including the earls of Pembroke, Salisbury and Norfolk. Isabella was one of three children; her elder sister, Eleanor, married Henry Percy and was the mother of Henry de Percy, first Baron Percy. Isabella's younger brother, William de Warenne, married Joan de Vere, daughter of the fifth Earl of Oxford, and was father to two children, a son and a daughter, John and Alice. Isabella's nephew, John de Warenne, was the last Earl of Warenne and Surrey, whose marital and extra-marital situation led to the extinction of the senior Warenne line. It was through John's sister, Alice de Warenne, that the title Earl of Surrey would eventually pass to her son Richard Fitzalan, tenth Earl of Arundel.

Alice de Lusignan died in 1256, shortly after giving birth to her youngest child, William, leaving the 25-year-old Earl Warenne to raise three young children alone. Countess Alice was buried at Lewes Priory, the family mausoleum. She was 'placed in the earth before the great altar in the presence of her brother Adelmar [Aymer de Valence], [bishop] elect of Winchester'.[22] Isabella was probably born around 1253, although some genealogical sources claim she was much younger and, therefore, must be the daughter of a second, unknown wife of John de Warenne. The theory is most likely based on the writings of chronicler Thomas Wykes.

During that period between the death of his older brother and his own succession to the family lands, the Balliol lands in Northumberland were taken into royal custody, and a contemporary chronicler, Thomas Wykes, recorded that John himself was also in royal custody at about this time. According to Wykes, Balliol needed Edward's consent for his proposed marriage to Isabella. He described John as a youth, *adolescens*, and Isabella, a young girl, *adolescentula*. In fact, at the date of their marriage, which probably took place in February 1281, John was about 30 years of age and Isabella was at least in her mid-20s. Clearly, Edward could not have been exercising rights of wardship in a minority but the true reasons for his heavy-handed intervention are not clear.[23] In addition, there is no evidence that John de Warenne ever remarried after Alice's death, so it seems just as likely – or more likely, in fact – that Isabella married late, perhaps because previous marriage proposals or arrangements had fallen through, either due to failed negotiations or the death of the proposed groom. Such instances often went unrecorded and are much more feasible than the suggestion that the earl had remarried but not one of the chroniclers of the time thought to mention it.

Isabella and John Balliol were distantly related. He was the great-grandson of Ada de Warenne's youngest son, David, Earl of Huntingdon, by David's daughter, Margaret, and therefore a great-great-great-grandson of the second Earl Warenne: Isabella was the second earl's great-great-great-granddaughter. John and Isabella were, therefore, fourth cousins, both being descended from William de Warenne, second Earl of Surrey, and his wife, Isabel de Vermandois. With thirteen claimants to the Scottish throne, it was Edward I of England who was given the duty of selecting Scotland's next king. Isabella's close family links to the English crown, and the fact her father was one of Edward's closest companions, may have helped Edward decide in John's favour and he was installed as King of Scotland in November 1292.

Very little is known of John and Isabella's life together. Her death date and final resting place are both unknown. It is by no means certain that Isabella was still alive when John became king. She may have died before 1292, when John succeeded to the Scottish throne. If she did become Queen of Scots when her husband was chosen to take the throne, her reign was short and, for the most part, miserable. There is no indication that she was present at his inauguration as King of Scots 'on the 26th day of December, though against the will of the first men of the kingdom, of all but a few, this John did homage to Edward I, king of England, for the kingdom of Scotland, as he had before promised in his ear, submitting to thraldom unto him for ever.'[24] King John did manage to institute a number of administrative reforms during his reign, calling annual parliaments. Alexander III's policy of expanding royal authority continued with the creation of three new sheriffdoms in the west Highlands, at Skye, Lorn and Kintyre.[25] John de Balliol was up against an expert manipulator in Edward I, who exploited the divisions among the Scots to undermine John's authority as king. King John was caught between the growing demands of King Edward and the rising resentment of the Scots. Edward allowed appeals from Scottish courts to be heard at the English court, inevitably leading to confrontations between John and Edward when the Scots king attempted to resist.[26] The final straw came when John and his leading earls were summoned to perform military service for Edward in his war against France in the summer of 1294. King John chose instead to make an alliance with Philip IV of France, which included the marriage of his eldest son, Edward, to the French king's niece:

The often-mentioned king of England more than once sent for the king of Scotland to compear at the marches and borders of the kingdom, and had him summoned before him to stand his trial for his disobedience and rebellion. But he would not deign to come when peremptorily summoned; so, because of his manifold contumacy, as well as because of his misconduct in breaking through his oath of fealty and homage, Edward passed against him a sentence of deprivation and deposition from the kingdom, as also from all other lands and possessions which John held of him; so that him whom he had, in spite of the law, promoted to the kingship, he, by the law, deprived, both by a sentence and in deed, of all the honours bestowed upon him.[27]

In 1296, John renounced his fealty to Edward, prompting the King of England to invade, sacking the port of Berwick, the city and castle being taken and the king, 'in his tyrannous rage, bade them put to the sword 7500 souls of both sexes; so that, for two days, streams flowed from the bodies slain'.[28]

Shortly before the French alliance, the Scots had held a parliament at Stirling where 'by common assent it was decreed that their king could do no act by himself, and that he should have twelve peers, after the manner of the French, and these they then and there elected and constituted'.[29] At the same parliament, according to the Lanercost chronicler, 'they insultingly refused audience to my lord the Earl of Warenne, father-in-law of the King of Scotland, and to the other envoys of my lord the King of England; nor would they even allow so great a man, albeit a kinsman of their own king, to enter the castle.'[30] The following year, April 1296, Isabella's own father, John de Warenne, defeated King John and the Scottish army at the Battle of Dunbar:

On the 27th of April, in the same year, was fought the battle of Dunbar, where Patrick of Graham and many nobles fell wounded; while a great many other knights and barons, in the hope of saving their lives, fled to Dunbar Castle, and were there readily welcomed. But they were all – to the number of seventy knights, besides famous squires, together with William, Earl of Ross – made over, like sheep offered to the slaughter, by Richard Seward, warden of the said castle, to the king of England.[31]

Following the battle, John fled to the north-east. He eventually surrendered to Edward and was forced to abdicate in July of the same year. Defeated and with his country occupied by the triumphant Edward I, King John was brought before the English king at Montrose and was taken to the churchyard at Strathcaro where he was stripped of his royal vestments and forced to denounce the French alliance.[32] Three days later, in another humiliating ceremony, on 10 July, the Scots king, 'stripped of his kingly ornaments, and holding a white wand in his hand, surrendered up, with staff and baton, and resigned into the hands of the king of England, all right which he himself had, or might have, to the kingdom of Scotland.'[33] This punishment earned John Balliol the nickname that has followed him down the centuries, 'Toom Tabard', meaning empty surcoat. John and his eldest son, Edward, were removed to London, along with the Stone of Destiny and Scotland's government records.[34] If Isabella was still alive, it is likely she accompanied her husband and son. John would never see Scotland again, though Scots, such as William Wallace and Andrew Murray, would continue to fight in his name, perhaps seeing his return as king as a symbol of Scottish independence.

John and Isabella may have had at least three, but possibly four, children together – the evidence is sketchy and incomplete. A daughter, Margaret, died unmarried. There is mention of another daughter, Anne; but there is doubt as to whether she ever existed. Their eldest son, Edward, was born around 1283. Following the deposition of his father, in November 1299, Edward was entrusted to the custody of his grandfather, John, Earl Warenne, who was then approaching his 70th year. After his grandfather's death in 1304, Edward was transferred into the custody of his cousin John, the seventh Earl Warenne, until he was delivered into royal custody in 1310. By the 1330s, Edward's prospects had improved. He was seen as a useful political tool, a rival claimant to the Scottish crown. With English support, Edward made his own bid for the throne, and was crowned king following his defeat of 8-year-old David II's forces at the Battle of Dupplin Moor in 1332. David II was the young son of King Robert I the Bruce, who had succeeded to the throne at the age of 5, on his father's death in 1329. David's supporters and Edward struggled against each other for years. Henry de Balliol, who was killed on 16 December 1332 at the Battle of Annan, has been identified as a possible younger son of John and Isabella. The battle in which he was killed was a resounding victory for supporters of David II against Henry's brother, Edward. Edward was deposed in favour of David II on 16 December 1332, and fled from Scotland. He was restored in March 1333 but was deposed again in 1334 and fled to England, restored again in 1335. David's forces eventually triumphed over Edward, and he was deposed for the last time in 1336. Edward Balliol finally resigned all rights to the crown of Scotland in favour of Edward III of England in 1356, pleading old age and infirmity.[35] In return, he was given an annuity of £2,000 and lived in retirement at Wheatley, in Doncaster, where he died, sometime between 1 and 24 January 1364. Although his final resting place has recently been claimed to be under Doncaster Post Office, the former site of Doncaster Priory, it remains elusive.

Edward Balliol's marital history is almost as tumultuous as his regnal history. In 1295, he was betrothed to Isabelle de Valois, daughter of Charles of France, Comte de Valois, a nephew of King Philip IV of France, and Marguerite of Sicily.[36] Two marriage contracts were signed in 1295, on 5 July and 23 October, confirming the marriage between the niece of the King of France and the son of the King of Scots.[37] The marriage never materialised, however, probably because of his father's forced abdication in 1296, making the match unattractive to the bride's family. It is possible that Edward was later – briefly – married to Margaret of Taranto, daughter of Philip I, Prince of Taranto, around 1331. If this marriage did take place, it was childless and had been annulled by the time Balliol made his bid for the Scottish crown in 1332. Neither Edward nor his younger brother, Henry, had any children.

In 1299, Edward I acceded to Franco–Scottish pressure and released John Balliol into papal custody at Avignon, from where he was transferred into French custody in October 1301, and allowed to reside on his family estates in Picardy, at Hélicourt-en-Vimeau, where he died sometime around April 1313.[38] By the time of his death, Scotland had a new king in Robert the Bruce, who had succeeded his grandfather as the other leading Competitor to the throne. John's claim to the Scottish throne had continued to be supported by the Comyns, which led to the murder of John Comyn, in the church at Dumfries in 1306, by Bruce. Shortly after the murder, he was crowned King Robert I at Scone but was only able to consolidate his rule after winning a resounding victory over the English at Bannockburn in 1314. In his first parliament as king, in 1309, John Balliol was denounced by the Scottish clergy as 'a willing puppet of Edward I'.[39] After which, all mention of the Balliol dynasty was forbidden by the Bruce regime.

This may explain why we know so little of Isabella de Warenne's role in her husband's reign. It is frustrating; although information about queens has a habit of being patchy and incomplete, the evidence of Isabella's life as queen is non-existent. It may be that she died before John came to the throne. Or maybe she survived to share some of his exile. We do not know. There are no charters issued in Isabella's name, or witnessed by her, and no mention of her in the Scottish chronicles of the time. Isabella is barely a shadow on the history of Scotland.

Chapter Nine

The King and Queen of the May

For the next ten years, Scotland would be without a king – or a queen. Until Robert the Bruce. Bruce suffered greatly for the crown, with his family and friends facing similar hardships. Through the murder of his greatest rival and the Battle of Bannockburn, Bruce proved himself determined and resourceful, overcoming defeat to emerge victorious and master of his realm. Robert the Bruce's wife endured a no less punishing life in support of her husband. It was a hard path to follow, punctuated by the Scottish Wars of Independence.

Once he had ceremonially stripped John Balliol of his royal vestments and kingly dignity, and sent the poor man south as prisoner, Edward I proceeded to establish his direct rule on Scotland. She was to be a province, the land of Scotland, no longer a kingdom. Having dispensed with John Balliol, King Edward undertook a victorious summer march through the country, accompanied by John, Earl Warenne, who was appointed custodian of Scotland on 3 September. By this point, John was 65 years old. He had been Earl of Surrey for fifty-six years. And he did not like Scotland. Finding the climate inhospitable to his ageing bones, the earl returned to northern England, leaving officials in charge of the day-to-day government, led by Hugh de Cressingham, the treasurer appointed by King Edward. The leading magnates of Scotland were either prisoners or had been accepted into King Edward's peace. Whoever did not swear loyalty to Edward were outlawed.

This did not mean that the Scots themselves accepted the new situation. Many of Scotland's officials, supported by 'the community of the realm', refused to accept the abdication of John Balliol and continued to govern in his name. Aided by church prelates, including Robert Wishart, Bishop of Glasgow, who outwardly swore his oath to Edward I, but continued to conspire against him, Scottish resistance continued.[1] The churchmen provided supplies, money, encouragement and guidance in the subsequent campaign; their network of communications would have come in useful. The Scots rose in revolt with William Wallace at their head in 1297. Even then, John de Warenne refused to return to Scotland until King Edward specifically ordered him to proceed north and lead the fight. The earl sent his grandson, Henry Percy, on ahead as he slowly made his way northward, reaching Berwick in July. Although Percy met with some success, a frustrated Edward attempted to replace Earl Warenne as keeper of Scotland, with Brian fitzCount; but pleading poverty, Brian claimed he was too poor to take on such an expensive responsibility. In the end, Edward managed to persuade John to remain in Scotland and deal with the Wallace rebellion:

> Now that the king was ready for the crossing to Flanders he put Earl Warenne in charge of all military forces in the county of Yorkshire from the Trent to Scotland, and ordered him to go with all speed to crush the insolence of the Scots and punish the ringleaders as they deserved.[2]

Warenne marched on Stirling, where the two armies faced each other, on the opposite banks of the Firth of Forth, on 9 September 1297. Warenne sought to negotiate but was rebuffed by Wallace, being told, 'Tell your commander that we are not here to make peace but to do battle to defend ourselves and liberate our kingdom. Let them come and we shall prove this in their very beards.'[3] John de Warenne appears to have been over confident, convinced that the defeat of Wallace and his comrade, Andrew Murray, would be a matter of a simple campaign, given the Scottish army was comprised of common soldiers, with no heavy cavalry to speak of and the majority of the Scottish lords were either on the English side or in English custody. The Scots set up a defensive position on the high ground at the Abbey of Craig, overlooking the bridge. In order to attack, the English had to cross the narrow Stirling Bridge, and then navigate a narrow causeway through boggy terrain. Battle began on 11 September amid some confusion; Earl Warenne had given orders for the men to prepare to cross the bridge that morning but had overslept. His infantry mobilised, ready to cross the bridge, without the earl's authority, and had to be called back. When the earl was finally ready for battle, he ordered Hugh de Cressingham to lead the cavalry over the bridge and crush the Scots.[4]

Only able to ride two abreast, the column of English cavalry was soon stretched out along the bridge and causeway, presenting Wallace and Murray with their opportunity. The Scots infantry attacked the English flank, forcing knights and horses from the causeway and into the boggy fields. The horses becoming trapped in the deep mud, the English knights were massacred. As this was unfolding, a second contingent of Scots were sent to the bridge, destroying it with their axes and thus preventing Earl Warenne and the remainder of his army from crossing and coming to the aid of the beleaguered cavalry. The Scots proceeded to finish off the cavalry, inflicting a significant and shocking defeat on the English. Seeing the battle lost, Earl Warenne turned his horse and rode straight for Berwick, not stopping until he was safe in the English-held town; his exhausted horse collapsed and died upon arrival.[5] Hugh de Cressingham, the English treasurer of Scotland, hated by the Scots, was not so lucky. He was cut down and killed in the rout, his body flayed, with small pieces of his skin sent as gifts throughout the country. Wallace is said to have made a belt of Cressingham's skin, which he wore as a reminder of his great victory.[6]

John de Warenne's defeat at Stirling Bridge was a devastating blow for England and a boost for the Scottish resistance. It proved that the English war machine, so long unstoppable, was not invincible. The Scots were quick to take advantage of their victory and opened their seaports to European trade. Wallace and Andrew Murray were named Guardians of the Kingdom of Scotland, though Murray had been mortally wounded at Stirling Bridge and was dead by the end of the month, leaving Wallace to lead the country and the army. He marched south, harrying the English population along the borders and forcing them to abandon their homes. Earl Warenne, though rattled by his defeat, rallied himself and, along with Robert de Clifford, led his men into Annandale, burning villages and tenements and further stretching the financial resources of the powerful Bruce family. In January 1298, Earl Warenne presided over a parliament at York, in King Edward's name, which confirmed Magna Carta. He then led a short campaign against Scotland, during which he reoccupied Berwick, recently abandoned by Wallace, who did not have the resources to hold it. By March 1298, William Wallace had been knighted and appointed sole Guardian of Scotland. King Edward had been fighting on the Continent during the disastrous Stirling Bridge campaign but returned to England on 14 March 1298. On arriving in England, he summoned John de Warenne to discuss the Scottish situation, warmly thanking the aged earl for his services in the campaign.[7] The king set out for the north almost immediately; on 1 July, his army entered Scotland. The English king had a force of 25,000 foot and 3,000 cavalry.[8] Wallace had retreated deeper into Scotland, leaving a devastated countryside behind him, with no sustenance available for the advancing English; the threat of starvation was a real possibility for Edward's army.

The King of England brought Wallace and the Scots to battle at Falkirk on 22 July 1298. Outnumbered, Wallace deployed his spearmen in four densely packed schiltroms on the southern aspect of Callendar Wood, protected to the front by a marsh and the Westquarter burn, which stood between the two armies. His archers were placed between the rings of spearmen, with the cavalry to the rear. The English vanguard was commanded by the earls of Norfolk and Hereford, the second battle by Anthony Bek, Bishop of Durham, and Edward was in command of the reserve. As the English advanced, the van and second battle veered left and right, respectively, to avoid the marshy ground, before delivering their attack. The Scottish cavalry fled the field without even engaging with the English, leaving the infantry to their fate. The archers were ridden down but the schiltroms did their job, stopping the English and inflicting a number of casualties. Whereupon Edward brought up his archers and the schiltroms disintegrated under the hailstorm of arrows. The English cavalry charged once again, this time filing into the gaps in the schiltroms left by the rain of arrows, slaughtering the Scottish rank and file.[9] Wallace escaped, but his prestige was gone, and he took ship for France. After the victory at Falkirk, the English advanced into Fife, occupying St Andrews and destroying Perth.

The Battle of Falkirk was a tragedy for the Scots, but it did serve to galvanise some of the country's magnates into action, and this was when Robert the Bruce came to the fore. Robert was the grandson of Robert de Brus, the Competitor, who had once been recognised as heir to the Scots throne by King Alexander II. After failing in his bid for the crown in 1292, the Old Competitor transferred his claim to his son, also called Robert. This Robert then passed on his earldom of Carrick, held by right of his wife, who died that year, to his son, Robert the Bruce, though he retained the title by courtesy until his death in 1304. The youngest Bruce was born on 11 July 1274 at Turnberry Castle, as the eldest son of Robert de Brus, sixth lord of Annandale and Marjory, Countess of Carrick in her own right. Apparently, the marriage of Robert de Brus and Marjory of Carrick had taken place without royal consent and resulted in a heavy fine.[10]

Robert the Bruce's first occurrence in the historical record appears to be as a witness, with his father, to the confirmation of the grant, of the church of Kilkerran in Kintyre, to Paisley Abbey by Alexander MacDonald, eldest son of Angus, lord of Islay.[11] At some point in the early 1290s, Robert was married to Isabella of Mar, the daughter of Domhnall I (Donald), Earl of Mar, and Elen, said to be a daughter of Llywelyn Fawr (Llywelyn the Great), Prince of Gwynedd. Isabella had been born around 1277. During the succession crisis, her father was already in a clan dispute with John Comyn, Lord of Badenoch. The Comyns were firm adherents of John Balliol and so the Bruce family would be a natural ally for Domhnall, 'For all the Comyns and their whole abettors stood by Balliol; while the Earls of Mar and Athol, with the whole strength of their power, cleaved, in the firm league of kinship, to the side of Robert of Bruce.'[12] Isabella of Mar was, therefore, to be a diplomatic pawn of her father, a tool by which he could strengthen his ties to the Bruce family. That Isabella may eventually wear the crown of Scotland was an added bonus. For the Bruce's part, the marriage would serve to strengthen their claim to the lordship of Garrioch, which sat just to the north of the earldom of Mar.

To secure the family alliance even further, Domhnall's son, Gartnait, was married to Robert's sister, Christian, 'the eldest – wedded Gartnay, Earl of Mar'.[13] Fordun misidentifies Christian as Robert's oldest sister, when she was probably younger than him. In fact, Robert's oldest sister, Isabella, was 'on Sunday following the feast of S. Martin … married to Magnus [Erik II] King of Norway'.[14] A charter dated 25 September 1293 records articles delivered to 'Lady Isabella de Brus, Queen of Norway'.[15] It was a small world; the Norwegian king was the same Erik who had married Princess Margaret of Scotland, daughter of Alexander III, and was the father of Margaret, Maid of Norway.

Robert the Bruce's marriage to Isabella of Mar did not last long. They were probably married in 1295, shortly after the death of Bruce's grandfather, the Old Competitor.[16] Within a few months, the teenage bride was pregnant. Isabella died in 1296, either during or shortly after the birth of her only child, a daughter, Marjorie Bruce. Death in childbirth was all too common in the medieval period. The perils of the birthing chamber were as dangerous for a countess as for a woman from the local village, with the woman risking death at every attempt to bring a child into the world, whether it was her first child or her tenth. Isabella was no more than 19 years of age:

> Now King Robert, when he was Earl of Carrick, took to wife Isabella, sister of the aforesaid Gartnay, Earl of Mar; and, of her, he begat an only daughter, named Marjory, who wedded Walter, Steward of Scotland, and of whom this Walter begat an only son, named Robert Stewart, afterwards king.[17]

As Bruce was welcoming his new daughter and grieving the loss of his wife, he was also deciding where his loyalties lay. Maybe it was the arrival of his daughter, and the thought of her future, that galvanised Bruce into joining the Scottish cause. He had not fought for John Balliol at Dunbar, but in June 1297, he had allied himself with James the Steward and Bishop Wishart as they opposed an English force at Irvine. The skirmish ended ignominiously, but Bruce had chosen his side and spent the next four and a half years taking part in, and sometimes leading, the resistance to English rule. Despite John of Fordun's claims to the contrary, Bruce did not fight for the English at Falkirk; he was at the time burning the castle at Ayr, to prevent it becoming an English base of operations.[18]

The defeat at Falkirk saw the southeast of Scotland come under English rule, but the fight was not over. By late 1298, Robert the Bruce had been made a Guardian of Scotland, alongside his greatest rival, John Comyn of Badenoch. William Wallace was sent to France to renew the alliance of 1295. Further approaches were made to the papacy in an effort to win support for the return of John Balliol, now in papal custody, to the Scots throne. And despite Edward's instructions that only Englishmen were to be appointed to church vacancies in Scotland, two new Scottish bishops were appointed in William Lamberton, as Bishop of St Andrews, and David Murray, as Bishop of Moray.[19] Lamberton was further appointed as chief Guardian of Scotland, with the hope that he could keep the bickering between Bruce and Comyn at bay. In 1299, Bruce and Comyn almost came to blows and had to be separated by James the Steward. By May 1300, Robert the Bruce was no longer a guardian. The reasons behind his departure are unclear, though it may have been the insistence on the reinstatement of King John Balliol, when Robert had ambitions for the throne himself. Despite his resignation, Robert the Bruce continued to make his resources available to the administration and led the resistance to an English invasion into Galloway led by the prince of Wales, as Edward I led a second force up the eastern side of the country. As his castle at Turnberry was captured, Bruce found himself isolated and without political influence. He continued to resist, carrying out lightning raids on the prince's army, inflicting casualties and forcing him to return to Carlisle.[20]

In February 1302, when it was believed that John Balliol would return imminently, and with his castle of Turnberry in English hands, Robert the Bruce renewed his allegiance to Edward I. We may judge Robert the Bruce harshly for his shifting loyalties, between Scotland and Edward I, but we must remember that Bruce had a foot in both camps. He was a Scottish lord. However, he was also a Norman one, with lands and titles on both sides of the border. He must have been conflicted. He had to decide where his own best interests lay. Balliol's return was thwarted in 1303 when, on 20 May, England and France made peace, leaving Scotland isolated. Moreover, the pope's declining interest in the Scottish cause allowed Edward to act as he saw fit with Scotland. In the same year that he had renewed his allegiance to the English king, Robert the Bruce married again, as Bower records: 'After the death of the aforesaid Isabella, the same Robert while still an earl married Elizabeth daughter of [Richard] de Burgh earl of Ulster.'[21] His bride was the daughter of Richard de Burgh, Earl of Ulster and Connaught, and his wife, Margaret. She was a goddaughter of King Edward I. Richard de Burgh was one of the most prominent of Edward's Anglo-Irish supporters and it may be that the king himself played a part in arranging the match. However, the earldoms of Carrick and Ulster had previously been close, and it may be that Robert had returned to Edward's peace in order to renew these family relations with Ulster.[22] At the age of just 13, Elizabeth de Burgh was married to 28-year-old Robert the Bruce, Earl of Carrick; probably at his father's manor of Writtle, near Chelmsford in Essex, or possibly at Canterbury.[23] If Edward did not personally arrange the marriage, he certainly encouraged it, as a way of keeping his young Scottish noble loyal to his cause.

In April 1303, Robert the Bruce was ordered to raise 1,000 infantry and as many men-at-arms as he could gather and join the retinue of the prince of Wales for the forthcoming campaign against Scotland. His father-in-law launched a sea-borne attack on the Isle of Bute which resulted in the capture of Rothesay Castle. Bruce was part of the successful campaign and, following the capture of Ayr, was given custody of its castle in December 1303, along with the sheriffdom of Lanarkshire, a lucrative position which was valued at £494.[24] Edward I was having similar success in his campaign on the eastern side of Scotland. He then established himself at Dunfermline Abbey for the winter, hoping that his continued presence in Scotland would add to the discomfort of the Scots. In the meantime, the Scottish leadership called on Wallace to raise an army. Which he duly did. With the assistance of Simon Fraser, Wallace carried out a campaign of harassing the English from the depths of Selkirk Forest. But with the English so entrenched in Scotland, resistance appeared hopeless and the Scottish lords, one by one, began to submit to Edward, seeking terms of surrender. By 9 February 1304, the acting Guardian of Scotland, John Comyn, had formally surrendered near Perth. Of the leading Scots still in France, Edward demanded that Bishop Wishart serve three years in exile, Sir John de Soules chose exile rather than returning to Edward's peace, and James Stewart and Sir Ingram de Umfraville reluctantly returned to the king's peace.[25]

For William Wallace, however, there was to be no compromise. Edward set the freedom fighter's former allies the task of finding and capturing Wallace. Simon

Fraser and John Comyn both failed in the task, as did Robert the Bruce and Sir John de Segrave, but Wallace was now a hunted man and in retreat in the dense Selkirk Forest. Bruce and Segrave were urged by Edward to complete their task, 'as the cloak is well made, also to make the hood'.[26] Robert took a respite from his service for Edward in March 1304, after the death of his father, Robert de Brus, Lord of Annandale, taking physical possession of the lands newly bequeathed to him. With his father's death, Robert not only inherited the Bruce patrimony, but he also inherited his father's claim to the throne of Scotland, not that he was in a position to act on such a claim, at the time. Robert returned to the English army in May, as Edward I prosecuted the siege of Stirling Castle. The castle was held by Sir William Oliphant, initially in the name of King John Balliol, until he realised the King of Scots was not bringing a French army to his relief. The castle was bombarded by siege engines for twelve weeks until the garrison gave its unconditional surrender. However, King Edward had not yet been able to deploy his largest siege engine, War Wolf. And so, he ordered the garrison to reoccupy the castle until he could try out the new weapon, in front of an audience comprising his young queen, Marguerite of France, his son, the prince of Wales, and several Scottish lords who were now in the English camp.[27]

Amidst all the excitement, no one noticed that Robert the Bruce, Earl of Carrick, had slipped away.

A mile away from Stirling, at Cambuskenneth Abbey, Robert met with William Lamberton, Bishop of St Andrews. The earl and the bishop made an agreement of mutual support, sealed in an indenture in which it was agreed that, if either broke the agreement, the offending party would pay a fine of £10,000. They agreed to help each other in their business and other affairs, to warn each other of danger, and to act to avert any such danger.[28] And with the bishop on his side, Robert could now start his campaign for the Scottish throne, discreetly, at first. Edward I was none the wiser. With Stirling subdued, he appointed Robert the Bruce, Bishop Wishart and Sir John de Mowbray to be the representatives of the Scottish Community of the Realm.[29] They were to offer ideas of how the future government of Scotland should be managed and suggest ten men who should be elected to represent Scotland in the English parliament, where the final details would be debated. With this aim in mind, a Scots parliament was held at Perth in May 1305, where two bishops, two abbots, two earls and two barons were elected, alongside one representative each from the north and south of the Forth. Neither Bishop Wishart nor Robert the Bruce were among those elected, though at the English parliament in September of the same year, Bruce was selected as one of the twenty-two-member Scots council. Bishops Lamberton and Crambeth and the earls of Buchan, Dunbar, Ross and Atholl, were all given places on the council. Among the barons on the council was Robert the Bruce's arch-rival, John Comyn of Badenoch.[30] However, Edward was to place loyal Englishmen in key positions throughout Scotland. The new Lieutenant of Scotland was Edward's nephew, John of Brittany, and 'by decree and assent from both sides, justiciars and clerks were deputed to act two by two both north and south of the Forth, to keep the peace in their native regions, decide lawsuits and settle fights.'[31] However, the sheriffs were replaced, with Edinburgh, Jedburgh, Linlithgow and Peebles now having English sheriffs, and most of Scotland's key castles were to remain in English lands.[32]

Where Elizabeth de Burgh was amidst all of these events is unrecorded. She may have been residing on one of Robert the Bruce's estates, only accompanying him when he attended King Edward's court. Neither do we know that Robert consulted with his wife before putting his thoughts into action. I cannot believe that she was totally ignorant of her husband's thoughts and ambitions. He surely discussed some parts of his plan with Elizabeth when they were alone in their chamber, though he may have been reticent in how much he trusted his young wife, when her father was a close ally of the King of England. We can only speculate.

As the political future of Scotland was being decided in the English parliament, a Scottish tragedy was being played out at Westminster and Smithfield. On 3 August 1305, William Wallace's luck in evading his pursuers had finally run out. He was 'craftily and treacherously taken', near Glasgow, by men in the service of Sir John Stewart of Menteith, keeper of Dumbarton Castle, and was handed over to the English.[33] Menteith was rewarded with £100.[34] Wallace was transported to London, where he arrived on 22 August. The following day, he was tried for treason at Westminster, though he argued that he could be no traitor, as he had never sworn allegiance to the King of England. His guilt was already decided:

> it was adjudged that he should be drawn and hanged, beheaded, disembowelled, and dismembered, and that his entrails should be burnt; which was done. And his head was exposed upon London Bridge, his right arm on the bridge of Newcastle-upon-Tyne, his left arm at Berwick, his right foot at Perth, and his left foot at Aberdeen.[35]

Edward was making an example of Wallace for all to see, and remember: 'By this that tyrant thought to destroy the fame of the noble William for ever, since in the eyes of the foolish his life seemed to be ended with such a contemptible death. But such a death does not count against him.'[36]

In trying to make an example of William Wallace, to stamp out the last vestiges of resistance, Edward I had made him into a hero and a martyr to the Scots. He was their Braveheart (sorry, couldn't resist). Rather than subduing and overawing the Scots, Wallace's brutal and unjust execution motivated them to re-establish Scottish sovereignty and divest themselves of English rule. It must have helped to galvanise Robert the Bruce into action. In the months since his meeting with Lamberton, Robert the Bruce must have been building up his support, sounding out the Scottish magnates and divining who would – and who would not – support his bid for the throne. There was one significant obstacle to his plans, however, and that was the Comyn faction, loyal adherents to John Balliol, who were still holding out for the return of King John or, failing that, the accession of his son and heir, Edward.

The leader of the Comyn family was John Comyn, Lord of Badenoch, who had served alongside Bruce as Guardian of Scotland. The two men had clashed many times and a lifetime of animosity festered between them. But Robert needed to come to terms with Comyn if he was to have any chance of taking the throne. A meeting was arranged and on 10 February 1306, the two men met at the Church of the Greyfriars in Dumfries, each accompanied by a small retinue of their most trusted men.

To meet in the Church of the Greyfriars was supposed to guarantee a safe, violence-free meeting. To shed blood in a church was the worst sacrilege and would merit a sentence of excommunication, condemning the perpetrator's soul to eternal damnation. That both sides believed in these dire consequences makes what happened next all the more shocking. Bruce and Comyn met at the high altar, whether their men were watching from a distance, or waiting outside the church, is unclear. Though we do not have a record of the discussion, we can assume that it went along the lines of Bruce asking what Comyn wanted in return for supporting Bruce's attempt on the throne. The discussion became an argument, insults were thrown and then a weapon was drawn:

> The same year, after the aforesaid Robert had left the king of England and returned home, no less miraculously than by God's grace, a day is appointed for him and the aforesaid John to meet together at Dumfries; and both sides repair to the above-named place. John Comyn is twitted with his treachery and belied troth. The lie is at once given. The evil-speaker is stabbed, and wounded unto death, in the church of the Friars; and the wounded man is, by the friars, laid behind the altar. On being asked by those around whether he could live, straightway his answer is: – 'I can.' His foes, hearing this, give him another wound.[37]

And here, in this act, we can see the distinct perspectives of the Scottish and English chroniclers. As far as the Scots are concerned, Bower and Fordun, although they each acknowledge that it was Bruce who drew the dagger, both have sympathy for Robert the Bruce's actions and place the blame on Comyn for his treachery, as 'John was attacked for his betrayal and breach of faith.'[38] The English, on the other hand, lay the blame at Robert the Bruce's feet:

> In the same year, on the fourth of the Ides of February, to wit, on the festival of S. Scholastica virgin, Sir Robert Bruce, Earl of Carrick, sent seditiously and treacherously for Sir John Comyn, requiring him to come and confer with him at the house of the Minorite Friars in Dumfries; and, when he came, did slay him and his uncle Sir Robert Comyn in the church of the Friars, and afterwards took [some] castles of Scotland and their wardens, and on the Annunciation of

the Blessed Virgin next following was made King of Scotland at Scone, and many of the nobles and commonalty of that land adhered to him.[39]

As Comyn lay wounded, Bruce's men ran to finish him off, also killing John's uncle, Robert Comyn. However, whilst the accounts of Fordun, Bower and even Lanercost can be read as Robert the Bruce acting in the heat of the moment, Walter of Guisborough suggested the murder was calculated and premeditated. According to him,

> Robert the Bruce greatly feared John Comyn, earl of Badenoch, who was a powerful man in Scotland and loyal to the king of England. Bruce knew that John Comyn might stand in the way of his scheme, so he sent him as a trick two of his brothers, Thomas and Nigel Bruce, to ask whether Comyn would come to see him at Dumfries to discuss with him matters which affected them both.[40]

The discussion became an argument, with Bruce accusing Comyn of treachery and

> when Comyn tried to pacify him and defend himself, Bruce refused to listen. Instead, as he had plotted, he kicked him and struck him with his sword, then departed. Bruce's men pursued Comyn, struck him down in the church on the paved floor in front of the altar, and left him there for dead.[41]

And just in case Robert the Bruce had not damned himself enough in killing Comyn, Guisborough adds horse stealing to his crimes when, as he left the church, 'seeing John Comyn's fine warhorse, he mounted it'.[42]

Whether Robert the Bruce always intended to kill John Comyn, or acted in the heat of the moment, is open to conjecture, and probably personal preference. Every historian has a bias, and those who admire Robert the Bruce, including myself, will tend towards a sudden act of violence, whereas those less enamoured of him would probably lean towards premeditated murder. The fact the two rivals met in a church, neutral, sanctified ground, would suggest that Bruce was trying to avoid shedding blood. However, he did have a sword, or maybe just a dagger, with him, suggesting he knew that the meeting could descend into violence. It is an intriguing dilemma. Whatever the motives, the result was the death of John Comyn and a race against time for Robert the Bruce to execute the plans he had put in place over the last few months. One of his first moves was to visit Bishop Wishart in Glasgow, to confess his sin and receive absolution. Robert's actions at Dumfries had not only endangered his immortal soul but risked everything he had worked for. Should the pope issue a sentence of excommunication before he could be crowned, his bid for the throne would be over before it had begun. Wishart absolved Robert of his crime and offered his public support in return for Robert's assurances that he would protect and obey the Church of Scotland.[43]

Bishop Wishart then gave Robert the royal standard of Scotland, the Lion Rampant, which he had kept hidden from King Edward, and the rich robes which were to be worn at Robert's inauguration as king. Robert then wrote to Edward I to demand recognition of his kingship and the sovereignty of the kingdom of Scotland, a demand Edward contemptuously dismissed. According to Walter of Guisborough, 'Robert Bruce then travelled through Scotland, occupying and fortifying Comyn's castles and devastating his lands, while the dead man's relatives fled from him, and all the English fled to their own country.'[44] At the same time, Robert was provisioning his own castles from the stores seized from the castles he had taken. Dumfries fell on 3 March, followed by Ayr, Dunaverty and Rothesay on the Isle of Bute.[45] He did not have everything his own way, however, and some resisted, such as Sir John of Menteith, who refused to surrender the castle of Dumbarton to Sir Alexander Lindsay.

From that fateful moment in Greyfriars Church in Dumfries when Robert the Bruce killed John Comyn, it was a race against time for Robert to establish himself as king. Almost immediately, Robert made the dash for Scone, hoping to achieve his inauguration before the Christian world erupted in uproar over his sacrilege. An excommunicate could not be crowned. And so, although he did not have the whole of Scotland behind him, Robert 'taking with him as many men as he could get, hastened to Scone'.[46] His sisters Christian and Mary accompanied him to Scone Abbey, as did his wife Elizabeth and daughter Marjorie. The Stone of Scone was the traditional seat for the making of the kings of Scotland and, although the stone had been stolen by the English and spirited away to London, holding the inauguration at the abbey sent a message of defiance to the English king.

Six weeks after the death of John Comyn, on 25 March 1306, Robert the Bruce was crowned King Robert I of Scotland, with Elizabeth by his side, by Isabella MacDuff, Countess of Buchan, daughter of Duncan, Earl of Fife. In the absence of the royal crown of Scotland, a gold circlet was placed on Robert's head. The Earls of Fife had, for centuries, claimed the hereditary right to crown Scotland's kings. However, in 1306, the earl was only a teenager, in English custody, and a loyal devotee of Edward I. It fell to the courageous Isabella MacDuff, the young earl's aunt, to claim the hereditary right to perform the ritual. Isabella's husband was John Comyn, Earl of Buchan, friend and cousin to the John Comyn killed in the church in Dumfries. Isabella knew that she was not only facing the wrath of King Edward but also her husband in participating in Robert's inauguration as king. Isabella's participation was an act of bravery and defiance. She would have known that her actions would mean there was no going back. In supporting Robert the Bruce, the man who stood accused of John Comyn's murder, Isabella turned against her husband and his entire family, people she had lived among for her entire married life. Isabella is said to have stolen one of her husband's destriers for the ride to Scone to place the crown on the new king's head. However, it is also suggested that Robert sent the Earl of Atholl to fetch Isabella from her lands, to perform the inauguration, indicating she was rather reluctant to play her part in the open defiance of Edward I. With the murder of Comyn hanging over him, Robert the Bruce wanted to ensure that his inauguration was an imitation of that of Alexander III, to reinforce his legitimacy and respectability as king.[47]

Elizabeth was present to see her husband crowned, though Scottish queens were, by tradition, not crowned themselves. Also present were the earls of Lennox, Atholl, Menteith and, possibly, the young Earl of Mar who was in Robert's wardship. Also present were the bishops of Dunkeld and Brechin, and lords and barons including James Stewart, Sir Christopher Seton and Alexander Scrymgeour, the royal standard bearer. Robert the Bruce's four brothers, Edward, Neil, Thomas and Alexander, were in attendance with two of their sisters, Mary and Christian. The king's daughter, Marjorie, no more than 10 years old, was there to see her father crowned. The ceremony may have been overseen by bishops Wishart and Lamberton, though both claimed they were not present when questioned by Edward I. Bishop Lamberton, as Bishop of St Andrews and senior prelate in Scotland, certainly celebrated High Mass for the new king and queen two days later, on 27 March.[48] The bishop then paid homage to King Robert and swore fealty to him for his temporalities. Over the two days, all the lords and clerics assembled would have done the same. According to one account, Elizabeth is said to have referred to herself and her husband as the king and queen of the May, suggesting that their royal tenure could be fleeting, or, perhaps, that they were playing at being king and queen, as children did during the May Day celebrations. By this point, while she was still only about 17 years of age, Elizabeth and Robert had been married for four years. Certainly, for them the inauguration was not the end of the struggle but the beginning. If anything, things were about to get much worse.

Edward's wrath was implacable. He raised the dragon banner, which signified that the normal rules of chivalry were suspended; mercy would not be shown to those who surrendered. He sent forces north, with Aymer de Valence taking command in the east while Henry Percy commanded the west.[49] They were to hunt down anyone complicit in Comyn's murder and anyone aiding Robert the Bruce. Edward's forces

> hanged those who had part in the aforesaid conspiracy, design and assistance in making him king, most of whom they caused first to be drawn at the heels of horses and afterwards hanged them; among whom were the Englishman Christopher de Seton, who had married the sister of the oft-mentioned Robert, and John and Humphrey, brothers of the said Christopher, and several others with them. Among those who were hanged were not only simple country folk and laymen, but also knights and clerics and prebendaries, albeit these protested that, as members of the Church, justice should be done to them accordingly.[50]

By early June, King Robert was in the north-east, attempting to recruit more troops in the Garioch. The difficulty he was having in recruitment demonstrates how divisive his kingship was to the Scots. Extraordinary efforts were made to encourage men to fight. David of Moravia (Murray), Bishop of Moray, promised all they would receive God's grace if they fought for Robert, as if they were fighting in the Holy Land. At the same time, the king's supporters were being gathered up by the advancing English, including William Lamberton and Robert Wishart:

> They also took to England and imprisoned the Bishop of S. Andrews, whom the King of England had appointed Guardian of Scotland, and who had entered into a bond of friendship with the said Robert, as was proved by letters of his which were found; also the Bishop of Glasgow, who had been principal adviser in that affair, and the Abbot of Scone, who assisted the aforesaid Robert when he was received into royal honour. Howbeit in the meantime Robert called de Brus was lurking in the remote isles of Scotland.[51]

It was a desperate time for King Robert. As the situation deteriorated, on hearing the news that Valence had taken Perth, Robert sent his wife and daughter north to what he hoped would be safety at Kildrummy Castle.[52] His sisters Mary and Christian, along with Isabella, Countess of Buchan, accompanied them. They were escorted by John of Strathbogie, Earl of Atholl and King Robert's brother, Sir Neil Bruce. In June, he headed for Perth and a showdown with Aymer de Valence. The two forces met on 19 June at Methven, when Valence attacked Robert's camp, taking him completely by surprise. The fighting was fierce and Robert barely escaped capture when Philip Mowbray caught his reins. The king's brother-in-law, Sir Christopher Seton, came to his aid. Bruce, his brothers and the earls of Lennox and Atholl all managed to escape; while others were killed or captured, including the king's nephew, Thomas Randolph and Alexander Scrymgeour, who were taken south to imprisonment. It was a summer of losses for Robert. Following his capture at Methven, Alexander Scrymgeour was hanged along with fourteen others. Sir Christopher Seton, Christian's husband, was captured after the fall of Loch Doon and executed at Dumfries. Simon Fraser was taken to London, where he was hanged, drawn and quartered.[53]

King Robert now sent word to his brother Neil, to bring the queen and her ladies south to meet with the king in the foothills of the Mounth. Once reunited, the royal party travelled at speed towards the shores of Loch Lomond. At the shrine of Saint Fillan of Glenlochart, Robert left an offering, venerated the relic, a pastoral staff, and was given absolution from Abbot Maurice of Inchaffray. The need for such spiritual consolation must have been acute, as on 5 June, the Archbishop of Canterbury and the Bishop of Carlisle had both pronounced pope Clement V's sentence of excommunication on the Scottish king. In late July, Robert and his party moved into Lorn, hostile territory, where 'he was again beaten and put to flight, on the 11th of August, at a place called Dalry. But there, also, he did not lose many of his men.'[54] With James Douglas and many others injured in the skirmishing, his numbers dwindling, and with the queen and her ladies in their company, the king realised it would be impossible to keep everyone safe. He sent the queen back to Kildrummy Castle under the protection of his brother, Neil Bruce.

It is thought that the eventual destination for the Bruce women was to be Orkney, so they could take a boat to Norway, where Robert's sister, Isabella, widow of King Erik II, was still living. Unfortunately, they would never make it. As well as Neil Bruce, their escort included the Earl of Atholl, Alexander Lindsay and his son David.[55] The English caught up with them at Kildrummy Castle and laid siege to it, not realising the queen and her ladies, escorted by the Earl of Atholl, had already escaped further north. Neil Bruce remained with the garrison to mount a desperate defence, in order to give the queen, his niece and sisters enough time to escape. The defenders were betrayed by someone in their garrison, a blacksmith who set fire to the barns, making the castle indefensible. Following their capitulation, the entire garrison was executed. Sir Neil Bruce was subjected to a traitor's death; he was hanged, drawn and quartered at Berwick in September 1306. The young queen and her companions did not escape for long; they made for Tain, in Easter Ross, probably in the hope of finding a boat to take them onwards. They were hiding in the sanctuary of St Duthac when they were captured by the Earl of Ross (an adherent of John Balliol), who breached sanctuary in order to apprehend the queen. Ross handed them over to the English. They were sent south, to Edward I at Lanercost Priory in Cumbria.

The Earl of Atholl was taken to London, where he was hanged and decapitated; his head was placed on a spike on London Bridge, beside those of Wallace and Fraser. The women would not face death, but Edward was not inclined to sympathy. Queen Elizabeth was sent south from Lanercost, to the royal manor of Burstwick-in-Holderness. She was assigned a meagre daily allowance for her keep and watched over by two women, specifically chosen for their dour, humourless personalities. No one was allowed to talk to her, nor address her as queen. Elizabeth wrote to Edward:

> Elizabeth de Brus to the K. Complains that though he commanded his bailiffs of Holderness to see herself and attendants honourably sustained, yet they neither furnish attire for her person or head, nor a bed, nor furniture of her chamber, saving only a robe of three 'garnementz' yearly, and for her servants one robe each for everything. Prays the K. to order amendment of her condition, and that her servants be paid for their labour, that she be not neglected; or that she may have a yearly sum allowed by the K. for her sustenance.[56]

The king was unmoved. Elizabeth, however, was treated more kindly than her stepdaughter, and the other ladies in her party. Her father was a close ally of Edward I and the king did not want to alienate him. In 1310, on 15 October, Edward II issued an order: 'The K. commands the sheriff of Oxford and Berkshire to buy 30 qrs. wheat and 30 qrs. malt for the use of Elizabeth wife of Robert de Brus, dwelling at Bistelesham by his orders.'[57] By this time, Elizabeth was staying at Bisham Manor in Berkshire but the king's order was not carried out and a month later, had to be reissued, with a rebuke, on 15 November: 'The sheriff of Oxford is commanded forthwith to deliver to John de Benteleye keeper of the household of Elizabeth de Brus, 30 qrs. of wheat and 10 *l.* in money for her expenses, which he had omitted to do.'[58]

At the start of 1312, with her husband gaining strength and raiding into Yorkshire, Elizabeth was moved to a more secure location and on 6 February, the king commanded 'the constable of Windsor castle to receive Elizabeth wife of Robert de Brus and her retinue, providing sufficient houses to accommodate them. John de Benteleye to be in attendance on her as hitherto.'[59] Elizabeth was later moved to Shaftesbury Abbey in Dorset. By this time, she was allowed six attendants and was given a regular allowance of '20s. a week for the support of herself and retinue at Shaftesbury'.[60] Elizabeth was still at Shaftesbury on 6 July 1313, when a payment was made of 'Respite of 12*l.* paid to Elizabeth de Brus wife of Robert de Brus for expenses of herself and retinue for 12 weeks (6th year) at 20s. a week.'[61] On 6 July 1314, three weeks after Edward II's defeat at Bannockburn – and Robert's victory – Elizabeth was moved once again, and allowed more freedom, though still guarded:

> The K. commands that Elizabeth, wife of Robert de Brus, be removed
> from the abbey of Barking to Rochester castle, where the constable
> is directed to assign her a sufficient chamber and 20s. weekly for
> expenses. That she may take exercise within the castle and the priory
> of St Andrew at suitable times, under sure guard.[62]

She would endure eight years of house arrest, in total. Throughout her years of captivity, Elizabeth was never acknowledged as Queen of Scots by the English, and nor was Robert acknowledged as king. She was always referred to as the wife of Robert de Brus, Earl of Carrick.

Elizabeth's capture would have been a hard blow for Robert the Bruce. The new King of Scotland still lacked a male heir, and had no chance of getting one while his wife was in English hands. This made his hold on the throne even more precarious than it already was. In addition, the king's only legitimate child, Marjorie, was also in English custody. Edward I had his own plans for her imprisonment and that of her aunts. Edward I's admirer, Sir Maurice Powicke, said Edward treated his captives with a 'peculiar ferocity'.[63] Orders for the 'farther ... custody of the countesses of Carrick and Buchan, Marie and Christine the sisters, and Margerie the daughter, of Robert de Brus', specifying that 'three of the ladies to be in kages', are dated 7 November 1306.[64] King Edward ordered that 24-year-old Mary Bruce and

Isabella, the Countess of Buchan, who had performed Robert the Bruce's coronation, should be imprisoned in specially constructed iron cages, the only privacy being a small privy, and kept within the tower rooms of two castles; Mary at Roxburgh and Isabella at Berwick. Much myth has risen around these orders, with suggestions that the cages were suspended from the castles' walls, exposed to the elements, on the Scottish borders, which would have been a certain death sentence.

As it was, the cages were hardly comfortable accommodations and were constructed with 'sparred sides that all might look in from curiosity'.[65] The construction of the cages was intended to humiliate their occupants and, at the same time, Scotland's new king. They were also a taunt; placing Isabella and Mary in these cages, in castles on the border with Scotland, it is possible they were intended as a challenge to Robert the Bruce, showing him that he was not powerful enough to protect his women, but also teasing him, hoping he would be drawn into a rescue attempt that would, almost certainly, lead to the destruction of his limited forces. The unfortunate women would be held in that way for four years, until Edward I's successor, Edward II, with Robert the Bruce making gains against the English, ordered their removal to convents in 1310. On 15 October 1311, payment was made for Mary's imprisonment of '48*s*. 8*d* to Mary de Brus sister of Robert de Brus, prisoner, from 29th January till 24th June last – 146 days at 4 *d*. a day.'[66] Isabella was transferred to a Carmelite convent, though still in Berwick. In 1313, she was placed in the custody of Sir Henry de Beaumont, who was married to Alice, niece and co-heir of Isabella's husband, John Comyn, Earl of Buchan. Mary was moved to Newcastle.[67] It seems Edward also ordered a cage to be made for Marjorie at the Tower of London, where she was first held. But he relented, possibly because of her age, and the child – not yet 11 years old – was sent to a Gilbertine convent at Watton in Yorkshire. Initial orders were given that she should be held in solitary confinement, with no one allowed to speak to her; but this may also have been rescinded. It must have been a terrifying time for the little girl, far away from home and separated from everyone she knew and loved. Marjorie's aunt and Mary's older sister, Christian, was also sent to a Gilbertine nunnery, at Sixhills in the Lincolnshire Wolds; we do not know when she received the news that her husband, Sir Christopher Seton, had been hanged, drawn, and beheaded at Dumfries.

The death of Edward I in 1307 brought no respite in the fight for Scotland. Edward II continued his father's policy of hunting down King Robert and his allies, though vicariously through various lieutenants. Edward II's unstable reign would present opportunities for Robert to advance his cause. Even before the old king's death, Robert had won a notable victory against Aymer de Valence at Loudoun Hill in May 1307. As the years passed, Robert the Bruce began to make progress in Scotland, winning ground and supporters, though not without setbacks. A later legend arose about this period in his career, that King Robert learned patience when he was hiding in a cave in a remote area of Carrick, watching a spider weave its web, failing time and again but never giving up, until it had succeeded. Despite his grave losses, including his wife in captivity and three of his brothers, Neil, Thomas and Alexander, executed by the English, Bruce continued the fight, his surviving brother Edward at his side. The opportunity for a showdown with the English came out of a rash, though chivalrous, agreement between Edward Bruce and the English commander of Stirling Castle; the castle would be surrendered to the Scots if an English army did not come to within three miles of Stirling within a year.[68]

With all of Europe watching, Edward II could not refuse the challenge and arrived at Stirling on 23 June 1314, with an army consisting of 3,000 cavalry and around 15,000 foot soldiers. King Robert was there to face him, with no more than 10,000 infantry and perhaps 500 light cavalry. The next day, 'an evil, miserable and calamitous day for the English', the Scots king achieved a not inconsiderable victory at the Battle of Bannockburn.[69] The English cavalry were easily beaten by a combination of marshy terrain, camouflaged pitfalls and the Scottish tactic of fighting in schiltroms.[70] The King of England narrowly escaped capture, fleeing the field with an escort of 500 knights. Several notable English lords were taken prisoner, including Humphrey de Bohun, Earl of Hereford. And the capture of such notable Englishmen gave King Robert a strong bargaining position in the ensuing negotiations. And the chance to reunite what was left of his family. Peace talks opened on 20 October. The English agreed to the release of Robert's wife, daughter and sisters, as well as Robert Wishart, Bishop of Glasgow, in exchange for King Edward's brother-in-law, Humphrey de Bohun, and the remaining English prisoners.[71] The talks collapsed on the issue of the English king recognising the legitimacy of Robert as King of Scots and Scottish independence from England. They continued sporadically, amid a series of skirmishes and political jostling, but little further was decided. The prisoner exchange was eventually completed by mid-February 1315:

> Among them was captured also the wealthy John of Brittany, who eventually offered for his release a considerable amount of money and immense wealth. An exchange was made for him to the effect that in return for him the queen was restored to freedom along with the venerable old man the bishop of Glasgow.[72]

And after eight years of imprisonment, Queen Elizabeth, her stepdaughter Marjorie and Robert's sisters, Mary and Christian, finally returned home: 'From that day forward, moreover, the whole land of Scotland not only always rejoiced in victory over the English, but also overflowed with boundless wealth.'[73]

It must have been a bitter-sweet reunion. Of their thirteen years of marriage, Robert and Elizabeth had spent two-thirds of it separated. Marjorie was now an 18-year-old woman, rather than the child she had been when Robert last saw her. It seems likely that Isabella MacDuff died whilst still in captivity, in the year leading up to Bannockburn, probably due to her health being destroyed by the years of deprivation; she was not among the hostages who were returned to Scotland following the Scots' victory.

Reunited at last, Robert set about consolidating his kingdom, with his queen at his side. In April, he summoned a parliament at Ayr, where the succession was decided in favour of any sons the king may have, followed by his brother, Edward Bruce, and any sons he may have. It was only if these two male lines failed that the succession would pass to Robert's daughter, Marjorie. At the same parliament, a marriage was arranged for Marjorie, to Walter Stewart, hereditary High Steward of Scotland. And in March 1316, Marjorie gave birth to a son, Robert Stewart, but we will look into that story later. In the meantime, Robert and Elizabeth hoped for children of their own, with two daughters being born between 1321 and 1323:

> Of her, this Robert, then king, begat two daughters – Matilda and Margaret. The said Margaret wedded the Earl of Sutherland, who, of her, begat an only son, named John. This John was, with his father, a hostage in England for the release of David ii., king of Scotland. But his mother departed this life just after she had given him birth. I will say nothing at all about her sister, Matilda; for she did nothing worth remembering. The aforesaid King Robert likewise begat, in the seventeenth year of his reign, an only son, named David, who succeeded him on the throne.[74]

Of their daughters, Margaret married William, fifth Earl of Sutherland and died in childbirth in 1346 or 1347; 'to them was born John earl of the same, who died as a hostage in England for his uncle King David.'[75] Despite his not wanting to mention her, John of Fordun records:

> In the year 1353, Matilda of Bruce, sister of the lord David, king of Scotland, died at Aberdeen, on the Feast of the blessed virgin Margaret, and was buried in Dunfermline, with her father and mother. She wedded a certain squire, named Thomas Isaac, who, of her, begat two daughters. The elder, named Joan, wedded a noble and mighty man, John of Lorne, lord of that ilk; who, of her, begat sons and daughters. Matilda's younger daughter, named Catherine, was taken away from this life at Strivelyn [Stirling].[76]

The much longed-for son, David, was born in 1324; 'In that year – on Monday the 5th of March, to wit, in the first week of Lent – David, King Robert's son, and the heir of Scotland, who succeeded his father in the kingdom, was born in the monastery of Dunfermline, after complines.'[77] The royal family had moved to Dunfermline Abbey at the end of 1323, celebrating Christmas there and settled in to await the arrival of the hoped-for prince. The relics of St Margaret of Wessex were housed within the abbey and were believed to assist women in labour. The queen – or the king – may well have asked for the birthing serk of St Margaret to be brought to Elizabeth when her time was near. The king had been absent, attending to tensions in the north, and was returning to Dunfermline when news reached him of the arrival of his son.[78]

David may have been the younger of a set of twins, his older brother, John, dying young.[79] However, it is also possible that John was born later, in 1327, shortly before the queen's death; the evidence is confusing. Either way, the child did not survive past infancy. If John was David's older twin, then he did not survive until his second birthday, when,

> the whole Scottish clergy, the earls and barons, and all the nobles, were gathered together, with the people, at Cambuskenneth, and, in presence of King Robert himself, took the oaths to David, King Robert's son and heir, – and to Robert Stewart, the aforesaid king's grandson, in case that same David died childless.[80]

The king was taking no chances and had both his son and grandson recognised as heirs, so that there would be no uncertainty to the succession, should the young prince die without a son of his own. The occasion also saw the celebration of a marriage when 'Andrew of Moray took to wife the lady Christina, that king's sister'.[81]

Elizabeth de Burgh, Queen of Scots suddenly fell ill in October 1327. She died on 26 October, aged around 38, at the royal residence at Cullen in Banffshire. The queen was buried beneath the choir in Dunfermline Abbey, while her viscera were entombed in the Lady Kirk of Cullen, where Robert founded a chaplaincy to pray for the queen's soul.[82] Robert the Bruce was buried beside her when he died eighteen months later: 'On the 7th of June 1329, died Robert of Bruce, of goodly memory, the illustrious king of Scots, at Cardross, in the twenty-fourth year of his reign. He was, beyond all living men of his day, a valiant knight.'[83]

We have little evidence of the closeness of Robert and Elizabeth's relationship. With the rancour between England and Scotland at the time, the chronicles tend to concentrate on the bigger picture, rather than the individuals. It cannot have been easy to rekindle a relationship after eight years apart, nor to overcome any recriminations each might have for the other over the paths their choices had taken them down. Elizabeth's remark at Robert's inauguration, of them playing at being king and queen, is often taken as a rebuke against Robert, but could also be read as her knowing they were baiting the bear, and that Edward I would be furious.[84] Robert is known to have had at least six illegitimate children, but that is not always the sign of an unhappy marriage, especially among kings. What we do know is that Elizabeth and Robert were able to overcome the emotional distance created by the years apart and secure the succession with the birth of Prince David. Robert was attentive to his family and saw to the comfort of his wife at Dunfermline, when she was close to going into labour. And he chose to be buried beside her. If there was not love between the king and queen, there was certainly affection, and that is all most medieval couples would have expected in a marriage.

Chapter Ten

Joan Makepeace and the Second War of Independence

I t was the success of Robert and Elizabeth's marriage, and of their determination to ensure the independence and sovereignty of Scotland, that meant their son, David, would succeed to the throne. King Robert's final years were marred by the loss of his wife and severe bouts of illness, often identified as leprosy. However, before his death, he had, also, finally, achieved the recognition of England. His more powerful southern neighbour had problems of its own in the 1320s, with increasingly violent challenges to the rule of Edward II culminating in his deposition by his estranged wife, Isabella of France. In 1326, Isabella had invaded with an army, captured King Edward, and replaced him on the throne with their son, Edward III. At such a time of internal strife, England – Isabella – needed peace with Scotland. Even before his death in 1329, King Robert had secured his son a bride. For King Robert, who knew that his own time was now short, peace with England would allow his son the time and stability he needed to grow into his role as king. Or so he hoped. And the deal would be sealed with a marriage.

In my research I frequently discover instances of happy medieval marriages – and even if a marriage was not based on love, it did not mean that it would not be successful. Indeed, in many such instances the young woman concerned found her own way of succeeding, whether it was through her children or the management of estates – or the fact that a lasting peace was achieved between her two countries. Unfortunately for Joan of the Tower, later to be known as Joan Makepeace, her marriage achieved none of these things. Joan was born in the Tower of London on 5 July 1321; hence her rather dramatic name. She was the youngest of the four children of Edward II and his queen, Isabella of France. Joan had two older brothers and a sister. Her eldest brother, Edward, who was nine years older than Joan, succeeded his father as King Edward III in 1327, following Edward II's deposition. Her second brother, John of Eltham, was born in 1316 and died of illness shortly after his 20th birthday, whilst campaigning against the Scots. Joan's only sister, Eleanor of Woodstock, born in 1318, was only three years older than her baby sister and would go on to marry Reginald II, Count of Guelders. Joan also had an illegitimate brother, Adam FitzRoy, a son of Edward II by an unknown woman. He was born in the early 1300s, but died whilst campaigning in Scotland with his father, in 1322.

Little Joan was named after her maternal grandmother, Queen Joan I of Navarre, wife of Philip IV of France. The king, also in London at the time of Joan's birth, but not at the Tower, granted an £80 respite on a £180 loan to Robert Staunton, the man who brought him 'news of her [Isabella's] delivery of Joan, the king's daughter'.[1] On 8 July, Edward arrived at the Tower of London to visit his wife and newborn daughter and stayed with them for several days. Little Joan was born at a time when her father was facing increasing opposition within the country. Calls for the exile of the hated favourites, the Despensers, father and son, saw an army led by Marcher barons surround the city of London, trapping Edward inside until he acquiesced to their demands. Edward II refused to accede to the pressure, until Queen Isabella, just weeks after giving birth, went down on her knees before her husband and begged him to send the Despensers away in order to prevent further violence. This act may well have been what finally drew a wedge between the king and queen, as Hugh Despenser the Younger, on his return from exile a few months later, blamed the queen for persuading the king to send him away.

As the last of the children of Edward II and Isabella, it seems likely that the royal couple's relationship changed shortly after her birth, their marriage heading for an irretrievable breakdown that would see the king deposed in favour of his son. Edward II was well known for having favourites; the first, Sir Piers Gaveston, met a sticky end in 1312, when he was murdered by barons angry at the influence he held over the king. Isabella's estrangement from her husband followed the rise of a new favourite, Sir Hugh Despenser the Younger, and, by the time of Joan's birth, his influence on the king was significant and alienating powerful barons at court. In March 1322, those barons were defeated at the Battle of Boroughbridge, Yorkshire, with many prominent lords killed, including the king's erstwhile brother-in-law Humphrey de Bohun, earl of Hereford, the man who had been taken prisoner at Bannockburn. The leader of the insurrection, the king's cousin Thomas, Earl of Lancaster, was executed six days later at Pontefract Castle. Joan was, therefore, growing up in the midst of a period of great turmoil, not only within England, but within her own family. It is doubtful that, as she grew, she was unaware of the atmosphere, but Isabella and Edward were both loving parents and probably tried to shield their children as much as they could, ensuring stability in their everyday lives. Joan was soon placed in the household of her older siblings, and put into the care of Matilda Pyrie, who had once been nurse to her older brother, John of Eltham.

Sometime before February 1325, Joan and her sister were established in their own household, under the supervision of Isabel, Lady Hastings and her husband, Ralph Monthermer. Isabel was the younger sister of Edward II's close companion, Hugh Despenser the Younger, and this act has often been seen by historians as the king removing the children from the queen's custody. Although it could have been a malicious act, it must be remembered, however, that Ralph Monthermer was the girls' uncle-by-marriage through his first wife, Joan of Acre, Edward II's sister, and it was a custom of the time that aristocratic children were fostered among the wider family. Joan and her elder sister, Eleanor, remained with Isabel even after Ralph's death in the summer of 1325; however, the following January, they were given into the custody of Joan Jermy, sister-in-law of the king's younger half-brother Thomas, Earl of Norfolk. Joan was the sister of Thomas's wife, Alice Hales, and took charge of the girls' household in January 1326. They lived mainly between Pleshey in Essex and Marlborough in Wiltshire.

As a consequence of the war with France, the little-known War of St Sardos, Queen Isabella saw her lands confiscated by the king, with Edward perhaps fearing that she would use her resources to support her brother, rather than her husband. According to the Lanercost chronicler, the king took action

> to resume possession of the lands and rents which he had formerly
> bestowed upon the queen, and they allowed her only twenty shillings
> a day for herself and her whole court, and they took away from her
> her officers and body servants, so that the wife of the said Sir Hugh
> was appointed, as it were, guardian to the queen, and carried her
> seal; nor could the queen write to anybody without her knowledge;
> whereat my lady the queen was equally indignant and distressed.[2]

Despenser's wife was Eleanor de Clare, King Edward's cousin, so it is questionable whether she was assigned to the queen as a jailor; it may be she was the queen's companion and friend. However, it is clear that life in England was becoming increasingly difficult for the queen, due to the war with France. The dispute had arisen over Edward II's refusal to travel to France to pay homage to Charles IV for the counties of Gascony and Ponthieu, which Edward had inherited from his parents, Edward I and Eleanor of Castile, respectively. Charles sent an army into the counties to confiscate them from the English king. As with all her siblings and many royal children throughout the centuries, Joan played a part in her father's diplomatic plans. In an attempt to form an alliance against France in 1324/5, Edward sought marriages in Spain for three of his four children, including 3-year-old Joan. While Eleanor was to marry Alfonso XI of Castile, Edward of Windsor, Edward II's oldest son and heir, was betrothed to Alfonso's sister, Leonor. Little Joan was proposed as the bride for the grandson of James II of Aragon – the future Pedro IV. The little prince was only two years older than Joan, but this would come to nought.[3]

On 9 March 1325, Queen Isabella departed England for France, to negotiate a peace settlement with her brother and bring an end to the War of St Sardos. Once at her brother's court, Queen Isabella

> astutely contrived that Edward, her elder son and heir of England,
> should cross over to his uncle, the King of France, on the plea that
> if he came and did homage to his uncle for Gascony and the other
> lands of the king beyond the sea, the King [of France] would transfer

> to him all these lands from the King [of England]; and he [Prince
> Edward] was made Duke of Aquitaine.[4]

Passing French lands into the hands of the eldest son was an established tactic of
English kings, in order to avoid paying homage to the King of France and therefore
appearing subservient or inferior to their fellow sovereign. By 1326, their mother,
Isabella, was living at the French court, along with her eldest son, Edward, refusing
to return to her husband whilst he still welcomed Hugh Despenser at his court.
Within months, Isabella and her companion (possibly her lover), Roger Mortimer,
were to invade England and drive Edward II from his throne, putting an end to the
proposed Spanish marriages. Edward II was captured and imprisoned in Berkley
Castle, forced to abdicate in favour of his eldest son, who was proclaimed King
Edward III in 1327.

On the deposition of Edward II, relations with Scotland became fractious.
The teenage Edward III marched north and narrowly escaped getting captured
or killed when the redoubtable Sir James Douglas raided his camp one night,
before returning to Scotland. Once the King of England had returned south, the
Scots crossed the border again and continued to harry parts of Northumberland,
so 'ambassadors were appointed between the kingdoms of England and Scotland
to arrange a temporary truce or confirm the former truce for thirteen years, or to
come to any treaty for a perpetual peace if that could be done'.[5] With the advice
of his mother and Roger Mortimer, the effective rulers of England, Edward 'was
forced to release the Scots by his public deed from all exaction, right, claim or
demand of the overlordship of the kingdom of Scotland on his part, or that of his
heirs and successors in perpetuity, and from any homage to be done to the Kings of
England.'[6] By the 1328 Treaty of Northampton, it was agreed that

> the aforesaid young king gave his younger sister, my lady Joan of
> the Tower, in marriage to David, son of Robert de Brus, King of
> Scotland, he being then a boy five years old. All this was arranged by
> the king's mother the Queen [dowager] of England, who at that time
> governed the whole realm. The nuptials were solemnly celebrated
> at Berwick on Sunday next before the feast of S. Mary Magdalene.[7]

With her father exiled or murdered (his fate remains a bone of contention to this
day), Joan became the central part of another plan – that of peace with Scotland.
The 7-year-old princess was to marry Robert the Bruce's only son and heir,
4-year-old David Bruce. The treaty provided that King Edward would supply an
alternative bride, if Joan were to die before the wedding. Conversely, were David
to die, Joan would marry King Robert's next heir instead – this would be the king's
grandson and namesake, Robert Stewart.[8] There is no reference to the provision of
a dowry in the treaty, but the Scots agreed to settle lands to the value of £2,000 on
Joan.[9] The English were so fearful that the Scots would renege on the agreement,

given that the marriage could be repudiated any time before David's 14th birthday, that they stipulated that King Robert would pay a fine of £100,000 if the marriage ceremony did not take place before Michaelmas 1338.[10] The treaty gave recognition to Scotland as an independent kingdom, and agreed to the return of the Black Rood (a portion of the Holy Cross), the Ragman Roll (a document showing the individual acts of homage by the Scottish nobility) and the Stone of Scone (the traditional stone on which Scotland's kings were crowned and which had sat in Westminster Abbey since being brought south by Edward I). The people of London, however, 'would no wise allow to be taken away from them the Stone of Scone, whereon the Kings of Scotland used to be set at their coronation at Scone'.[11] In return, King Robert was to make a payment of 30,000 marks in reparations for damages recently inflicted by the Scots.[12] The 1328 Treaty of Northampton was seen as a major humiliation by Edward III – and the 16-year-old king made sure his displeasure was known. However, he was obliged to sign it, resigning all rights and claims to the kingdom of Scotland:

> To all Christ's faithful people who shall see these letters, Edward, by the grace of God, King of England, Lord of Ireland, Duke of Aquitaine, greeting and peace everlasting in the Lord. Whereas, we and some of our predecessors, Kings of England, have endeavoured to establish rights of rule or dominion or superiority over the realm of Scotland, whence dire conflicts of wars waged have afflicted for a long time the kingdoms of England and Scotland: we, having regard to the slaughter, disasters, crimes, destruction of churches and evils innumerable which, in the course of such wars, have repeatedly befallen the subjects of both realms, and to the wealth with which each realm, if united by the assurance of perpetual peace, might abound to their mutual advantage, thereby rendering them more secure against the hurtful efforts of those conspiring to rebel or to attack, whether from within or from without: We will and grant by these presents, for us, our heirs and successors whatsoever, with the common advice, assent and consent of the prelates, princes, earls and barons, and the commons of our realm in our parliament, that the kingdom of Scotland, within its own proper marches as they were held and maintained in the time of King Alexander of Scotland, last deceased, of good memory, shall belong to our dearest ally and friend, the magnificent prince, Lord Robert, by God's grace illustrious King of Scotland, and to his heirs and successors, separate in all things from the kingdom of England, whole, free and undisturbed in perpetuity, without any kind of subjection, service, claim or demand. And by these presents we renounce and demit to the King of Scotland, his heirs and successors, whatsoever right we or our predecessors have put forward in any way in bygone times to the aforesaid kingdom

of Scotland. And, for ourselves and our heirs and successors, we cancel wholly and utterly all obligations, conventions and compacts undertaken in whatsoever manner with our predecessors, at whatsoever times, by whatsoever kings or inhabitants, clergy or laity, of the same kingdom of Scotland concerning the subjection of the realm of Scotland and its inhabitants. And wheresoever any letters, charters, deeds or instruments may be discovered bearing upon obligations, conventions and compacts of this nature, we will that they be deemed cancelled , invalid, of no effect and void, and of no value or moment. And for the full, peaceful and faithful observance of the foregoing, all and singular, for all time, we have given full power and special command by our other letters patent to our well-beloved and faithful Henry de Percy, our kinsman, and William de la Zouche of Ashby, and to either of them to make oath upon our soul. In testimony whereof we have caused these letters to be executed.

Given at York on the first day of March, in the second year of our reign.[13]

Although the Stone of Scone and Ragman Roll were never returned to Scotland, the marriage between Joan and David did go ahead, with a proviso that, should the marriage not be completed, within two months of David reaching his 14th birthday, the treaty would be declared invalid. Neither king was present at the nuptials. Wholly opposed to the marriage, Edward III refused to attend. Robert the Bruce stayed away, also, claiming illness; the Lanercost chronicler claims that King Robert 'had become leprous'.[14] The children were married at Berwick-on-Tweed on 17 July 1328, 'to the unspeakable joy of the people of either kingdom'.[15] Although the king was not present, 'the queen mother was there, with the king's brother and his older Sister and my lords the Bishops of Lincoln, Ely and Norwich, and the Earl of Warenne, Sir Roger de Mortimer and other English barons, and much people, besides those of Scotland, who assembled in great numbers at those nuptials.'[16] Despite the absence of the two kings, the wedding was a lavish occasion, costing the Scots king over £2,500.[92] In his *Scotichronicon*, Walter Bower described the wedding as 'an occasion of unutterable joy among all the people of both kingdoms'.[17]

Following the wedding, and nicknamed Joan Makepeace by the Scots, Joan was taken to Scotland to be raised alongside her child-groom. Her first stop was Cardross, where she and David stayed with King Robert for a short time. The little princess had been accompanied by a number of English ladies, most of whom returned to England at this point. Everything was to change for the two children the following year, when 'On the 7th of June 1329, died Robert of Bruce, of goodly memory, the illustrious king of Scots, at Cardross, in the twenty-fourth year of his reign. He was, beyond all living men of his day, a valiant knight.'[18] Five-year-old David Bruce was now King

David II, and Joan was his queen. Joan and David attained the dubious record of being the youngest married monarchs in British history. They were crowned, jointly, at Scone Abbey in Perthshire, on 24 November 1331. David was the first Scottish monarch to have a coronation which included the anointing with holy oil, thanks to a bull of John XXII granted on 13 June 1329, something David's predecessors, Alexander II and Alexander III, had both argued for, but been denied:

> On the 24th of November 1331, David, son and heir of King Robert, was anointed king of Scots, and crowned at Scone, by the lord James Ben, bishop of Saint Andrews, specially appointed thereunto by a Bull of the most holy father John xxii., then sovereign Pontiff. We do not read that any of the kings of Scotland, before this David, were anointed, or with such solemnity crowned. The same day, John Stewart, Earl of Angus – Thomas Randolph, son and heir of Thomas Earl of Moray – and other nobles of the kingdom of Scotland, received the order of knighthood.[19]

It was also the first time a Scottish Queen Consort was crowned: 'In the same year and on the same day Joan of the Tower was crowned queen.'[20] Virtually nothing is known of Joan's early years in Scotland. We can assume she continued her education and maybe spent some time getting to know her husband, as the country was ruled by a series of guardians. Scotland, however, was in turmoil and Edward III was not about to let his sister's marriage get in the way of his own ambitions for the country. Unfortunately for Joan, Edward Balliol, son of the erstwhile king, John Balliol, and Isabella de Warenne, had a strong claim to the crown and was, as opposed to her young husband, a grown man with the backing of Edward III. What followed was a tug-of-war for Scotland's crown, lasting many years. In 1332, Edward Balliol had even proposed to King Edward that Joan's marriage could be annulled, given the young couple were still too young to consummate it, and that Balliol himself could marry Joan. Balliol must have been in his 50s by that time, and Joan was 10 years old. Luckily, nothing came of the suggestion. David's supporters suffered a heavy defeat at Halidon Hill in July 1333. The little king and queen had been staying in the relative safety of Dumbarton Castle, one of the few Scottish castles not in the possession of the English.

Ten months after the defeat at Halidon Hill, with the situation still precarious, Joan and

> king David de Bruce, then a nine-year old boy, who was not strong enough to take revenge on his enemies, being only a child, retired to the kingdom of France with Rankin More and the queen under the supervision of his foster-father Sir Malcolm Fleming the keeper of Dumbarton, after the kingdom of Scotland had been put under Sir Andrew Moray as governor; and he was honourably received by the king and people of France.[21]

The Lanercost chronicler lays the blame for his departure firmly at King David's door, omitting to mention the king was still a child whose kingdom was beset by the English king:

> Meanwhile David, whom the Scots had formerly anointed as their king, and who had remained in the strong castle of Dunbarton, betook himself to France, and did homage to the King of France, so that he should hold his realm from him as from a Lord Paramount, on condition that he should assist him in recovering his kingdom from the aforesaid Kings of England and Scotland. Rumour of this being spread through Scotland, the number of Scots in rebellion against their king increased daily.[22]

The departure of the King of Scots would have definitely affected the moral of the forces he was leaving behind, but what choice did his guardians have? Exile in France was the better alternative to capture by the English.

An ally of Scotland and first cousin of Joan's mother, Philip VI of France gave the king and queen, and their Scottish attendants, accommodation in the famous Château Gaillard, built by Richard the Lionheart, in Normandy. Although very little is known of David and Joan's time in France, David was involved in the failed negotiations between Edward III and Philip VI of France in 1335 and 1336, which were aimed at resolving the respective claims, to the Scottish throne, of David and Edward Balliol. David is also thought to have accompanied the French king on campaigns in Picardy in 1339 and at Tournai in 1340.[23] Joan would have still been living in France when she heard of the demise of her older brother, John of Eltham, who had just turned 20 the month before his death in September 1336. John had been serving as one of Edward III's commanders in Scotland. He had been with his brother, the king, at Perth, when he fell ill, most likely of a fever though there were rumours of murder. It cannot have been an easy time for Joan. Far away from family, one brother dies suddenly whilst the other brother was attempting to secure her husband's throne for his rival, Edward Balliol. Joan must have known Edward had not wanted her married to David Bruce, but it would not have made the situation any more acceptable. He was her brother, after all.

The struggle against Edward Balliol continued in Scotland, with David's nephew, Robert Stewart, who was eight years the king's senior, acting as guardian of the kingdom from 1338.[24] In 1341, it was finally deemed safe enough for the royal couple to come home and they returned to Scotland, on 2 June. Joan was a month shy of her 20th birthday, while David was 17:

> On the 17th of April 1341, Edinburgh Castle was taken with the strong hand, no less fortunately than cleverly, by the lords William of Douglas, William Fraser, and William Bullock, with their party, after

they had subdued the whole garrison of that castle. The same year –
in 1341, to wit – on the 2nd of June, David, by the grace of God the
illustrious king of Scots, came back from France to Scotland. He and
the queen were brought over by a fleet to Inverbervie, and landed
safe and sound.[25]

The arrival of the young couple was greeted with widespread rejoicing as 'all
Scots were delighted beyond belief at his arrival, and held feasts with joy and
dancing'.[26] The celebrations proved to be short-lived. Scotland was still caught up
in the dynastic wranglings of England and France. The French asked for help in
their conflict with the English, invoking his obligations under the treaty of Corbeil,
whereby, in return for French support, the Scots had promised to invade England
whenever the French king required it.[27] David led his forces south into England.
He fought valiantly in the disastrous battle at Neville's Cross on 17 October 1346,
suffered a serious arrow wound to his face and was captured by the English; he
was escorted to a captivity in England that would last for the next eleven years,
save for a short return to Scotland in 1351–52, when he had reached agreement
with the English that should he fail to produce an heir, the Scottish crown would
pass to a son of Edward III. As his heir, Robert Stewart, who had ruled Scotland
in David's absence, had been outraged by the idea. The Scots parliament rejected
the proposal and David, threatened with war by the English, was forced to return
to captivity. Joan and David's marriage had proved to be an unhappy, loveless and
childless union and, while a safe conduct was issued for Joan to visit her husband
at Windsor for the St George's Day celebrations of 1348, there is no evidence that
she took advantage of it. Although we know little of Joan's movements, it seems
she remained in Scotland at least some of the time, possibly held as a hostage to
David's safety by his Scottish allies.

There are numerous examples, during 1349 and 1350, of the queen using her
patronage to various clerics. On 4 June 1350, from Avignon, the pope granted to,
'Joan, queen of Scotland, and William, bishop of Aberdeen. On behalf of William
Boyl the bishop's nephew, scholar of civil law, for a dignity or office in the church
of Aberdeen; notwithstanding that he has the vicarage of Samery, in the same
diocese.'[28] And in the same year Alexander Bur, licentiate in civil law, received
'confirmation of the papal provision made to him, at the instance of the king and
queen of Scots, of the canonry, prebend, and archdeaconry of Moray, now void by
the death of Adam Perry; or for provision to him anew of the same'.[29] The queen
also sought benefices for her secretary and her clerk, as well as the king's chaplain
and almoner and the nephew of the Bishop of Moray. A dispensation was issued to
Joan's clerk:

The same queen and countess. On behalf of their clerk, Theodoric de
Hesewic, M.A. of Paris, bachelor of medicine, rector of the chapel
of St. Emedame, in the diocese of Maestricht, already dispensed

on account of illegitimacy so as to hold two benefices, for a further dispensation to hold two additional benefices.[30]

It is highly likely that Joan visited David during his captivity in England, taking it as an opportunity to visit with her own family, including her mother; Queen Isabella is said to have supported Joan financially while her husband was imprisoned, feeding and clothing her. Joan does not appear to have taken an active role in the negotiations for David's release, despite her close familial ties to the English court:

> In the year 1357, about Michaelmas, King David of Scotland was released from prison, after having been, for twelve years, kept in close confinement in sundry places in England. There were given, for his ransom, 100,000 merks sterling, to be honestly paid within the ten years immediately following, without any treaty, dismemberment or subjection of the kingdom, or any exaction whatsoever. As security that the whole of this money would be paid to the king of England, the sons and heirs of nearly all the nobles and lords of the kingdom of Scotland were given, as hostages, into the hands of the English.[31]

When King David did return to Scotland in 1357, he was not alone. He brought his lover, Katherine Mortimer, with him. They had met in England, and it was said 'the king loved her more than all other women, and on her account the queen was entirely neglected while he embraced his mistress'.[32] Katherine met a grisly fate in the summer of 1360, when she was stabbed to death on the road near Soutra, by men said to be in the service of the Earl of Angus.[33] David had allowed Katherine to wield too much power in Scotland, exasperating his barons, who felt the need to take drastic action to remove her influence. David's relationship with Katherine appears to have sundered altogether his relationship with Joan of the Tower. As David returned to Scotland in 1357, Queen Joan travelled south, receiving a safe conduct at Christmas 1357 from her brother, Edward III 'on business touching us and David' and again in May 1358 'by our licence for certain causes'.[34] Although the licences are understandably vague on the matter, Joan had, in fact, left David and Scotland: 'In 1357 the Lady Joan of the Tower queen of Scotland and sister of Edward de Windsor king of England made for England after seeking permission from King David her husband; and after spending a little time there as a pilgrim she died.'[35] Joan spent the rest of her life in England, living on a pension of £200 a year provided by her brother, Edward III. The pension was paid quarterly and on 9 October 1359, it was paid 'To Johanna Queen of Scotland, by John Dodelle's hands, the quarter due her at Michaelmas of the 200*l*. a year granted her by the K. during her stay in England — 50*l*.'[36] Joan renewed family connections and was able to visit her mother and spend time with her, and nurse the dowager queen until her death in August 1358.

Although her health was failing, Queen Isabella was able to attend the great tournament, hosted by King Edward III at Windsor, for which Joan had travelled south from Scotland.[37] It was part of a series of festivities following the return of the Black Prince from campaigning in France, with John, King of France, the prince's prisoner since his capture at the Battle of Poitiers in 1356. Held at Windsor on St George's Day, the tournament attracted nobility from Gascony, Germany, Hainault and France and was followed a few days later by the signing of the Treaty of London, between England and France.[38] As Queen of Scotland, Joan occasionally acted on her husband's behalf. In February 1359, David acknowledged her assistance in the respite of ransom payments granted by Edward III, saying it was 'at the great and diligent request and instance of our dear companion the Lady Joan his sister'.[39] Payment of Joan's pension is recorded again on 6 May 1362, this time with a deduction for payments already received:

> To Johanna Queen of Scotland, by the hands of Helmingus Leget, in payment of 50*l.* due at Easter term of the 200*l.* allowed her yearly by the K. for necessaries of her chamber during her stay in England, less a prest of 29 *l.* given to her on 4th April last – 21*l.* To same Queen, by said Helmingus' hands a prest for the Midsummer quarter next – 9*l.*[40]

Little is known of Joan's appearance or personality. Several years after her death she was described as 'swete, and debonare, Curtas, hamely, plesande, and faire' by the chronicler Andrew of Wyntoun, although this description is standard fare for the time.[41] Having led an adventurous life, through no choice of her own, if unhappy in love, Joan of the Tower, Queen of Scots, died at the age of 41 on 7 September 1362, and was buried in the Church of the Greyfriars, Newgate, in London, where her mother had been laid to rest just four years earlier. Payments were made 'To Gilbert Prince painter of London, by his own hands for banners and other things bought from him for the exsequies of Johanna, late Queen of Scotland, as appears by bill of the late keeper of the wardrobe – 24*l.*'[42] A further payment is made when 'On 16th February following Peter of Preston of Scotland, is repaid 13 marks laid out by him in jewels bought for Johanna, late Queen of Scotland.'[43]

Joan of the Tower had been Queen of Scots for thirty-three years. She had never borne a child, nor is there any mention of her ever having become pregnant. So, on her death, David II was still without an heir of his own, other than Robert Stewart, the nephew he despised, who had six legitimate sons by 1362. Following the death of his lover, Katherine Mortimer, in 1360, and before Joan's death, David had fallen in love with Margaret Drummond. The first reference to Margaret and David's relationship is in a charter of 20 January 1363, to the Friars Preacher, for the souls of David himself and of 'our beloved' Margaret Logie.[44] Margaret was the daughter of a lowly Scottish knight, Sir Malcolm Drummond. She had been married to Sir John Logie of Logie and had at least one son, also called John. The relationship further alienated David's heir, Robert, who was involved in a violent feud with Margaret's brothers, John and Maurice Drummond. The relationship also threatened to disinherit Robert, should Margaret give birth to a son. This could explain Robert's involvement in a rebellion early in 1363, in which a petition was presented to the king, demanding that he set aside Margaret and dismiss his current advisers.[45]

Despite the opposition to the relationship, 'in the year 1363, the aforesaid lord David, king of Scotland, took to wife, at Inchmurdach, a great lady, named Margaret of Logie, of high and noble birth, and born in his kingdom; and he endowed her with many lands and possessions, and raised her to reign in honour with him, with the royal diadem.'[46] They were married at Inchmurdoch, in the Fife manor house of the Bishop of St Andrews, though 'Thai ware togiddyr bot schort quhile.'[47] According to the chroniclers, Margaret was very beautiful, but her character left much to be desired, 'With the aim therefore of providing for the succession to the kingdom from the fruit of her womb (if God granted it), King David chose a most beautiful lady, Margaret Logie, the widow of John Logie, perhaps not so much for the excellence of her character as a woman as for the pleasure he took in her desirable appearance.'[48] Once married, David gave preferential treatment to Margaret's family, granting them lands and prestigious marriages. One such marriage, possibly inspired by Margaret herself, was between her niece, Annabella Drummond, and John, the eldest son and heir of Robert Stewart. If Margaret herself did not produce a son and heir for Scotland, her niece might one day become queen. This must have angered Robert Stewart, who was still embroiled in the feud with Margaret's brothers. Demonstrating her own influence over King David, in the winter of 1368, the queen went as far as to persuade her husband to order the arrest and imprisonment of Robert and some of his sons. David also favoured his stepson. On 6 December 1363, John Logie, 'the son of the Queen of Scotland', was among the 'divers lords and others, who came to England in the retinue of the K. of Scotland about a treaty of peace between the Kings' and was gifted 'a parcel-gilt cup, weight 75s., value 6*l*. 5s. 4*d*'.[49] He received further gifts such as that on 16 December 1365, when the king 'of Scotland, Sir Archibald, and other lords of Scotland came to Annandale, and gave seisin of it to one John de Logy son of the Queen of Scotland'.[50]

The continued lack of an heir, however, may have begun to rankle with King David, who released his nephew after a short time. The *Liber Pluscardensis* suggests that the queen, knowing David was tiring of her, faked a pregnancy in order to maintain her influence over her husband, and save her marriage.[51] It did not work. Margaret is always portrayed as an 'arrogant, demanding wife', and it may be that she was, though I cannot help but wonder that harsh words are used to describe her because she was lowly born, the daughter of a mere knight, rather than a princess.[52] She was seen as unworthy for the high office to which David had elevated her. It cannot have been easy for her, being reminded constantly of her low social position in respect of the others who surrounded the king. It would go some way to explain her haughty attitude; she was trying to live up to her queenship. David had also started an affair with Agnes Dunbar, sister of George,

Earl of March. Whether it was for the lack of an heir, the demanding nature of his wife, or a desire to marry a new love, the result was the same: 'he lived with her for a short time, [but following animosity that arose between them,] he divorced her about the beginning of Lent 1369.'[53] King David applied for a divorce, which was granted, relegating Margaret to the position of 'Lady Margaret Logie, onetime Queen'.[54] Margaret, however, was not going to go quietly and live in retirement on the pension of £100 a year the king had awarded her. Margaret decided to appeal to a higher power and

> On this account she secretly boarded a ship in the Firth of Forth [well supplied with money] and made for the papal court. She arrived at Avignon where the pope was then to be found. By making an appeal she transferred her case there, and disturbed the whole kingdom by her legal action. And so once the king's proctors had travelled to the apostolic see, the case was bitterly disputed, and the pleading between the advocates of the contending parties was so prolonged that a book compiled from that source and certified by notarial marks is longer [in] wordage (in my judgment, for I who have written this have seen this pleading) than the contents of the text of four Psalters. For her case was many times committed for hearing by auditors and cardinals, so that if she had lived, she would have subjected the kingdom to an interdict; but she died on a pilgrimage to Rome.[55]

King David II Bruce died, childless, at Edinburgh Castle on 22 February 1371, having reigned for forty-two of his forty-seven years. The king's death did not stop Margaret from continuing with her lawsuit against him for some years, despite how much it was costing the former queen. There was a

> Notarial instrument dated 23d June 1372, attesting obligation of same date by the Lady Margaret Queen of Scotland, widow of the late David Bruys K. of Scotland, acknowledging a loan of 500 marks from Adam Franceys and two other London merchants, made to her at Avignon, repayable at Caleys at Pentecost following. Done in the house of the said Queen Margaret at Avignon ut supra.[56]

Scotland was under the threat of a papal interdict as a result. Reprieve only came with Margaret's death, during a pilgrimage to Rome in early 1375. The rule of the house of Bruce had lasted just sixty-five years and had been punctuated by the country's fight for Scotland's sovereignty. Robert the Bruce's struggle for independence from England had seen his wife, daughter and sisters imprisoned by an implacable Edward I. The enforced absence of Elizabeth de Burgh for eight years had prevented King Robert from ensuring the security of his kingdom with a son and heir. This absence also contributed to the fact that when a son, David, was finally born, he was still only a child when he inherited the throne. Edward III took advantage of Scotland having a child-king to promote his own candidate for the throne, Edward Balliol, even if that was at the expense of his sister, Joan of the Tower, Queen of Scots as David's consort. It was a game of thrones, in the most literal sense!

One cannot fail to feel sorry for the child-bride, living in a new country, surrounded by strangers and knowing that her brother was against her marriage. Worse still, he actively – militarily and politically – worked to deprive her husband and, by extension, herself, of the throne she sat on. Things could have been so different, had David and Joan had children shortly after reaching adulthood, but the empty nursery would have added more pressure to the strained marriage. There was simply too much for David and Joan to overcome, leaving them both miserable and isolated.

Eventually, however, it was not England that ensured the downfall of the House of Bruce. It was the failure of King David to have an heir. There is always a tendency to blame the woman when a king dies childless, but the fact that David was married twice and had a number of mistresses, but never became a father, even of an illegitimate child, would suggest that the problem lay with David. Though the point is moot. In the end, David's heir was his nephew, as he had been from the moment David ascended the throne. David was succeeded by the first of the Stewart kings, Robert II, son of Robert the Bruce's eldest daughter, Marjorie.

Chapter Eleven

The Rise of the House of Stewart

As with Ada de Warenne, although she never became a queen, Marjorie Bruce should not be left on the sidelines. For many years she was the only living legitimate child of King Robert the Bruce. Her marriage became a matter of national importance as the king remained childless with his second wife, Elizabeth de Burgh. And she is the 'lass' with which the Stewart dynasty was founded. As James V is famously recorded as saying on his deathbed, on hearing of the birth of his daughter, Mary – the future Mary, Queen of Scots – 'it cam wi' a lass, it'l gang wi' a lass'.[1]

I have always had a soft spot for little Marjorie Bruce. Dead before her 20th birthday, her short life was filled with tragedy and adversity from the moment of her birth. I could find no pictures of her, just ones of her tomb, which just about sums it up for poor Marjorie. Marjorie Bruce was born at a time of great upheaval for Scotland. Edward I was claiming overlordship of the country, and the right to choose its next king. John Balliol was picked as king, ahead of Marjorie's great-grandfather, only for Edward to humiliate and dethrone him a short time later. Marjorie's father, Robert the Bruce, was one of those with royal blood who had a claim to the Scots crown. Marjorie was the only daughter of Robert the Bruce, Lord of Annandale and Earl of Carrick, and Isabella of Mar. Isabella was the daughter of Donald, sixth Earl of Mar, and Ellen, an illegitimate daughter of Llewelyn the Great, Prince of Wales.

Isabella and Robert had married in about 1295 and Marjorie was born a year or two after. At the age of only 19, Isabella died shortly after giving birth and poor Marjorie was left motherless, with a father who was fighting, alternately, for and against the English. Marjorie was named after her paternal grandmother, Marjory, Countess of Carrick in her own right. Even when still a baby, Marjorie was seen as a political pawn, when on 9 July 1297, Edward I demanded that she be handed over as a hostage to her father's good behaviour. Three of Robert's allies, 'Robert bishop of Glasgow, James the Steward of Scotland, and Alexander de Lindesye, become guarantees for the Earl of Carrick's loyalty till he delivers his daughter Margerie as a hostage.'[2] However, there is no record that Marjorie was ever handed over to the English at this time. And it seems highly likely that Marjorie's care was handed to one of her father's sisters, probably Mary or Christian. Marjorie was about 6 years old when she acquired a new, teenage stepmother. Robert married Elizabeth de Burgh, daughter of Richard de Burgh, Earl of Ulster, and goddaughter of Edward I. Although Edward I appears to have arranged the marriage in order to keep the Bruce's loyalty, it was only a short while after that Robert the Bruce finally decided to join William Wallace and fight for Scotland.

In March 1306, following his murder of his political rival, John Comyn, Robert the Bruce defied Edward I by having himself crowned King of Scots at Scone Abbey. Little 8-year-old Marjorie was suddenly a Princess of Scotland as the daughter of King Robert I, although her uncle Edward Bruce was designated Robert's heir. Unfortunately, Robert's coronation infuriated Edward I even more. After King Robert was brought to battle, and defeated, at Methven in June 1306, he and his family became fugitives in their own land, Marjorie Bruce with them. Edward I of England was determined to hunt him down, sending men after Robert and all his adherents. In August 1306, Robert divided his party; while he headed west, Robert sent Marjorie and Elizabeth to the north-east, possibly hoping they could escape to Orkney and take a boat to Norway, where his sister, Isabella, was queen. Accompanying Elizabeth and Marjorie were two of Robert's sisters, Christian and Mary, and Isabella, Countess of Buchan, who had crowned King Robert at Scone. They were escorted by John of Strathbogie, Earl of Atholl, and Robert's younger brother, Sir Neil Bruce. Having escaped Kildrummy Castle before it was besieged by the English, the women travelled further north, but were captured by the Earl of Ross, a supporter of John Balliol and the Comyns, at the shrine of St Duthac at Tain in Inverness. They were sent south, to King Edward.

Although Edward did not order the executions of the women folk, it cannot be said he treated them kindly. They were used to set an example, a demonstration of the price for rebellion against Edward. On 7 November 1306, Edward issued 'Farther orders for the custody of the Countesses of Carrick and Buchan, Marie and Christine the sisters, and Margerie the daughter, of Robert de Brus, and other Scottish prisoners; three of the ladies to be in "kages".'[3] Isabella, Countess of Buchan, who had set the crown of Scotland on Robert the Bruce's head, was imprisoned in one such cage at Berwick Castle. The same was ordered for Mary Bruce at Roxburgh. It was horrendous treatment for two noblewomen and a deliberate taunt to King Robert, not only that he could not keep his women safe but also that he did not have the means to rescue them, even though they were held in castles on the Anglo-Scottish border. Christian Bruce, whose husband had recently been executed as a traitor at Dumfries, was ordered to be confined at a convent at Sixhills in Lincolnshire; while Elizabeth de Burgh was confined to various manors in England and treated more kindly, due to her father's friendship with the king.

For Marjorie Bruce, these events must have been terrifying. Edward ordered her confined in an iron cage in the Tower of London, where no one was to speak to her. Whether Edward relented of his own free will, or was advised against such treatment of a child who was not yet 10 years old, the order was rescinded and she was confined to a convent at Watton in Yorkshire. Although loyal to their king, we can only hope that the nuns took pity on the poor child and treated her kindly. On 15 March 1307, Edward sent orders for financial provision for Marjorie:

'The K. commands the sheriff of York, by view of the Prior of Wattone, to allow Margery daughter of Robert de Brus, staying in Wattone by the K.'s order, 3*d*. a day for her expenses, from the morrow of All Souls last year, when she came there; and a mark yearly for her dress.'[4] Marjorie was held at Watton for eight years. There is no record of her being assigned tutors in order to continue her education, though the nuns there may well have taught her to read and write and, of course, the religious offices of the day. It was only her father's victory at the Battle of Bannockburn, in 1314, that eventually secured Marjorie's freedom. Many English noble prisoners were taken, 'for whose ransom not only were the queen and other Scottish prisoners released from their dungeons, but even the Scots themselves were, all and sundry, enriched very much.'[5]

Robert the Bruce's resounding victory over Edward I's son and successor, Edward II, in the 1314 battle meant Bruce was finally in a position to insist on the return of his queen, daughter, sisters and the Countess of Buchan. With so many English nobles taken prisoner, the women were the price demanded in the exchange of hostages. Shortly after the defeat at Bannockburn, on 18 July 1314 King Edward ordered 'that Robert bishop of Glasgow, Elizabeth wife of Robert de Brus, Donald de Mar, and other Scots in England, be brought to him at York'.[6] No doubt Marjorie was among those captives brought to York. We then have record of her on 2 October, when 'The K. sends Robert bishop of Glasgow, the Countess of Carrick wife of Robert de Brus, with his sister and daughter and Donald de Mar, to Carlisle castle, to be taken thence to a place arranged by the Earl of Essex and Hereford and the sheriff.'[7]

Her release would take some time yet to achieve, as negotiations were protracted and broke down in October 1314. Her father's victory at Bannockburn had been overwhelming, however, and England could not put off the exchange of prisoners indefinitely. In February 1315, 'not only were the queen and many other captives from Scotland set free from prisons in England, but also the Scots themselves from the lowest to the highest were greatly enriched, not so much from the booty as from the ransoming of the captives.'[8]

On Marjorie's return to Scotland, King Robert almost immediately set about arranging her marriage. With the queen not yet having produced a child, the now 17-year-old Marjorie was needed to produce an heir for the Bruce dynasty, just in case. The husband chosen for her was just five years older than Marjorie. Walter Stewart was the wealthy and powerful sixth High Steward of Scotland. His father had been one of Robert the Bruce's closest allies. Walter had distinguished himself as a commander at the Battle of Bannockburn, and was the man who had been entrusted by the king to bring his family home from their English captivity. At least he was not a total stranger to Marjorie, and they may have spent some time getting to know each other on their journey north. Walter and Marjorie were married shortly after 27 April in 1315.[9] The couple received a wedding gift of the Baronies of Bathgate and Ratho in West Lothian from King Robert.[10]

Whatever happiness – if any – Marjorie derived from the marriage, however, was short-lived. The traditional narrative is that in 1316, whilst heavily pregnant,

Marjorie fell from her horse when out riding near Paisley Abbey. Going into premature labour, she was taken to the abbey, where she was delivered of a son, Robert, on 2 March 1316. It is possible that Robert was delivered by caesarean as his mother was close to death. Tragically, Marjorie is said to have survived the birth by just a few hours and died the same day. While it is believed that Marjorie died after a fall from her horse, some historians suggest that this was in 1317, rather than 1316.[11] I must say, it does make some sense; no one has ever explained why Marjorie would be out riding so close to giving birth, a practice that was heavily frowned upon, especially for a princess carrying a possible heir to the throne. It may well be that Marjorie's story has been convoluted so that she appears to have died in the same manner as her mother, who had died giving birth to Marjorie at the age of 19. Either way, Marjorie was no more than 19 or 20 years of age at her death. She had lived through some of the most turbulent years of Scottish history and died giving birth – or in the year following – to the country's future king, the first of the royal house of Stewart. Had she lived, Marjorie would have seen her son succeed the brother she never met, David II, to the Scots throne as King Robert II.

Initially, baby Robert was not his grandfather's immediate heir, as a device of 27 April 1315 entailed the crown to any sons of Robert the Bruce, followed by his brother Edward and his heirs, before falling to Marjorie and her heirs. Although he had a prominent place in the royal succession, it still appeared that Robert's chances of succeeding to the crown were remote. When Edward Bruce died in battle in Ireland on 14 October 1318, still childless, however, 2-year-old Robert was named as the king's heir. It was arranged

> that if it happens (may it not be so!) that the said lord king comes to the end of his life without a male heir generated legitimately from his body surviving and remaining, Robert the son of the Lady Marjorie of worthy memory the daughter of the said lord king legitimately fathered by the noble man Sir Walter Steward of Scotland her husband is to succeed the same lord king fully as his nearest legitimate heir in that kingdom.[12]

When David Bruce was born in 1324, Robert was relegated to the position of a spare heir. In July 1326, in a parliament at Cambuskenneth, the magnates of Scotland pledged their fealty to David as heir to the throne. The same parliament acknowledged Robert's position as the next heir should David die childless.[13] Within a year, 10-year-old Robert was an orphan, his father, Walter Stewart, dying on 9 April 1327, leaving Robert to inherit the title Steward of Scotland. After the death of his mother, Robert's father had remarried, to Isabel de Graham, and had three further children, Robert's half-siblings, two boys and a girl, John, Andrew and Egidia. Robert grew up on the Stewart family lands in Renfrew, Clydeside and the Isle of Bute, and may have been fostered into an Isles or Argyll family, a region of which he was particularly fond.[14]

With his recognition as heir after Prince David, Robert was given new estates in Knapdale (Argyll), the Lothians and Roxburghshire. It was expected that Robert would be a senior member of the government of Scotland, a stalwart of his uncle's administration, as High Steward, although there was always the awareness that one day, he could be king. So, when Edward Balliol made a bid for the Scots throne, following the death of Robert's grandfather, Robert the Bruce, Robert Stewart was to play a crucial role in the recovery of the kingdom for his young uncle, David II. At the age of just 16, on 19 July 1333, he led a division of his own retainers against Edward III's forces at the Battle of Halidon Hill, which ended in a Scottish defeat. A year later, he escaped capture, or worse, when his lands were overrun by a force of Anglo-Balliol men, by taking a boat to Dumbarton Castle.[15] As 10-year-old King David and his queen were whisked to exile and safety in France, Robert remained in Scotland to continue the fight, earning himself a reputation and the admiration of the Scots people:

> While they were thus swarming towards him in groups from all sides, he began to attract certain brave men to his side, and to draw Scots of good sense towards him, to enlarge his army every day, and to attach their hearts to himself in mutual affection and firm loyalty. For he was then beginning to grow into a young man of attractive appearance above the sons of men, broad and tall in physique, kind to everyone, and modest, generous, cheerful and honest. In him innate goodness produced such charm that he was fervently loved by nearly all the faithful Scottish peoples.[16]

However, Robert's popularity and attempts to increase his own lands during the wars brought him into conflict with David's chief councillors, when he was King's Lieutenant in 1334–35 and 1338–41. By the time of David's return in 1341, the lines were drawn between the crown and the heir presumptive, a rivalry that would fester throughout David's personal rule. It cannot have helped the relationship between David and his nephew, that Robert was credited with saving Scotland: 'And thus, through the activity of Sir Andrew Moray and the work of that guardian, Robert Steward, the kingdom was rescued from the hands of the English, with the exception at this stage of the castles of Edinburgh, Roxburgh, Berwick, Jedburgh and Lochmaben, and a few small towers round about.'[17] Although King David was able to intimidate and frustrate Robert Stewart in his landed ambitions, until the king had a son Robert's position as his heir was unassailable. And they both knew it. Robert was a constant presence at court and could use his position to limit the king's power and sabotage his plans. It was Robert's own troops who broke and fled the battle at Neville's Cross in 1346, leaving King David to be captured by the English.[18] Afterwards, Robert acted to delay David's release from English captivity, joined a rebellion against the crown in 1363 and roused parliament to oppose David's attempts to alter the Scottish succession to admit an English royal.

Robert and at least one of his sons were even imprisoned, in 1368, due to the influence of David's second wife, Margaret Logie, although he was released after a short time.

Robert's strength, however, lay not only in his proximity to the throne, but also in the fact he had managed to do what David had not, produce an heir. Six, in fact. Robert's rather unusual marital situation, and perhaps the growing awareness that there was less and less likelihood of David producing an heir, saw him apply for a papal dispensation to marry Elizabeth Mure, which was supported by King David, the King of France, the seven Scottish bishops and parliament. It was granted on 22 November 1347, at least ten years after the start of their relationship. The dispensation allowed for the retrospective legitimisation of their children:

> This Robert took to his bed one of the daughters of Adam More, knight; and of her he begat sons and daughters, out of wedlock. But he afterwards – in the year 1349, to wit – bespoke and got the dispensation of the Apostolic See, and espoused her regularly, according to the forms of the Church.[19]

An earlier dispensation, issued in 1345, had annulled Elizabeth's betrothal to Hugh Giffard.[20] Elizabeth was the daughter of Adam Mure of Rowallon, Ayrshire. Though whether her mother was his first wife, Joan Cunnigham, or his second wife, Janet, is undetermined.[21] The unusual nature of their relationship and marital situation has given rise to questions over the legitimacy of their children. According to John Riddell, the facts of the relationship are that:

> Robert II, when related to Elizabeth Mure, in the third and fourth forbidden degrees of affinity, and the fourth forbidden degree of consanguinity, lived for a long space in concubinage with her, during which 'prolis utriusque sexus multitudinem procrearunf' – during that unhallowed, and in law, incestuous connection; till at last, resolving to marry, but discovering the double relationship between them, which was a bar to their marriage at common (Ecclesiastical) law, they then obtained a dispensation from Clement VI, in 1347, for the purpose, in ordinary form. After which it is in proof, that they did marry under authority of the dispensation, – Robert founding in 1364, in compliance with an injunction there, a Chaplainry, in expiation of his former offence, which was, by received doctrine at the time, deemed an aggravated one.[22]

It has been argued that the children of Robert and Elizabeth were not only born outside of marriage, but also that their parents were related within the limited degrees, and therefore the relationship was incestuous. This, however, ignores the possibility that Robert and Elizabeth did go through a form of marriage in the 1330s, when Scotland was deeply involved in its war with England and, with David II sent to France for his safety, Robert was the senior representative of the Bruce family in Scotland. Moreover, it may have been thought prudent that Robert should marry sooner, rather than later, for dynastic considerations. With Edward Balliol unmarried and with no heir, the fact that the king's heir was married with children was significant, a sign that the Bruce–Stewart dynasty was secure, at least. That the marriage was not regularised until the war was over could be excused by the fact there were more urgent matters to attend to and the financial and legal obligations of obtaining a dispensation could wait. This would certainly explain the papacy's willingness to regulate the marriage by issuing a retroactive dispensation. Alternatively, they may have only recently discovered a familial relationship within the prohibited degrees, and therefore applied for a dispensation. Elizabeth and Robert then underwent a second, formal, marriage ceremony in 1349.

Their first child, John, had been born in about 1337 and was created Earl of Carrick in 1369, the title held by his great-grandfather, Robert the Bruce, before he became king.[23] He would ascend the throne as Robert III on his father's death in 1390. Although the birth order could be slightly different, it seems likely that John was followed by a sister, Margaret, who was married to John MacDonald, Lord of the Isles, as his second wife, for which a papal dispensation was issued on 14 June 1350.[24] The couple were granted the island of Colowsay by Margaret's father in a charter dated to July 1376.[25] Three more sons followed, Walter, Robert and Alexander. Walter was married to Isabel, Countess of Fife, in April 1360 or 1361. He died sometime after 14 August 1362 but before the end of the year, as his widow married again, to Thomas Bisset of Upsetlington on 10 January 1363. She resigned the earldom of Fife to Walter's brother, Robert Stewart, Earl of Menteith, on 30 March 1371.[26]

Robert Stewart is identified as the 'second born of the king' in the *Liber Pluscardensis*.[27] Robert was Earl of Menteith by right of his wife, Margaret Graham, a title she herself had inherited from her mother, Mary. Margaret had been married three times before; her first husband, Sir John Moray, was the son of Christian Bruce, King Robert I's sister, by her last husband, Sir Andrew Murray. Robert was later created Duke of Albany and acted as regent during his brother's reign. The third son, Alexander, has a significant reputation as a cruel and rapacious character, earning him the nickname, the Wolf of Badenoch. He married Euphemia, Countess of Ross and was Earl of Ross in her name. Euphemia resigned her share of Buchan to the king, who regranted it to Alexander and Euphemia, in July 1382, so that they were Earl and Countess of Ross and Buchan. The marriage had its difficulties and Alexander left his wife, for 'Mariota's daughter Athyn' but was ordered to return to her, in a charter dated 2 November 1389, by the Bishop of Moray and Ross.[28] Apparently, the breach was irretrievable, as Pope Clement VII 'issued a commission to dissolve her marriage' on 9 June 1392, and in December 1392 Euphemia was granted a divorce 'from bed and board'.[29] Although Alexander had seven illegitimate children, he and Euphemia had remained childless.

Robert II and Elizabeth Mure also had four more daughters, although their order of birth is unknown. Marjory married John Dunbar, the son of Patrick Dunbar and Isabel Randolph of Moray. He was created Earl of Moray by his father-in-law in March 1372.[30] Marjory's second husband was Alexander Keith of Grandown. Jean, or Joan, Stewart was married three times, firstly to John Keith, son of William de Keith, the Marischal, in January 1374. John died just fourteen months later. A year after that, in either June or October 1376, Jean married Sir John Lyon of Glamis. On 4 October 1376, King Robert II granted land, the thanedom of Tannadyce in Forfar, possibly a wedding gift, 'to his dearest son John Lyon and Johanna his wife, the King's beloved daughter'.[31] The marriage was initially kept secret and only publicly acknowledged on 10 May 1378 when the king, with the consent of his surviving sons, 'granted to the spouses letters of acknowledgement and remission for any clandestine marriage formerly contracted by them, in regard a marriage had been solemnly celebrated between them in face of the Church, in presence of the King and his sons and other friends and relatives.'[32] Further grants followed, but Sir John was killed, apparently murdered by Sir James Lindsay on 4 November 1382. According to the *Liber Pluscardensis*, the deed was done at night when the 'victim was in bed and unsuspecting'.[33] Their only child was John's son and successor, also called John Lyon. On 20 November 1384, Jean married for a third and final time, to Sir James Sandilands of Calder. Ahead of the marriage, Sir James was granted the baronies of Dalzell, Motherwell and Wiston, to be held by Sir James and Jean, the king's daughter, 'whom God willing he is about to take to wife'.[34] The princess is last mentioned in 1404, as 'Lady Johanna of Glammys'. She was buried beside her second husband, Sir John Lyon, at Scone Abbey.[35]

Another daughter, Elizabeth Stewart, married Thomas Hay, Baron of Erroll and Constable of Scotland. A charter issued by King Robert II granted an annuity to 'Thomas Hay and Elizabeth the king's daughter, and the children born and to be born of them' dated 7 September 1372, the day of their marriage.[36] Isabel Stewart was married twice, firstly to James Douglas, son of William Douglas, Earl of Douglas, and his wife, Margaret, Countess of Mar. A papal dispensation was issued for the marriage in September 1371 and James succeeded his father as Earl Douglas in 1384. Sir James died in 1388 and sometime in the next two years, Isabel married John Edmonstone of Duntreath. Isabel most likely died before 22 July 1410, when accounts record payments to 'John Edmonstone ... for the reason that he was once married to the Countess of Douglas'.[37]

Through the marriages of his sons and daughters, Robert Stewart created a familial network that extended his influence over the greater part of central, western and north-eastern Scotland. He formed unions with eight of the country's fifteen existing earldoms as well as gaining other lordships, royal castles and offices north of the Forth-Clyde line.[38] However, the unusual nature of the marriage of Robert and Elizabeth would always leave a question mark hanging over the legitimacy of their children, an uncertainty that the children of Robert's second marriage would highlight and try to exploit. But it was Elizabeth's eldest son, John, Earl of Carrick, who would succeed his father as King Robert III. Elizabeth herself, though married to David II's heir, was never to become queen. She died sometime before 1355, possibly in childbirth as she would have been no more than in her late 30s, or perhaps from complications arising from having borne at least nine children, and possibly as many as thirteen. We have so little information about her that her place of burial is also unknown, though Paisley Abbey or Scone Abbey are possibilities. We only know that poor Elizabeth was dead by 1355 because 2 May of that year is the date of the papal dispensation for Robert Stewart's second marriage, to Euphemia Ross.

Whatever the nature of their marriage, and the reason for the dispensation, it was not an arranged marriage for dynastic purposes. Robert and Elizabeth appear to have chosen each other. The number of children born, even during times of war, suggests that Robert and Elizabeth had a close and loving relationship. This did not, however, preclude Robert from marrying again, possibly only a short time after Elizabeth's death. Walter Bower suggests that, although Robert's relationship with Elizabeth Mure was earlier, the marriage only occurred after Queen Euphemia's death.

> It is noteworthy that the said King Robert fathered three sons by the Lady Elizabeth daughter of Sir Adam More, namely John who was later king, and Robert duke of Albany, and the said Alexander earl of Buchan, who was commonly called 'The Wolf of Badenoch'. Later he married the Lady Euphemia daughter of Hugh earl of Ross, by whom he fathered Walter earl of Athol and lord of Brechin, and David earl of Strathearn. But on the death of Queen Euphemia he married the said Lady Elizabeth, and so by virtue of subsequent marriage, a second marriage ceremony, the said brothers John, Robert and Alexander were legitimated, for according to canon law a subsequent marriage legitimates sons born before the marriage.[39]

This timeline, of course, does not work, as the papal dispensation, legitimising the children, was issued in 1347 and there is every indication that Elizabeth was dead before 1355.

Euphemia was the daughter of Hugh, Earl of Ross, and his second wife, Margaret Graham. Hugh's first wife had been Maud Bruce, sister of Robert the Bruce, and Hugh was a friend of King Robert. So, although the family lived away from court, they were still part of the royal family's circle. Euphemia was probably born in around 1322, though it is possible that it was as late as 1329, when her parents received a papal dispensation for their marriage, issued after an impediment was discovered, which included legitimising any children already born of the marriage.[40] Euphemia was probably raised at Dingwall Castle, the family's principal residence in the north of Scotland.[41] Dingwall was considered one of the largest and most important strongholds north of Stirling, covering a site of more than an acre, with four towers enclosing a courtyard.[42] She would also have spent time at the family residences at Delny, Balcony Castle in Evanton, in Easter Ross, and Balloan at Tarbat Ness.[43] Euphemia had an older, full brother, Hugh, and two older half-siblings, William and Maud, and possibly two younger sisters, Janet and Lilias.[44] She would later have at least one more half-sister, Janet, after her mother's remarriage to John de Barclay. Euphemia's education would have included all that was needed for a high-born lady to manage a noble household and the family estates, entertain guests and follow the religious offices of the day. She would also have learnt music and dancing and needlework. She was betrothed when still a child, to John Randolph, second son of Thomas Randolph, first Earl of Moray, a great-nephew of King Robert the Bruce. The betrothal may well have been arranged by the king himself, which would mean it took place before his death in 1329, and united the two most important families in the north.

A nephew of Robert the Bruce, Thomas Randolph had been a firm supporter of his uncle and was the first regent for David II. He led the army against Edward Balliol's forces in the summer of 1332, but died at Musselburgh on 20 July that year, amid the usual rumours of poison but most likely of a sudden illness. His two oldest sons had campaigned alongside him, and just three weeks later, his oldest son, also called Thomas, was killed at the Battle of Dupplin Moor. John inherited the earldom and, shortly after the battle, escaped to France, returning a few months later, at which time he was appointed a joint Guardian of Scotland alongside the young king's nephew, Robert Stewart. John and Robert were the same age, just 17. One cannot help but wonder at the wisdom of putting two teenage boys, with their reckless energy, in charge of a country that was being invaded by its more powerful neighbour, in support of a rival dynasty. But Scotland had lost so many of its senior barons in the war, their options were severely limited. It is, perhaps, no surprise that the teenagers soon quarrelled, and their guardianship was dissolved in 1335 and placed in the hands of Sir Andrew Moray, husband of Robert the Bruce's sister, Christian. Later in that same year, young John was captured by the English and held in various English strongholds from Bamburgh to Winchester, before being moved to the Tower of London. Poor Euphemia must have wondered whether her marriage would ever take place. Or maybe she was grateful for the delay, though not John's incarceration. Her father had been killed, fighting the English at the Battle of Halidon Hill in July 1333, and the grief and uncertainty must have affected her.

When John was finally released from the Tower after five long years, in February 1341, he again left for France, but had returned by 1343. By this time, the young king had already returned from his French exile and taken over the reins of government from his uncle, Robert Stewart. The king appointed John Randolph justiciar of Annandale and Mar and a warden of the Marches.[45] John and Euphemia's wedding was probably celebrated shortly afterwards. Euphemia was now about 21 years old and John Randolph 27. On her marriage, Euphemia became Countess of Moray and would have resided at her husband's principal castle of Darnaway in

Moray and in his island castle of Lochmaben, in Dumfriesshire, which had been built by the English and was back in Scottish hands by 1343.[46]

The marriage produced no living children, although we do not know if Euphemia suffered the grief of a miscarriage or still birth, events which often go unrecorded. The lack of an heir may have put strain on the marriage, as the earldom was entailed in the male line and would revert to the crown on John's death, unless a son was born to the couple. Whatever marital bliss Euphemia and John experienced was cut short when John was killed at the Battle of Neville's Cross, on 17 October 1346. The long list of dead included some of the most senior knights and royal officers in Scotland: 'John of Randolph, Earl of Moray; the Earl of Stratherne; the constable of Scotland; the marshal of Scotland; the chamberlain of Scotland; and numberless other barons, knights, squires, and good men.'[47] In the same battle, King David II was captured and taken to imprisonment in England. Of the leaders of the realm, only 'Patrick of Dunbar, Earl of March, and Robert, steward of Scotland ... took to flight, and got away unhurt.'[48]

In the aftermath of the battle, Robert Stewart was once again appointed Guardian of Scotland. Euphemia would have received a dower settlement from the earldom of Moray, but little else, as she had no children to maintain her interest in the earldom. She was to remain a widow for the best part of the next decade, perhaps enjoying the freedom that widowhood conferred on a woman. The fact Euphemia had not borne a child during her marriage to John Randolph has been used to explain the lack of possible suitors for her hand, but this seems unlikely. Euphemia and John had only been married for three years, and in a time of war, the opportunities for the couple to be together may have been limited. Euphemia was still young, no more than 24 years of age when she was widowed. We know not how or when Euphemia developed a relationship with Robert Stewart. They had always known each other, the quarrel between John and Robert when they were guardians may have caused some friction, and there may have been rivalry over David II's favouritism towards John Randolph. However, the Randolph and Stewart families, as a whole, remained close. Following Elizabeth Mure's death, Euphemia may have felt sympathy for Robert's now-motherless children. Having no family of her own, she may have been drawn to the ready-made one offered by Robert. As members of the Scottish court, Elizabeth and Euphemia would have known each other well, and may even have been friends. Unfortunately, it is not something we can know from the chronicles. The Steward was an attractive prospect as a groom, he 'was humble and gentle, friendly in appearance, a cheerful man, an honourable king, witty in his responses, admirable in the way he carried himself, surpassing others in stature and the height of his body'.[49]

For his part, Robert already had nine legitimate children, including four sons, so having a wife with proven child-bearing ability was not a requirement. We have no contemporary description of Euphemia, and therefore cannot say whether Robert was primarily attracted to the woman, or to her lands. As the widow of John Randolph, Euphemia held one-third of his property rights, which likely included the lordship of Badenoch. A marriage would also ease the discord that had arisen between Robert and Euphemia's brother, William, Earl of Ross, who both had interests in the earldom of Strathearn, which was adjacent to Robert's earldom of Atholl; however, Earl William's daughter had been recognised as heir of her uncle-by-marriage, Malise, former earl of Strathearn, Caithness and Orkney. [50] Malise was married to Euphemia and William's sister, Marjorie. The marriage of Robert and Euphemia could be seen as a reconciliation of the conflicting interests of William and Robert. If it was a marriage of convenience, it was one that suited both parties, and Euphemia does not appear to have been put off by knowing that Robert kept mistresses. She was not a woman without powerful family connections and would have been able to refuse Robert's proposal, had she so desired. The papal dispensation for the marriage was issued from Avignon, by Pope Innocent VI, on 2 May 1355:

> To the bishop of Glasgow. Mandate to dispense Robert Stiuard, steward of Scotland, and Euphemia, relict of John, earl of Moray, to intermarry, in order to put an end to the strife between Robert and William, earl of Ross, Euphemia's brother, the said Robert and John having been related in the third degree of kindred, and Robert and Euphemia being therefore related in the fourth degree of kindred and the third of affinity.[51]

Second marriages were usually quieter affairs, especially when both parties had been through the ceremony before, but it appears that Euphemia was escorted to her second wedding with some considerable pomp. According to the Wardlaw manuscript *History of Clan Fraser*, Euphemia was escorted south in style by her maternal uncle, the Lord of Lovat, at the request of her half-brother, the Earl of Ross. The ceremony, probably held at Robert's castle of Dundonald, in the heart of his family estates in Ayrshire, was a private celebration.[52] With her marriage, Euphemia had a ready-made family; the eldest of her nine stepchildren would have been teenagers, but the youngest will have been under 10, possibly only toddlers. For a woman in her early 30s, who had no children of her own, it would have been a steep learning curve, especially if some, or all, of Robert's eight illegitimate children were also growing up in the household. We can only wonder if the older children accepted their new stepmother or resented her.

Euphemia would have divided her time between Robert's castles, including Dundonald, a thirteenth-century concentric castle that would be rebuilt as a tower house once Robert became king.[53] She would have also stayed at his strongholds of Renfrew and Rothesay, when Dundonald was in need of cleaning, or Robert was attending to business in those areas. Castle households were predominantly male, housing not only knights, squires and men-at-arms, but also the lord's senior officials, stewards responsible for managing the castle and surrounding lands, and a legion of servants working in the kitchen, hall, stables and stores. Euphemia would have been accompanied by her ladies, nurses for the children, maids and launderesses. During the first few years of their marriage, Robert was ruling Scotland as guardian while King David was still a prisoner in England, as well as negotiating for David's release. Becoming embroiled in France's war with England, when the French king asked for Scotland's assistance, resulted in the destruction of Lothian by Edward III. A further French defeat, at the Battle of Poitiers in 1356, led to a renegotiation of the terms for King David's release. The Treaty of Berwick now required the payment, in instalments, of 100,000 merks, a long truce and the delivery of twenty noble hostages. It was now stipulated that three named, supplementary, hostages were to be held in reserve, one of which was Robert himself.[54]

This did not mean that Robert did not have time for his new wife. Indeed, not long after the wedding, Euphemia was to discover she was pregnant; her first child, a boy named David after the king, was born sometime between 1356 and 1360.[55] David married a daughter of Alexander Lindsay, by whom he had one child, a daughter named for her grandmother, Euphemia, who inherited her father's titles as Countess Palatine of Strathearn and Countess of Caithness, when he died sometime before 15 March 1390.[56] A second son, Walter, was probably born after the death of his older half-brother, also called Walter, who died towards the end of 1362. Walter Stewart would be created Earl of Atholl in 1404 but would meet a sticky end after being implicated in the murder of his nephew, James I, in 1437. He was executed for high treason. Euphemia also gave birth to two daughters, Egidia and Elizabeth (or Jean). Egidia married, in 1387, the same year her mother died, William Douglas of Nithsdale, who was killed at the Battle of Danzig in 1391, fighting against the pagan Lithuanians. Elizabeth, who is named Jean in some sources, married after 22 February 1375 – when the papal dispensation was issued – David Lindsay, who was later created Earl of Crawford.[57]

Although King David was still only in his mid-30s when he returned from his English captivity, he and Joan had been married since childhood, and still had no children. Neither had the king fathered any children by his various mistresses. In 1364, the king married his second wife, Margaret Drummond, a widow with one son by her first marriage. David must have hoped that Margaret would give him a son, but it was not to be. Euphemia and Robert must have always had the possibility, in the back of their minds, of the crown passing to Robert's descendants in the not-too-distant future. Robert himself, given he was eight years older than David, may not have expected to become king but there was an increasing possibility that his eldest son, John, recently given the Bruce earldom of Carrick by King David, would succeed his great-uncle. This must have been tempered by the worry that Edward III had his eye on the crown and would try to claim it, should David die without an heir. Robert may well have had this in mind in the late 1350s and early 1360s, when he was arranging the marriages of his older children, aimed at consolidating and extending Stewart influence in Scotland, marrying his sons into various earldoms and lordships, bringing the earldoms of Atholl, Carrick, Fife,

Mentieth, Ross and Strathearn into Stewart hands. His daughters, likewise, made advantageous marriages which tied the earldoms of Crawford, Douglas, March and Moray, to the family, as well as the lordship of the Isles, and the offices of hereditary constable and Marischal.[58]

Robert and David's relationship was always fractious and resulted in Robert and his sons becoming involved in some form of rebellion against the king in 1368. Robert and his son Alexander were imprisoned in Lochleven Castle and only released in 1369, the same year that David sought an annulment of his marriage with Queen Margaret. By the New Year of 1371, Robert and Euphemia had been married for almost sixteen years as King David was planning to marry his latest mistress, Agnes of Dunbar. It was never to be. The king suddenly fell ill at Edinburgh Castle and died on 22 February. Unexpectedly, Robert was now King Robert II, and Euphemia was his queen. His accession was confirmed by a parliament at Linlithgow. Almost immediately after his accession, Robert had to deal with an armed demonstration led by William, Earl of Douglas, though the nature of William's grievances is unknown. It certainly did not manage to unseat Robert from the throne and his coronation took place a month later, at Scone, on 27 March 1371: 'So on the following feast of the Annunciation of Our Lady the said Sir Robert Stewart was crowned at Scone with due ceremony.'[59] Euphemia, however, was not crowned alongside her husband. Her coronation came the following year:

> In the same year [1372] the coronation of the Lady Euphemia the queen daughter of lord Hugh earl of Ross, was performed at Scone at a solemn ceremony conducted by the bishop of Aberdeen. By her [the king] fathered [two] sons, namely Walter earl of Atholl and lord of Brechin, who was later convicted of treacherously killing King James I, and was on this account drawn, hanged, disembowelled and beheaded. His limbs were hung up at Edinburgh and Perth as a warning, and are still hanging [there]. The queen also bore David earl of Strathearn.[60]

Robert was 55 years old when he ascended the throne, while Euphemia was about 48. The family moved from their Stewart residences into the royal castles at Edinburgh and Stirling. A seal, dating to 1375, depicts the queen in a conventional pose, standing between the arms of Scotland and the earldom of Ross.[61] As queen, Euphemia would have been expected to attend the formal entertainments and gatherings of the court, welcome ambassadors from diverse countries, be they clerics or lords and knights. She was also a patron of the arts, encouraging artists, poets and musicians. One such writer, John Barbour, archdeacon of Aberdeen, was patronised by the Stewarts. He had left for France during David's reign, but returned to Scotland at King Robert's accession, writing his epic poem *The Bruce* for the new king.[62] The queen would also have been called upon to act as an intermediary, for those seeking justice or mercy, hearing petitions and speaking with the king on an individual's behalf. Her diplomatic skills may also have been called upon to heal rifts between her children and stepchildren. As a Christian queen, she would have been expected to practise charity and to dispense alms to the poor and disadvantaged. She was also expected to be a patron of merchants, taking an interest in fashion and jewellery, as well as plate and furniture for the royal castles. The queen's coronation gown, for example, would have been made from the finest materials, hand-embroidered and accessorised with the finest jewels. Her portrait in the Seton Armorial, created in the sixteenth century, shows her gown embroidered with the three lions of the coat of arms of the earls of Ross.[63] The queen was also expected to reward those who have given dutiful service to the crown. One such reward was given to Sir John Lyon, when 'On 10 October 1375, Queen Euphemia, the second wife of Robert II. assigned to him certain liferent duties payable to her out of the revenue of the Castle of Edinburgh, of which John Lyon was then Keeper.'[64]

Robert's long years as Guardian of Scotland, first during David II's minority and, later, his imprisonment in England, meant he was more than up to the task of kingship, despite his advancing years. Although Robert's reign has been seen as lacklustre by historians in the past, recent assessments have shown the king in a more positive light, emphasising the financial and political stability of his reign, alongside the diplomatic successes.[65] The negative view of Robert that prevailed so long arises from Froissart's portrayal of the king following a French expedition to Scotland to assist in border warfare with England. According to Froissart, the first Stewart king had 'red bleared eyes, of the colour of sandalwood, which clearly showed that he was no valiant man, but one who would rather remain at home than march to the field'.[66] This rather harsh assessment of the ageing king ignores Robert's extensive, if not always impressive, military record, portraying him as a coward who shied away from conflict. On the contrary, Robert's increasingly aggressive policy in his border warfare with England and campaign to recover Scottish lands and castles achieved some success before Edward III's death in 1377.

As the reign progressed, however, tensions developed within the kingdom, many of them arising out of the activities of Robert's grown sons from his first marriage. Tensions within the king's own family also arose, with Queen Euphemia eager to promote the interests of her own sons. Prince David was created Earl Palatine of Caithness in 1377 and began claiming that he was the rightful heir to the throne, raising questions over the legitimacy of his elder half-siblings due to the irregularities in their parents' marriage. It is unknown whether or not Euphemia encouraged David's claims. By 1384, King Robert II's health was beginning to fail and his eldest son John, Earl of Carrick, took on many of his responsibilities. The king retired to Dundonald Castle, no doubt accompanied by Queen Euphemia. She died at the age of about 65, her passing recorded in Bower's *Scotichronicon*, almost as an aside: 'In 1387 Sir Walter de Wardlaw bishop of Glasgow the cardinal and legate died. Also in that year the lady Euphemia queen of Scotland died.'[67]

Tradition has Euphemia and Robert buried together at Scone Abbey. However, in a later addition to Bower's fifteenth-century manuscript, it is recorded that Euphemia died on 20 February 1388 and was buried at Dunfermline.[68] Furthermore, there is some indication that Euphemia was still alive on 19 June 1388, which would place her death before 23 February 1389.[69] It is a conundrum.

King Robert II died at Dundonald Castle on 19 April 1390 and was buried at Scone Abbey.[70] He had spent almost his entire life as heir presumptive to the Scottish throne, always waiting on the sidelines. It is a sad fact of history that we have very little insight into the personalities and appearances of Robert's wives. We do not know, for instance, what either wife thought of his various mistresses, nor his illegitimate children. They cannot have been happy about his philandering but may have accepted it, reluctantly. It was certainly not an unusual trait in the men of the family, as both Robert the Bruce and David II had had a string of mistresses. Robert's first wife, Elizabeth Mure, never got to wear the crown, though her influence, through her children, would set the tone for the Scottish royal house of Stewart into the next century. Euphemia Ross would ascend the throne in her 40s, the first queen of the Stewart dynasty, wearing the crown for the last sixteen years of her life. Euphemia's second marriage had given her the opportunity she may have thought had eluded her, to have children of her own. It would not be her children who succeeded to the throne, but their older half-sibling John, Earl of Carrick, who would rule as King Robert III. On her death, however, it was Euphemia's oldest son, David, who inherited her own earldom of Strathearn.

Chapter Twelve

Family Feuds

King Robert II was succeeded by his eldest son John, Earl of Carrick, who took the regnal name of Robert III, John being considered an unlucky name for a king after the disastrous rule of John Balliol. John had been born around 1337, possibly before the marriage of his parents, Robert the Steward and Elizabeth Muir. He was legitimised, along with his brothers and sisters, in the papal dispensation of November 1347. When it became clear that David II was not going to have a son of his own, he began to favour John as his heir, giving him the earldom of Carrick, which had once belonged to David's father – John's great-grandfather – Robert the Bruce. Although he was the king's nephew, John's father was eight years older than David II and so it was expected that it would be John who inherited the crown, rather than his father. However, when David died of a sudden illness in 1171, Robert the Steward succeeded his uncle and would reign for the next nineteen years, dying just over a month after his 74th birthday.

John, Earl of Carrick, therefore, succeeded to the throne in 1390, aged 53. He is first recorded in the chronicles in the 1350s, when he 'collected an army together and made a stay in Annandale for as long as needed until he brought all the people of that region to the allegiance and firm peace of our lord the king, and arranged for them to swear allegiance to him'.[1] In 1363, John, then Lord of Kyle, joined his father in rebellion against David II. The Stewarts were angered by David's alleged misuse of the money collected to pay David's ransom, the possibility that hostages, including John's father, would be sent to England as surety for the ransom payments, and the threats to their territorial interests posed by David's policies. Added to this was the impending marriage of David to Margaret Drummond, with whose family the Stewarts had a long-standing dispute. The situation was not helped by the difficult relationship that Robert Stewart had with his uncle, the king, and the fact the king was actively supporting alternate claims to the throne, undermining Robert's position as his heir. The dispute was resolved with a marriage, that of John to Queen Margaret's niece, Annabella Drummond.

Annabella was the daughter of John Drummond and his wife, Mary de Montefichet. She was probably born in the early 1350s and therefore in her mid-teens when she married. A papal dispensation for the marriage was sought in March 1366. The wedding had taken place sometime before 31 May 1367, when the king granted the earldom of Atholl to 'John Stewart of Kyle … his wife Annabella' by charter.[2] And on 22 June 1368, David granted to John and Annabella, and their heirs, the earldom of Carrick, which is often seen as David's acknowledgement of John as his heir.[3] In the same year, apparently due to pressure from Queen Margaret, '[while the king was boiling with passion,] at her suggestion he arrested his nephew Robert Steward along with three of his sons, namely John, Robert and Alexander, and arranged for them to be warded in various castles. But after the divorce he released them and restored them to favour as before.'[4]

On his father's accession to the throne, the new king transferred the ancestral Stewart lordships around the Firth of Clyde, which were known collectively as the Stewartry, to John. And on the day of his coronation, Robert II formally named John as heir to the throne, with the assembled prelates and magnates being obliged to acknowledge John's rights and promise to defend them.[5] This recognition of his position as heir to the crown ended any doubts over the legitimacy of John, given his parents' unconventional marriage. By 1373, John and Annabella had at least two children together, both daughters, Margaret and Elizabeth. They had no sons. As a consequence, a further amendment was made to the succession. On 4 April, a parliament, held at Scone, approved an entail which excluded John's daughters from the throne. The crown was to pass to John, and any son of John, but then to the five surviving younger sons of Robert II, from both his marriages, who were named in the entail in order of seniority. This change to the succession may well have been engineered by the king's second son, Robert, Earl of Fife, who had designs on the throne himself.[6] This Robert, later Duke of Albany, already had a son of his own by 1373, named Murdoch.

The exclusion of their daughters from the royal succession prompted John and Annabella to move to secure the girls' futures by John resigning the earldom of Carrick to the king, so that it would be regranted, jointly, to John and Annabella, the grant stipulating that if they had no sons, the earldom could descend through the female line.[7] The succession was finally secured when Annabella gave birth to the much-desired son, David, named for David II, on 24 October 1378. In 1384, John took over many of his father's responsibilities as King Robert II's health declined. This changed, however, in December 1388 when a general council in Edinburgh forced John to relinquish the office of guardian in favour of his brother, the Earl of Fife, citing defects in John's government due to his infirmity:

> In 1389 in view of the fact that the king was unfit to govern because of his great age, and that his eldest son John earl of Carrick had become lame following a kick from a horse belonging to Sir James Douglas of Dalkeith, [the king] summoned a council of the three estates to Edinburgh. There with their consent he appointed his second son Sir Robert earl of Fife as guardian of the kingdom. From then on the name 'guardian' was changed, and he desired Robert to be called governor'. Therefore to establish his office once the governor had taken the oath, the prelates and magnates were sworn to support him in office and to give him faithful counsel.[8]

Although John's brother, Fife, had used his accident to claim the governorship of Scotland in their father's final year, he was not able to secure the succession. When their father died the following year, it was John who was proclaimed king, as Robert III, despite his injury. The strange situation in which Scotland found itself, with a king who the magnates had already decided was incapable of ruling, appears to have caused a delay in John's coronation, which did not take place until 14 August 1390: 'King Robert III was crowned at Scone in royal fashion the same year, after changing his name; and on the morrow Anabella Drummond was in like manner graced with the Royal diadem at the same place.'[9] King Robert III was crowned and anointed at Scone, by Walter Trail, Bishop of St Andrews. In a separate ceremony, the next day, Annabella was crowned queen by the bishop of Dunkeld. The coronation must have been quite the spectacle as Bower noted in his *Scotichronicon* that 'So great was the crowd from every part of the kingdom that gathered for the king's coronation that all the standing crops of the monastery of Scone nearby and in other places and granges round about were ruined by the horses.'[10]

In the two years that he had acted as Governor of Scotland, the Earl of Fife had proven himself to be a capable administrator, negotiating a generous truce with the English and making some progress in restoring order in the north. He also had the support of influential figures, who he had been careful to reward with offices and patronage, whereas the king's chief supporter, James, Earl Douglas, had been killed at the Battle of Otterburn in August 1388.[11] It was whilst preparing for the invasion of England, in which Douglas died, that the future king was severely and permanently injured by a kick from a horse. Those magnates who had previously backed the Earl of Fife had every reason to stay faithful to him. It was in their best interests. They would have feared retribution should Robert III be allowed to reassert his personal authority. We do not know Annabella's own thoughts on the matter, but, given her animosity towards the Earl of Fife and her own behaviour throughout the reign, we can surmise that she supported her husband's attempts to reclaim power. It was not to be, however, as it was decided that, although John was crowned as King Robert III, his brother the Earl of Fife would retain his position as Governor of Scotland:

> Once therefore the body of the most highly regarded King Robert II had been placed in its tomb and the kingdom had been entrusted to the guardianship of his son (that is Robert his second son), John earl of Carrick the first-born son of the dead king was crowned at Scone in the royal manner on the eve of the Assumption of Our Lady following, 1390 (which was a Sunday). He was thereafter with the consent of the estates known as King Robert III. Then on the following day his wife the Lady Annabel, daughter of the noble John de Drummond and a lady of great distinction, was invested with a royal crown. On the Tuesday next following the king took fealty and

homage from his lieges, and everyone passed these days of festivity most pleasantly.[12]

Unfortunately, we have no description of Queen Annabella, but we do have one, given by Walter Bower, of King Robert III:

> The said king was tall in stature though lame; he had a very handsome face with a luxuriant beard; he had the attractiveness of a snowy-white old age, with lively eyes which always spread good humour, and rather long and ruddy cheeks blooming with every mark of handsome aimiability [sic]. Wherever he went, moreover, he took with him humility as attendant of the virtues, that is as his constant companion. This had made him so beloved by his men that all his subjects thought it agreeable to look on him, both for his gentle countenance and for the proof of his humility.[13]

At the time of their coronations, Annabella and Robert's only son, David, was approaching his 12th birthday and the young prince was created Earl of Carrick. It was perhaps two years after her coronation that Annabella finally gave birth to a second son, named Robert, but the little boy died sometime after 8 February 1393, when he is recorded in a charter issued by King Robert III as 'our son'.[14] And in December 1394, another son was born. He was given the name James and would go on to rule as King James I. At the same time that she was pregnant with James, the queen was engaging in correspondence with King Richard II. The English king was engaged in negotiations with her husband over the possibility of arranging marriages between the two royal families. King Richard's letter has not survived, but Annabella's reply has. Written from Dunfermline Abbey on 1 August 1394, it says:

> To the most high and mighty prince Richard, by the grace of God king of England, our very dear cousin, Annabella, by the selfsame grace queen of Scotland, sends health and greeting. We give you hearty and entire thanks for your loving letters presented to us by our well-beloved Douglas, herald-at-arms, from which we have learned to our great pleasure and comfort your good health and estate. And, dearest cousin, as touching the marriage-treaty to be made between some nearly allied to you by blood and some children of the king my lord and of us, be pleased to know that it is agreeable to the king my said lord and to us, as he has signified to you by these letters. And in especial, that, although the said treaty could not be held on the third day of July last past for certain and reasonable causes contained in your letters sent to the king my aforesaid lord, you consented that the treaty should in like manner take place another day, namely, the

first day of October next coming, which is agreeable to the king my aforesaid lord and to us; and we thank you heartily and with good will, and affectionately pray you that you will continue the said treaty, and have the said day kept, for it is the will of my said lord the king and of us that as far as in us lies the said day should be kept without fail. And, dearest cousin, we affectionately require and entreat you that your highness will not be displeased that we have not sooner written to you; for we were lying in childbed of a male infant named James, of whom we are now well and graciously delivered, thanks to God and our Lady. And also because at the coming of your letters, the king my said lord was far away in the isles of his kingdom, we did not receive these letters sent to us on this matter till the last day of July last past. Most high and puissant prince, may the Holy Ghost ever keep you! Given under our signet, at the abbey of Dunfermline, the first day of August.[15]

The letter gives a wonderful insight into Queen Annabella's favourable opinions on the prospect of a marriage alliance with England, but also demonstrates her practical mind, looking to the details of the arrangements, and her position as a mother, announcing the safe delivery of her son. It also demonstrates that Annabella was intimately involved in the business of Scotland, not only in securing the Stewart dynasty, but also in furthering treaties and corresponding with foreign courts. In the end, no marriage treaty was agreed between England and Scotland. Robert and Annabella's daughters all married Scottish noblemen, though their youngest son, James, whose birth is announced in the letter, would go on to marry Joan Beaufort, a cousin of Richard II, in a love match, but more of that later. The letter serves to demonstrate that Queen Annabella was involved in Scottish affairs. We have no details regarding the queen's household, but we do know that in March 1391, parliament granted her an annual pension of 2,500 merks for 'her adornment and other things necessary for rank and livelihood'.[16] The Fife burgh of Inverkeithing is believed to have been a favourite residence of the queen. She presented the parish church with a sandstone font, decorated with angels and heraldry, which survives today.[17]

King Robert III never fully recovered from the injuries he sustained two years before his accession and, as a result, he was also prone to depression. As the reign progressed, Annabella increasingly looked to her eldest son, David, to counteract the power and influence of her brother-in-law, the Earl of Fife. From 1393, Robert III tried to impose his own authority and rule for himself but caused more division between the Highlands of the north and the Lowlands of the south; bribery and corruption were rife. David was now 14, and able to start taking on some of the responsibilities of government and, with this, Fife's guardianship was annulled. The influence of his mother's family is clear in that David's first two chamberlains were her relatives, William Drummond and

John Logie.[18] The Earl of Fife retained the post of chamberlain, and his friends continued to occupy positions of influence within the administration, both central and regional, but power was increasingly in the hands of Robert III's son and heir. The more influential David became, the more his parents were able to exert their own control on the governance of the realm.

Queen Annabella's influence is clearly demonstrated when in

> 1398 [the lady queen arranged] a great tournament for twelve knights [among whom the leading figure was her son the prince of the realm David Stewart, who was made duke of Rothesay in the same year, a title that would, from that moment on, be borne by all heirs to the Scottish throne. This occasion for the conferment of knighthood on him was staged close to the north side of the town of Edinburgh where there is now a loch].[19]

As Bower says, it was in the same year that, newly knighted,

> King Robert III held a great council at Perth where he raised his eldest son David Stewart from earl of Carrick to duke of Rothesay and Sir Robert his brother (then governor of the realm) from earl of Fife and Menteith to duke of Albany. Before this time there is no record of a duke since the death of Fulgentius who killed the Emperor Severus in Britain in a pitched battle. This ceremony was performed at Scone on 28 April, with sir Walter Trail bishop of St Andrews celebrating mass and preaching [about the state of the realm] before the king and queen.[20]

That Fife (from now on referred to as Albany) was also made a duke clearly demonstrates he still held considerable influence in the kingdom. As the king's health deteriorated, it was Albany who secured himself the place as Robert III's chief adviser.[21] The queen, however, continued to advance the interests of her son and it was for this reason that she was at, and may have helped to arrange, a meeting at Falkland Castle in Fife, at which were also present her son, Albany, and Archibald 'the Grim' Earl of Douglas. The result of the conference was that on 27 January 1399, 19-year-old David was made Lieutenant of the Realm, effectively excluding his father from the business of government.[22] This was also seen as a means of ensuring that David would succeed his increasingly frail father. This appointment essentially gave him the rule of Scotland, in his father's place; although he was to consult with the full council, with his Uncle Robert as his primary adviser. David would hold the position for three years.

A power struggle developed between Albany and David. As their rivalry grew more intense, the country was effectively divided into two factions. David, it seems, was of a 'dissolute and licentious' nature and almost as inept as his father.[23] In a kinder assessment, Nigel Tranter says he was 'high-spirited' and 'not always noted for good judgement'.[24] In 1399, David was betrothed to Elizabeth Dunbar, daughter of the Earl of March.[25] However, the marriage never took place and in 1400, the prince married Marjory Douglas, the daughter of Archibald 'the Grim', Earl of Douglas, and his wife, Jean Moray of Strathearn.[26] The couple were married at Bothwell Church, but the marriage would be childless. The marriage itself caused the Earl of March – father of David's erstwhile fiancée – to renounce his allegiance to Scotland and swear fealty to Henry IV of England. For his part, Henry IV claimed that the Scots had slandered him in letters to the King of France, shortly after he had usurped the throne from his cousin, Richard II. He launched an invasion.[27] Henry managed to reach Edinburgh without much opposition. Once there, he summoned the dukes of Rothesay and Albany to pay homage to him, but neither did. David held Edinburgh Castle against Henry, whilst Albany had mustered an army 15 miles away at Calder Muir; but he failed to march to Rothesay's aid. Henry IV was eventually forced to retire for lack of supplies, with the Scots powerless to take the advantage. David was blamed for provoking the English invasion, though the chronicles claim little damage was done: 'the King of England, for want of provisions some say, went back again to England after doing some trifling damage to the country; and as nothing worth remembering was done there we pass on'.[28] It was noted that 'the aforesaid King Henry, out of respect for Queen Anabella of Scotland, who was at Dunfermline, behaved the more kindly in all he did in the kingdom of Scotland'.[29]

King Robert III is barely given consideration by this time. Walter Bower describes a scene in which Queen Annabella asks her husband why he had given no thought to the construction of his tomb. His response is a sad indication of how the unfortunate king saw himself:

> One day when the noble Queen Annabel (the wife of this most gentle king in her lifetime) asked him why he was not making arrangements for an honourable monument like other kings who had been his predecessors, and what words of appreciation he had in mind to be written as his epitaph, the king replied to her thus: 'You have spoken like a worldly woman, for if I think carefully over what, who and of what kind I am – on what is my nature (because I am a stinking seed), on what is my personality (because I am food for worms), and on what is the nature of my life (because I am the most wretched of men) – I should as a result have no desire to erect a proud tomb. Therefore let these men who strive in this world for the pleasures of honour have shining monuments. I on the other hand should prefer to be buried at the bottom of a midden, so that my soul may be saved in the day of the Lord. Bury me therefore, I beg you, in a midden, and write for my epitaph: "Here lies the worst of kings and the most wretched of men in the whole kingdom."'[30]

In the end, it was Queen Annabella who died first, passing away in the autumn of 1401, at Scone. She was buried at Dunfermline Abbey. Her death was greatly lamented by the chroniclers of the time, the *Liber Pluscardensis* calling the queen 'the pride and ornament of the kingdom while she lived'.[31] The death of the queen, and of the Bishop of St Andrews a few weeks before, robbed Scotland of two of the most influential and steadying forces in the kingdom:

> In 1401 sir Walter Trail bishop of St Andrews died, a very solid pillar of the church, a vehicle for eloquence, a repository of knowledge and defender of the church. Also [a little later] the queen, the Lady Annabel, died at Scone and was buried at Dunfermline. While these two lived, they raised high the honour of the kingdom as it were by recalling to amity princes and magnates who had been roused to discord, by entertaining foreigners and strangers brilliantly with feasting, and by delighting them munificently on departure, so that it was almost a proverbial saying then that with the deaths of the queen of Scotland, the earl of Douglas and the bishop of St Andrews dignity departed, honour withdrew and the integrity of Scotland died away.[32]

Another chronicler, Andrew Wyntoun, described Annabella as 'fair, honourable and pleasant', saying the queen was 'Cunning [meaning intelligent], courteous in her affairs/ Loving and large [generous] to strangers/ They she treated honourably/ And them rewarded largely.'[33] With Queen Annabella's death went David's chief supporter and last protector. She had also been a calming influence on her eldest son and 'on the death of the queen his noble mother, who used to curb him in many things, it was as if a noose had become worn: he hoped to free himself and, spurning his council of honourable men, gave himself up wholly once more to his previous frivolity.'[34] The extent to which Annabella had been able to limit her son's excesses is evident in his lack of control when she was no longer around:

> Now, after the death of the said Queen Anabella, the prince of Scotland, duke of Rothesay, who was wanton in life and behaviour, but had been kept in check and led by sounder advice, after his mother's death went back to his former wantonness, altogether rejected the advice of the lords who had been assigned him by his father and mother to rule, advise and govern him and guide him away from his wantonness to uprightness of conduct and went back to his former wantonness, leading a most wanton life, as his end showed.[35]

The council of magnates, set up to advise and assist David in the government of the realm, offered their resignations to the king, claiming they 'could not divert him to a serious way of life'.[36] Still grieving for his queen and with his health declining daily, a desperate King Robert III must have been at the end of his tether when he called upon his brother to act: 'Thereupon the weak and decrepit king wrote to his brother the duke of Albany as governor that [the said duke of Rothesay should be arrested by him] and put into custody for a time until, after punishment by the rod of discipline, he should know himself better.'[37] Albany, in alliance with David's brother-in-law, the fourth Earl of Douglas, took action and had David waylaid on the road to St Andrews, arrested and held captive in St Andrews Castle, before being moved to Falkland Palace, 'upon a small packhorse and clad in a grey jerkin, after the manner of a varlet, so that he might not be noticed on the way'.[38] According to Tranter, David was flung into a cellar, with no food and water, taking him eighteen days to die.[39] Stories arose, explaining why it took him so long to succumb to starvation. One suggested that he was sustained by grains of corn that trickled through the floorboards from a granary above. While another tells how 'a sympathetic serving woman, a nursing mother, managed to squeeze milk from her breast through a straw poked through a crack in the masonry to the starving prince'.[40] Walter Bower suggests that David may have died of dysentery, but whether he died of starvation or disease the result was the same.[41] David died between 25 and 27 March 1402, before news of his imprisonment could reach his allies, and a rescue attempt could be made. He was 23 years old. David was buried in Lindores Abbey, Fife. The king founded a chaplaincy at the parish church of Dundee to pray for David's soul, and the soul of Queen Annabella, and ordered daily masses to be said in the prince's memory at Deer Abbey and Culross.

Following David's death, his widow, Marjorie, went on to marry Sir Walter Haliburton in 1403; she died sometime before 11 May 1421. With the death of David, the king roused himself to protect and promote the interests of his surviving son, James, now Earl of Carrick and heir to the throne. The king began to appear regularly in Edinburgh and Linlithgow and lent his support to the territorial ambitions of members of Prince James's household, most notably Sir David Fleming of Cumbernauld. However, Fleming was killed in February 1406, in a battle with Sir James Douglas of Balvenie at Long Hermiston Moor. The loss of Fleming and his own declining health prompted the king to send James to France, in secret. Aged just 12, the prince was smuggled out of Scotland by ship, in March 1406, 'in order that he might there be instructed in manners and virtue and be the more safely kept'.[42] The ship was captured by English pirates off Flamborough Head, and the prince began what would be eighteen years of imprisonment in England and

No sooner had King Robert III heard his son had been taken a prisoner to England, than he began to heave piteous sighs from his heart, inwardly giving way to the most bitter grief; and by reason of the fierce anguish of his heart he was as it were half dead, and his spirits drooped, so that after this day, namely the 4th of April, he never took his food with a good heart, until he gave up the ghost to the Most High at the said place, namely the castle of Bute; and he lies honourably buried at Paisley, in front of the high altar.[43]

King Robert III died on 4 April 1406. Albany was, thereafter, the effective ruler of Scotland until his own death in 1420. The disintegration of the fragile alliance between Rothesay and Albany so soon after the death of Queen Annabella is a clear demonstration of how it was her tireless efforts, and strength of will, that had maintained the peace between the prince and his uncle. She had been a driving force in promoting her son's interests and career while she was alive. Her death was a devastating loss, not only to her family but to the country as a whole. Her surviving son, James, who was 10 years old when she died, was probably raised in her household. A number of the queen's servants would staff his own household after her death, including Annabella's marshal, William Giffard, who was still in James's household in 1428.[44] And it may have been Annabella's example, as a queen, that James remembered when promoting the interests of his own wife and queen, Joan Beaufort.

The story of King James I of Scotland and his queen, Joan Beaufort, is probably the greatest love story of the medieval era. He was a king in captivity and she a beautiful young lady of the court of the Lancastrians. After his capture by pirates in 1406, James was handed over to the English king, Henry IV, and imprisoned in the Tower of London. Within a couple of months of his capture, after his father's death, James was proclaimed King of Scots, but the English would not release their valuable prisoner. James was closely guarded and regularly moved around, but he was also well educated while in the custody of the English king and became an accomplished musician and poet. He was held at various castles including the Tower of London, Nottingham Castle, where he was allowed to go hunting, and Windsor. He was even taken to France with the English court and attended the wedding at Troyes Cathedral, in 1420, of Herny V to Catherine of Valois. The young Scots king was knighted by Henry V on St George's Day, 23 April 1421, and was made a member of the Order of the Garter the same day.[45] However honourably he was treated, James was still a captive and must have felt frustrated being kept from his own kingdom, especially when it was still governed by his hated uncle, the Duke of Albany. He wrote of his imprisonment in his autobiographical poem, *The Kingis Quair*:

> The bird, the beast, the fish eke in the sea
> They live in freedom, everyone in his kind
> And I, a man, and lacking liberty![46]

James's future bride, Joan Beaufort, was probably born in the early 1400s. Lady Joan was the daughter of John Beaufort, first Earl of Somerset and the legitimated son of John of Gaunt (himself the third son of Edward III) by his mistress and, later, wife Katherine Swynford. Joan's mother was Margaret Holland, granddaughter of

Joan of Kent (later the wife of Edward the Black Prince), from her first marriage to Thomas Holland, first Earl of Kent. The Lady Joan was very well connected; she was a niece of Henry IV, cousin to Henry V, great-niece of Richard II and great-granddaughter of Edward III. Her uncle, Henry Beaufort, was a cardinal and the Chancellor of England. Little seems to be known of her early life, but she would have been educated in the skills needed for a woman of the high nobility, in the management of a noble household, as well as dancing, music and needlework. Joan was at court by the early 1420s, when James first set eyes on her. James wrote of his love for Joan in his famous poem, *The Kingis Quair*. According to Nigel Tranter, James was with the court at Windsor, when he saw Joan for the first time; she was walking her little lapdog in the garden, below his window.[47] The narrow window afforded him only a limited view but the Lady Joan walked the same route every morning and James wrote of her:

> And with the streamers of your piercing light
> Convey my heart that is so woe begone.
> Again unto that sweet and heavenly sight.
> That I within the walls as cold as stone.
> So sweetly saw this morning walk and gone,
> Low in the garden, right before mine eye:
> Now, mercy. Queen! allow me not to die.[48]

One morning, James managed to drop a plucked rose down to Lady Joan, which he saw her wearing the following evening at dinner. Nigel Tranter suggests Lady Joan grieved over James's imprisonment and even pleaded for him to be released.[49] It is as a result of James's poetic musings that we have a description of Joan's appearance and dress:

> Of her array the form if I should write,
> To wit her golden hair and rich attire
> In fretwise trimmed and set with pearls so white
> And balas rubies sparkling as the fire,
> With many an emerald and fair sapphire;
> And on her head a chaplet fresh of hue,
> Of plumes part coloured red, and white, and blue;
> ....
> In her was beauty, youth, and humble port.
> And bounty, riches, womanly facture,
> God better wot than pen of mine report:
> Wisdom, laigess, estate, discretion sure
> In ev'ry point so guided her mesure,
> In word, in deed, in shape, in contenance,
> That nature could no more her child advance.[50]

Their romance grew apace but was interrupted when James had to accompany Henry V on his campaign against France. Henry was hoping that James's presence would make the Scots, who were fighting with the French, think twice about engaging with him. However, the strategy had little effect. James's imprisonment lasted for eighteen years. His uncle Robert Stewart, Duke of Albany and Guardian of Scotland in James's absence, refused to ransom him, in the hope of gaining the throne himself. He never quite garnered enough support but managed to keep the Scottish nobles in check. However, when he died in 1420, control passed to his son Murdoch, who had also been imprisoned by the English for twelve years but was ransomed – instead of James – in 1414, and Scotland fell into a state of virtual anarchy.

Henry V had finally decided that it was time for James to return to Scotland, having been pressured by the Beauforts and his own wife, Catherine of Valois. However, his untimely death left the details to Henry's brother, John, Duke of Bedford. On the Scottish side, James's heir presumptive, Murdoch, Duke of Albany and Governor of Scotland, sent an impressive embassy to England to negotiate the king's release. As regent for the infant Henry VI, it was Bedford who set the terms of James's freedom. Following a draft treaty agreed at York on 10 September, the details were finalised in London on 4 December.[51] James was charged 60,000 marks in ransom – although it was claimed that this was to cover the costs for his upkeep and education for the last eighteen years, rather than a ransom. The agreement included a promise for the Scots to keep out of England's wars with France, and twenty-one Scottish hostages would be handed over to the English against the payment of the remaining money. James was to marry an English noblewoman, Joan Beaufort, of course, who was to be given a dowry of 10,000 marks, though the Scots would not see the money; the amount was to be subtracted from the outstanding ransom. This marriage clause was not an onerous one, if James and Joan had already fallen in love, as King James's poetry suggests. Written in the winter of 1423/24, his autobiographical poem gives expression to James's feelings for Joan:

> I declare the kind of my loving
> Truly and good, without variance
> I love that flower above all other things[52]

James and Joan were married at the Church of St Mary Overie in Southwark (now Southwark Cathedral) on 2 February 1424: 'In this same yeer in the moneth of feuerer Sir James Styward, kyng of Scotland, espoused dame Joan, the duchesse douhter of Clarence goten by her ffirst hosbond the Erle of Somersete, at seynt Marye Oueree in Sothewerke.'[53]

The wedding feast took place in the adjoining hall, the official residence of Joan's uncle Henry Beaufort, Bishop of Winchester. James and Joan made their way north shortly afterwards. They were met in York by a large number of Scottish nobles, who had gathered to escort their king and queen home. They reached Durham by 28 March, where James signed an indenture agreeing to a seven-year truce between England and Scotland. The couple were in Scotland by the end of the month. They were crowned together at Scone in a ceremony officiated by Henry de Warlaw, Bishop of St Andrews, on 21 May 1424.[54] Although he was no longer Governor of Scotland after the king's return, Murdoch Stewart, Duke of Albany, could not be ignored. Until James and Joan had a son, Murdoch was still James's heir. He had arranged the negotiations for James's release and played a major role in the subsequent coronation:

> But on his [Robert, Duke of Albany's] death the prelates and lords of the kingdom took counsel and delivered their King James, the first of this name, out of the hands of his enemies, giving hostages for a hundred thousand marks and contracting a marriage with the niece of the king of England and daughter of the earl of Somerset, now duke thereof, and brought him back to the kingdom; and all the chief men of the kingdom assembled in a body at Scone and crowned him with glory and honour, after the manner of his predecessors. As security for his liberation and the foregoing sum, many magnates of the kingdom were sent as hostages into England in the year 1424. Now this queen Joan was the daughter of John Beaufort marquess of Dorset and earl of Somerset, who was the son of the lord John of Gaunt, the father of Henry duke of Lancaster and fourth king of England of that name. The queen's mother was the daughter of the earl of Kent, brother of King Richard ii. who was driven out into Scotland, and his name was Thomas of Holland. Because of the marriage, however, and as the said queen's dowry, the king was let off half the said sum. So they were both crowned by the bishop of Saint Andrews on the twenty-first day of May in the year 1424. But Murdach Stewart, by a special privilege granted to him as duke of Albany and earl of Fife, set the said king upon the royal seat; and many aspirants were girded and decorated with the belt of knighthood by the king, as will be shown later, together with the names of the hostages given and the king's expenses in England.[55]

The ceremony was conducted in the presence of the bishops, prelates and magnates of the kingdom and the day after, King James held a parliament at Perth, 'where various statutes were enacted for the public good'.[56]

James and Joan had eight children, seven of whom survived childhood. Their six daughters, though barred from the succession by the 1373 entail of the crown through the male line, helped to strengthen alliances across Europe. Their oldest daughter, Margaret, was born in the royal apartments at the Dominican Friary in Perth, on Christmas Day in 1424. In 1425, an embassy arrived from France, seeking little Margaret's hand in marriage for Louis, son and heir of Charles VII:

> The king [of Scots] was pleased to respond favourably to so distinguished an embassy, and forthwith sent as a solemn embassy to the king of France with a specific brief and commission the venerable men sir Henry Lychton bishop of Aberdeen, sir Edward Lauder archdeacon of Lothian, and Sir Patrick Ogilvie knight (the sheriff of Angus and justiciar of Scotland). Whereupon there was an agreement on both sides; and five years later, when each was of marriageable age, there came as envoys from the king of France La Hire the king's maitre d'hôtel along with the distinguished cleric Master Aymer; and in terms of their commission they arranged the betrothal of the said eldest daughter of the king. The girl was sent to France by her father a little later, namely 1436, surrounded by a distinguished following of attendants, and in the following year she was married.[57]

At the age of 11, Margaret was sent to France, narrowly escaping her father's fate when the English fleet attempted to capture her en route:

> the dauphiness luckily made her escape and landed at La Rochelle. She rested at Nieul Priory which is two leagues from La Rochelle without notice being taken of her until such time as the [arch-] bishop of Rheims, with the bishops of Poitiers and Saintes and the worthy sires de Graville, Gaucourt and 'Pontissey' welcomed her and lodged her honourably in a splendid place for more than two months until the marriage was celebrated at Tours in Touraine. This was performed there by the archbishop of Rheims with the greatest possible ceremony, in the presence of the king and queen and also of the queen of Sicily (the mother of the queen of France). Once the wedding had been formally celebrated, the Scots (except the few who remained with the dauphiness) were much gratified with various presents and after a safe voyage arrived home.[58]

Sadly, Margaret never became Queen of France as she died in 1445, leaving no children. Five more daughters were born to James and Joan in the next nine years, Isabella, Eleanor, Joan, Mary and Anabella. The royal couple finally had twin sons on 16 October 1430, born at Holyrood Abbey, amidst great rejoicing. Bonfires were lit, wine and food distributed to the people of Edinburgh. The king was delighted and knighted the baby boys at their baptism.[59] Alexander died within a year of his birth, leaving the younger twin, James, as Duke of Rothesay and heir to the throne.

On his return to Scotland, James proved to be an energetic king, both in the business of government and in his pastimes. He jousted, wrestled, travelled widely, was skilled in several musical instruments, wrote poetry and painted, among other things.[60] He apparently loved and trusted his wife Joan and in 1428 and 1435, when he was preparing to visit the northern parts of his kingdom, he elicited an oath from his barons, of fealty to the queen in case anything should happen to him.[61] In 1431, after the birth of their son, the king granted Joan an annuity of £360 and proceeded to pursue a policy of expanding her landed interests into Perthshire, rather aggressively, at the expense of the interests of his uncle Walter, Earl of Atholl.

The king also set about getting his revenge on the Duke of Albany's family and its adherents; executing some, including Murdoch, Albany's son and heir. Two other claimants to James's throne were sent to England, as hostages for the payment of his ransom. James and Joan ruled Scotland for thirteen years; James even allowed Joan to take some part in the business of government. Although the Scots were wary of her being English, Queen Joan became a figurehead for patronage and pageantry; she granted her chaplain the hospital at Linlithgow in 1426.[62] Unusually, we know the name of Joan's personal physician from a writ issued on 15 March 1431: 'William of Forest physician of the Queen of Scots, now in England, to go with 8 attendants to Hainault and thence to Scotland at pleasure. Westminster.'[63] In recognition of her piety, Pope Eugene IV corresponded with her, in 1436, requesting that she aid the king in his reforms of the Scottish church.[64] She acted as intercessor with the king, appealing for mercy for Alexander Macdonald, Lord of the Isles, after he had led a campaign of violence across the Highlands in 1429.[65] After Joan pleaded for his life, Macdonald escaped execution and was instead imprisoned in Tantallon Castle.[66] The chronicler Walter Bower tells us of another incident in which the queen pleaded with her husband for mercy:

> I have indeed known (which is why I speak) a certain great nobleman, a near relative of the king, who was on some occasion which I cannot now recall staying at the royal court. Because he slapped another man in the king's hall [at which the man who had been struck complained to the king], the king ordered the same hand as had struck the blow to be stretched out on the dining table, and handing a little knife to the young man who had been slapped, ordered him under pain of death to strike the hand that was pinioned in this way and pierce the palm. On hearing this the queen with her ladies and the prelates with their clerics prostrated themselves on the floor. They had difficulty for an hour in securing pardon for the culprit, and then only on the basis that the man who had struck the blow was forbidden the court and the king's presence for a time.[67]

The English hope that Joan's marriage to James would also steer the Scots away from their alliance with France was short-lived. The 1436 marriage of Margaret to the

French dauphin formed part of a renewal of the Auld Alliance and, when the seven-year truce expired, James laid siege to Roxburgh Castle, on the Anglo-Scottish border. James's political reforms, combined with his desire for a firm but just government, made enemies of some nobles, including his own chamberlain Sir Robert Stewart, grandson of Walter, Earl of Atholl, who had been James's heir until the birth of his son. Sir Robert and his grandfather hatched a plot to kill the king and queen.

After so many years of imprisonment in English strongholds, King James had developed an aversion to castles and avoided them as much as he could. And so, in February 1437, the regal couple was staying in the royal apartments at the Dominican Friary in Perth, having celebrated Christmas there. Sir Robert Stewart had dismissed the guard and allowed the assassins into the friary. The king was relaxing with the queen and her ladies when they heard the men approaching. The locking bar to the king's quarters had been surreptitiously removed and on seeing it missing, Joan's lady, Kate Douglas, used her own arm to bar the door, earning her the name 'Kate Bar-lass'. The queen hid the king in an underground vault as Kate's arm broke and the plotters gained entry. There is a legend that the vault had originally been an underground passage; however, the king had ordered the far end to be sealed, when his tennis balls kept getting lost down there. Unfortunately, that also meant James had blocked off his own escape route. The assassins dragged the king from his hiding place and stabbed him to death; Joan herself was injured in the scuffle, taking a wound to the shoulder, but she managed to escape outside. As the assassins fled north, the queen made her way to Edinburgh, where her children were staying.

The plotters, led by Walter, Earl of Atholl, had expected to seize power, but were arrested and executed as the nobles rallied around the new king, 6-year-old James II. James I was buried at Perth. It being too dangerous to make their way to Scone, little James was crowned on 25 March 1437, at Holyrood Abbey, by the Bishop of Dunblane.[68] The new king's great-uncle Walter, Earl of Atholl, was executed as a traitor the following day. In his late 70s, the ageing prince had endured three days of torture before his execution. There was limited support for Joan as regent; the usual objections to a woman ruling over men were raised and, eventually, Joan had to be satisfied with retaining the guardianship of her son, while the government of the kingdom went to Archibald Douglas, Earl of Douglas. The queen took her young family to the security of Dunbar Castle. When Douglas died two years later, a power struggle erupted, between the rival factions of Douglas, Livingstone and Crichton. Alexander Livingstone came out on top and took possession of the child-king. To shore up her own position, and possibly with some affection on both sides, Joan married a loyal supporter of the late Archibald Douglas, 40-year-old Sir James Stewart, the Black Knight of Lorne and son of the Scottish ambassador to England. However, the newlyweds had little time to enjoy their marital bliss and were arrested on 3 August, just days or weeks after their July wedding. Joan was held under house arrest in the castle apartments at Linlithgow, while her husband was sequestered in the castle dungeons.

They were only freed after parliament met at Stirling and negotiated the queen's release. In a document known as 'the Appoyntement', Joan agreed to Livingstone keeping custody of the king, although Joan would have access to her son, and the annuity parliament had assigned her would be used to pay for her son's maintenance.[69] Joan retreated to Dunbar Castle, with her daughters. Over the next five years, Joan gave birth to three sons, John, James and Andrew. Queen Joan also arranged the marriages of her five younger daughters. Isabella married Francis I, Duke of Brittany; she had two daughters and died in 1494. Eleanor married Sigismund, Archduke of Austria, and died in 1480. Joan was born mute and, after several false starts on the marriage market, she married James Douglas, Earl of Morton, and had four children – her eldest son, Sir John Douglas, second Earl of Morton, was probably killed at Flodden in 1513. Joan herself died in 1486. Another daughter, Mary, was created Countess of Buchan in 1444; she married Wolfert, Count of Grandpre, of the Netherlands, and gave birth to two sons who died young. She died in 1465. A last daughter, Anabella, initially married Louis of Savoy but, following their divorce in 1458, she married George Gordon, second Earl of Huntly. They had two children before divorcing on the grounds of consanguinity in 1471.

The rivalry between the Livingstones and the Crichtons continued and flared up again in 1444, when King James II turned 14. Livingstone still held the king in his custody at Edinburgh Castle. Queen Joan and her husband sided with Sir William Crichton and his chief ally, James Kennedy, Bishop of St Andrews, and civil war erupted. In 1445, Sir James Stewart was arrested and arraigned before parliament for speaking out against Livingstone's management of the kingdom. Queen Joan retreated to her stronghold of Dunbar Castle, where she was besieged by Livingstone's forces. The queen and the castellan, Adam Hepburn of Hailes, prosecuted a stout defence of the castle. However, whether it was as a result of falling masonry, murder, a missile, or illness, Joan died during the fighting on 15 July 1445. Hepburn was forced to surrender. Shortly after Joan's death, on 22 November, a safe conduct warrant was issued, for a year, at Westminster for 'Sir James Stewart, husband of the late Queen of Scotland, John Stewart his son, and William Dicson, Scotsmen, with 20 other Scotsmen in their company.'[70] Although it was asserted by the Auchinleck chronicler that Stewart was killed at sea by Flemings, a second safe conduct, was issued on 20 November 1447, 'for four years for James Stewart, late husband of the Queen of Scotland deceased, John and James Stewart his sons, John Ysaac, Robert Galle, Robert Flemyng, and ten persons in their company, to pass through England to France or elsewhere'.[71]

Queen Joan was laid to rest beside her first love, King James I, in the Charterhouse at Perth. Their magnificent tomb was destroyed in 1559, during the Scottish Reformation. Their story of true love was cut short by an assassin's dagger in 1437, but the literary story lives on in King James's own work, *The Kingis Quair*, written in Middle Scots when the royal lover was still imprisoned by the English.

The unrest that arose, out of the rivalry of the many sons of Robert II, meant that both Annabella Drummond and Joan Beaufort had to fight to protect the rights of their sons and guarantee their succession to the crown. Where Annabella's husband was incapacitated by injury and depression, Joan's had succumbed to an assassin's dagger. While she was alive, Annabella could protect her children from the machinations of her husband's brother, but her death left both boys, David and James, without their greatest protector, resulting in the eldest dying in prison and the youngest being held captive by the English for eighteen years. Joan, on the other hand, fought desperately to protect herself and her children following the murder of James I. As a consequence, each queen was forced to fill at least some of the void left by their husbands. While neither wholly succeeded, they proved capable of accepting the challenge and demonstrated their ability and courage in the face of adversity. Neither gave up. To some extent, both women set the tone for queenship in medieval Scotland for the remainder of the fifteenth century.

Chapter Thirteen

Renaissance Queens

U ntil the mid-fifteenth century, the majority of Scotland's queens had been either English or native Scots. Only Yolande de Dreux and Marie de Coucy had come from farther afield in France. It must have come as a culture shock for both the Scots and the bride, then, when James II married Mary of Guelders (or Gueldres). King since he was only 6 years old, James's childhood – and the accompanying regency – had been marked by a bitter rivalry between the most powerful Scottish barons, Sir William Crichton, Lord Chancellor of Scotland, and Sir Alexander Livingstone, warden of Stirling Castle, fighting over the custody of the king, and therefore Scotland. As Nigel Tranter so elegantly puts it, 'these two beauties, Crichton and Livingston, now began a tug-of-war which was to last for years, pulling their youthful liege-lord between them, heedless of his needs and feelings.'[1] The most notorious incident of the regency has become known as the Black Dinner, and has become a trope among historical fiction writers, in particular.

Archibald Douglas, fifth Earl of Douglas, the king's first cousin, had been lieutenant-general of the realm until his death in 1439. His demise had left a power vacuum which Crichton and Livingstone both hoped to fill. Douglas had been succeeded as Earl of Douglas by his 16-year-old son, William. On 24 November 1440, William and his younger brother, David, who was just 12 years old, were invited to Edinburgh Castle to dine with the king. Only 10 years of age himself, the king was charmed by the older boys. However, as they ate, a black bull's head was brought in and placed in front of the earl. It symbolised death. The two boys were bundled from the table and beheaded in the castle yard, with the young king still pleading for their lives. He was powerless to save them.

King James had been with his mother at Stirling when she was arrested in 1439, following her marriage to James Stewart, the Black Knight of Lorne. Her negotiated release saw custody of the young king handed over to Livingstone, with the queen's annual pension to pay for his keep. Her political influence was much reduced, although she sided with Crichton and his ally, James Kennedy, Bishop of St Andrews, when civil war broke out between Livingstone and Crichton. In 1445, with her second husband arraigned for speaking out against the administration of the country, Joan was besieged in Dunbar Castle. Her death during the siege, whether from physical injury or illness, must have been a hard blow to the young king. James was now 15 years of age but still dominated by the Livingstone faction, who now enjoyed the support of the new Earl of Douglas, James the Gross, whose complicity in the murder of his great-nephews at the Black Dinner saw him and the Livingstones achieve dominance at court.[2]

James II was very much like his father and was not one to acquiesce when seeing his royal authority challenged or impeded, especially having endured the frustration of a long minority. And it was in the arrangements for his marriage that James was finally able to assert his independence. In January 1448, the king may have sought the assistance of his kinsman, Charles VII, King of France, in arranging his marriage to Mary of Guelders. King Charles was the father-in-law of his eldest sister, Margaret, dauphine of France until her death in 1445. Margaret's marriage to the son and heir of the King of France had vicariously increased the marriage prospects of all her siblings, establishing the Scottish royal family as a presence in the courts of Europe. It is also possible that the marriage was mooted through James's female relations. Guelders was a large province in the Netherlands, occupying some 5,000 square kilometres of fertile land. Mary of Guelders was the daughter of Arnold, Duke of Guelders, and Catherine, Duchess of Cleves. Through her mother, she was the great-niece of the powerful Duke of Burgundy, Philip the Good, and was brought up at his highly cultivated court in Brussels. Duke Philip was married to Isabella of Portugal, a first cousin of James's mother, Joan Beaufort. Isabella had already arranged the marriage of her son, the future Charles the Bold, Duke of Burgundy, to Catherine of France, Charles VII's 6-year-old daughter, in 1439, as well as the marriages of various other relatives. It is not a stretch of the imagination to see Isabella taking a lead role in arranging Mary's marriage to James.[3] The Scots king was not Mary's first marriage prospect, however. When she was only 12, it was proposed that she marry Charles, Comte de Maine, brother of René of Anjou, as part of an alliance between Anjou and Burgundy. René was the father of Margaret of Anjou, future queen of England as the wife of King Henry VI. The marriage negotiations fell through, however, when Mary's father sent Duchess Isabella a message, saying that he was unable to provide the required dowry.

Mary remained at court, in the household of Duchess Isabella's daughter-in-law, Catherine of France. She appears in the duchess's accounts, where there is mention of Mary's ten attendants, including her carver, Robert de Harpe, and an expense, 'For the Count, the Countess [of Charolais] and Mademoiselle Mary of Gueldres ... fur for their robes.'[4] Living at the court of Isabella and Philip would have given Mary first-hand experience of how a woman could wield power. Isabella was an impressive administrator who ruled Burgundy during her husband's absences, negotiated treaties and managed the finances, in addition to raising the children. The marriage of Mary and James may well have been first proposed before the death of James's mother as in June 1446, the young king's ambassador visited Arnhem, the capital of Guelders, and the following month the Scottish herald visited 'the Maiden of Gueldres', who was staying with her parents at the time.[5] Unfortunately, little Princess Catherine died in Brussels on 28 July and all thoughts of marriage were abandoned as the court went into mourning. As the princess's household had been an extension of that of Duchess Isabella, it is likely that Mary was transferred into the duchess's household.[6]

In 1448, King James approached Charles VII of France, reminding him of their old alliance against England and asking that he recommend a suitable queen for Scotland. The French king had no suitable female relative within his close family but advised James to approach the Duke of Burgundy. Given the previous tentative approaches, it seems likely that Charles, James and, indeed, Duchess Isabella, had already decided on Mary of Guelders as the bride for the Scots king. Indeed, the Franco–Scottish alliance was renewed, on 31 December 1448, while the marriage negotiations were ongoing. James II gave full powers to his ambassadors, including the chancellor, Sir William Crichton, in May of the same year, to negotiate the contract. In February 1449, in the festivities that surrounded the talks at Stirling, a great tournament was held in which three Burgundian knights faced three Scottish knights, with 'lances, axes, swords and daggers'.[7] James Douglas led the Scottish contingent as he jousted with Jacques de Lalain, eldest son of the Lord of Lalain. The combat was to continue until one side admitted defeat, or as long as the king wished, as he was the judge.[8] The protracted discussions were not resolved until 1 April 1449, when the marriage treaty was sealed in Brussels by Mary's father. Scotland, Burgundy and Guelders agreed a treaty of mutual assistance against all enemies, and to promote each other's interests.[9] Duke Philip would provide Mary's dowry, which amounted to 60,000 crowns (£30,000 Scots), to be paid over two years. For his part, King James would provide Mary a considerable jointure of 10,000 crowns (£5,000), for which King Charles VII would provide surety, in the event of James's death. Mary's income would come from the lands of Strathearn and Atholl and the lordship of Methven, with the palace of Linlithgow as her residence, should Mary be widowed.[10]

Duke Philip levied a subsidy of 400 livres from the town of Courtrai towards the marriage but it was Duchess Isabella who took charge of the preparations in earnest. She made the arrangements for the bride's trousseau and paid the costs of it. A tournament was held in Brussels, as those who were to escort Mary to her wedding gathered in the city, by which time she was being referred to as 'the Queen of Scotland'.[11] Mary was to be accompanied by two of the duchess's ladies-in-waiting, an illegitimate sister of the Duke of Burgundy, who was married to Anthoine de Rochebaron, and Isabelle, daughter of the Lord of Lalain and sister of Jacques, who had jousted in the tournament at Stirling in February. Her retinue also included the Keeper of her Wardrobe, the Master of her Stable and Henry Vandervelde, Mary's former tutor.[12] And it was at the Duke of Burgundy's expense that Mary was to be conveyed to her new realm, in a fleet of fourteen splendid vessels, commanded by Henric, Lord of Veere, Admiral of Holland. The admiral's son, Jean, was married to James II's sister Mary and the Scottish princess sailed with her new sister-in-law. Sir William Crichton, the Scottish Chancellor, and John Ralston, Bishop of Dunkeld, arrived from Scotland to escort Mary to her new home. The fleet departed Sluys on 9 June 1449, visiting the chapel of St Adrian on the Isle of May en route and arriving at Leith on 18 June:

> 1449 brought the arrival of Queen Mary, a daughter of the duke of Guelders, with many nobles including the lord of Veere and the lord of 'Rochbarron'. The marriage of King James II and the coronation of the said Mary were most solemnly celebrated at the monastery of Holyrood in the month of July in the same year.[13]

According to the French chronicler, Mathieu d'Escouchy, there were 'many tears and lamentations' from Mary and others as she said her farewells to the Duke of Burgundy and his son, Charles, and the other members of the court who had come to see her off.[14] On her arrival at Leith, before continuing her journey, Mary was visited by members of the court, the clergy, and diverse people. D'escouchy commented that many 'seemed to be wild people'.[15] From Leith, Mary travelled on to Edinburgh, where she was to stay in the guest house at Holyrood Abbey. As many as 10,000 people are said to have turned out to welcome their new queen, though d'Escouchy may have exaggerated, with some playing musical instruments.[16] Bishop Ralston and Chancellor Crichton took their leave of Mary and went to report to the king. James himself visited Mary 'very late, around midnight' and at his arrival the 'queen went down on her knees before him and he raised her gently to her feet and after kissed Dame de Baresy and Isabelle de Lalain'.[17] The king spent three hours with Mary and her ladies, before taking his leave. In the ensuing days, Mary was visited by the leading lords and ladies of the realm, and the king sent her a horse as a gift. On 24 June 1449, James was at Stirling, where he ratified the marriage treaty under the Great Seal of Scotland, giving his final consent to a number of conditions, including renouncing the right of any future sons to the duchy of Guelders and promising to return Mary's dowry should she die childless within a year of the marriage being consummated.[18]

James and Mary were married at Holyrood Abbey on 3 July. D'escouchy provides us with a wonderful account of the ceremonies: Mary was escorted to her wedding by the Lord of Veere, Anthoine de Rochebaron, those who had accompanied her from Burgundy and all the Scottish noblewomen. The king arrived shortly afterwards with a retinue of knights, dismounted at the door and entered the church. There, the guarantees of the queen's dower were made, letters read, and the king and queen were married. The king led the queen to the great altar, where they remained on their knees for the duration of the mass. The queen was then led to a side chapel, where she removed her wedding clothes and was dressed in her coronation robes of violet trimmed with ermine, her long hair hanging loose. The king was similarly dressed. The queen then was taken before the altar, 'where she was crowned'.[19] A lavish banquet was to follow:

> When the king and queen were seated, the first dish to be brought
> in and presented to them was a boar's head, which had been painted

and stuffed, on a huge plate. Round the head were a good thirty-two banners, with the arms of the king and the other lords of the country. Then, the stuffing was set on fire, to the great joy of everyone in the room. Next, a fine and beautifully-made ship was brought in, which had a forecastle, masts with a top, and cords of silver. Then the earl of Orkney entered, with four knights, followed by the meat course, comprising various dishes. Each dish was brought in by some thirty to forty people, all carrying plates … and, as each plate was set down, the waiter knelt until the person served had started eating…

At another table, a patriarch, three bishops, an abbot and other clerics, were merrily celebrating their king's wedding. These five prelates were drinking heavily from a huge wooden goblet, without pouring anything back; for wine and other drinks seemed in as plentiful supply as sea-water. The same thing happened at the table of knights and squires of Scotland. This feast lasted four or five hours, during which time a very large number of dishes were served.[20]

The Burgundians were disappointed that there was no dancing or supper afterwards. D'escouchy remarks on how the Burgundians found Scottish customs and dress strange and very unlike what they were used to in their part of France.[21] Five or six days after the wedding celebrations, Mary's Burgundian entourage bade their farewells to the king and queen. The king gave them expensive gifts and the queen 'felt a great sorrow in her heart as they took their leave of her and cried tenderly'.[22] Only Isabelle de Lalain stayed with her, with two or three female servants and two or three men.[23]

King James was now 19, but still officially supervised by the Livingstone family. His marriage seems to have given him the impetus to break away from their control, perhaps emboldened by his new bond with Burgundy and France. No doubt never having forgotten the treatment of his mother at the hands of Sir Alexander Livingstone, the justiciar, and in need of lands in order to pay Mary's jointure, so that Duke Philip would have no excuse to withhold Mary's dowry, the king moved against the Livingstones on 23 September. Sir Alexander, his son James, his brother Alexander, Captain of Methven and Robert Livingstone the Comptroller, and two leading Livingstone supporters were arrested. They were tried and convicted the following January. The Captain of Methven and Robert the Comptroller were beheaded, the others suffered forfeiture of their lands. The next day, Queen Mary's jointure was finalised by a charter agreed by parliament, granting Mary the earldoms of Strathearn and Atholl with various other lordships and revenues, including the customs of Linlithgow and Methven Castle. Though Menteith was later substituted for Methven.[24]

Having now assumed personal rule as King of Scots, James held his first parliament at Edinburgh in January 1450; Queen Mary was also present. She gave her support to the Scottish bishops in their complaint to the crown that the estates of deceased prelates were being requisitioned by royal officers, rather than bequeathed to their friends and relatives, leaving their executors unable to settle any outstanding debts. The bishops knelt in the full parliament and expressed their grievances. When they were done, the queen added her pleas on their behalf, acting in the traditional queen's role of intercessor.[25] The king then ceremoniously granted the bishops' request. In the same parliament, Mary also secured the widest possible support for the payment of her dower, the jointure assigned her out of the forfeiture of the Livingstone lands.

There is one peculiar incident that was attended to by parliament. And that was the order to introduce measures against strangers importing poisons into the country. We have few details as to the background to this, but it seems to originate from rumours of an attempt to bribe one of Mary's Burgundian attendants to assassinate her. It seems likely that this plot gave rise to the sending home of those attendants who had accompanied the queen to Scotland, including Isabelle de Lalain and Mary's confessor, Gerard Boot.[26]

Although she was still only a teenager, Mary had grown up at the sophisticated Burgundian court, where she developed her artistic sensibilities and a love of music.[27] Having the example of Isabella of Portugal to learn how a woman with power should behave, Mary was a confident young woman and, what's more, she was pregnant. The Duke of Burgundy was so satisfied with the provisions made for Mary, and with the news of her pregnancy, that he paid a further 20,000 crowns of her dowry. In May 1450, the queen gave birth to her first child, but the baby was three months premature and only lived for six hours. Whether the child was a boy or girl has gone unrecorded. King Charles VII of France sent letters of commiseration, to which Mary replied on 1 July 1450, informing him that she was in good health and sending him wishes that the Holy Trinity would keep Charles and his realm in happiness and prosperity. Written in Latin, the letter was penned by a scribe but signed in Mary's own hand as 'Marie R'.[28] A papal writ from 1450 demonstrates that James and Mary, and their households, were closely entwined:

> 1450. 17 Kal. Oct. (15 Sept.) Fabriano. (f. 216.) To James, king of Scots [*Scotorum*]. Indult for the dean of his chapel to hear the confessions of the domestic members of the household, of both sexes, of him and the queen of Scotland [*Scocie*], and grant absolution and enjoin penance, in cases reserved to the apostolic see once only, in all other cases as often as opportune, administer the Eucharist and other sacraments, and commute any their vows, except only those of pilgrimage to the Holy Land [*transmarino*], SS. Peter and Paul, and St. James, and receive and convert to his uses the oblations of the said queen and household. *Eximie devotionis*.[29]

The following year, the queen was once again acting as intercessor, in the parliament of April 1451, when the king seized the earldom of Wigtown, which had been held by William Douglas, eighth Earl of Douglas. The Douglas earldom had long been a bone of contention between the crown and the Douglases as it had been granted by James I to his sister Margaret, widow of the fifth earl, for her lifetime. Margaret died whilst the eighth earl was in Rome for the Papal Jubilee and James acted to recover the earldom for the crown, transmitting it and the lordship of Galloway to Mary as part of her jointure. When the earl heard what was afoot, he hastened back to Scotland and was cordially welcomed by the king 'at the request of the Queen and the Three Estates'.[30] Mary was confirmed in her existing properties and granted further land and revenues in a charter issued on 1 July. The enmity between the king and Douglas continued and Wigtown was only returned – reluctantly – to the earl in October 1451.[31] The following year, James's rivalry with Douglas came to a head amid heated discussions at Stirling and the earl was fatally stabbed twenty-six times, with the king issuing two of the blows, the rest committed by his courtiers.[32]

By the end of 1450, the grief of losing their first child was replaced with news that Mary was once again pregnant with the royal couple's second child. Her pregnancy must have been apparent when she spoke up for Douglas in the April parliament as she gave birth in July 1451. Historians cannot seem to agree as to whether the child was a daughter, Mary, or a son, James – the future James III.[33] Most, however, seem to believe that James was not born until 1452, which would mean that Princess Mary was born in 1451. Whether the queen gave birth to a girl or a boy, it must have been a worrying time for her and James. Having previously given birth prematurely to a short-lived child, all would have been anxious that everything would go well, this time. There is a record in the Exchequer accounts of a payment of six shillings to William Craig, who had brought the shirt of St Margaret, a holy relic, from Dunfermline for the queen's use during her confinement. Scotland's sainted queen was believed to be a help for women in childbirth.[34] The child born in 1451 was born at Stirling Castle but in 1452, when Mary was pregnant again, James sent her to the relative safety of the episcopal castle at St Andrews, due to rising tensions in the aftermath of Douglas's murder. Three more sons, Alexander, David (who died aged about 3) and John, and a second daughter, Margaret, would complete the royal nursery over the ensuing years:

> 1452 brought the birth of King James III, the son of King James II. And it is noteworthy that King James II fathered by the said Queen Mary King James III, Alexander duke of Albany and John earl of Mar, and two daughters, besides a fourth son David and a third daughter who died young.[35]

The future King James III would be the first king to grow up with royal brothers of a similar age since Robert III, with just as much brotherly love, or lack thereof, between them. In 1479, both brothers were arrested, accused of conspiring against the king, but we will look into that in greater detail later. James III's youngest sister, Margaret, was considered as a bride for George, Duke of Clarence, the unstable brother of Edward IV, and Anthony Woodville, Edward IV's brother-in-law, but neither scheme came to fruition. Rather scandalously, Margaret was the mistress of William Lord Crichton, by whom she had a daughter, also called Margaret. There's no evidence the couple ever married and the younger Margaret was considered illegitimate.[36]

As the queen continued to fill the royal nursery, King James pursued his policy of enriching the queen. In May 1454, Mary was present in person to witness the king besieging Blackness Castle, which had been seized by James Crichton. Once he had taken it, James handed the castle to Mary. She was becoming a very wealthy woman. From the Exchequer rolls, we can see that Mary spent considerable sums on her charitable interests, having a hospital built for the poor and needy, just outside Edinburgh and establishing a friary for the Franciscans in the city, with the help of Bishop Kennedy.[37] In 1451, salmon costing £240 was purchased for the queen's table and she also spent money on wine and furs for her clothing.[38] Mary was very devout and is mentioned as a petitioner, alongside King James, in a papal writ authorising an investigation into the nefarious activities of the Trinitarian friars of Glasgow:

> 1459: To the bishops of Glasgow and Whiteherne and the archdeacon of Glasgow. Mandate, as below. The recent petition of James and Mary, king and queen of Scots, contained that the minister and friars of the Trinitarian house of Fale in the diocese of Glasgow, instead of the redemption of captives and hospitality engage in uncleanness etc., so publicly and notoriously that there is a great rumour among all the inhabitants of the realm; that on account of exemption from the ordinaries and the dangers of sea and land and the negligence of their superiors, their enormities and shameful life are not corrected, and that they are so much involved in evil that they cannot be brought back to decency and the observance of their rule; and that the said queen has built and erected a certain great hospital, with church, houses, etc., and a number of dignities etc. therein, and has endowed the same. At the said petition, the pope hereby orders the above three, if they find the statements made therein to be true, to remove the said minister and friars, place them in other houses of the same order in the realm, suppress the said order in the said house, and unite and appropriate the said house, value with its annexes not exceeding 70*l.* sterling, to the said church and hospital in perpetuity, so that the rectors thereof may take possession of the said house etc., without requiring the licence [of the ordinary or] of any other, etc. *Ad ea ex apostolice servitutis.*[39]

Mary of Guelders' wedded bliss was to come to a sudden and tragic end in the summer of 1460, when King James was besieging Roxburgh Castle, which had been taken by the English. The king held a fascination for artillery and had been sent several guns by Philip, Duke of Burgundy. One such was the famous Mons Meg, made in 1449 at Mons, which can still be seen guarding the ramparts at Edinburgh Castle. Cannons, however, were notoriously fickle. During the prosecution of the siege, the king was standing too close to one of the cannon as it fired, possibly in a salute to greet the Earl of Huntly or the queen, sources are unsure.[40] The queen may have still been in Edinburgh with her children as she had recently given birth to her last child, Margaret. Whatever the reason for the gun firing, the effects were not those desired. The cannon exploded and a fragment of flying metal shattered the king's leg at the thigh. The dying king was carried to the nearby friary of St Peter, where he received the last rites before breathing his last. He was 29 years old. The Auchinleck chronicler reported the event: 'the third sonday of august king Iames the secund with ane gret ost was At the sege of Roxburgh and wnhappely was slane with ane gwn the quhilk brak in the fyring.'[41] The chronicle goes on to say there 'was gret dolour throu all Scotland'.[42]

In spite of the shock of the king's death, it was decided that the siege should continue. The queen brought her young son, the new King James III, to the Scottish camp and mother and son reached Roxburgh just as the castle fell, on 8 August. Two days later, the 8-year-old was crowned King of Scots at the Abbey of Kelso, watched by his mother. As part of the ceremony 'there was made more than a hundred knights'.[43] That autumn, the dowager queen founded a Collegiate Church of the Holy Trinity beside her hospital, just outside Edinburgh, as a permanent memorial to her husband, 'the late most illustrious prince, James, King of Scots, our most tender husband'.[44] The queen herself laid down the regulations for services and the attendant clerics, ordering that any priest absent without permission for fifteen days, or who kept a concubine, would be dismissed after three warnings.[45] King James III was given into the custody of his mother, who was given the regency of the kingdom, with the help of a council. The Auchinleck chronicler was critical of the decision, claiming 'there was little good worth both spiritual and temporal that gave the keeping of the kingdom to a woman'.[46]

Mary, however, was to prove a more than capable regent and administrator. Many of the officers she appointed remained in place into her son's personal reign, giving a much-needed stability to the government of the realm. The queen was to continue many of her husband's policies, especially in her foreign policy, which included playing the Yorkists off against the Lancastrians in the continuing war in England, known as the Wars of the Roses. This brought her into disagreement with Bishop Kennedy, who favoured Henry VI and the Lancastrian cause. In the winter of 1460, Margaret of Anjou and her son, Edward of Westminster, arrived in Scotland

> to get help and supplies against the duke of Yorke. And thai came
> to Dumfries and the quene of Scotland, the duke Guelders daughter,
> met the forsaid prince and his moder at Kyncloudaine and thai

remanit thar togidder x or xii days. And thai said tha war spekand of marriage betuix the forsaid prince and king James the thridis sister, and sum said that thai war accordit on baith the sydis.[47]

It was suggested that Prince Edward should marry Mary's eldest daughter, also called Mary. Shortly after the meeting, on 30 December 1460, Richard, Duke of York, was killed at the Battle of Wakefield and Margaret and her son were back in England to try to take advantage of the victory. A further victory at St Albans was countered by the victory at Towton of York's oldest son Edward, on 4 March 1461. With Edward triumphant and about to be crowned King Edward IV, Margaret, Prince Edward and Henry VI all sought shelter in Scotland. A papal report of 1 June 1461 summed up the state of play in England, Scotland and France:

Francesco Coppino, Bishop of Terni, Papal Legate to Pope Pius II: Although I have frequently written to your Holiness upon the events of these parts, yet I think it right to lay before you a brief compendium of the affairs of France, England, Scotland and Burgundy and all the western shore, so that where your Holiness is present you may also absolve. The affairs of England are in the following position. Edward has not yet made himself supreme over the whole kingdom or reduced it to peace, because Henry, the late king, with his wife and son and the Duke of Somerset and Lord de Ros are with the Scots. There it is announced they have married the daughter of the late King of Scots and sister of the present little king to the son of the said Henry, King of England. They have received from the same Henry the town of Berwick, on the frontiers of Scotland, which the Scots have long claimed as their right from the English, as the excellently well furnished guardian of their frontiers, and the place to which King Henry repaired as an asylum after the battle. Hence it is suspected on all sides, that something fresh is in preparation for Edward to chew, and that these Scots are about to break into England with Henry, his son and wife to recover the realm. And because of the ancient alliance by which the Scots are united with the French, it is thought that the French also will assist, and render support both by land and sea, because they also are inflamed against the English, especially under these new conditions, for old-standing reasons well known to all ... The Duke of Burgundy here, however, seeing from afar, and having been warned frequently and for a long time by those who love his state, fears all these things and has attempted to prevent such an alliance by approaching the Queen of Scotland, his niece ... I also have not neglected to do what I could. I have also fully instructed the most reverend patriarch here upon all things, and as one who has quite recently come out of sad troubles, he would ask for very little favour so long as the wish of that prince awaited complete fulfilment; but he himself will report what he has done. But, as we anticipated, although that announcement could not accomplish what was desired, yet it is believed that on this account the Duke here will finally strike up a treaty with Edward, although some fear that he may have delayed longer than he should, through his innate longing for peace, which the other side are believed to abhor.[48]

Reports were being written throughout Europe, summing up the state of affairs in England and Scotland and speculating on how much aid Queen Mary would give to Henry VI and his wife, and whether the French would send their assistance in accordance with the long-standing treaty they had with the Scots:

18 June 1461 Prospero di Camulio, Milanese Ambassador to the French Court to Francesco Sforza, Duke of Milan: Accordingly there is a report, which so far has not been confirmed, of the conclusion of a marriage alliance between the prince and the sister of the late King of Scotland. If that alliance took place, the Scots were to make an effort to recover the kingdom for King Henry. In favour of that king there was a most powerful French fleet at sea, to attack England, so that Henry's party cherished great hopes. I sent word about this, their plans, the course of this fleet, its attack and return … It is thought that the Queen of Scotland will give up the idea, but I cannot shut my eyes to the fact that up to the present *the Duke of Burgundy* still hesitates about those affairs, although they have a good appearance. I am of those who think it would be as well for *your Excellency* to do the like and make no further demonstration until we see things more settled. For this reason I have not told the legate to cross, but have even advised him to wait awhile until I should be willing to go with all that *your lordship* commits to me. I have no letters of credence and it does not seem decent to me to base one's operations upon mere words without the guarantee of letters.[49]

Keeping her options open, the politically astute queen allowed Henry VI and his family to stay in Scotland for a year, but avoided committing to aiding their return to England, in spite of Queen Margaret surrendering Berwick and promising to return Carlisle to the Scots.[50] The queen also sent an embassy to Edward IV, to discuss a possible truce. Philip of Burgundy was urging her to ally with the Yorkists and sent Louis de Gruuthuse to her to try and persuade her. By March 1462, Queen Mary had given the Lancastrian family a large sum of money to persuade them to leave Scotland and was in discussions with the Yorkist Earl of Warwick, proposing a marriage between herself and King Edward, though this came to nothing. And Margaret of Anjou, a fugitive once again, was back in Scotland by October 1462, though this time without her husband, who was hiding out in the northern regions of England.

As the war in England progressed, Queen Mary was also dealing with internal matters. She had bought land at Ravenscraig with the intention of building a castle designed for the use of artillery and to provide a secure refuge across the River Forth from Edinburgh, should she need it. The queen was also making renovations at Falkland Palace, though more for comfort, with a new chamber, fireplace and stable for the queen's use.[51] In 1462, the queen also received confirmation from the pope with regard to the foundation of the hospital and Collegiate Church in Edinburgh:

> Confirmation etc., as below. The recent petition of Mary queen of Scots contained that whilst the late James II king of Scots, her husband, was alive, she caused a poor hospital to be built without the royal burgh of Edinbourgh in the diocese of St. Andrews and endowed it, and erected hard by a church or chapel for a college of a provost and ten or twelve priests and clerks, has continued it with magnificent and sumptuous work, and intends as soon as possible to finish it, has assigned as the endowment of the said church a certain good barony and other possessions etc. to the sum of about 100 marks [sterling], and intends to increase the said endowment. Seeing that Nicholas V caused the poor hospital of Soltre in the said diocese, of the patronage of the king of Scots, which was in ruin and in which no hospitality was kept, to be erected into the chancellorship of the church of St. Andrews, and that the present pope, at the said queen's petition, has undone the said union and erection, and has ordered the same hospital to be united to the said new hospital, James the present king of Scots, son of the said queen, and the said queen also have petitioned the pope to confirm the said foundation, endowment and union, and also the union, made by authority of the ordinary, of the chapel of Ochterogarte in the said diocese, likewise of the patronage of the said king, the yearly value of which and of the said hospital of Soltre does not exceed 70*l.* sterling, and to erect anew the said church into a collegiate church with the *insignia* of a college, etc., the pope therefore approves and confirms hereby the said foundation, endowment and unions, and moreover erects anew the said church into a collegiate church with the *insignia* of a college, decrees that all obventions to the said church are to be applied to its fabric and repair, and grants power and faculty to the master or rector of the said new hospital, present and future, to administer all the sacraments to all of both sexes who dwell and to others who serve therein. *Ad fut. rei mem. Inter multiplices curas.* 6 Id. July. [10 July] Abbadia S. Salvatore in the diocese of Chiusi.[52]

Queen Margaret was still eager to continue the struggle against Edward IV and it may have been her, but more likely Bishop Kennedy, who was still supportive of the Lancastrian cause, who persuaded Mary to approve an attack on Norham, in Northumberland. The queen, James III and Bishop Kennedy were all present, but the assault failed utterly. Shortly afterwards, Margaret of Anjou left for Burgundy, hoping to persuade Duke Philip to aid her cause. That autumn, Queen Mary fell seriously ill, dying on 1 December 1463, possibly at Edinburgh. Her funeral did not take place until June 1464 and was held at Brechin.[53] The queen was eventually laid to rest in the Holy Trinity Collegiate Church that she had founded in memory of James II, in Edinburgh. Her lasting legacies were to be Ravenscraig Castle and the Holy Trinity Church in which she was buried, which was demolished in the nineteenth century. The peace process with the Yorkists in England, which she had started, was to continue after her death, which Bishop Kennedy, a long-time supporter of the Lancastrians, was even brought into. Rumours of illicit affairs with Edmund Beaufort, Duke of Somerset, and Adam Hepburn are probably without foundation and may have originated with the supporters of her political rival, Bishop Kennedy.[54] Mary of Guelders had proved to be a politically adept and capable regent for her young son, James III.

Queen Mary's death left her son in the hands of Bishop Kennedy, who would continue with Mary's policy towards England and the negotiations with the House of York. In 1464, the bishop took the 12-year-old king on a northern progress as far as Inverness. The bishop died in May 1465, leaving the king in the care of his brother Gilbert, Lord Kennedy. However, in 1466, as the young king was out hunting near Linlithgow, he was seized by Sir Alexander Boyd of Drumcoll, his own chamberlain, who was his instructor in the use of arms. The Boyd faction, led by Sir Alexander's older brother, Robert Lord Boyd, could not take control of the minority government, as the major offices remained in the hands of men not allied with the Boyds. Robert Lord Boyd proved to be ambitious and acquisitive, creating his son, Thomas, Earl of Arran by securing his marriage to the king's oldest sister, Mary, sometime before 26 April 1467, with the Isle of Arran as her dower.[55] Boyd's actions caused considerable animosity within the Scots court, not least with the king himself.

King James's own marriage had been mooted as early as 1456. When he was still a toddler his father, James II, had made diplomatic overtures towards King Christian I of Denmark. As part of his expansionist policies, James II was looking towards the islands of Orkney and Shetland, which remained nominally in Danish hands. A thorn in the negotiations was the matter of an annual payment of 100 marks that the Scots had promised (but only intermittently paid) in the Treaty of Perth in 1266, and the payment of which the king of Denmark now demanded, including the arrears. In the summer of 1460, shortly after James II's death, the king's ambassadors in Paris proposed the betrothal of James's 8-year-old eldest son and heir, James III, to King Christian's 3-year-old daughter, Margaret, with the cancellation of the annual payment and the surrendering of Orkney and Shetland to the Scots forming Margaret's dowry. The proposal was rejected at the time, with the Scots then turning their attention to England in search of a bride for their young king.[56] Nothing came of it and the idea of a Danish match was revived a few years later. In January 1468, the Scots decided to send an embassy to Copenhagen to discuss the question of the annual payment, and a bride for King James. King Christian I's situation had changed drastically; where he had been at the height of his power in 1460, he was now facing rebellion in Sweden, opposition in Denmark and financial troubles with growing debts. An alliance with Scotland would help to strengthen an existing alliance with Burgundy. Princess Margaret was now 11 years of age. Although she had three brothers, Margaret was the only daughter of King Christian and his wife, Dorothea von Brandenburg.

Queen Dorothea was a capable and practical consort for her husband Christian, King of Denmark, Norway and Sweden, and it was she who helped the king reorganise his finances, even paying off his debts. She administered her own estates and was involved in the founding of the University of Copenhagen.[57] Margaret was probably raised in her mother's household, though we have no information about her childhood or education. In the summer of 1468, having been granted £3,000 towards the costs, an embassy of eight leading magnates set out for Denmark. They were led by Lord Chancellor Avandale and included Thomas Boyd, Earl of Arran, the king's brother-in-law as the husband of Princess Mary.[58] More desperate than in 1460, the Danish royal administration agreed to terms almost identical to those initially proposed. The Treaty of Copenhagen, of 1468, agreed to a dowry of 60,000 florins of the Rhine, with an initial payment of 10,000 florins while Orkney was to stand surety for the outstanding 50,000 florins. However, when it came to paying the first instalment, King Christian could only raise 2,000 florins and so Shetland was pledged for the remaining 8,000. As neither the Danish king nor his successors were ever able to pay the balance of the dowry, Shetland and Orkney – the Northern Isles – became part of Scotland. For his part, James III was to settle on Margaret Linlithgow Palace, Doune Castle and one-third of his royal revenues, the largest possible jointure allowed according to a parliamentary ordinance of 1466.[59]

By the time the marriage treaty was signed, on 8 September 1468, it was too late in the year for the Danish princess to embark for Scotland and so it was not until the following spring that the Earl of Arran arrived in Denmark to escort the princess to Leith. As the princess landed in Scotland, Arran was met by his wife Mary, the king's sister, saying that the king had turned against him and the rest of the Boyd family. Arran and Princess Mary immediately took ship, fleeing back to Denmark. Arran's father, Robert Lord Boyd, also managed to escape to the Continent, while Sir Alexander, the one who had seized the king at Linlithgow, was not so fortunate and was executed. Princess Margaret continued on her journey, meeting James III for the first time shortly before her wedding, which took place at Holyrood Abbey on 13 July 1469, no doubt accompanied by the usual celebrations and festivities.[60] After his marriage, now aged 17, the king assumed control of the government, bringing an end to his minority.[61] A year later, in July and August

1470, the king took his new wife on a progress through northern Scotland. Riding via Aberdeen, Fyvie and Banff, they spent a month at Inverness. After returning south, they settled into the usual routine of the Scottish court, sharing their time between Holyroodhouse, Linlithgow, Stirling and Falkland.[62] Earlier in the year, the king had granted the queen the barony of Kilmarnock, specifically to pay for her gowns and headdresses. The revenues from the queen's estates were collected each year by her husband's officials and the Lord Treasurer paid her expenses.

The Treasurer's Accounts for 1473–74 have survived and show that Queen Margaret spent a considerable amount, £757.9.10, the majority of it on clothing. From this, we know more about Margaret's wardrobe than we do any other medieval Queen of Scots. During this period, she bought fifteen new gowns, six of which were black, two purple and two crimson, as well as gowns in tawny, brown and blue.[63] The materials used included velvet, damask, satin and silk, with the gowns lined with cloth, fur, velvet, buckram and silk. Five new cloaks were made for her, all black and lined with either damask or grey squirrel fur. New kirtles, made in damask, velvet, silk and satin, were also made for her, at least twelve were ordered in that year alone, in various colours including black, crimson, green and blue.[64] The queen's purchases also included elaborate headdresses, gloves from a skinner in Stirling and shoes made by Hude, the royal shoemaker, as well as fine hose and white foot socks. Margaret also bought cloth for a number of ceremonial gowns, including seven ells of crimson satin at a cost of £31.10/, supplied by Will of Rynd, and a further ten ells for the same garment provided by Tom of Stanley, at a cost of £40.[65] A further fifteen ells of damask were purchased from Isabel Williamson, at a cost of £28.10/, for another ceremonial gown.[66] Both gowns may have been for the queen's use during the May parliament of 1474 and would have been accessorised with lengthy trains and sparkling jewels.

A surviving inventory of the queen's possessions at her death, from Stirling Castle, gives us a glimpse into the types and quality of jewels owned by a Queen of Scots. There were five belts, one of crimson ornamented with gold braid and four of gold. Two gold chains, one of sixty-one links and one of fifty-eight. There was a collar of chalcedony with a filigree pomander as a pendant, another collar made of gold enamelled roses and a third, engraved and set with sixteen rubies, in addition to diamonds and pearls, featuring eight white swans. Margaret also had strings of pearls, and a small chain, with a pendant in the shape of an M, set with diamonds and pearls. A jewel in the shape of a golden heart, with a pearl hanging from it, may have been a wedding gift from the king, or possibly a gift on the birth of their first child. There was also a jewelled hairnet, brooches, pendants and rings, set with numerous stones including diamonds, rubies, and sapphires. The inventory included several rosaries, serpent's tongue and a unicorn horn, as well as many items of plate, including silver-gilt basins, cups and a lamp of silver.[67]

Margaret of Denmark is the first Scottish queen of whom a contemporary portrait survives. It is part of an altarpiece commissioned for the Holy Trinity Church in Edinburgh, founded by Margaret's mother-in-law, Mary of Guelders, and completed by James III. Painted by Hugo van der Goes, one wing of the altarpiece has James III kneeling in prayer with a boy, most likely his eldest son, James, while the other wing shows Queen Margaret kneeling at a prie-dieu. The portrait is conventional for the time, with a meek expression, oval face and arched eyebrows above small eyes. The queen has a long nose and neat mouth with the suggestion of a double chin. Her hair is completely covered, so we have no indication as to whether she was blonde or brunette. The queen is dressed in royal robes, though the colours have faded over time, and an elaborate headdress, with a gold collar, set with diamonds and pearls and a pendant, about her neck. As we have nothing to compare the image to, we cannot attest to the accuracy of the portrait, unfortunately.

Margaret of Denmark was only 12 years old when she married James III, so it is no surprise that she did not become pregnant immediately after the wedding. Indeed, one would hope that King James held off consummating the marriage for at least a couple of years, until the queen was more mature, in body and mind. Her first child was born at Stirling Castle on 17 March 1473, a son named James after his father, grandfather and great-grandfather; he was created Duke of Rothesay at his birth. He would eventually succeed to the throne as James IV. From the Treasury Accounts, we know that the young prince slept in a cradle lined with white, with a silk canopy. He wore 'linen shirts, lawn baby caps and a white coat lined with miniver'.[68] A second son followed, also named James, which must have been confusing, three years later, and a third, this one named John, three years after that in 1479. The younger James was created Marquess of Ormond at his baptism, and Duke of Ross on 29 January 1488. He was later nominated as Archbishop of St Andrews, before 22 May 1497 and was appointed papal legate in 1500.[69] John Stewart was created Earl of Mar and Garrioch in 1486 and died unmarried in March 1503.[70]

The *Calendar of Papal Registers* provides us with an insight into Queen Margaret's involvement in the religious life of Scotland. Queen Margaret's own confessor was granted three benefices in 1474:

> To John Cant, priest, perpetual beneficiary called a prebendary in the church of Dalkeith, in the diocese of St. Andrews, M.A. Dispensation to him, who is by both parents of noble and baronial birth, and confessor and continual commensal chaplain of Margaret, queen of Scots, to receive and retain for life any three benefices with cure or otherwise incompatible, even if they be dignities, etc. or parish churches, etc., and to resign them, etc., provided that not more than two of such benefices be parish churches.[71]

The Lateran Regista clearly demonstrates the close relationship between Denmark and Scotland, forged by the marriage of James and Margaret. Dorothea, Queen of Denmark, successfully petitioned for benefices in Glasgow for a priest she favoured in 1475:

> To Alexander Gyffard, rector of the parish church of Newlands [*de Neulandis*] in the diocese of Glasgow, M.A. Dispensation, out of consideration for Dorathea [sic], queen of Denmark [*Datie*], and at her and his petition, to receive and retain for life with the said church *de Neullandis* one other benefice, etc.[72]

This and a similar papal writ involving King Christian, which had achieved similar results in 1474, demonstrates clearly that Margaret's parents also showed an interest in their daughter's country:

> To John Malison, rector of Stobo in the diocese of Glasgow, bachelor in decrees. Dispensation for him, who is well-beloved of Christian, king of Denmark, to receive and retain for life with the said church (value not expressed) any two benefices, or without it any three benefices, with cure or otherwise incompatible, even if major or principal and elective dignities, etc., and to resign or exchange them, etc.[73]

While the accounts and papal register provide us with an insight into the material and spiritual life of Queen Margaret, respectively, her relationship with King James is far more elusive. The couple appear to have shared a confessor, approved by the papacy:

> To James and Margaret, king and queen of Scots. Indult that the confessor of their choice, secular or regular of any order, may absolve them, being contrite and having confessed, from all sentences of excommunication, etc., and from any vows and oaths, perjuries, and other sins, etc., however enormous, short of the laying of violent hands on any ecclesiastical prelate, even in cases reserved to the apostolic see, every year for life on the feasts of St. John Baptist and All Saints, and in other cases as often as opportune, grant them plenary remission of all their sins and enjoin a salutary penance, grant them in the hour of death plenary remission of all their sins, and commute any vows and release any oaths; with further grant that by visiting yearly on the said feasts seven altars in any church or churches they may gain the same indulgence as they would gain by personally visiting certain churches within and without Rome in the year of Jubilee. If, trusting to the present grant, they commit any [sins], it shall be null and void as far as regards the said plenary remission.[74]

Queen Margaret appears to have played the traditional queenly role of intercessor, as in the parliament of July 1476, when John MacDonald, Earl of Ross, was stripped of his earldom, which was annexed to the crown. The queen's intercession did not restore his earldom, but did see him appointed to parliament as Lord of the Isles.[75] The three-year gaps between each of their children suggests they were not close, physically, and some near-contemporary sources allude to the king lusting after other women, with George Buchanan, in the sixteenth century, accusing James III of seducing Lady Crichton, while another poem charges him with the seduction of a burgess's daughter.[76] Giovanni Sabadino degli Arienti, an Italian who wrote a life of Queen Margaret and may have had a source at the Scottish court, suggested that the queen would only lie with the king in order to get pregnant, and would have no relations with her husband otherwise. James is often seen as a difficult character. Although he was cultured and had a love for music, he was a distant ruler, establishing himself in and around Edinburgh, rather than travelling through the country, thus inaccessible to the majority of his people and unable to fulfil his role of curbing local feuds and dispensing royal justice in the regions.[77] James was accused of ignoring the advice of his nobles and relying on a handful of low-born favourites.

However, most of these accusations seem to have come from later writers, perhaps justifying the opposition against James that would ultimately see him defeated. Parliament was also opposed to the king's idea of leaving Scotland for a pilgrimage to the shrine of St John the Baptist at Amiens, during which journey he also hoped to meet with King Louis XI to negotiate the renewal of the Franco–Scottish alliance. In the end, the opposition was moot as James simply did not have the money to undertake the journey. In fact, his financial problems forced the king to debase the coinage. And in 1478 he moved against his own brothers, imprisoning both of them; John died – or was murdered – in prison, while the younger Alexander, Duke of Albany, fled abroad and, for a time, was recognised as King of Scots by Edward IV of England. When the English invaded, led by Richard, Duke of Gloucester, in 1482, James III's sister Mary, forcibly married to Lord Hamilton, joined the rebellion of her brother, Albany, as did the king's half-uncles, John, Earl of Atholl, James, Earl of Buchan and Andrew, Bishop of Moray, who seized James and took him to Edinburgh as a prisoner.

Queen Margaret was at Stirling, where she appears to have spent most of her time, with her children, but may also have been involved, as Albany visited the queen there. They discussed the education of the heir to the throne. There is a suggestion that they discussed replacing the king with his oldest son, the Duke of Rothesay. If they did consider this, the queen and Albany decided against it, as no such move was ever made. It is just as likely that Margaret urged Albany to besiege Edinburgh Castle and release the king, as Albany later played a part in releasing King James from captivity.

The brief rebellion ended after two months with James recovering power. Edward IV of England had died suddenly on 9 April 1483 and Albany lost his chief supporter, fleeing the country, only to return the following year, when he was defeated at Lochmaben. His lands declared forfeit, he again fled, returning one final time in 1485, when he was captured and imprisoned in Edinburgh, only to escape and flee – yet again – to France.

Many historians suggest that King James believed that Margaret was in collusion with Albany as his distrust of the queen was evident and they appear to have been estranged once the crisis was ended, with Sabadino claiming 'The more gentle and affectionate the love which she showed to her husband ... the more anguish she received from him.'[78] Their relationship not aided by the fact that Margaret was 'much more loved and revered by the people than was the King, since she possessed more aptitude than he for ruling the kingdom'.[79] However, a charter of 17 January 1483 suggests otherwise. Issued after his release by King James III, the charter rewarded John Dundas, one of the squires of the king's chamber, for risking his life in the liberation of the king from Edinburgh Castle, stating it was made 'with the consent and assent of our dearest consort, Margaret, Queen of Scots'.[80] Although the words are quite formulaic, the mere mention of the queen suggests that James may not have harboured the resentment for her that has been suggested. The Exchequer accounts for the time also show Queen Margaret making a payment to John Stewart, Lord Darnley, for custody of the castle.[81]

Although there is no evidence that the king and queen ever met after 1482, neither is there evidence that they did not. The queen continued to dwell at Stirling Castle, with the children, as she had done before the crisis. James resided at Edinburgh and elsewhere. But that does not preclude his visiting his wife and children, occasionally, not least to check on the progress of his three sons, whose ages ranged from 4 to 10 in 1483. Three years later, in the summer of 1486, Queen Margaret fell seriously ill and died at Stirling on 14 July; she had just turned 30. After her burial at Cambuskenneth, the king paid for daily masses for her soul. He also sent a supplication to the pope, asking that Margaret be made a saint, though nothing came of it. As with many of James III's acts, this reverence for his late wife has contradictory explanations: either James was feeling guilty for the way he treated his wife, or it was a sign of his genuine affection and love for his queen, and regret at her passing. Two years after the queen's death, James's enemies sent messages to Denmark, accusing the king of poisoning his wife. Although the accusations were dismissed out of hand, they do demonstrate the widely held belief that the king and queen were on bad terms.

After his wife's death, James III contemplated marrying again, and had set his sights on Elizabeth Woodville, widow of Edward IV, but the plan never came to fruition. In 1488, King James faced his final rebellion, following the dismissal of his chancellor, Colin Campbell, until that point a committed supported of the king. The king's oldest son, 15-year-old James, Duke of Rothesay, sided with the rebels. The two armies met near Stirling, close to the historic battlefield of Bannockburn, fighting a battle on 11 June 1488 that would become known as the battle of Sauchieburn. King James III's forces were defeated, and he was killed, either during the battle itself or in the subsequent rout. He was succeeded by his son, James IV, who was crowned on 24 June at Scone Abbey, but did not assume personal rule until 1495, using the years of his minority to acquire an impressive education. James III was buried at Cambuskenneth Abbey, beside Queen Margaret.[82]

I cannot help but think that the childhood experiences of the last three medieval kings, James I, James II and James III, had a deep impact on their lives, and the lives of their wives. Imprisonment, murder and being violently seized whilst still children must have traumatised them. Where James I found solace and love with Joan Beaufort, his inability to forgive and deep distrust of his family and magnates ultimately led to his murder. That Joan Beaufort was left to pick up the pieces and continue the fight, for the sake of her son, is testament to her strength and tenacity. She may not have always made the right decision but she never gave up. James II, too, had witnessed more than any child should. The victim of rival factions at court, taken from his mother's custody and forced to be part of a murder plot, at only 10 years old, at the Black Dinner, must have taken their toll – added to that his guardians actually made war on his mother, laying siege to her at Dunbar Castle. But he appears to have found a strong, capable helpmate in Mary of Guelders. Mary proved to be an intelligent, politically adept queen. She may have expected to grow old with James but the freak accident at Roxburgh that killed the king brought her to the fore as regent for James III. She proved to be more than equal to the task, protecting Scotland first and foremost, both in the domestic and the foreign sphere, taking advantage of the unrest in England to advance Scotland's aims. She was an accomplished and influential Queen of Scots. That Mary died when James III was only 12 was a tragedy for the young king. If she had lived just that little bit longer, until James reached his majority, maybe he would not have experienced the factionalism of the Boyds. Maybe he would have trusted those around him, especially his wife. Margaret of Denmark, however, leaves her own legacy. Hers is the first contemporary portrait we have of a Scottish queen, even though there are doubts as to accuracy. It provides us with an insight into the queen's dress and appearance. And the Treasurer's Accounts supplement this, providing us with an understanding of Margaret's spending habits, demonstrating the glamour and ceremony of queenship.

With the 1480s, the medieval era drew to a close in England and Scotland, Henry Tudor's victory at Bosworth in 1485 and the accession of James IV in 1488 marking the advent of the early modern period in history. Although those living through it would have seen no line of demarcation. The world was changing and both Mary of Guelders and Margaret of Denmark had risen to the challenge. Between them, Mary and Margaret showcase the various duties and roles a fifteenth-century queen was expected to fulfil.

Postscript

The Queens of Scots of the medieval era are a fascinating variety of women and I can only hope that I have done them justice in this tome. From the highly educated and pious St Margaret to the glamorous Margaret of Denmark, their lives and experiences tell the story of their nation. Some, such as Matilda de Senlis and Ermengarde de Beaumont, barely make an impression on history, though merely by producing a son, they each guaranteed that Scotland would persevere. And it is not that they made no impression. Their influence was in the domestic sphere, raising children and supporting their husbands, rather than on the political or the international stage. Marrying an English princess, for example, did not always guarantee the peace with England that was intended. As the wife of Alexander II, Joan of England did her best to maintain peaceful relations with her brother Henry III, often using private letters to broker diplomatic solutions. And Henry III's own daughter Margaret, in marrying Alexander III, brought Scotland years of peace with England. Edward III's sister Joan of the Tower was to have no such legacy, however, as her brother's ambition would blight her marriage for years. If Edward III had not been so keen to exploit Scotland's dynastic divisions, maybe Joan and David II would have had a happier marriage. We will never know.

Although we have charters and chronicles, and evidence of religious and charitable donations, most of these women remain elusive. They are enigmas. We do not – and cannot – know them intimately as the one thing that is missing is their own voice. Their thoughts and personalities are lost to us. Even letters to family members are often formulaic and rarely speak of their true feelings, of their happiness – or not – and their cares and concerns for themselves. We know what they endured for the sake of Scotland, the risk of death in childbirth, the grief of lost children, or the grief of no children. Every woman in medieval Europe was exposed to similar experiences. Scottish queens, however, had to endure imprisonment, scheming noblemen and the early deaths of their husbands more times than they should have had to. One cannot help but feel sympathy for Elizabeth de Burgh, seeing her fortunes rise and fall at the whim of England's king, Edward I, held captive for eight years when she should have been sitting in splendour on Scotland's throne. Or poor Marjorie Bruce, whose childhood was torn from her by that same English king, held far away from everyone she loved, only to be married as she tasted freedom, and dead in childbirth by the age of 19. Passed over for the throne because she was a woman, she still managed to give birth to a dynasty, the Stewarts. Scotland was the first nation in the British Isles to accept a queen regnant when Margaret, Maid of Norway, was recognised as its queen in 1290. How her queenship would have developed, we have no way of knowing. The poor girl died before she even landed in mainland Scotland. Her significance is in that she was proclaimed queen and the possibilities that heralded, even if it got no further. We can only speculate as to how a successful rule by a queen regnant in the thirteenth century may have changed the lives and experiences of women in subsequent centuries. Her death was a tragedy, not just to her family, but to women's rights to rule.

As I said in my introduction, Scotland's story is often violent and suffered greatly from the machinations if its powerful southern neighbour. However, Scotland did emerge from the Middle Ages as, still, an independent, sovereign nation. And Scotland's medieval queens had each made their own contribution to the country's continuing survival and independence. From Saint Margaret – even from Gruoch – to Margaret of Denmark, each queen, to varying degrees of success, made their own indelible imprint on Scotland's remarkable story.

Notes

Prologue

1. Shakespeare, William, *Macbeth*, New York, Dover Publications, 1963, pp. 76–82.
2. Ibid., pp. 103–104.
3. Dauvit Broun, Macbeth [Macbethad mac Findlaich] (d. 1057), king of Scots, Oxforddnb.com, 23 September 2004.
4. David Ross, *Scotland: History of a Nation*, Broxburn, Lomond Books Ltd, 2014, p. 53.
5. Ibid.
6. Kate Braithwaite, *Gruoch: The Real Lady Macbeth*, historyofroyalwomen.com
7. *Annals of Ulster*, 1033.7, p. 473, quoted in fmg.ac/Projects/MedLands/SCOTLAND
8. fmg.ac/Projects/MedLands/SCOTLAND
9. 'Macbeth son of Finlach ... and Gruoch daughter of Boite, king and queen of the Scots', *Early Scottish Charters V*, p. 5, quoted in fmg.ac/Projects/MedLands/SCOTLAND
10. 'nephew of the son of Boite', Skene (1867), XVI, *Chronicle of the Scots*, 1165, *Cronica Regum Scottorum*, p. 131, quoted in fmg.ac/Projects/MedLands/SCOTLAND
11. Ross, *Scotland*, p. 55.
12. Dauvit Broun, *Malcolm II [Mael Coluim mac Cinaeda] (d. 1034)*, Oxforddnb.com, 23 September 2004.
13. Ibid.
14. *Annals of Ulster*, 1020.6, p. 458, quoted in fmg.ac/Projects/MedLands/SCOTLAND
15. Broun, *Macbeth*.
16. *Annals of Ulster*, 1032.1, p. 472, quoted in fmg.ac/Projects/MedLands/SCOTLAND
17. 'Malcolm, son of Kenneth king of Scotland', *Annals of Tigernach II*, p. 266, quoted in fmg.ac/Projects/MedLands/SCOTLAND
18. Rosalind K. Marshall, *Scottish Queens 1034–1714*, Edinburgh, Truckwell Press, 2003, p. 1.
19. Mike Ashley, *A Brief History of British Kings and Queens*, London, Robinson Publishing, 2014, p. 106.
20. Ibid., p. 107.
21. Ross, *Scotland*, p. 55.
22. Ashley, *A Brief History of British Kings and Queens*, p. 107.
23. *Chronicles of the Picts, chronicles of the Scots, and other early memorials of Scottish history*, edited by W. F. Skene, 1867 Edinburgh, HM General Register House, p. cxlvii.
24. Richard Oram, editor, *The Kings and Queens of Scotland*, Cheltenham, The History Press, 2021, p. 56.
25. Ibid.
26. Anderson, *Early Sources*, 1.588, quoted in Broun, *Macbeth*.
27. Oram, editor, *The Kings and Queens of Scotland*, p. 56.

28. *The Chronicle of John of Worcester*, edited by R. R. Darlington and P. McGurk, 2 volumes, OMT, Oxford, 1995, p. 573.
29. Oram, editor, *The Kings and Queens of Scotland*, p. 57.
30. *Henry of Huntingdon: The History of the English People 1000-1154*, edited by Diana Greenway, Oxford, Oxford University Press, 2009, p. 21.
31. *The Chronicle of John of Worcester*, edited by R. R. Darlington and P. McGurk, p. 575.
32. Oram, editor, *The Kings and Queens of Scotland*, p. 57.
33. Mike Ashley, *The Mammoth Book of British Kings and Queens*, London, Robinson Publishing, 1998, p. 394.
34. 'Macbeth mac Fingel 17 annis regnauit et interfectus es in Limfanan a Malcolim mac Dunchat et sepultus est in Hyona insula', *Chronicles of the Picts, chronicles of the Scots, and other early memorials of Scottish history*, edited by Skene, p. 302.
35. Oram, editor, *The Kings and Queens of Scotland*, p. 57.
36. Broun, *Macbeth*.
37. Kate Braithwaite, *Gruoch: The Real Lady Macbeth*, historyofroyalwomen.com
38. *Early Scottish Charters I*, p. 2, quoted in fmg.ac/Projects/MedLands/SCOTLAND
39. fmg.ac/Projects/MedLands/SCOTLAND
40. Ashley, *The Mammoth Book of British Kings and Queens*, p. 393.
41. Broun, *Macbeth*.
42. 'Macbeth filius Finlach ... et Gruoch filia Bodhe, Rex et Regina Scottorum', *Early Scottish charters prior to A.D. 1153: with notes and an index*, edited by Archibald Campbell Lawrie, Glasgow, J. MacLehose, 1905, p. 5.
43. *Liber Cartorum Prioratus S. Andree in Scotia*, cited in Marshall, *Scottish Queens 1034–1714*, p. 5.
44. *The Chronicle of John of Worcester*, edited by R. R. Darlington and P. McGurk, p. 553.
45. Act V, Scene VIII, Shakespeare, William, *The tragedie of Macbeth; a new edition of Shakspere's works with critical text in Elizabethan English and brief notes, illustrative of Elizabethan life, thought and idiom*, edited by Mark Harvey Liddell, New York, New York Doubleday, 1903, p. 227.

Chapter One: St Margaret, Queen of Scots

1. G. W. S. Barrow, Malcolm III [Mael Coluim Ceann Mór, Malcolm Canmore] (d. 1093), Oxford Dictionary of National Biography (Oxford: Oxford University Press, 2008) [online edition: oxforddnb.com].
2. Marshall, *Scottish Queens 1034–1714*, pp. 6–7.
3. Ibid.
4. Barrow, Malcolm III.
5. *The Chronicle of John of Worcester*, edited by R. R. Darlington and P. McGurk, p. 481.
6. Ibid.
7. Ibid.
8. Edmund II [known as Edmund Ironside] (d. 1016) (article) by M. K. Lawson, *Oxford Dictionary of National Biography* (Oxford: Oxford University Press, 2004) [online edition: oxforddnb.com].
9. *The Chronicle of John of Worcester*, edited by R. R. Darlington and P. McGurk, p. 485.
10. Ibid.
11. Ibid.
12. Ibid., p. 487.

13. Ibid.
14. M. K. Lawson, Edmund II.
15. *The Chronicle of John of Worcester*, edited by R. R. Darlington and P. McGurk, p. 505.
16. Alan J. Wilson, *St Margaret Queen of Scotland,* Edinburgh, John Donald Publishers Ltd, 1993, p. 30.
17. Turgot, Bishop of St Andrews, *The Life of St Margaret Queen of Scotland*, edited by William Forbes-Leith, Edinburgh, William Paterson, 1884, pp. 27–28.
18. *The Chronicle of John of Worcester*, edited by R. R. Darlington and P. McGurk, p. 607.
19. Turgot, *Life of St Margaret Queen of Scotland*, pp. 11–12.
20. Symeon of Durham's *Historia Regum*, Vol ii, p. 190, quoted in Wilson, *St Margaret Queen of Scotland*, p. 55.
21. *The Anglo-Saxon Chronicle*, translated by James Ingram, London, 1823, reprinted by Dodo Press, pp. 143–144.
22. Nigel Tranter, *The Story of Scotland*, ebook, 4th edition, Neil Wilson Publishing, 2011, p. 492.
23. Turgot, Bishop of St Andrews, *The Life of St Margaret Queen of Scotland*, edited by William Forbes-Leith, London, Forgotten Books, 2012, p. 28.
24. Marshall, *Scottish Queens 1034–1714*, p. 9.
25. *A Dangerous Saint: St Margaret of Scotland* by Claire Havrill, DangerousWomenProject. org.
26. Turgot, *Life of St. Margaret Queen of Scotland*, p. 28–29.
27. Ibid., p. 55.
28. Ibid., p. 57.
29. Ibid., pp. 40–41.
30. Ibid., p. 41.
31. Ibid.
32. *The Ecclesiastical History of England and Normandy* by Ordericus Vitalis 1075–1143, London, Bohn, 1853, p. 198.
33. Elizabeth M. Tyler, *England in Europe: English Royal Women and Literary Patronage c.1000–c.1150*, Toronto, University of Toronto Press, 2017, p. 272.
34. Nigel Tranter, *The Story of Scotland*, p. 484.
35. Ibid.
36. Ibid., p. 536.
37. Turgot, *Life of St. Margaret Queen of Scotland*, p. 48.
38. G. W. S. Barrow, Margaret [St Margaret] (d. 1093), queen of Scots, consort of Malcolm III (article), Oxford Dictionary of National Biography (Oxford: Oxford University Press, 2004) [online edition: oxforddnb.com].
39. Turgot, *Life of St Margaret Queen of Scotland*, p. 29.
40. *Letters of Lanfranc Archbishop of Canterbury*, ed. and transl. by Helen Clover and Margaret Gibson. Quoted by epistolae.ccnmtl.columbia.edu
41. G. W. S. Barrow, Margaret [St Margaret], oxforddnb.com.
42. Turgot, *Life of St Margaret Queen of Scotland*, pp. 29–30.
43. Ibid., p. 30.
44. Fairweather, Kathleen Margaret, editor, *St Margaret Queen of Scotland and Her Chapel*, p. 5.
45. Turgot, *Life of St Margaret Queen of Scotland*, p. 33.
46. Ibid.
47. Ibid.
48. David Williamson, *Brewer's British Royalty*, London, Cassell, 1996, p. 275–275.

49. Christina (fl. 1057–1093) (article) by Nicholas Hooper, *Oxford Dictionary of National Biography* (Oxford: Oxford University Press, 2004) [online edition: oxforddnb.com].
50. Eadmer, quoted in *Saint Margaret, Queen of Scotland* (article) by Susan Abernethy, thefreelancehistorywriter.com
51. Manuscript D, *The Anglo-Saxon Chronicles*, edited and translated by Michael Swanton, London, Phoenix Press, 2000, p. 210.
52. *The Chronicle of Florence of Worcester with the two continuations*, translated and edited by Thomas Forester, A. M., London, Henry G. Bohn, 1854, p. 196.
53. Manuscript E, *The Anglo-Saxon Chronicles*, edited and translated by Michael Swanton, p. 228.
54. Turgot, *Life of St Margaret Queen of Scotland*, p. 71.
55. Ibid., pp. 77–78.
56. Ibid., p. 81.
57. Ibid., p. 28.
58. Manuscript E, *The Anglo-Saxon Chronicles*, edited and translated by Michael Swanton, p. 202.
59. Forester, *The Chronicle of John Florence of Worcester with the two continuations*, p. 196.
60. David W. and Michael P. Peyton, *Saint Margaret of Scotland circa 1045–1093: Relics and Some Recent Commemorations*, academia.edu, accessed 6 November 2023.
61. Thomas Morrison, quoted in *Saint Margaret, Queen of Scotland* (article) by Susan Abernethy, thefreelancehistorywriter.com

Chapter Two: The Daughters-in-Law of St Margaret

1. fmg.ac/Projects/MedLands/SCOTLAND
2. Forester, *The Chronicle of John Florence of Worcester with the two continuations*, pp. 196–197.
3. Ibid., p. 198.
4. *Annals of Inisfallen*, 1094.4, p. 249, quoted in fmg.ac/Projects/MedLands/SCOTLAND
5. *John of Fordun's Chronicle of the Scottish Nation*, edited by W. F. Skene, Edinburgh, Edmonston and Douglas, 1872, p. 213.
6. Annals of Ulster, 1094.7, p. 530, quoted in fmg.ac/Projects/MedLands/SCOTLAND
7. *John of Fordun's Chronicle of the Scottish Nation*, p. 213.
8. Dugdale *Monasticon* III, Wetherall Priory, Cumberland, XVI, *Cronicon Cumbriæ*, p. 585, quoted in fmg.ac/Projects/MedLands/SCOTLAND
9. Ibid.
10. *John of Fordun's Chronicle of the Scottish Nation*, pp. 263–264.
11. fmg.ac/Projects/MedLands/SCOTLAND
12. *John of Fordun's Chronicle of the Scottish Nation*, p. 213.
13. Ibid.
14. Ibid., p. 214.
15. Ibid.
16. Ibid., p. 215.
17. Sharpe, Rev. J. (trans.), revised Stephenson, Rev. J. (1854) *William of Malmesbury, The Kings before the Norman Conquest* (Seeleys, London, reprint Llanerch, 1989) 400, p. 349, quoted in fmg.ac/Projects/MedLands/SCOTLAND

18. *Chronicles of the Picts, chronicles of the Scots, and other early memorials of Scottish history*, edited by W. F. Skene, p. 207.
19. Oram, editor, *The Kings and Queens of Scotland*, p. 69.
20. Malmesbury, 400, p. 349, quoted in fmg.ac/Projects/MedLands/SCOTLAND
21. Oram, editor, *The Kings and Queens of Scotland*, p. 70.
22. "*Edgarus ... Rex Scottorum*" made grants for the souls of "*Malcolmi patris nostri et Margaretæ matris nostræ ... ac Edwardi et Duncani fratrum nostrorum*" by charter dated 1095. *Early Scottish Charters XVII*, p. 14, quoted in fmg.ac/Projects/MedLands/SCOTLAND
23. Oram, editor, *The Kings and Queens of Scotland*, p. 71.
24. Manuscript E, *The Anglo-Saxon Chronicles*, edited and translated by Michael Swanton, p. 241.
25. *John of Fordun's Chronicle of the Scottish Nation*, pp. 217–218.
26. Ross, *Scotland*, p. 62.
27. Oram, editor, *The Kings and Queens of Scotland*, p. 71.
28. Ibid., p. 73.
29. Forester, *The Chronicle of John Florence of Worcester with the two continuations*, p. 213.
30. A. A. M. Duncan, *Alexander I*, Oxforddnb.com, 4 October 2008.
31. Oram, editor, *The Kings and Queens of Scotland*, p. 73.
32. *John of Fordun's Chronicle of the Scottish Nation*, pp. 208.
33. Walter Bower, *Scotichronicon*, Vol. 3, books 5 and 6, Edinburgh, The Mercat Press, 1995, p. 111.
34. *John of Fordun's Chronicle of the Scottish Nation*, p. 218.
35. Ibid.
36. Duncan, Alexander I.
37. Ashley, *A Brief History of British Kings and Queens*, p. 117.
38. Duncan, Alexander I.
39. Ibid.
40. Bower, *Scotichronicon*, Vol. 3, p. 105.
41. 'filiam Henrici regis Anglorun ex concubine', Orderic Vitalis cited in Danna Messer, *Medieval Monarchs, Female Illegitimacy and Modern Genealogical Matters: Part 1: Sybilla, Queen of Scotland, c. 1090–1122*, fmg.ac accessed 9 May 2023.
42. Jessica Nelson, Sybilla (d. 1122), queen of Scots and consort of Alexander I, oxforddnb.com, 4 October 2008.
43. Messer, *Medieval Monarchs, Female Illegitimacy and Modern Genealogical Matters: Part 1: Sybilla, Queen of Scotland, c. 1090–1122*.
44. fmg.ac/Projects/MedLands/ENGLAND
45. Nelson, Sybilla (d. 1122), queen of Scots and consort of Alexander I.
46. 'Alexander ... rex Scottorum filius regis Malcolmi et regine Margerete et...Sibilla regina Scottorum filia Henrici regis Anglie', Scone, 1, p. 1. Quoted in fmg.ac/Projects/MedLands/SCOTLAND
47. Messer, *Medieval Monarchs, Female Illegitimacy and Modern Genealogical Matters: Part 1: Sybilla, Queen of Scotland, c. 1090–1122*.
48. William of Malmesbury, 400, p. 349, quoted in fmg.ac/Projects/MedLands/SCOTLAND
49. William of Malmesbury, quoted in Messer, *Medieval Monarchs, Female Illegitimacy and Modern Genealogical Matters: Part 1: Sybilla, Queen of Scotland, c. 1090–1122*.

50. For an unhappy marriage, see Oram, editor, *The Kings and Queens of Scotland*, p. 72. For a loving marriage, see Marshall, *Scottish Queens 1034–1714*, p. 15.
51. Marshall, *Scottish Queens 1034–1714*, p. 15.
52. Ashley, *A Brief History of British Kings and Queens*, p. 117.
53. Nelson, Sybilla (d. 1122), queen of Scots and consort of Alexander I.
54. Ibid.
55. *Extracta ex Cronicis Scocie*, p. 68, quoted in fmg.ac/Projects/MedLands/SCOTLAND
56. Nelson, Sybilla (d. 1122), queen of Scots and consort of Alexander I.
57. Orderic Vitalis (Prévost), Vol. III, Liber VIII, XXII, p. 403, quoted in fmg.ac/Projects/MedLands/SCOTLAND
58. fmg.ac/Projects/MedLands/SCOTLAND
59. *John of Fordun's Chronicle of the Scottish Nation*, edited by W. F. Skene, p. 221.
60. Nelson, Sybilla (d. 1122), queen of Scots and consort of Alexander I.
61. G. W. S. Barrow, David I (c. 1085–1153) (article), *Oxford Dictionary of National Biography* (Oxford: Oxford University Press, 2006) [online edition: oxforddnb.com].
62. Ibid.
63. Oram, editor, *The Kings and Queens of Scotland*, p. 74.
64. Ibid.
65. Ibid.
66. *John of Fordun's Chronicle of the Scottish Nation*, edited by W. F. Skene, p. 222.
67. Ingulph, *Ingulph's Chronicle of the Abbey of Croyland*, edited by Henry T. Riley, H. G. Bohn, London, 1854, p. 146.
68. Ibid.
69. 'The Development of Northampton', in *An Inventory of the Historical Monuments in the County of Northamptonshire, Volume 5, Archaeology and Churches in Northampton* (London, 1985), pp. 27–71. British History Online, www.british-history.ac.uk/rchme/northants/vol5/pp27-71 [accessed 16 November 2023].
70. fmg.ac/Projects/MedLands/ENGLAND
71. Ibid.
72. Ashley, *The Mammoth Book of British Kings and Queens*, p. 405.
73. G. W. S. Barrow, David I.
74. Andrew Wyntoun, *The orygynale cronykil of Scotland*, edited by David Laing, Edinburgh, Edmonston and Douglas, 1872, p. 184.
75. Oram, editor, *The Kings and Queens of Scotland*, p. 76.
76. G. W. S. Barrow, David I.
77. Oram, editor, *The Kings and Queens of Scotland*, p. 76.
78. *Early Scottish Charters XXXV*, p. 26, quoted in fmg.ac/Projects/MedLands/SCOTLAND
79. Kelso, Tome I, 1, p. 3, quoted in fmg.ac/Projects/MedLands/SCOTLAND
80. *John of Fordun's Chronicle of the Scottish Nation*, edited by W. F. Skene, p. 220–221.
81. Oram, editor, *The Kings and Queens of Scotland*, p. 76.
82. G. W. S. Barrow, David I.
83. Ibid.
84. *Early Scottish Charters L*, p. 46, quoted in fmg.ac/Projects/MedLands/SCOTLAND
85. G. W. S. Barrow, David I.
86. *Early Scottish Charters LXXXIII*, p. 69, quoted in fmg.ac/Projects/MedLands/SCOTLAND
87. *Mediaeval chronicles of Scotland: the chronicles of Melrose and Holyrood*, translated by Joseph Stephenson, London, Seeleys, 1850, p. 9.

88. *Early Scottish charters prior to A.D. 1153: with notes and an index*, edited by Archibald Campbell Lawrie, Glasgow, J. MacLehose, 1905, p. 333.
89. Ibid.
90. Oram, editor, *The Kings and Queens of Scotland*, p. 76.
91. Ibid.
92. Nigel Tranter, *The Story of Scotland*, p. 677.
93. Oram, editor, *The Kings and Queens of Scotland*, p. 77.
94. Ibid.
95. Ibid.
96. fmg.ac/Projects/MedLands/SCOTLAND
97. *Early Scottish charters prior to A.D. 1153*, p. 339.
98. Ibid., p. 417.
99. 'David vero Rex de Matilda Comitissa … filia Ivette Willelmi conquestoris neptis genuit Henricum Comitem patrem Willelmi Regis [qui genuit] Alexandmm Regem patrem Alexandri ultimi', *Chronicles of the Picts, chronicles of the Scots, and other early memorials of Scottish history*, edited by W. F. Skene, 1867, Edinburgh, HM General Register House, p. 213.
100. Bower, *Scotichronicon*, Vol. 3, pp. 126–127.

Chapter Three: Peace with a Marriage

1. Victoria Chandler, Ada de Warenne, Queen Mother of Scotland (c. 1123-1178) (article), *The Scottish Historical Review*, vol. 60, no. 170 Part 2 (Oct. 1981).
2. David Crouch, *The Reign of King Stephen 1135–1154*, p. 72.
3. David Williamson, *Brewer's British Royalty*.
4. *John of Fordun's Chronicle of the Scottish Nation*, edited by W. F. Skene, p. 222.
5. G. W. S. Barrow, David I (c. 1185–1153) (article), oxforddnb.com.
6. Oram, editor, *The Kings and Queens of Scotland*, p. 79.
7. Keith Stringer, Henry, earl of Northumberland (c. 1115–1152) (article), oxforddnb.com.
8. Ibid.
9. *Gesta Stephani*, translated by K. R. Potter, London: Thomas Nelson and sons, 1955, p. 35.
10. Ibid.
11. Ibid., p. 36.
12. Ibid.
13. Forester, *The Chronicle of John Florence of Worcester with the two continuations*, p. 256.
14. Crouch, *The Reign of King Stephen 1135–1154*, p. 74.
15. Matthew Lewis, *Stephen and Matilda's Civil War: Cousins of Anarchy*, p. 58.
16. Ibid., p. 52.
17. William of Malmesbury quoted in ibid., p. 53.
18. Ibid., p. 59.
19. John of Worcester quoted in Patricia A. Dark, *The Career of Matilda of Boulogne as Countess and Queen in England, 1135–1152*, p. 32.
20. Oram, editor, *The Kings and Queens of Scotland*, pp. 79–80.
21. Lewis, *Stephen and Matilda's Civil War*, p. 60.
22. David Smurthwaite, *The Complete Guide to the Battlefields of Britain*, p. 67.

23. *The Chronicle of Henry of Huntingdon. Comprising the history of England, from the invasion of Julius Caesar to the accession of Henry II. Also, the Acts of Stephen, King of England and duke of Normandy*, translated and edited by Thomas Forester, p. 268.
24. *Henry of Huntingdon: The History of the English People 1000–1154*, edited by Diana Greenway, pp. 71–72.
25. *The Chronicle of Henry of Huntingdon*, translated and edited by Thomas Forester, p. 269.
26. Ibid.
27. Ibid., pp. 269–270.
28. Smurthwaite, *The Complete Guide to the Battlefields of Britain*, p. 68.
29. *Henry of Huntingdon: The History of the English People 1000–1154*, edited by Diana Greenway, p. 72.
30. Ordericus Vitalis, *The Ecclesiastical History of Orderic Vitalis, 1075–1143*, book XIII, pp. 523–525.
31. Richard of Hexham, quoted in Patricia A. Dark, *The Career of Matilda of Boulogne as Countess and Queen in England, 1135–1152*, p. 34.
32. Ibid.
33. Lewis, *Stephen and Matilda's Civil War*, p. 75.
34. Richard of Hexham, quoted in Dark, *The Career of Matilda of Boulogne as Countess and Queen in England, 1135–1152*, p. 35.
35. *Mediaeval chronicles of Scotland*, translated by Joseph Stephenson, p. 8.
36. Vitalis, book XIII, p. 525.
37. Lewis, *Stephen and Matilda's Civil War*, p. 75.
38. Keith Stringer, Ada [née Ada de Warenne], Countess of Northumberland (c. 1123–1178), oxforddnb.com.
39. 'Ada, Countess of the king of Scots', Victoria Chandler, 'Ada de Warenne, Queen Mother of Scotland (c.1123–1178)'.
40. Ibid.
41. *Early Scottish charters prior to A.D. 1153*, p. 194.
42. Keith Stringer, Henry, earl of Northumberland (c.1115–1152) (article), oxforddnb.com
43. Ibid.
44. *Mediaeval chronicles of Scotland*, translated by Joseph Stephenson, p. 10.
45. *Gesta Stephani*, translated by K. R. Potter, London; Thomas Nelson and sons, 1955, pp. 142–143.
46. *Mediaeval chronicles of Scotland*, translated by Joseph Stephenson, p. 10.
47. Keith Stringer, Henry, earl of Northumberland (c. 1115–1152) (article), oxforddnb. com
48. *John of Fordun's Chronicle of the Scottish Nation*, p. 224.
49. Ibid.
50. Stringer, Ada [née Ada de Warenne], Countess of Northumberland (c.1123–1178).
51. Chandler, 'Ada de Warenne, Queen Mother of Scotland (c.1123–1178)'.
52. Ibid., charter no. 4, 6, 8.
53. Ibid., charter no. 9.
54. Ibid., charter no. 11.
55. Ibid., charter no. 25.
56. Ibid., charter no. 27.
57. Ibid.
58. Ibid., charter no. 10, 12, 13, 29.
59. *Early Scottish charters prior to A.D. 1153*, p. 405.

60. Chandler, 'Ada de Warenne, Queen Mother of Scotland (c.1123–1178)', charter no. 17
61. Ibid., charter no. 3, 4.
62. Stephen Spinks, *Robert the Bruce: Champion of a Nation*, p. 60.
63. Ross, *Scotland*, p. 68.
64. Chandler, 'Ada de Warenne, Queen Mother of Scotland (c.1123–1178)'.
65. Oram, editor, *The Kings and Queens of Scotland*, p. 87.
66. W. W., Malcolm IV (c. 1141–1165), oxforddnb.com, 3 January 2008.
67. *Mediaeval chronicles of Scotland*, translated by Joseph Stephenson, p. 11.
68. Ibid.
69. Ibid.
70. Oram, editor, *The Kings and Queens of Scotland*, p. 89.
71. *Mediaeval chronicles of Scotland*, translated by Joseph Stephenson, p. 11.
72. Ibid., pp. 11–12.
73. Ross, *Scotland*, p. 68.
74. *Mediaeval chronicles of Scotland*, translated by Joseph Stephenson, p. 12.
75. Ibid.
76. Ibid.
77. Ibid.
78. Ibid., p. 13.
79. Ibid., p. 14.
80. *Early Scottish charters prior to A.D. 1153*, pp. 405 and 422.
81. Bower, *Scotichronicon*, Vol. 3, p. 365.

Chapter Four: Queen Ermengarde

1. Oram, editor, *The Kings and Queens of Scotland*, p. 84.
2. *John of Fordun's Chronicle of the Scottish Nation*, p. 252.
3. Oram, editor, *The Kings and Queens of Scotland*, p. 89.
4. Chandler, 'Ada de Warenne, Queen Mother of Scotland'.
5. Oram, editor, *The Kings and Queens of Scotland*, p. 89.
6. *Mediaeval chronicles of Scotland*, translated by Joseph Stephenson, p. 14.
7. *John of Fordun's Chronicle of the Scottish Nation*, p. 255.
8. W. W. Scott, William I [known as William the Lion] (c.1142–1214), oxforddnb.com
9. Oram, editor, *The Kings and Queens of Scotland*, p. 89.
10. Scott, William I [known as William the Lion] (c. 1142–1214).
11. *Mediaeval chronicles of Scotland*, translated by Joseph Stephenson, p. 18.
12. Ibid.
13. Scott, William I [known as William the Lion] (c. 1142–1214).
14. *Mediaeval chronicles of Scotland*, translated by Joseph Stephenson, pp. 18–19.
15. Ross, *Scotland*, p. 69.
16. *Mediaeval chronicles of Scotland*, translated by Joseph Stephenson, p. 19.
17. Oram, editor, *The Kings and Queens of Scotland*, p. 90.
18. Chandler, 'Ada de Warenne, Queen Mother of Scotland'.
19. Scott, William I [known as William the Lion] (c. 1142–1214).
20. *Mediaeval chronicles of Scotland*, translated by Joseph Stephenson, p. 19.
21. Roger of Hoveden, *The annals of Roger de Hoveden. Comprising the history of England and of other countries of Europe from A.D. 732 to A.D. 1201*, edited by Herny T. Riley, London, H. G. Bohn, 1853, p. 32.

22. Scott, William I [known as William the Lion] (c. 1142–1214).
23. *Chronicles of the Picts, chronicles of the Scots, and other early memorials of Scottish history*, edited by W. F. Skene, p. clxix.
24. Gerald of Wales, quoted in *John of Fordun's Chronicle of the Scottish Nation*, p. lix.
25. Chandler, 'Ada de Warenne, Queen Mother of Scotland'.
26. Scott, William I [known as William the Lion] (c. 1142–1214).
27. Scott, William I [known as William the Lion] (c. 1142–1214).
28. Oram, editor, *The Kings and Queens of Scotland*, p. 92.
29. Ibid.
30. Bower, *Scotichronicon*, Vol. 3, p. 373.
31. Ibid.
32. Ibid., p. 375.
33. Ibid., p 377.
34. Ibid., p. 373.
35. Roger of Hoveden, *The annals of Roger de Hoveden*, p. 15.
36. Ibid., p. 16.
37. Ibid., pp. 93–94.
38. Bower, *Scotichronicon*, Vol. 3, p. 393.
39. *John of Fordun's Chronicle of the Scottish Nation*, p. 275.
40. Ross, *Scotland*, p. 69.
41. Ibid.
42. *Mediaeval chronicles of Scotland*, translated by Joseph Stephenson, p. 22.
43. Ibid., p. 27.
44. Ibid., p. 28.
45. Bower, *Scotichronicon*, V. 4, p. 393.
46. Ibid., p. 411.
47. fmg.ac/Projects/MedLands/SCOTLAND
48. Oram, editor, *The Kings and Queens of Scotland*, p. 91.
49. *Mediaeval chronicles of Scotland*, translated by Joseph Stephenson, p. 24.
50. Marshall, *Scottish Queens 1034–1714*, pp. 17–18.
51. W. W. Scott, Ermengarde [Ermengarde de Beaumont], oxforddnb.com, 23 September 2004.
52. Ibid.
53. Ibid.
54. *Mediaeval chronicles of Scotland*, translated by Joseph Stephenson, p. 30.
55. Marshall, *Scottish Queens 1034–1714*, p. 18.
56. Ibid.
57. Ibid.
58. *John of Fordun's Chronicle of the Scottish Nation*, pp. 267–268.
59. Scott, William I [known as William the Lion] (c. 1142–1214).
60. Ibid.
61. Ibid.
62. *John of Fordun's Chronicle of the Scottish Nation*, pp. 270–271.
63. *Mediaeval chronicles of Scotland*, translated by Joseph Stephenson, p. 31.
64. Scott, William I [known as William the Lion] (c.1142–1214).
65. Marshall, *Scottish Queens 1034–1714*, p. 18.
66. Scott, William I [known as William the Lion] (c.1142–1214).
67. Bower, *Scotichronicon* V. 4, p. 455.
68. Ibid., pp. 467–469.

69. Ibid., p. 455.
70. Ibid., p. 457.
71. Scott, William I [known as William the Lion] (c.1142–1214).
72. Ibid.
73. *John of Fordun's Chronicle of the Scottish Nation*, pp. 274.
74. Bower, *Scotichronicon V. 4*, pp. 471–472.
75. Scott, William I [known as William the Lion] (c.1142–1214).
76. *Mediaeval chronicles of Scotland*, translated by Joseph Stephenson, p. 38.
77. *John of Fordun's Chronicle of the Scottish Nation*, p. 275.
78. Marshall, *Scottish Queens 1034–1714*, p. 19.
79. Scott, Ermengarde [Ermengarde de Beaumont].
80. Ross, *Scotland*, p. 70.
81. *Mediaeval chronicles of Scotland*, translated by Joseph Stephenson, p. 46.
82. Keith Stringer, Alexander II (1198–1249), oxforddnb.com, 23 September 2004.
83. *Mediaeval chronicles of Scotland*, translated by Joseph Stephenson, p. 52.
84. Ibid., p. 56.
85. Ibid., p. 57.
86. Ibid., p. 58.
87. Samuel Lewis, 'Bachies – Baneton', in *A Topographical Dictionary of Scotland* (London, 1846), pp. 91–101. *British History Online*, www.british-history.ac.uk/topographical-dict/scotland/pp91-101 [accessed 29 November 2023].
88. Scott, Ermengarde [Ermengarde de Beaumont].
89. *John of Fordun's Chronicle of the Scottish Nation*, p. 288.
90. Scott, Ermengarde [Ermengarde de Beaumont].
91. *Mediaeval chronicles of Scotland*, translated by Joseph Stephenson, p. 63.
92. Ibid., p. 60.

Chapter Five: The Foundations of Peace

1. Roger of Hoveden, *The annals of Roger de Hoveden*, p. 427.
2. *Mediaeval chronicles of Scotland*, translated by Joseph Stephenson, p. 31.
3. Ibid.
4. Bower, *Scotichronicon*, V. 4, p. 468.
5. Ibid., p. 469.
6. *John of Fordun's Chronicle of the Scottish Nation*, pp. 273–274.
7. Ibid., p. 274.
8. Ibid., p. 276.
9. Ibid.
10. Ibid., p. 276.
11. Keith Stringer, Alexander II (1198–1249), oxforddnb.com, 23 September 2004.
12. Oram, editor, *The Kings and Queens of Scotland*, p. 99.
13. Ibid.
14. Magna Carta, British Library, transcript from bl.uk
15. *Mediaeval chronicles of Scotland*, translated by Joseph Stephenson, p. 43.
16. Ibid., p. 44.
17. Ibid.
18. Ibid.
19. Ibid.

20. Ibid., p. 45.
21. Oram, editor, *The Kings and Queens of Scotland*, p. 100.
22. *John of Fordun's Chronicle of the Scottish Nation*, pp. 280.
23. Oram, editor, *The Kings and Queens of Scotland*, p. 101.
24. *John of Fordun's Chronicle of the Scottish Nation*, pp. 284.
25. Oram, editor, *The Kings and Queens of Scotland*, p. 101.
26. Ibid., pp. 101–102.
27. Danny Danziger and John Gillingham, *1215: The Year of Magna Carta*, Hodder & Stoughton, London, 2004, p. 228.
28. Roger of Hoveden, *The annals of Roger de Hoveden*, p. 501.
29. Danny Danziger and John Gillingham, *1215*, p. 228.
30. Anne Crawford, editor and translator, *Letters of the Queens of England*, Stroud, Sutton Publishing, 2002, p. 53.
31. Bower, *Scotichronicon*, V. 4, p. 107.
32. Matthew Lewis, *Henry III: The Son of Magna Carta*, Amberley, Stroud, 2016, p. 74.
33. finerollshenry3.co.uk/ content/calendar/roll_015.html#it192_005, 19 June 1221.
34. *John of Fordun's Chronicle of the Scottish Nation*, p. 284.
35. *Mediaeval chronicles of Scotland*, translated by Joseph Stephenson, p. 56.
36. Keith Stringer, Joan (1210–1238), oxforddnb.com, 23 September 2004.
37. Ibid.
38. Ibid.
39. Ibid.
40. Ibid.
41. Keith Stringer, Alexander II (1198–1249).
42. Bower, *Scotichronicon*, V, p. 161.
43. finerollshenry3.co.uk/content/calendar/roll_005E.html#it019_004, 5 May 1238.
44. Matthaei Parisiensis, *Chronica majora*.
45. *Mediaeval chronicles of Scotland*, translated by Joseph Stephenson, p. 64.
46. Keith Stringer, Alexander II (1198–1249).
47. David Carpenter, *Henry III: The Rise to Power and Personal Rule 1207–1258*, London, Yale University Press, 2021, p. 421.
48. Keith Stringer, Marie [née Marie de Coucy] (d. 1284), oxforddnb.com, 23 September 2004.
49. Ibid.
50. *Mediaeval chronicles of Scotland*, translated by Joseph Stephenson, p. 64..
51. *John of Fordun's Chronicle of the Scottish Nation*, p. 287.
52. *Mediaeval chronicles of Scotland*, translated by Joseph Stephenson, pp. 67–68.
53. Marshall, *Scottish Queens 1034–1714*, p. 20.
54. Ibid.
55. Stringer, Marie [née Marie de Coucy] (d. 1284).
56. Ibid.
57. Carpenter, *Henry III*, p. 421.
58. Bower, *Scotichronicon*, V. 5, p. 179.
59. Ibid.
60. Ibid.
61. Wyntoun, *The orygynale cronykil of Scotland*, p. 246.
62. *Mediaeval chronicles of Scotland*, p. 69.
63. Carpenter, *Henry III*, pp. 421–422.

64. *Scottish Annals from English Chroniclers A.D. 500 to 1286*, edited by Alan Orr Anderson, London, Nutt, 1908, p. 352.
65. Ibid.
66. *John of Fordun's Chronicle of the Scottish Nation*, p. 287.
67. Carpenter, *Henry III*, pp. 423–424.
68. *Mediaeval chronicles of Scotland*, p. 87.
69. *John of Fordun's Chronicle of the Scottish Nation*, p. 287.
70. Ibid., p. 289.
71. Ibid.
72. Ibid., pp. 289–290.
73. Ibid., p. 290.
74. Stringer, Marie [née Marie de Coucy] (d. 1284).
75. *John of Fordun's Chronicle of the Scottish Nation*, p. 290.
76. Bower, *Scotichronicon*, V. 5, p. 299.
77. *John of Fordun's Chronicle of the Scottish Nation*, p. 291.
78. *Scottish Annals from English Chroniclers A.D. 500 to 1286*, p. 363.
79. Ibid.
80. *John of Fordun's Chronicle of the Scottish Nation*, p. 291.
81. *Scottish Annals from English Chroniclers A.D. 500 to 1286*, p. 365.
82. Ibid., p. 364.
83. Ibid., p. 365.
84. Ibid.
85. Stringer, Marie [née Marie de Coucy] (d. 1284).
86. Marshall, *Scottish Queens 1034–1714*, p. 21.
87. Ibid., p. 22.
88. Bower, *Scotichronicon*, V. 5, p. 371.
89. Stringer, Marie [née Marie de Coucy] (d. 1284).

Chapter Six: An Enduring Peace

1. Norman H., Alexander III (1241–1286), oxforddnb.com, 19 May 2011.
2. Bower, *Scotichronicon*, V. 5, p. 295.
3. Watt, D. (1971). The Minority of Alexander III of Scotland. *Transactions of the Royal Historical Society*, 21, 1–23. doi:10.2307/3678917, p. 6.
4. Ibid., p. 7.
5. Ibid.
6. *Scottish Annals from English Chroniclers A.D. 500 to 1286*, pp. 348–349.
7. *John of Fordun's Chronicle of the Scottish Nation*, p. 291.
8. Ibid.
9. Ibid.
10. Ibid.
11. *Scottish Annals from English Chroniclers A.D. 500 to 1286*, p. 364.
12. Ibid., p. 366.
13. Marshall, *Scottish Queens 1034–1714*, p. 22.
14. *Scottish Annals from English Chroniclers A.D. 500 to 1286*, pp. 365–366.
15. Ibid., p. 366.
16. *Mediaeval chronicles of Scotland*, p. 88.

17. Ibid.
18. Ibid.
19. *John of Fordun's Chronicle of the Scottish Nation*, p. 291.
20. Ibid.
21. Marshall, *Scottish Queens 1034–1714*, p. 22.
22. Ibid., p. 23.
23. Watt, *The Minority of Alexander III of Scotland*, p. 10.
24. Ibid.
25. *Scottish Annals from English Chroniclers A.D. 500 to 1286*, p. 370.
26. Ibid., p. 371.
27. *Mediaeval chronicles of Scotland*, p. 89.
28. *Scottish Annals from English Chroniclers A.D. 500 to 1286*, p. 372.
29. Oram, editor, *The Kings and Queens of Scotland*, p. 110.
30. *Scottish Annals from English Chroniclers A.D. 500 to 1286*, pp. 371–372.
31. Watt, *The Minority of Alexander III of Scotland*, p. 11.
32. *Mediaeval chronicles of Scotland*, p. 90.
33. Marshall, *Scottish Queens 1034–1714*, p. 24.
34. *Mediaeval chronicles of Scotland*, p. 90.
35. Watt, *The Minority of Alexander III of Scotland*, pp. 13–15.
36. Marshall, *Scottish Queens 1034–1714*, p. 24.
37. *Scottish Annals from English Chroniclers A.D. 500 to 1286*, p. 373.
38. Bower, *Scotichronicon*, V. 5, p. 319.
39. Norman, Alexander III (1241–1286).
40. Bower, *Scotichronicon*, V. 5, p. 319.
41. *Scottish Annals from English Chroniclers A.D. 500 to 1286*, p. 376.
42. Ibid.
43. Watt, *The Minority of Alexander III of Scotland*, p. 18.
44. *Scottish Annals from English Chroniclers A.D. 500 to 1286*, p. 376.
45. Marshall, *Scottish Queens 1034–1714*, p. 25.
46. Watt, *The Minority of Alexander III of Scotland*, p. 21.
47. *John of Fordun's Chronicle of the Scottish Nation*, p. 295.
48. Marshall, *Scottish Queens 1034–1714*, p. 25.
49. *John of Fordun's Chronicle of the Scottish Nation*, p. 295.
50. Norman, Alexander III (1241–1286).
51. *Mediaeval chronicles of Scotland*, pp. 95–96.
52. Ibid., p. 118.
53. Bower, *Scotichronicon*, V. 5, p. 353.
54. Ibid., p. 355.
55. Ibid., p. 371.
56. Ibid., p. 367.
57. Bower, *Scotichronicon*, V. 5, p. 371.
58. *The Chronicle of Lanercost*, edited by Sir Herbert Maxwell, J. Maclehose, Glasgow, 1913, p. 7.
59. Marshall, *Scottish Queens 1034–1714*, p. 25.
60. The Chronicle of Lanercost, pp. 7–8.
61. Susan Abernethy, *Margaret of England, Queen of Scots*, thefreelancehistorywriter.com, 26 October 2012.
62. Bower, *Scotichronicon*, V. 5, p. 401.

63. *The Chronicle of Lanercost*, pp. 8–9.
64. *John of Fordun's Chronicle of the Scottish Nation*, p. 300.
65. The Chronicle of Lanercost, p. 9.
66. Bower, *Scotichronicon* V. 5, pp. 409–411.
67. Marshall, *Scottish Queens 1034–1714*, p. 26.
68. 'A thousand two hundred years, four score over to reckon clear, of David, this third Alexander's son, of this life all his days were done. Dead he was at Stirling, and interred in Dunfermline', Wyntoun, *The orygynale cronykil of Scotland*, p. 259.
69. *John of Fordun's Chronicle of the Scottish Nation*, p. 302.
70. *The Chronicle of Lanercost*, p. 32.
71. *John of Fordun's Chronicle of the Scottish Nation*, p. 302.
72. *Theiner*, 134 ('Regesta 43: 1286', in *Calendar of Papal Registers Relating To Great Britain and Ireland: Volume 1, 1198–1304*, ed. W. H. Bliss (London, 1893), pp. 479–491. *British History Online*, www.british-history.ac.uk/cal-papal-registers/brit-ie/vol1/pp479-491 [accessed 6 December 2023]).
73. Bower, *Scotichronicon*, V. 5, p. 413.
74. Ibid., p. 417.
75. Marshall, *Scottish Queens 1034–1714*, p. 26.
76. Ibid.
77. Samuel Lewis, 'Jamestown – Jura', in *A Topographical Dictionary of Scotland* (London, 1846), pp. 584–592. *British History Online*, www.british-history.ac.uk/topographical-dict/scotland/pp584-592 [accessed 6 December 2023].
78. Bower, *Scotichronicon*, V. 5, p. 419.
79. Ibid.
80. Ibid., pp. 419–421.
81. Ibid., p. 421.
82. *The Chronicle of Lanercost*, p. 32.
83. *John of Fordun's Chronicle of the Scottish Nation*, pp. 304–305.
84. *The Chronicle of Lanercost*, pp. 43–44.
85. Marshall, *Scottish Queens 1034–1714*, p. 27.
86. *CSP Scot*. 3. no. 829 quoted by Jessica Nelson, Yolande (d. in or after 1324), oxforddnb.com, 4 October 2008.

Chapter Seven: Scotland's First Queen Regnant

1. Oram, editor, *The Kings and Queens of Scotland*, pp. 115–116.
2. Wyntoun, *The orygynale cronykil of Scotland*, pp. 259–260.
3. Bower, *Scotichronicon*, V. 5, p. 411.
4. *The Chronicle of Lanercost*, p. 21.
5. Ibid.
6. Ibid., pp. 22–23.
7. Bower, *Scotichronicon*, V. 5, p. 411.
8. Wyntoun, *The orygynale cronykil of Scotland*, p. 262.
9. Bower, *Scotichronicon*, V. 5, p. 413.
10. Ibid., notes, pp. 502–504.
11. Oram, editor, *The Kings and Queens of Scotland*, p. 123.
12. Bower, *Scotichronicon*, V. 6, p. 3.

13. Ibid.
14. Marc Morris, *Edward I: A Great and Terrible King*, London, Windmill Books, 2008, p. 235.
15. Bower, *Scotichronicon*, V. 6, p. 3.
16. Oram, editor, *The Kings and Queens of Scotland*, p. 123.
17. Ibid.
18. Morris, *Edward I*, p. 236.
19. Ibid., pp. 236–237.
20. Bower, *Scotichronicon*, V. 6, pp. 3–5.
21. Oram, editor, *The Kings and Queens of Scotland*, pp. 122–124.
22. *John of Fordun's Chronicle of the Scottish Nation*, p. 306.
23. Oram, editor, *The Kings and Queens of Scotland*, p. 124.
24. Ibid., p. 124.
25. Bower, *Scotichronicon*, V. 5, p. 411.
26. *John of Fordun's Chronicle of the Scottish Nation*, p. 306.

Chapter Eight: The House of Balliol

1. Bower, *Scotichronicon*, V. 6, p. 5.
2. Ibid.
3. Elizabeth Hallam, editor, *Chronicles of the Age of Chivalry*, Twickenham, Tiger Books, 1995, p. 134.
4. Stephen Spinks, *Robert the Bruce: Champion of a Nation*, Stroud, Amberley, 2019, p. 60.
5. Ibid.
6. Ibid.
7. Ibid.
8. Walter of Guisborough, quoted in Elizabeth Hallam, editor, *Chronicles of the Age of Chivalry*, p. 134.
9. Bower, *Scotichronicon*, V. 6, p. 7.
10. Stephen Spinks, *Robert the Bruce*, p. 60.
11. Forester, *The Chronicle of John Florence of Worcester with the two continuations*, p. 399.
12. Bower, *Scotichronicon*, V. 6, p. 31, *John of Fordun's Chronicle of the Scottish Nation*, p. 309.
13. *John of Fordun's Chronicle of the Scottish Nation*, p. 309.
14. Walter of Guisborough, quoted in Elizabeth Hallam, editor, *Chronicles of the Age of Chivalry*, p. 134.
15. G. P. Stell, John [John de Balliol] (c. 1248x1250–1314), oxforddnb.com, 22 September 2005.
16. Ibid.
17. Ibid.
18. fmg.ac/Projects/MedLands/SCOTLAND
19. *Calendar of Documents Scotland* (Bain), Vol. II, 189, p. 60, quoted in fmg.ac/Projects/MedLands/SCOTLAND
20. Waugh, Scott L., 'Warenne, John de, sixth earl of Surrey [earl of Surrey and Sussex, Earl Warenne] (1232–1304)', *Oxford Dictionary of National Biography* (Oxford: Oxford University Press, 2004) [online edition: oxforddnb.com].

21. Ibid.
22. Ibid.
23. *John of Fordun's Chronicle of the Scottish Nation*, p. 315.
24. Waugh, 'Warenne, John de, sixth earl of Surrey [earl of Surrey and Sussex, Earl Warenne] (1232–1304)'.
25. Oram, editor, *The Kings and Queens of Scotland*, p. 129.
26. *John of Fordun's Chronicle of the Scottish Nation*, p. 316.
27. Ibid., p. 318.
28. *The Chronicle of Lanercost*, p. 115.
29. Ibid.
30. Ibid., p. 116.
31. *John of Fordun's Chronicle of the Scottish Nation*, p. 318–319.
32. Oram, editor, *The Kings and Queens of Scotland*, p. 130.
33. *John of Fordun's Chronicle of the Scottish Nation*, p. 320.
34. Oram, editor, *The Kings and Queens of Scotland*, p. 130.
35. Waugh, 'Warenne, John de, sixth earl of Surrey [earl of Surrey and Sussex, Earl Warenne] (1232–1304)'.
36. fmg.ac/Projects/MedLands/SCOTLAND
37. Rymer (1745), Tome I, Pars III, p. 152, quoted in fmg.ac/Projects/MedLands/SCOTLAND
38. Oram, editor, *The Kings and Queens of Scotland*, p. 131.
39. Ibid.

Chapter Nine: The King and Queen of the May

1. Ross, *Scotland*, p. 81–82.
2. Walter of Guisborough, quoted in Elizabeth Hallam, editor, *Chronicles of the Age of Chivalry*, p. 142.
3. Ibid., p. 144.
4. *Chronicle of Walter of Guisborough*, quoted in Spinks, *Robert the Bruce*, pp. 84–85.
5. Spinks, *Robert the Bruce*, p. 85.
6. Ibid.
7. Waugh, 'Warenne, John de, sixth earl of Surrey [earl of Surrey and Sussex, Earl Warenne] (1232–1304)'.
8. Spinks, *Robert the Bruce*, p. 86.
9. Ibid.
10. CP III 55, quoted in fmg.ac/Projects/MedLands/SCOTLAND
11. G. W. S. Barrow, Robert I [Robert the Bruce], *Oxford Dictionary of National Biography* (Oxford: Oxford University Press, 2004) [online edition: oxforddnb.com].
12. *John of Fordun's Chronicle of the Scottish Nation*, p. 319.
13. Ibid., p. 311.
14. *The Chronicle of Lanercost*, p. 103.
15. *Calendar of Documents Scotland* (Bain), Vol. II, 675, p. 158, quoted in fmg.ac/Projects/MedLands/SCOTLAND
16. Spinks, *Robert the Bruce*, p. 72.
17. *John of Fordun's Chronicle of the Scottish Nation*, p. 311.
18. G. W. S. Barrow, Robert I.
19. Ross, *Scotland*, p. 84.

20. Spinks, *Robert the Bruce*, p. 91.
21. Bower, *Scotichronicon*, V. 6, p. 37.
22. G. W. S. Barrow, Robert I.
23. Spinks, *Robert the Bruce*, p. 93.
24. Ibid., p. 94.
25. Ibid., p. 95.
26. CDS, ii, no. 1465, quoted in Spinks, *Robert the Bruce*, p. 96.
27. Spinks, *Robert the Bruce*, pp. 96–97.
28. Ibid., p. 98.
29. Ibid., p. 99.
30. Ibid.
31. *Flores Historiarum, per Matthaeum Westmonasteriensem collecti*, quoted in Elizabeth Hallam, editor, *Chronicles of the Age of Chivalry*, p. 157.
32. Spinks, *Robert the Bruce*, p. 100.
33. *John of Fordun's Chronicle of the Scottish Nation*, p. 332.
34. Spinks, *Robert the Bruce*, p. 100.
35. *The Chronicle of Lanercost*, p. 176.
36. Bower, *Scotichronicon*, V. 6, pp. 313–315.
37. *John of Fordun's Chronicle of the Scottish Nation*, pp. 332–333.
38. Bower, *Scotichronicon*, V. 6, p. 311.
39. *The Chronicle of Lanercost*, p. 176.
40. Walter of Guisborough, quoted in Elizabeth Hallam, editor, *Chronicles of the Age of Chivalry*, p. 157.
41. Ibid., p. 158.
42. Ibid.
43. Spinks, *Robert the Bruce*, p. 105.
44. Walter of Guisborough, quoted in Elizabeth Hallam, editor, *Chronicles of the Age of Chivalry*, p. 158.
45. Spinks, *Robert the Bruce*, p. 106.
46. *John of Fordun's Chronicle of the Scottish Nation*, p. 333.
47. My thanks to Dr Fiona Watson for helping me to work out the intricacies of Robert the Bruce's inauguration.
48. G. W. S. Barrow, Robert I.
49. *The Chronicle of Lanercost*, p. 178.
50. Spinks, *Robert the Bruce*, p. 109.
51. *The Chronicle of Lanercost*, p. 178.
52. Spinks, *Robert the Bruce*, pp. 110–111.
53. Ibid., p. 112.
54. *John of Fordun's Chronicle of the Scottish Nation*, p. 334.
55. Spinks, *Robert the Bruce*, p. 113.
56. Calendar of documents relating to Scotland preserved in Her Majesty's Public Record Office, London, Vol. 2, Edinburgh, H. M. General Register House, 1881, archive.org, no, 1963, p. 521.
57. Ibid., no. 169, p. 31.
58. Ibid., no. 174, p. 32.
59. Ibid., no. 244, p. 49.
60. Ibid., no. 305, p. 60.
61. Ibid., no. 323, p. 62.

62. Ibid., no. 354, p. 68.
63. Morris, *Edward I*, p. 358.
64. *Calendar of Documents Scotland* (Bain), Vol. II, 1851, p. 495 quoted in fmg.ac/ Projects/MedLands/SCOTLAND
65. CDS, ii, no 1910, quoted in Spinks, *Robert the Bruce*, p. 115.
66. Calendar of documents relating to Scotland, Vol. 3, p. 47.
67. Spinks, *Robert the Bruce*, p. 115.
68. Ross, *Scotland*, p. 90.
69. *The Chronicle of Lanercost*, p. 207.
70. Laffin, John, *Brassey's Battles: 3,500 Years of Conflict, Campaigns and Wars from A–Z*, London, Brassey's, 1995, p. 68.
71. Spinks, *Robert the Bruce*, p. 174.
72. Bower, *Scotichronicon*, V 6, p. 353.
73. *John of Fordun's Chronicle of the Scottish Nation*, p. 340.
74. Ibid., p. 312.
75. Bower, *Scotichronicon*, V. 6, p. 377.
76. *John of Fordun's Chronicle of the Scottish Nation*, p. 360.
77. Ibid., p. 343.
78. Spinks, *Robert the Bruce*, p. 232.
79. Ibid.
80. *John of Fordun's Chronicle of the Scottish Nation*, p. 343.
81. Ibid.
82. Spinks, *Robert the Bruce*, p. 254.
83. *John of Fordun's Chronicle of the Scottish Nation*, p. 345.
84. Colm McNamee, *Robert Bruce: Our Most Valiant Prince and Lord*, Edinburgh, Birlinn Limited, 2006, p. 297.

Chapter Ten: Joan Makepeace and the Second War of Independence

1. *CPR 1321–4*, 23 quoted in Kathryn Warner, *Isabella of France: The Rebel Queen*, Stroud, Amberley Publishing, 2016, p. 137.
2. Warner, *Isabella of France*, p. 167.
3. *The Chronicle of Lanercost*, p. 249.
4. Ibid., pp. 249–250.
5. Ibid., p. 259.
6. Ibid., pp. 259–260.
7. Ibid., p. 260.
8. Marshall, *Scottish Queens 1034–1714*, p. 36.
9. Ibid.
10. Ibid.
11. *The Chronicle of Lanercost*, p. 260.
12. Walter Bower, *Scotichronicon*, V 7 Bks 13 & 14, open source, archive.org, 1440, p. 39.
13. *The Chronicle of Lanercost*, pp. 261–262 notes and Bower, *Scotichronicon*, V 7, pp. 37–39.
14. Ibid., p. 257.
15. *John of Fordun's Chronicle of the Scottish Nation*, p. 345.
16. *The Chronicle of Lanercost*, pp. 260–261.

17. Bower, *Scotichronicon*, V 7, p. 43.
18. Bruce Webster, Joan [Joan of the Tower], oxforddnb.com, 23 September 2004.
19. *John of Fordun's Chronicle of the Scottish Nation*, p. 346.
20. Bower, *Scotichronicon*, V 7, p. 73.
21. Ibid., p. 83.
22. *The Chronicle of Lanercost*, p. 287.
23. *John of Fordun's Chronicle of the Scottish Nation*, p. 346.
24. Bruce Webster, *David II*, oxforddnb.com, 23 September 2004.
25. *John of Fordun's Chronicle of the Scottish Nation*, p. 356.
26. Bower, *Scotichronicon*, V 7, p. 151.
27. Hallam, editor, *Chronicles of the Age of Chivalry*, p. 235.
28. 'Volume XX: 9 Clement VI', in *Petitions to the Pope 1342–1419*, ed. W. H. Bliss (London, 1896), pp. 197–208. *British History Online*, www.british-history.ac.uk/no-series/petitions-to-pope/1342-1419/pp197-208 [accessed 24 January 2024].
29. Ibid.
30. Ibid.
31. *John of Fordun's Chronicle of the Scottish Nation*, p. 366.
32. Bower, *Scotichronicon*, V 7, p. 321.
33. Ibid.
34. *RotS*, 1.817, 822 quoted in Webster, Joan [Joan of the Tower].
35. Bower, *Scotichronicon*, V 7, p. 305.
36. *Calendar of documents relating to Scotland*, Vol. 4, no. 37, p. 10.
37. Ian Mortimer, *The Perfect King: The Life of Edward III, Father of the English Nation*, London, Random House, 2006, p. 502.
38. Ibid., pp. 497–498.
39. *Regesta regum Scottorum*, vol. 6, ed. B. Webster, 1982, 237, quoted in Webster, Joan [Joan of the Tower].
40. *Calendar of documents relating to Scotland*, Vol. 4, no. 65, p. 16.
41. 'sweet and debonair, courteous, homely, pleasant and fair', Wyntoun, *The orygynale cronykil of Scotland*, p. 502.
42. *Calendar of documents relating to Scotland*, Vol. 4, no. 94, p. 22.
43. Ibid.
44. Marshall, *Scottish Queens 1034–1714*, p. 38.
45. Ibid., p. 38.
46. *John of Fordun's Chronicle of the Scottish Nation*, p. 370.
47. 'They were together but a short while', Wyntoun, *The orygynale cronykil of Scotland*, p. 506.
48. Bower, *Scotichronicon*, V 7, p. 333.
49. *Calendar of documents relating to Scotland*, Vol. 4, no. 93, p. 22.
50. Ibid., no. 128, p. 28.
51. Bruce, Webster, Margaret [née Margaret Drummond], *Oxford Dictionary of National Biography* (Oxford: Oxford University Press, 2004) [online edition: oxforddnb.com].
52. Marshall, *Scottish Queens 1034–1714*, p. 39.
53. Bower, *Scotichronicon*, V 7, p. 359.
54. Marshall, *Scottish Queens 1034–1714*, p. 39.
55. Bower, *Scotichronicon*, V 7, p. 359.
56. *Calendar of documents relating to Scotland*, Vol. 4, no. 197, pp. 44–45.

Chapter Eleven: The Rise of the House of Stewart

1. Quote attributed to John Knox recounting the death of James V, Oram, editor, *The Kings and Queens of Scotland*, p. 277.
2. *Calendar of documents relating to Scotland*, Vol. 2, no. 910, p. 237.
3. Ibid., no. 1851, p. 495.
4. Ibid., no. 1910, p. 508.
5. *John of Fordun's Chronicle of the Scottish Nation*, p. 339.
6. *Calendar of documents relating to Scotland*, Vol. 3, no. 372, p. 71.
7. Ibid., no. 393, p. 74.
8. Bower, *Scotichronicon*, V 6, p. 353.
9. S. I. Boardman, Robert II (1316-1390), *Oxford Dictionary of National Biography* (Oxford: Oxford University Press, 2006) [online edition: oxforddnb.com].
10. Spinks, *Robert the Bruce*, p. 179.
11. Oram, editor, *The Kings and Queens of Scotland*, p. 163.
12. Bower, *Scotichronicon*, V 7, p. 41.
13. Boardman, Robert II (1316–1390).
14. Oram, editor, *The Kings and Queens of Scotland*, p. 163.
15. Ibid., p. 164.
16. Bower, *Scotichronicon*, V 7, p. 105.
17. Ibid., p. 145.
18. Oram, editor, *The Kings and Queens of Scotland*, p. 165.
19. *John of Fordun's Chronicle of the Scottish Nation*, pp. 311–312.
20. Theiner (1864), DLXV, p. 284, quoted in fmg.ac/Projects/MedLands/SCOTLAND
21. fmg.ac/Projects/MedLands/SCOTLAND
22. John Riddell, Stewartiana, containing the case of Robert II and Elizabeth Mure, Edinburgh, Thomas G. Stevenson, 1843, pp. 1–2.
23. Burnett (1880) *Exchequer Rolls*, Vol. IV, Appendix to Preface, I, Stewart Genealogy, p. clxx, quoted in fmg.ac/Projects/MedLands/SCOTLAND
24. fmg.ac/Projects/MedLands/SCOTLAND
25. Macdonald, A. and Macdonald, A. (1896) *The Clan Donald* (Inverness), Vol. I, p. 503, quoted in fmg.ac/Projects/MedLands/SCOTLAND
26. CP V 375, quoted in fmg.ac/Projects/MedLands/SCOTLAND
27. 'regis secundo genitus', *Liber Pluscardensis*, Vol. I, Liber X, CVIII, p. 324, quoted in fmg.ac/Projects/MedLands/SCOTLAND
28. *Registrum Episcopatus Moraviensis* (Edinburgh, 1837), 271, p. 353, quoted in fmg.ac/Projects/MedLands/SCOTLAND
29. Balfour Paul *Scots Peerage*, Vol. VII, p. 241, quoted in fmg.ac/Projects/MedLands/SCOTLAND
30. fmg.ac/Projects/MedLands/SCOTLAND
31. Sir James Balfour Paul, editor, *The Scots Peerage*, Vol. VIII, Edinburgh, David Douglas, 1911, p. 266.
32. Ibid., p. 268.
33. Ibid., p. 267.
34. Ibid., p. 269.
35. Ibid.
36. Burnett (1880) *Exchequer Rolls*, Vol. IV, Appendix to Preface, I, quoted in fmg.ac/Projects/MedLands/SCOTLAND

37. Burnett (1880) *Exchequer Rolls*, Vol. IV, p. 120, quoted in fmg.ac/Projects/MedLands/ SCOTLAND
38. Susan Abernethy, *The Two Wives of Robert II, King of Scots – Elizabeth Mure and Euphemia Ross*, thefreelancehistorywriter.com, March 2014.
39. Bower, *Scotichronicon*, V 7, p. 447.
40. Dr Amy Hayes, *Euphemia Ross: The surprise queen*, www.historyscotland.com/ history/the-stewart-queens-of-scotland-1371-1513, 30 May 2018.
41. Marshall, *Scottish Queens 1034–1714*, p. 42.
42. Elizabeth Sutherland, *Five Euphemias: Women in Medieval Scotland 1200–1420*, London, Constable, 1999, p. 131.
43. Ibid.
44. Ibid., p. 133.
45. Ibid., p. 140.
46. Ibid., p. 141.
47. *John of Fordun's Chronicle of the Scottish Nation*, p. 358.
48. Ibid.
49. Bower, *Scotichronicon*, V 7, p. 367.
50. Hayes, *Euphemia Ross*.
51. Theiner, 307; Cal. Pet. i. 287. 'Regesta 231: 1355', in *Calendar of Papal Registers Relating To Great Britain and Ireland*, Volume 3, 1342–1362, ed. W. H. Bliss and C. Johnson (London, 1897), pp. 568–580. British History Online, www.british-history. ac.uk/cal-papal-registers/brit-ie/vol3/pp568-580 [accessed 12 January 2024].
52. Sutherland, *Five Euphemias*, p. 150.
53. Ibid., p. 151.
54. Ibid., p. 155.
55. fmg.ac/Projects/MedLands/SCOTLAND
56. Ibid.
57. Ibid.
58. Sutherland, *Five Euphemias*, p.156.
59. Bower, *Scotichronicon*, V 7, p. 367.
60. Ibid., p. 373.
61. S. I. Boardman, Euphemia [née Euphemia Ross], *Oxford Dictionary of National Biography* (Oxford: Oxford University Press, 2004) [online edition: oxforddnb.com].
62. Sutherland, *Five Euphemias*, p. 158.
63. Ibid., p. 159.
64. Sir James Balfour Paul, editor, *The Scots Peerage*, Vol. VIII, p. 263.
65. Boardman, Robert II (1316–1390).
66. Froissart, 2.48, quoted in Boardman, Robert II (1316-1390).
67. Bower, *Scotichronicon*, V 7, p. 409.
68. Boardman, Euphemia.
69. Ibid.
70. fmg.ac/Projects/MedLands/SCOTLAND

Chapter Twelve: Family Feuds

1. Bower, *Scotichronicon*, V 7, p. 297.
2. Burnett (1880) *Exchequer Rolls*, Vol. IV, Appendix to Preface, I, Stewart Genealogy, p. clxx, citing 'Harleian MSS. 4695', quoted in fmg.ac/Projects/MedLands/SCOTLAND

3. S. I. Boardman, Robert III (1316–1390), *Oxford Dictionary of National Biography* (Oxford: Oxford University Press, 2004) [online edition: oxforddnb.com].
4. Bower, *Scotichronicon*, V 7, p. 359.
5. Boardman, Robert III.
6. Marshall, *Scottish Queens 1034–1714*, p. 45.
7. Ibid., p. 46.
8. Bower, *Scotichronicon*, V 7, p. 443.
9. *Liber pluscardensis*, Vol. 2 edited by Felix James Henry Skene, Edinburgh, W. Paterson, 1877, pp. 252–253.
10. Bower, *Scotichronicon*, V 8, p. 3.
11. Ibid.
12. Callum, *'Ane Lady Bricht': A Life of Annabella Drummond, Queen of Scots, c. 1350–1401*, https://drcallumwatson.blogspot.com, 15 August 2019.
13. Bower, *Scotichronicon*, V 8, pp. 63–65.
14. Burnett (1880) *Exchequer Rolls*, Vol. IV, Appendix to Preface, quoted in fmg.ac/Projects/MedLands/SCOTLAND
15. Mary Anne Everett Wood, *Letters of Royal and Illustrious Ladies of Great Britain: From the Commencement of the Twelfth Century to the Close of the Reign of Queen Mary*, Volume 1, Henry Colburn, London, 1846, pp. 68–70.
16. Nicholson, *Later Middle Ages*, 215, quoted in Marshall, *Scottish Queens 1034–1714*, p. 47.
17. stewartsociety.org/history-of-the-stewarts
18. Marshall, *Scottish Queens 1034–1714*, p. 47.
19. Bower, *Scotichronicon*, V 8, p. 11.
20. Ibid., p. 13.
21. Marshall, *Scottish Queens 1034–1714*, p. 47.
22. Callum Watson, *'Ane Lady Bricht': A Life of Annabella Drummond, Queen of Scots, c. 1350–1401*, https://drcallumwatson.blogspot.com, 15 August 2019.
23. Mike Ashley, *The Mammoth Book of British Kings and Queens*, p. 554.
24. Nigel Tranter, *The Story of Scotland*, ebook loc. 1457.
25. Liber pluscardensis, Vol. 1, p. 339.
26. Ibid.
27. Marshall, *Scottish Queens 1034–1714*, p. 48.
28. Liber pluscardensis, Vol. 2, p. 257.
29. Ibid.
30. Bower, *Scotichronicon*, V 8, p. 65.
31. *Liber pluscardensis*, Vol. 2, p. 257.
32. Bower, *Scotichronicon*, V 8, p. 37.
33. Wyntoun, *The orygynale cronykil of Scotland*, vi, pp. 396–397.
34. Bower, *Scotichronicon*, V 8, p. 39.
35. *Liber pluscardensis*, Vol. 2, pp. 257–258.
36. Bower, *Scotichronicon*, V 8, p. 39.
37. Ibid.
38. *Liber pluscardensis*, Vol. 2, p. 258.
39. Nigel Tranter, *The Story of Scotland*, ebook loc. 1481.
40. Ibid.
41. Bower, *Scotichronicon*, V 8, p. 39.
42. *Liber pluscardensis*, Vol. 2, p. 262.
43. Ibid.

44. Watson, 'Ane Lady Bricht'.
45. Marshall, *Scottish Queens 1034–1714*, p. 49.
46. James I, King of Scots, *The Kingis Quair*, edited by William MacKean James and Walter W. Skeat, Alexander Gardner, London, 1886, p. 10.
47. Nigel Tranter, *The Story of Scotland*, ebook loc. 1583.
48. James I, King of Scots, *The Kingis Quair*, p. 35.
49. Nigel Tranter, *The Story of Scotland*, ebook loc. 1592.
50. James I, King of Scots, *The Kingis Quair*, pp. 16–17.
51. Marshall, *Scottish Queens 1034–1714*, p. 50.
52. James I, King of Scots, *The Kingis Quair*, p. 47.
53. *Liber pluscardensis*, Vol. 2, p. 75.
54. Marshall, *Scottish Queens 1034–1714*, p. 51.
55. *Liber pluscardensis*, Vol. 2, pp. 278–279.
56. Bower, *Scotichronicon*, V 8, p. 221.
57. Ibid., p. 249.
58. Ibid., p. 251.
59. Marshall, *Scottish Queens 1034–1714*, p. 51.
60. Ibid.
61. Ibid.
62. M. H. Brown, Joan [née Joan Beaufort], *Oxford Dictionary of National Biography* (Oxford: Oxford University Press, 2004) [online edition: oxforddnb.com].
63. [Privy Seals (Tower), 9 Hen. VI. File I.], *Calendar of documents relating to Scotland*, Vol. 4, no. 1044, p. 215.
64. Amy Licence, *Red Roses: Blanche of Gaunt to Margaret Beaufort*, Stroud, Amberley Publishing, 2016, p. 209.
65. Ibid., p. 208.
66. Marshall, *Scottish Queens 1034–1714*, p. 52.
67. Bower, *Scotichronicon*, V 8, p. 221.
68. Marshall, *Scottish Queens 1034–1714*, p. 53.
69. Ibid., p. 54.
70. [Privy Seals (Tower), 24 Hen. VI. File 8.] *Calendar of documents relating to Scotland*, Vol. 4, no. 1181 p. 240.
71. [Privy Seals (Tower), 26 Hen. VI. File 5.] *Calendar of documents relating to Scotland*, Vol. 4, no. 1203 p. 244.

Chapter Thirteen: Renaissance Queens

1. Nigel Tranter, *The Story of Scotland*, ebook loc. 1670.
2. Oram, editor, *The Kings and Queens of Scotland*, p. 240.
3. Marshall, *Scottish Queens 1034–1714*, p. 57.
4. Ibid., p. 58.
5. Ibid.
6. Ibid.
7. *Chronique de Mathieu d'Escouchy*, Mme. Ve. J. Renouard, Paris, 1863, p. 149.
8. Ibid.
9. Marshall, *Scottish Queens 1034–1714*, p. 59.
10. Ibid.

11. Ibid.
12. Ibid., p. 60.
13. Bower, *Scotichronicon*, V 9, p. 141.
14. *Chronique de Mathieu d'Escouchy*, p. 177.
15. Ibid., p. 178
16. Ibid.
17. Ibid., p. 179.
18. *Marshall, Scottish Queens 1034–1714*, p. 61.
19. *Chronique de Mathieu d'Escouchy*, p. 181.
20. Ibid., pp. 181–182.
21. Ibid., p. 182.
22. Ibid., pp. 182–183.
23. Ibid., p. 183.
24. Marshall, *Scottish Queens 1034–1714*, p. 63.
25. Ibid.
26. Ibid.
27. Marshall, *Scottish Queens 1034–1714*, p. 71.
28. *Letters and papers: illustrative of the wars of the English in France during the reign of Henry the Sixth, King of England*, edited by Joseph Stevenson, Public Records Office, London, 1863, pp. 303–304.
29. lxxxx. H. Senselebin [sic]. P. Davidis. [In the margin: Mar(tii).] ('Vatican Regesta 414: 1450–1451', in *Calendar of Papal Registers Relating To Great Britain and Ireland*, Volume 10, 1447–1455, ed. J. A. Twemlow (London, 1915), pp. 211–215. British History Online, www.british-history.ac.uk/cal-papal-registers/brit-ie/vol10/pp211-215 [accessed 24 January 2024].
30. Marshall, *Scottish Queens 1034–1714*, p. 64.
31. Oram, editor, *The Kings and Queens of Scotland*, p. 242.
32. Ibid., p. 243.
33. Oram in *The Kings and Queens of Scotland*, p. 243 states that James was born in May 1452, whereas Marshall in *Scottish Queens 1034–1714*, p. 64 states James was born in July 1451.
34. Marshall, *Scottish Queens 1034–1714*, p. 64.
35. Bower, *Scotichronicon*, V 9, p. 143.
36. fmg.ac/Projects/MedLands/SCOTLAND
37. Marshall, *Scottish Queens 1034–1714*, p. 65.
38. Ibid., p. 64.
39. 1459. 3 Non. Nov. (3 Nov.) Mantua. (f. 100.) 'Vatican Regesta 476: 1460', in *Calendar of Papal Registers Relating To Great Britain and Ireland: Volume 11, 1455-1464*, ed. J. A. Twemlow (London, 1921), pp. 401–407. British History Online, www.british-history.ac.uk/cal-papal-registers/brit-ie/vol11/pp401-407 [accessed 24 January 2024].
40. Marshall, *Scottish Queens 1034–1714*, p. 65.
41. *The Auchinleck chronicle*, Thomas Thomson, Edinburgh, 1819, p. 20.
42. Ibid., p. 57.
43. *The Auchinleck chronicle*, p. 58.
44. Marshall, *Scottish Queens 1034–1714*, pp. 65–66.
45. Ibid., p. 66.
46. *The Auchinleck chronicle*, p. 59.
47. Ibid., p. 58.

48. June 1. 'Milan: 1461', in *Calendar of State Papers and Manuscripts in the Archives and Collections of Milan 1385–1618*, ed. Allen B Hinds (London, 1912), pp. 37–106. British History Online, www.british-history.ac.uk/cal-state-papers/milan/1385-1618/pp37-106 [accessed 24 January 2024].

49. 'Milan: 1461', in *Calendar of State Papers and Manuscripts in the Archives and Collections of Milan 1385–1618*, ed. Allen B Hinds (London, 1912), pp. 37–106. British History Online, www.british-history.ac.uk/cal-state-papers/milan/1385-1618/pp37-106 [accessed 24 January 2024].

50. Marshall, *Scottish Queens 1034–1714*, p. 67.

51. Ibid.

52. 'Vatican Regesta 486: 1462', in *Calendar of Papal Registers Relating To Great Britain and Ireland*, Volume 11, 1455–1464, ed. J. A. Twemlow (London, 1921), pp. 443–453. British History Online, www.british-history.ac.uk/cal-papal-registers/brit-ie/vol11/pp443-453 [accessed 24 January 2024].

53. Marshall, *Scottish Queens 1034–1714*, p. 68.

54. Ibid., p. 69.

55. Oram, editor, *The Kings and Queens of Scotland*, p. 249.

56. Marshall, *Scottish Queens 1034–1714*, p. 72.

57. Ibid., p. 72.

58. Ibid., p. 73.

59. Ibid., p. 74.

60. Oram, editor, *The Kings and Queens of Scotland*, p. 249.

61. Ibid., p. 249.

62. Marshall, *Scottish Queens 1034–1714*, p. 73.

63. Ibid., p. 76.

64. Ibid.

65. Ibid., p. 77.

66. Ibid.

67. Ibid.

68. Ibid., p. 79.

69. fmg.ac/Projects/MedLands/SCOTLAND

70. Ibid.

71. 1475. 7 Id. Nov. (7 Nov.) St Peter's, Rome. (f. 242*r*.) 'Lateran Regesta 790: 1474–1480', in *Calendar of Papal Registers Relating To Great Britain and Ireland*, Volume 13, 1471–1484, ed. J. A. Twemlow (London, 1955), pp. 642–648. British History Online, www.british-history.ac.uk/cal-papal-registers/brit-ie/vol13/pp642-648 [accessed 24 January 2024].

72. 5 Id. Oct. (11 Oct.) St Peter's, Rome. (f. 287*v*.) in ibid.

73. 1474. 7 Kal. May. (25 April.) St Peter's, Rome. (f. 343*v*.) in ibid.

74. 7 Kal. Sept. (26 Aug.) St Peter's, Rome. (f. 507*r*.) in ibid.

75. Oram, editor, *The Kings and Queens of Scotland*, p. 253.

76. Marshall, *Scottish Queens 1034–1714*, p. 79.

77. Oram, editor, *The Kings and Queens of Scotland*, p. 250.

78. Giovanni Sabadino degli Arienti, quoted in Marshall, *Scottish Queens 1034–1714*, p. 81.

79. Ibid.

80. Marshall, *Scottish Queens 1034–1714*, p. 82.

81. Ibid.

82. Ibid., p. 83.

Bibliography

Primary Sources

Annales Monastici: Annales prioratus de Dunstaplia (A.D. 1–1297) Annales monasterii de Bermundesia (A.D. 1042–1432). Edited by Henry Richards Luard, London, Longmans, 1866

Bower, Walter, *Scotichronicon*, V 3 Bks 5 & 6, Edinburgh, The Mercat Press, 1995

Bower, Walter, *Scotichronicon*, V 4, Bks 7 & 8, open source, archive.org, 1440

Bower, Walter, *Scotichronicon*, V 5 Bks 9 & 10, open source, archive.org, 1440

Bower, Walter, *Scotichronicon*, V 6 Bks 11 & 12, open source, archive.org, 1440

Bower, Walter, *Scotichronicon*, V 7 Bks 13 & 14, open source, archive.org, 1440

Bower, Walter, *Scotichronicon*, V 8 Bks 15 & 16, open source, archive.org, 1440

Bower, Walter, *Scotichronicon*, V 9, open source, archive.org, 1440

Calendar of documents relating to Scotland preserved in Her Majesty's Public Record Office, London, Edinburgh, H. M. General Register House, 1881, archive.org

Chronicles of London, edited by Charles Lethbridge Kingsford, Alan Sutton, Dursley, 1977

Chronicles of the Picts, chronicles of the Scots, and other early memorials of Scottish history, edited by W. F. Skene, 1867, Edinburgh, HM General Register House

Chronique de Mathieu d'Escouchy, Mme. Ve. J. Renouard, Paris, 1863

Domesday Book: A Complete Translation, edited by A. Williams and G. H. Martin, 2002

Eadmer's History of Recent Events in England, edited by G. Bosanquet, 1964

Early Scottish charters prior to A.D. 1153: with notes and an index, edited by Archibald Campbell Lawrie, Glasgow, J. MacLehose, 1905

Encomium Emma Reginae, edited by A. Campbell and S. Keynes, Cambridge, 1998

Fine Rolls of Henry III Project, finerollshenry3.co.uk

Flores Historiarum by Roger of Wendover (d. 1236), translated by Matthew of Westminster *c.*1300–1320

Gervase of Canterbury, *The Deeds of Kings*, edited by W. Stubbs in *The Historical Works of Gervase of Canterbury*, Rolls Series, 1880

Gesta Normanorum Ducum by William of Jumièges, edited and translated by Elizabeth Van Houts, Oxford, 1992

Gesta Stephani, translated by K. R. Potter, London, Thomas Nelson and sons, 1955

Great Domesday Book: A Facsimile, edited by R. W. H. Erskine, London, 1986, fol. 164

Heimskringla: The Chronicle of the Kings of Norway, by Snorre Sturluson, translated by Samuel Laing, London, 1844

Henry of Huntingdon, *The Chronicle of Henry of Huntingdon, Comprising the history of England, from the invasion of Julius Caesar to the accession of Henry II. Also, the Acts of Stephen, King of England and duke of Normandy* edited by Thomas Forester, London, H. G. Bohn, 1853

Henry of Huntingdon: The History of the English People 1000–1154, edited by Diana Greenway, Oxford, Oxford University Press, 2009

Historia Novorum in Anglia by Eadmer of Canterbury, edited by Martin Rule, London, 1866

History of the Kings of England by Symeon of Durham, translated by J. Stevenson, facsimile reprint, Lampeter, 1987

Ingulph, *Ingulph's Chronicle of the Abbey of Croyland*, edited by Henry T. Riley, H. G. Bohn, London, 1854

James I, King of Scots, *The Kingis Quair*, edited by James, William MacKean, Walter W. Skeat, Alexander Gardner, London, 1886

John of Fordun's Chronicle of the Scottish Nation, edited by W. F. Skene, Edinburgh, Edmonston and Douglas, 1872

King Harald's Saga by Snorri Sturluson, edited by M. Magnusson and H. Pálsson, 1966

La Vie de S. Edouard le Confesseur par Osbert de Clare, edited by M. Bloch, Analecta Bollandiana, 41, 1923

Letters and papers: illustrative of the wars of the English in France during the reign of Henry the Sixth, King of England, edited by Joseph Stevenson, Public Records Office, London, 1863

Liber pluscardensis, edited by Felix James Henry Skene, Edinburgh, W. Paterson, 1877

Magna Carta, British Library, transcript from bl.uk

Mediaeval chronicles of Scotland: the chronicles of Melrose and Holyrood, translated by Joseph Stephenson, London, Seeleys, 1850

Opera: S. Anselmi Opera Omnia by Anselm, edited by F. S. Schmitt, Edinburgh, 1938–61

Paris, Matthew, Robert de Reading and others, *Flores Historiarum*, volume III, edited by Henry Richards Luard, H. M. Stationary Office, 1890

Ralph of Coggeshall, *The English Chronicle*, edited by J. Stevenson, in *Chronicon Anglicanum*, Rolls Series, 1875

Ralph of Diceto, *Images of History*, edited by W. Stubbs, in *The Historical Works of Master Ralph of Diceto*, Rolls Series, 1876

Richard of Devizes, *Chronicle*, Objective Systems Pty Ltd., ebook, 2008

Richard of Devizes, *The Chronicle of Richard of Devizes: Concerning the Deeds of Richard the First King of England also Richard of Cirencester's Description of Britain*, edited and translated by J. A. Giles, London, 1841

Rodolfus Glaber, Historiarum Libri Quinque, edited by J. France, N. Bulst and P. Reynolds, Oxford, Clarendon Press, 1993

Roger of Hoveden, *The annals of Roger de Hoveden. Comprising the history of England and of other countries of Europe from A.D. 732 to A.D. 1201*, edited by Henry T. Riley, London, H. G. Bohn, 1853

Roger of Wendover's Flowers of history, Comprising the history of England from the descent of the Saxons to A.D. 1235, volume II, by Roger of Wendover, edited by J. A. Giles, London, H. G. Bohn, 1849

Sawyer, P. H., *Anglo-Saxon charters: an annotated list and bibliography*, Royal Historical Society Guides and Handbooks, 1968

Saxo Grammaticus Danonum Regum Heroumque Hiistoria Books X–XVI, edited by Eric Christiansen, 2 volumes, BAR International Series 84, 1980

Scottish Annals from English Chroniclers A.D. 500 to 1286, edited by Alan Orr Anderson, London, Nutt, 1908

The Anglo-Saxon Chronicle, translated by James Ingram, London, reprinted by Dodo Press, 1823

The Anglo-Saxon Chronicles, Swanton, Michael, edited and translated, London, Phoenix Press, 2000

The Anglo-Saxon Chronicle, Whitelock, D., Douglas, D. C. & Tucker, S. I., editors and translators, London, 1961

The Auchinleck chronicle, Thomas Thomson, Edinburgh, 1819

The Carmen de Hastingi Proelio of Guy, Bishop of Amiens, edited by Catherine Morton and Hope Muntz, London, 1972

The Chronicle of Florence of Worcester with the two continuations, translated and edited by Thomas Forester, A. M., London, Henry G. Bohn, 1854

The Chronicle of Henry of Huntingdon. Comprising the history of England, from the invasion of Julius Caesar to the accession of Henry II. Also, the Acts of Stephen, King of England and duke of Normandy, translated and edited by Thomas Forester. London, H. G. Bohn, 1807

The Chronicle of John of Worcester, edited by R. R. Darlington and P. McGurk, 2 volumes, OMT, Oxford, 1995, 1998

The Chronicle of Lanercost, edited by Sir Herbert Maxwell, J. Maclehose, Glasgow, 1913

The Ecclesiastical History of England and Normandy by Ordericus Vitalis 1075–1143(?), London, Bohn, 1853

The Ecclesiastical History of England and Normandy by Ordericus Vitalis 1075–1143(?), Vol. 6, Oxford, Clarendon Press, 1969

The Gesta Guillielmi of William of Poitiers, edited by R. H. C. Davis and Marjorie Chibnall, OMT, Oxford, 1998

The Gesta Normannorum Ducum of William of Jumièges, Oderic Vitalis and Robert of Torigni, edited by E. M. C. van Houts, 2 volumes, Oxford, 1992–95

The historie and cronicles of Scotland ... by Robert Lindesay of Pitscottie, 3 volumes, Mackay, A. J. G., editor, Scottish Text Society, 42–3, 60 (1899–1911)

The History of the Kings of England and of his Own Times by William Malmesbury, Sharpe, J., translator, Seeleys, 1854

The Life of King Edward Who Rests at Westminster, edited by F. Barlow, OMT, 2nd edition, London, 1992

The Lives of Edward the Confessor, edited by Henry Richards Luard, London, Longman, archive.org., 1858

The Prosopography of Anglo-Saxon England, pase.ac.uk, August 2010

The Waltham chronicle, edited and translated by I. Watkiss and M. Chibnall, Oxford, Oxford University Press, 1998

Turgot, Bishop of St Andrews, *The Life of St Margaret Queen of Scotland,* edited by William Forbes-Leith, Edinburgh, William Paterson, 1884

Turgot, Bishop of St Andrews, *The Life of St Margaret Queen of Scotland*, edited by William Forbes-Leith, London, Forgotten Books, 2012

Vita Sanctae Margaretae Scotorum reginae, Symeonis Dunelmensis opera et collectanea by Symeon of Durham, ed. J. H. Hinde, Surtees Society, 1868

Vita Wulfstani of William of Malmesbury, edited by R. R. Darlington, PR new series 40, 1928

William of Malmesbury, *Chronicles of the Kings of England, From the Earliest Period to the Reign of King Stephen c. 1090–1143*, by William of Malmesbury, edited by John Sharpe and J. A. Giles, London, H. G. Bohn, 1847

William of Malmesbury, *Chronicles of the Kings of England, From the Earliest Period to the Reign of King Stephen*, ebook, Perennial Press, 2016

William of Malmesbury, *Gesta Regum Anglorum*, edited by R. A. B Mynors, R. M. Thomson and M. Winterbottom, OMT, 2 volumes, Oxford, 1998

Wood, Mary Anne Everett, *Letters of Royal and Illustrious Ladies of Great Britain: From the Commencement of the Twelfth Century to the Close of the Reign of Queen Mary*, Volume 1, Henry Colburn, London, 1846

Wyntoun, Andrew, *The orygynale cronykil of Scotland*, edited by David Laing, Edinburgh, Edmonston and Douglas, 1872

Secondary Sources

Abernethy, Susan, *Ermengarde de Beaumont, Queen of Scots* (article), thefreelancehistorywriter.com, 26 January 2013

Abernethy, Susan, *Joan Plantagenet, Queen of Scots* (article), thefreelancehistorywriter.com, 25 October 2014

Abernethy, Susan, *Marie de Coucy, Queen of Scots* (article), thefreelancehistorywriter.com, 4 July 2014

Abernethy, Susan, *Margaret of England, Queen of Scots*, thefreelancehistorywriter.com, 26 October 2012

Abernethy, Susan, *Saint Margaret, Queen of Scotland* (article), thefreelancehistorywriter.com, 1 June 2012

Abernethy, Susan, *The Two Wives of Robert II, King of Scots – Elizabeth Mure and Euphemia Ross*, thefreelancehistorywriter.com, 21 March 2014

Abernethy, Susan, *The Wedding Feast of James II, King of Scots and Mary of Guelders*, thefreelancehistorywriter.com, 11 August 2017

Abernethy, Susan, *Yolande de Dreux, Queen of Scots*, thefreelancehistorywriter.com, 25 July 2014

Adams, George Burton, *The History of England from the Norman Conquest to the Death of John*, ebook

Aird, William M., *Tostig, earl of Northumbria (c. 1029–1066)* (article), *Oxford Dictionary of National Biography* (Oxford: Oxford University Press, 2004) [online edition: oxforddnb. com]

Allan, A. (1878). Historical Notices of the Family of Margaret of Logy, Second Queen of David the Second, King of Scots. *Transactions of the Royal Historical Society*, 7, 330–361. doi:10.2307/3677892

Ashley, Mike, *A Brief History of British Kings and Queens*, London, Robinson Publishing, 2014

Ashley, Mike, *The Mammoth Book of British Kings and Queens*, London, Robinson Publishing, 1998

Atherton, David W. and Michael P. Peyton, *Saint Margaret of Scotland circa 1045–1093: Relics and Some Recent Commemorations*, academia.edu, accessed 6 November 2023

Balfour Paul, Sir James, editor, *The Scots Peerage*, Edinburgh, David Douglas, 1911

Barlow, Frank, *Edward the Confessor*, Berkeley and Los Angeles, University of California Press, 1984

Barrow, J. S. (editor), *Prebendaries: Norton*, in *Fasti Ecclesiae Anglicanae 1066–1300: Volume 8, Hereford*, London, Institute of Historical Research, 2002, british-history.ac.uk

Barrow, G. (1978). The Aftermath of War: Scotland and England in the late Thirteenth and early Fourteenth Centuries. *Transactions of the Royal Historical Society*, 28, 103–125. doi:10.2307/3679203

Barrow, G. W. S., David I (c. 1085–1153) (article), *Oxford Dictionary of National Biography* (Oxford: Oxford University Press, 2006) [online edition: oxforddnb.com]

Barrow, G. W. S., Elizabeth [née Elizabeth de Burgh], *Oxford Dictionary of National Biography* (Oxford: Oxford University Press, 2004) [online edition: oxforddnb.com]

Barrow, G. W. S., Malcolm III [Mael Coluim Ceann Mór, Malcolm Canmore] (d. 1093), *Oxford Dictionary of National Biography* (Oxford: Oxford University Press, 2008) [online edition: oxforddnb.com]

Barrow, G. W. S., Margaret [St Margaret] (d. 1093), queen of Scots, consort of Malcolm III (article), *Oxford Dictionary of National Biography* (Oxford: Oxford University Press, 2004) [online edition: oxforddnb.com]

Barrow, G. W. S., Robert I [Robert the Bruce], *Oxford Dictionary of National Biography* (Oxford: Oxford University Press, 2004) [online edition: oxforddnb.com]

Bartlett, Robert, *England Under the Norman and Angevin Kings, 1075–1225*, Oxford, Oxford University Press, 2000

Boardman, S. I., Euphemia [née Euphemia Ross], *Oxford Dictionary of National Biography* (Oxford: Oxford University Press, 2004) [online edition: oxforddnb.com]

Boardman, S. I., Robert II (1316–1390), *Oxford Dictionary of National Biography* (Oxford: Oxford University Press, 2006) [online edition: oxforddnb.com]

Boardman, S. I., Robert III (1316–1390), *Oxford Dictionary of National Biography* (Oxford: Oxford University Press, 2004) [online edition: oxforddnb.com]

Braithwaite, Kate, *Gruoch – The Real Lady Macbeth*, historyofroyalwomen.com, 23 November 2017

Broun, Dauvit, Macbeth [Macbethad mac Findlaich] (d. 1057), king of Scots, *Oxford Dictionary of National Biography* (Oxford: Oxford University Press, 2004) [online edition: oxforddnb.com]

Broun, Dauvit, Malcolm II [Mael Coluim mac Cinaeda] (d. 1034), *Oxford Dictionary of National Biography* (Oxford: Oxford University Press, 2004) [online edition: oxforddnb.com]

Brown, M. H., Joan [née Joan Beaufort], *Oxford Dictionary of National Biography* (Oxford: Oxford University Press, 2004) [online edition: oxforddnb.com]

Cannon, John, editor, *Oxford Companion to British History*, Oxford, Oxford University Press, 1997

Carpenter, David, *Henry III: The Rise to Power and Personal Rule 1207–1258*, London, Yale University Press, 2021

Carradice, Phil, *Robert the Bruce: Scotland's True Braveheart*, Barnsley, Pen and Sword, 2022

Chambers, James, *The Norman Kings*, London, Weidenfeld and Nicolson, 1981

Chambers, Robert, *Biographical Dictionary of Eminent Scotsmen*, Glasgow, Blackie & Son, 1856

Chandler, Victoria, Ada de Warenne, Queen Mother of Scotland (c. 1123–1178) (article), *The Scottish Historical Review*, vol. 60, no. 170, Part 2 (Oct. 1981) pp. 119–139, JSTOR, jstor.org/stable/25529417, accessed 28 Nov. 2019

Clarke, H., The Picts and Preceltic Britain. *Transactions of the Royal Historical Society*, 3(2) (1886), 243–280. doi:10.2307/3677846

Cole, Teresa, *The Norman Conquest: William the Conqueror's Subjugation of England*, Stroud, Amberley Publishing, 2016

Courtney, Joanna, *The Queens of 1066*, joannacourtney.com

Crawford, Anne, editor and translator, *Letters of Medieval Women*, Stroud, Sutton Publishing, 2002

Crawford, Anne, editor and translator, *Letters of the Queens of England*, Stroud, Sutton Publishing, 2002

Crouch, David, *The Reign of King Stephen 1135-1154*, Harlow, Longman, Pearson Education, 2000

Danziger, Danny and John Gillingham, *1215: The Year of Magna Carta*, Hodder & Stoughton, London, 2004

Dark, Patricia A., *The Career of Matilda of Boulogne as Countess and Queen in England, 1135–1152*, academia.edu

Davies, R., Presidential Addres: The Peoples of Britain and Ireland 1100–1400 II Names, Boundaries and Regnal Solidarities. *Transactions of the Royal Historical Society*, 5 (1995), 1–20. doi:10.1017/S0080440100016157

Duncan, A., The War of the Scots, 1306–23. *Transactions of the Royal Historical Society*, 2 (1992), 125–151. doi:10.2307/3679102

Duncan, A. A. M., Alexander I, *Oxford Dictionary of National Biography* (Oxford: Oxford University Press, 2008) [online edition: oxforddnb.com]

Farrer, William and Charles Travis Clay, editors, *Early Yorkshire Charters, Vol. 8: The Honour of Warenne*, Cambridge, Cambridge University Press, 2013 edition, first published 1949

Fell, Christine, *Anglo-Saxon England*, Vol. 3, Cambridge, Cambridge University Press, 1974

Fraser, Antonia, *The Warrior Queens: Boadicea's Chariot*, London, George Weidenfeld & Nicolson Ltd., 1993

Foundation for Medieval Genealogy, fmg.ac/Projects/MedLands

Gillingham, John, John (1167–1216) (article), *Oxford Dictionary of National Biography* (Oxford: Oxford University Press, 2010) [online edition: oxforddnb.com]

Gardiner, Juliet and Wenborn, Neil, editors, *The History Today Companion to British History*, London, Collins & Brown Ltd, 1995

Graham, Henry Grey, *Margaret Queen of Scotland*, ebook, Leonaur, 2011

Green, Mary Anne Everett, *Lives of the Princesses of England from the Norman Conquest*, Vol. 2, London, Longman, Brown, Green, Longman, & Roberts, 1857

Hallam, Elizabeth, editor, *Chronicles of the Age of Chivalry*, Twickenham, Tiger Books, 1995

Havrill, Claire, *A Dangerous Saint: St Margaret of Scotland* (article), DangerousWomenProject.org, 28 October 2016

Hayes, Dr Amy, *Euphemia Ross: The surprise queen*, www.historyscotland.com/history/the-stewart-queens-of-scotland-1371-1513, 30 May 2018

Hicks, Leonie, *Norman Women: the power behind the thrones* (article), BBC History, historyextra.com, October 2016

Hill, Justin, *The 1016 Danish Conquest that led to the Battle of Hastings* (article), historyextra.com

Hilliam, David, *Kings, Queens, Bones and Bastards*, Stroud, The History Press, 1999

Hilton, Lisa, *Queens Consort: England's Medieval Queens*, London, Phoenix, 2008

Hindley, Geoffrey, *A Brief History of the Anglo-Saxons*, London, Robinson, 2015

Hooper, Nicholas, Christina (fl. 1057–1093) (article), *Oxford Dictionary of National Biography* (Oxford: Oxford University Press, 2004) [online edition: oxforddnb.com]

Huneycutt, Lois L., *Margaret of Scotland: A Study in Queenship*, Woodbridge, The Boydell Press, 2003

Jones, Terry, and Ereira, Alan, *Terry Jones' Medieval Lives*, London, BBC Books, 2005

Keats-Rohan, Katharine, *Domesday People Revisited* (article), academia.edu, October 2011

Kendrick, T. D., *A History of the Vikings*, New York, Dover Publications Inc., 2004

Klinder, Hermann and Hilgemann, Werner, *The Penguin Atlas of World History, Vol. 1: From the Beginning to the Eve of the French Revolution*, London, Penguin Books Ltd, 1978

Koenigsberger, H. G., *Medieval Europe 400–1500*, New York, Longman, 1987

Laffin, John, *Brassey's Battles: 3,500 Years of Conflict, Campaigns and Wars from A–Z*, London, Brassey's, 1995

Lawson, M. K., Edmund II [known as Edmund Ironside] (d. 1016) (article), *Oxford Dictionary of National Biography* (Oxford: Oxford University Press, 2004) [online edition: oxforddnb.com]

Lewis, Matthew, *Henry III: The Son of Magna Carta*, Amberley, Stroud, 2016

Lewis, Matthew, *Stephen and Matilda's Civil War: Cousins of Anarchy*, Barnsley, Pen and Sword, 2019

Leyser, Henrietta, *Medieval Women: A Social History of Women in England 450–1500*, Phoenix, ebook, 2013

Licence, Amy, *Red Roses: Blanche of Gaunt to Margaret Beaufort*, Stroud, Amberley Publishing, 2016

Marlow, Joyce, *Kings and Queens of Britain* (sixth edition), London, Artus Publishing, 1979

Marshall, Rosalind K., *Scottish Queens 1034–1714*, Edinburgh, Truckwell Press, 2003

Matthew, Donald, *King Stephen*, London, Hambledon and London, 2002

McNamee, Colm, *Robert Bruce: Our Most Valiant Prince and Lord*, Edinburgh, Birlinn Limited, 2006

Messer, Danna, *Medieval Monarchs, Female Illegitimacy and Modern Genealogical Matters: Part 1: Sybilla, Queen of Scotland, c. 1090–1122*, fmg.ac, accessed 9 May 2023

Morris, Marc, *Castle Acre and the Warennes* (article), marcmorris.org.uk, 30 June 2016

Morris, Marc, *Edward I: A Great and Terrible King*, London, Windmill Books, 2008

Morris, Marc, *The Norman Conquest*, London, Windmill Books, 2013

Morris, Marc, *William I, England's Conqueror*, London, Penguin Books, 2016

Mortimer, Ian, *The Perfect King: The Life of Edward III, Father of the English Nation*, London, Random House, 2006

Mount, Toni, *A Year in the Life of Medieval England*, Stroud, Amberley Publishing, 2016

Nelson, Jessica, Sybilla (d. 1122), queen of Scots and consort of Alexander I, *Oxford Dictionary of National Biography* (Oxford: Oxford University Press, 2008) [online edition: oxforddnb.com]

Nelson, Jessica, Yolande (d. in or after 1324), *Oxford Dictionary of National Biography* (Oxford: Oxford University Press, 2008) [online edition: oxforddnb.com]

Oram, Richard, editor, *The Kings and Queens of Scotland*, Cheltenham, The History Press, 2021

Pelteret, David A. E., *Catalogue of English Post-Conquest Vernacular Documents*, Woodbridge, 1990

Reid, Norman H., Alexander III (1241–1286), *Oxford Dictionary of National Biography* (Oxford: Oxford University Press, 2011) [online edition: oxforddnb.com]

Rex, Peter, *Edward the Confessor, King of England*, Stroud, Amberley Publishing, 2013

Riddell, John, *Stewartiana, containing the case of Robert II and Elizabeth Mure*, Edinburgh, Thomas G. Stevenson, 1843

Roberton, George, *Queen Margaret – How important was she to Scotland?*, Dunfermline Historical Society, 2023, dunfermlinehistsoc.org.uk

Rogers, C., Memoir of George Wishart, the Scottish Martyr. with his Translation of the Helvetian Confession, and a Genealogical History of the Family of Wishart. *Transactions of the Royal Historical Society, 4* (1876), 260–363. doi:10.2307/3677925

Ross, David *Scotland, History of a Nation*, Broxburn, Lomond Books Ltd, 2014

russiapedia.rt.com, *Prominent Russians: Anna Yaroslavna* (article), russiapedia.rt.com/prominent-russians/the-ryurikovich-dynasty/anna-yaroslavna

Saul, Nigel and Nicholas Vincent, *English Medieval Government and Administration: Esssays in Honour of J. R. Maddicott*, Woodbridge, The Boydell Press, 2023

Scott, W. W., Ermengarde [Ermengarde de Beaumont], *Oxford Dictionary of National Biography* (Oxford: Oxford University Press, 2004) [online edition: oxforddnb.com]

Scott, W. W., Malcolm IV, *Oxford Dictionary of National Biography* (Oxford: Oxford University Press, 2008) [online edition: oxforddnb.com]

Scott, W. W., William I [known as William the Lion] (c. 1142–1214), *Oxford Dictionary of National Biography* (Oxford: Oxford University Press, 2004) [online edition: oxforddnb.com]

Shakespeare, William, *Macbeth*, New York, Dover Publications, 1963

Shakespeare, William, *The Tragedie of Macbeth*, Harlow, Longman, 2010

Shakespeare, William, *The Tragedie of Macbeth; a new edition of Shakspere's works with critical text in Elizabethan English and brief notes, illustrative of Elizabethan life, thought and idiom*, edited by Mark Harvey Liddell, New York, New York Doubleday, 1903

Smurthwaite, David, *The Complete Guide to the Battlefields of Britain*, London, Michael Joseph Ltd, 1993

Southern, R. W., *The Making of the Middle Ages*, 4th edition, London, The Folio Society, 1998

Spinks, Stephen, *Robert the Bruce: Champion of a Nation*, Stroud, Amberley Publishing, 2019

Spitzmiller, Kate, *Gruoch: The Real Lady Macbeth*, katespitzmiller.com, 8 May 2016

Stafford, P., Women and the Norman Conquest. *Transactions of the Royal Historical Society*, 4 (1994), 221–249. doi:10.2307/3679222

Stell, G. P., John [John de Balliol] (c. 1248x1250–1314), *Oxford Dictionary of National Biography* (Oxford: Oxford University Press, 2005) [online edition: oxforddnb.com]

stewartsociety.org/history-of-the-stewarts

Stringer, Keith, Ada [née Ada de Warenne], Countess of Northumberland (c. 1123–1178), *Oxford Dictionary of National Biography* (Oxford: Oxford University Press, 2004) [online edition: oxforddnb.com]

Stringer, Keith, Alexander II (1198–1249), *Oxford Dictionary of National Biography* (Oxford: Oxford University Press, 2004) [online edition: oxforddnb.com]

Stringer, Keith, Henry, earl of Northumberland (c. 1115–1152) (article), *Oxford Dictionary of National Biography* (Oxford: Oxford University Press, 2006) [online edition: oxforddnb.com]

Stringer, Keith, Joan (1210–1238), *Oxford Dictionary of National Biography* (Oxford: Oxford University Press, 2004) [online edition: oxforddnb.com]

Stringer, Keith, Marie [née Marie de Coucy] (d. 1284), *Oxford Dictionary of National Biography* (Oxford: Oxford University Press, 2004) [online edition: oxforddnb.com]

Sturdy, David *Alfred the Great*, London, Constable, 1995

Sutherland, Elizabeth, *Five Euphemias: Women in Medieval Scotland 1200–1420*, London, Constable, 1999

Tout, T. F., Margaret [Margaret of England] (1240-1275), revised by Norman H. Reid, *Oxford Dictionary of National Biography* (Oxford: Oxford University Press, 2004) [online edition: oxforddnb.com]

Tranter, Nigel, *The Story of Scotland*, ebook, 4th edition, Neil Wilson Publishing, 2011

Tyler, Elizabeth M., *England in Europe: English Royal Women and Literary Patronage c.1000–c.1150*, Toronto, University of Toronto Press, 2017

Undiscoveredscotland.co.uk, *King Malcolm III Canmore* (article)

Wall, Martin, *The Anglo-Saxon Age: The Birth of England*, Stroud, Amberley Publishing, 2015

Wall, Martin, *The Anglo-Saxons in 100 Facts*, Stroud, Amberley Publishing, 2016

Warner, Kathryn, *Isabella of France: The Rebel Queen*, Stroud, Amberley Publishing, 2016

Watson, Dr Callum, 'Ane Lady Bricht': A Life of Annabella Drummond, Queen of Scots, c. 1350–1401, https://drcallumwatson.blogspot.com, 15 August 2019

Watson, Dr Callum, 'King Iames the secund that had the fyre mark in his face': A life of King James II of Scotland, 1430–1460, https://drcallumwatson.blogspot.com, 3 August 2020

Watson, Fiona J., *Robert the Bruce*, Stroud, The History Press, 2014

Watt, D., The Minority of Alexander III of Scotland. *Transactions of the Royal Historical Society, 21* (1971), 1–23. doi:10.2307/3678917

Waugh, Scott L., Warenne, John de, sixth earl of Surrey [earl of Surrey and Sussex, Earl Warenne] (1232–1304), *Oxford Dictionary of National Biography* (Oxford: Oxford University Press, 2004) [online edition: oxforddnb.com]

Webster, B., David II and the Government of Fourteenth-Century Scotland. *Transactions of the Royal Historical Society, 16* (1966), 115–130. doi:10.2307/3678798

Webster, Bruce, David II, *Oxford Dictionary of National Biography* (Oxford: Oxford University Press, 2004) [online edition: oxforddnb.com]

Webster, Bruce, Joan [Joan of the Tower], *Oxford Dictionary of National Biography* (Oxford: Oxford University Press, 2004) [online edition: oxforddnb.com]

Webster, Bruce, Margaret [née Margaret Drummond], *Oxford Dictionary of National Biography* (Oxford: Oxford University Press, 2004) [online edition: oxforddnb.com]

Weir, Alison, *Britain's Royal Families: The Complete Genealogy*, London, Pimlico, revised edition 1996

White, G., King Stephen's Earldoms. *Transactions of the Royal Historical Society, 13* (1930), 51–82. doi:10.2307/3678488

Williams, Ann, *The English and the Norman Conquest*, Woodbridge, The Boydell Press, paperback edition, 2000

Williamson, David, *Brewer's British Royalty*, London, Cassell, 1996

Wilson, Alan J., *St Margaret Queen of Scotland*, Edinburgh, John Donald Publishers Ltd, 1993

Woodruff, Douglas, *The Life and Times of Alfred the Great*, London, George Weidenfeld and Nicolson Ltd and Book Club Associates, 1974

Woolf, Alex, The 'Moray Question' and the Kingship of Alba in the Tenth and Eleventh Centuries. *The Scottish Historical Review*, Volume LXXIX, 2: No. 208 (October 2000), 145–164

Index